ACCA

STUDY TEXT

PAPER F3

FINANCIAL ACCOUNTING
(UNITED KINGDOM)

In this edition approved by ACCA

- We **discuss** the **best strategies** for studying for ACCA exams
- We **highlight** the **most important elements** in the syllabus and the **key skills** you will need
- We **signpost** how each chapter links to the syllabus and the study guide
- We **provide** lots of **exam focus points** demonstrating what the examiner will want you to do
- We **emphasise key points** in regular **fast forward summaries**
- We **test your knowledge** of what you've studied in **quick quizzes**
- We **examine your understanding** in our **exam question bank**
- We **reference all the important topics** in our **full index**

BPP's **i-Learn** and **i-Pass** products also support this paper.

FOR EXAMS IN DECEMBER 2009 AND JUNE 2010

BPP
LEARNING MEDIA

First edition April 2007

Third edition June 2009

ISBN 9780 7517 6363 8
(Previous ISBN 9780 7517 4722 5)

British Library Cataloguing-in-Publication Data
A catalogue record for this book
is available from the British Library

Published by

BPP Learning Media Ltd
BPP House, Aldine Place
London W12 8AA

www.bpp.com/learningmedia

Printed in the United Kingdom

We are grateful to the Association of Chartered Certified
Accountants for permission to reproduce past
examination questions. The suggested solutions in the
exam answer bank have been prepared by BPP Learning
Media Ltd, unless where otherwise stated.

Your learning materials, published by BPP
Learning Media Ltd, are printed on paper
sourced from sustainable, managed forests.

Contents

A note about copyright

Dear Customer

What does the little © mean and why does it matter?

Your market-leading BPP books, course materials and e-learning materials do not write and update themselves. People write them: on their own behalf or as employees of an organisation that invests in this activity. Copyright law protects their livelihoods. It does so by creating rights over the use of the content.

Breach of copyright is a form of theft – as well as being a criminal offence in some jurisdictions, it is potentially a serious breach of professional ethics.

With current technology, things might seem a bit hazy but, basically, without the express permission of BPP Learning Media:
- Photocopying our materials is a breach of copyright
- Scanning, ripcasting or conversion of our digital materials into different file formats, uploading them to facebook or emailing them to your friends is a breach of copyright

You can, of course, sell your books, in the form in which you have bought them – once you have finished with them. (Is this fair to your fellow students? We update for a reason.) But the e-products are sold on a single user licence basis: we do not supply 'unlock' codes to people who have bought them second-hand.

And what about outside the UK? BPP Learning Media strives to make our materials available at prices students can afford by local printing arrangements, pricing policies and partnerships which are clearly listed on our website. A tiny minority ignore this and indulge in criminal activity by illegally photocopying our material or supporting organisations that do. If they act illegally and unethically in one area, can you really trust them?

How the BPP ACCA-approved Study Text can help you pass – AND help you with your Practical Experience Requirement!

Before you can qualify as an ACCA member, you do not only have to pass all your exams but also fulfil a three year **practical experience requirement** (PER). To help you to recognise areas of the syllabus that you might be able to apply in the workplace to achieve different performance objectives, we have introduced the '**PER alert**' feature. You will find this feature throughout the Study Text to remind you that what you are **learning to pass** your ACCA exams is **equally useful to the fulfilment of the PER requirement**.

Tackling studying

Studying can be a daunting prospect, particularly when you have lots of other commitments. The **different features** of the text, the **purposes** of which are explained fully on the **Chapter features** page, will help you whilst studying and improve your chances of **exam success**.

Developing exam awareness

Our Texts are completely **focused** on helping you pass your exam.

Our advice on **Studying F3** outlines the **content** of the paper, the **necessary skills** the examiner expects you to demonstrate and any **brought forward knowledge** you are expected to have.

Exam focus points are included within the chapters to provide information about skills that you will need in the exam and reminders of important points within the specific subject areas.

Using the Syllabus and Study Guide

You can find the syllabus, Study Guide and other useful resources for F3 on the ACCA web site:

www.accaglobal.com/students/study_exams/qualifications/acca_choose/acca/fundamentals

The Study Text covers **all aspects** of the syllabus to ensure you are as fully prepared for the exam as possible.

Testing what you can do

Testing yourself helps you develop the skills you need to pass the exam and also confirms that you can recall what you have learnt.

We include **Exam-style Questions** – lots of them – both within chapters and in the **Exam Question Bank**, as well as **Quick Quizzes** at the end of each chapter to test your knowledge of the chapter content.

Chapter features

Each chapter contains a number of helpful features to guide you through each topic.

Topic list

Topic list	Syllabus reference

Tells you what you will be studying in this chapter and the relevant section numbers, together with the ACCA syllabus references.

Introduction

Puts the chapter content in the context of the syllabus as a whole.

Study Guide

Links the chapter content with ACCA guidance.

Exam Guide

Highlights how examinable the chapter content is likely to be and the ways in which it could be examined.

 FAST FORWARD

Summarises the content of main chapter headings, allowing you to preview and review each section easily.

Examples

Demonstrate how to apply key knowledge and techniques.

Key terms

Definitions of important concepts that can often earn you easy marks in exams.

Exam focus points

Provide information about skills you will need in the exam and reminders of important points within the specific subject area.

Formula to learn

Formulae that are not given in the exam but which have to be learnt.

 PER alert

This is a new feature that gives you a useful indication of syllabus areas that closely relate to performance objectives in your PER.

 Question

Give you essential practice of techniques covered in the chapter.

 Case Study

Provide real world examples of theories and techniques.

Chapter Roundup

A full list of the Fast Forwards included in the chapter, providing an easy source of review.

Quick Quiz

A quick test of your knowledge of the main topics in the chapter.

Exam Question Bank

Found at the back of the Study Text with more comprehensive chapter questions.

Studying F3

As the name suggests, this paper examines basic financial accounting topics and is fundamental for all financial accountants.

The examiner for this paper is **Nicola Ventress**. She is a member of the ICAEW and an experienced accounting and financial reporting author and tutor.

1 What F3 is about

Paper F3 aims to develop your knowledge and understanding of the underlying principles, concepts and regulations relating to financial accounting. You will need to demonstrate technical proficiency in the use of double entry techniques, including the preparation of basic financial statements for sole traders, partnerships and limited liability companies. The skills you learn at F3 will be built upon in papers F7 and P2.

2 What skills are required?

You are expected to demonstrate Level 1 skills throughout the syllabus. This means that you need to show 'knowledge and comprehension'. It is not sufficient to merely know the subject, you need to understand it and show that you understand. Therefore you will need to not only know an accounting standard but also show how to use it in practice.

Double entry bookkeeping is a basic skill that you will need throughout all the financial accounting papers. Therefore it is essential that you master it at this stage or you will find the higher papers very difficult to understand.

For paper F3, you also need to be able to prepare basic financial statements. Once again, your basic knowledge from paper F3 will be built upon in papers F7 and P2. Therefore you must understand the basics of preparing financial statements now.

3 How to improve your chances of passing

Examiners have repeatedly emphasised that students must know the **whole syllabus**. This is particularly important for paper F3, as all fifty questions are compulsory and the examiner aims to cover most of the syllabus. If you miss out a syllabus area, you will severely limit your chances of passing the exam.

Above all you must practise questions. The text gives you some exam style questions but you really need a large question bank to practise on as given in BPP's Practice and Revision Kit. Do keep to the timing specified. The exam is 2 hours for 90 marks, which means 1.3 minutes per mark or just over 2.5 minutes for a 2 mark question. In the exam question bank we suggest that you allow 1 minute for a 1 mark question and 2 minutes for a 2 mark question.

The exam paper

The exam is a two-hour paper.

There will be fifty questions and they are all compulsory. The format of the paper based Pilot Paper is 50 MCQs, 40 being 2 mark questions and 10 being 1 mark questions. The examiner has confirmed that this will be the format for future exams.

All exams are marked by computer and so no marks will be given for workings.

Analysis of pilot paper

		Number of marks
40	2 mark compulsory MCQs	80
10	1 mark compulsory MCQs	10
		90

Computer based exam

You can also sit the exam as a computer based assessment. Feedback from students implies that the 40 2 mark questions are divided approximately 50:50 between MCQs and data entry style questions. Data entry style questions may require you to enter the answer to a calculation or words to complete a sentence and are very similar to the non-MCQ style questions found in the Quick Quizzes.

Technical articles

There have been a number of technical articles on exams in recent editions of *Student Accountant*.

Fundamental Knowledge, 7 February 2008 (why all the questions in Fundamentals level exams are compulsory)

Be prepared – multiple choice questions, 7 July 2008 (practical guidance on how to maximise marks in MCQs)

Computer-based exams put to the test, 19 August 2008.

P
A
R
T

A

The context and purpose
of financial reporting

Introduction
to accounting

Topic list	Syllabus reference
1 The purpose of financial reporting	A 1(a)
2 Types of business entity	A 1(b)-(d)
3 Nature, principles and scope of accounting	A 1(e)
4 Users' and stakeholders' needs	A 2(a)
5 The main elements of financial reports	A 3(a)-(b)

Introduction

We will begin by looking at the aim of Paper F3, as laid out in ACCA's syllabus and Study Guide and discussed already in the introductory pages to this text (if you haven't read through the introductory pages, do so now – the information in there is extremely important).

> 'Aim of Paper F3
>
> To develop knowledge and understanding of the underlying principles and concepts relating to financial accounting and technical proficiency in the use of double-entry accounting techniques including the preparation of basic financial statements.'

Before you learn **how** to prepare financial reports, it is important to understand **why** they are prepared. Sections 1 – 3 of this chapter introduce some basic ideas about financial reports and give an indication of their purpose. You will also be introduced to the **functions** which accountants carry out: financial accounting and management accounting. These functions will be developed in detail in your later studies for the ACCA qualification.

Section 4 identifies the main **users** of financial statements and their **needs**.

Finally, in Section 5, we will look at the **main financial statements**: the **balance sheet** and the **profit and loss account**. We also look at the definitions of the main elements: assets, liabilities, equity, revenue and expenses.

Study guide

			Intellectual level
A1	**The reasons for and objectives of financial reporting**		
(a)	Define financial reporting – recording, analysing and summarising financial data.		1
(b)	Identify and define types of business entity – sole trader, partnership, limited company		1
(c)	Recognise the legal differences between a sole trader, partnership and a limited company		1
(d)	Identify the advantages and disadvantages of operating as a limited company, sole trader or partnership		1
(e)	Understand the nature, principles and scope of financial reporting		1
A2	**Users' and stakeholders' needs**		
(a)	Identify the users of financial statements and state and differentiate between their information needs		1
A3	**The main elements of financial reports**		
(a)	Understand and identify the purpose of each of the main financial statements		1
(b)	Define and identify assets, liabilities, equity, revenue and expenses		1

Exam guide

The exam consists of 10 1 mark and 40 2 mark MCQs. Any of these topics could form the basis of a 1 mark question. However, be prepared for a 2 mark question (eg on users).

Remember that all fifty questions are compulsory and will cover most of the syllabus. Therefore, do not neglect these introductory topics. Just because the exam is composed of MCQs do not assume that it will be easy (it's not). Also the format means that no method marks are available.

Exam focus point

> At the 2009 ACCA Teachers' Conference, the examiner reminded students that they need to study the full breadth of the syllabus.

1 The purpose of financial reporting

1.1 What is financial reporting?

FAST FORWARD

> **Financial reporting** is a way of recording, analysing and summarising financial data.

Financial data is the name given to the actual transactions carried out by a business eg sales of goods, purchases of goods, payment of expenses.

These transactions are **recorded** in **books of prime entry** (which we will study in detail in Chapter 4).

The transactions are **analysed** in the books of prime entry and the totals are posted to the ledger accounts (see Chapter 5).

Finally, the transactions are **summarised** in the financial statements, which we will meet in section 5 of this chapter (and will study in detail in Chapter 6).

Question

Financial reporting means the financial statements produced only by a large quoted company.

Is this statement correct?

A   Yes
B   No

Answer

The correct answer is B. Financial reporting is carried out by all businesses, no matter what their size or structure.

2 Types of business entity

2.1 What is a business?

FAST FORWARD Businesses of whatever size or nature exist to make a **profit**.

There are a number of different ways of looking at a business. Some ideas are listed below.

- A business is a **commercial or industrial concern** which exists to deal in the manufacture, re-sale or supply of goods and services.
- A business is an **organisation which uses economic resources** to create goods or services which customers will buy.
- A business is an **organisation providing jobs** for people.
- A business **invests money in resources** (for example it buys buildings, machinery and so on, it pays employees) in order to make even more money for its owners.

This last definition introduces the important idea of profit. Business enterprises vary in character, size and complexity. They range from very small businesses (the local shopkeeper or plumber) to very large ones (ICI, IKEA, Corus). But the objective of earning profit is common to all of them.

Key term

> **Profit** is the excess of income over expenditure. When expenditure exceeds income, the business is running at a loss.

One of the jobs of an accountant is to measure income, expenditure and profit. It is not such a straightforward problem as it may seem and in later chapters we will look at some of the theoretical and practical difficulties involved.

2.2 Types of business entity

There are three main types of business entity.

- Sole traders
- Partnerships
- Limited companies

Sole traders are people who work for themselves. Examples include the local shopkeeper, a plumber and a hairdresser. Note that sole traders can employ people, the term 'sole trader' refers to the **ownership** of the business.

Partnerships occur when two or more sole traders decide to share the risks and rewards of a business together. Examples include an accountancy practice, a medical practice and a legal practice.

Limited companies are incorporated to take advantage of 'limited liability' for their owners (shareholders). This means that, while sole traders and partners are personally responsible for the amounts owed by their businesses, the shareholders of a limited company are only responsible for the amount to be paid for their shares. Limited companies are dealt with in more detail in Chapter 20.

In law sole traders and partnerships are not separate entities from their owners. However, a limited company is legally a separate entity from its owners and it can issue contracts in the company's name.

For **accounting purposes**, all three entities are treated as separate from their owners. This is called the **business entity concept**. We will see the practical consequences in Chapter 5.

2.3 Advantages of trading as a limited company

(a)   **Limited liability** makes investment less risky than investing in a sole trader or partnership. However, lenders to a small company may ask for a shareholder's personal guarantee to secure any loans.

(b)   It is **easier to raise finance** because of limited liability and there is no limit on the number of shareholders.

(c)   A limited company has a **separate legal identity** from its shareholders. So a company continues to exist regardless of the identity of its owners. In contrast, a partnership ceases, and a new one starts, whenever a partner joins or leaves the partnership.

(d)   There are **tax advantages** to being a limited company. The company is taxed as a separate entity from its owners and the tax rate on companies may be lower than the tax rate for individuals.

(e)   It is relatively easy to **transfer shares** from one owner to another. In contrast, it may be difficult to find someone to buy a sole trader's business or to buy a share in a partnership.

2.4 Disadvantages of trading as a limited company

(a)   Limited companies have to **publish annual financial statements**. This means that anyone (including competitors) can see how well (or badly) they are doing. In contrast, sole traders and partnerships do not have to publish their financial statements.

(b)   Limited company financial statements have to comply with **legal and accounting requirements**. In particular the financial statements have to comply with accounting standards. Sole traders and partnerships may comply with accounting standards, but are not compelled to do so.

(c)   The financial statements of larger limited companies have to be **audited**. This means that the statements are subject to an independent review to ensure that they comply with legal requirements and accounting standards. This can be inconvenient, time consuming and expensive.

(d)   **Share issues** are regulated by law. For example, it is difficult to reduce share capital. Sole traders and partnership can increase or decrease capital as and when the owners wish.

3 Nature, principles and scope of accounting

FAST FORWARD

You should be able to distinguish the following:

*   Financial accounting
*   Management accounting

You may have a wide understanding of what accounting and financial reporting is about. Your job may be in one area or type of accounting, but you must understand the breadth of work which an accountant undertakes.

3.1 Financial accounting

So far in this chapter we have dealt with **financial** accounts. Financial accounting is mainly a method of reporting the results and financial position of a business. It is not primarily concerned with providing information towards the more efficient running of the business. Although financial accounts are of interest to management, their principal function is to satisfy the information needs of persons not involved in running the business. They provide **historical** information.

3.2 Management accounting

The information needs of management go far beyond those of other account users. Managers have the responsibility of planning and controlling the resources of the business. Therefore they need much more detailed information. They also need to **plan for the future** (eg budgets, which predict future revenue and expenditure).

Key term

> **Management (or cost) accounting** is a management information system which analyses data to provide information as a basis for managerial action. The concern of a management accountant is to present accounting information in the form most helpful to management.

You need to understand this distinction between management accounting and financial accounting.

Question	Accountants

They say that America is run by lawyers and Britain is run by accountants, but what do accountants do in your organisation or country? Before moving on to the next section, think of any accountants you know and the kind of jobs they do.

4 Users' and stakeholders' needs

4.1 The need for accounts

FAST FORWARD

> There are various groups of people who need information about the activities of a business.

Why do businesses need to produce accounts? If a business is being run efficiently, why should it have to go through all the bother of accounting procedures in order to produce financial information?

A business should produce information about its activities because there are various groups of people who want or need to know that information. This sounds rather vague: to make it clearer, we will study the classes of people who need information about a business. We need also to think about what information in particular is of interest to the members of each class.

Large businesses are of interest to a greater variety of people and so we will consider the case of a large public company whose shares can be purchased and sold on the Stock Exchange.

4.2 Users of financial statements and accounting information

The following people are likely to be interested in financial information about a large company with listed shares.

(a)   **Managers of the company** appointed by the company's owners to supervise the day-to-day activities of the company. They need information about the company's financial situation as it is currently and as it is expected to be in the future. This is to enable them to manage the business efficiently and to make effective decisions.

(b)   **Shareholders of the company**, ie the company's owners, want to assess how well the management is performing its stewardship function. They will want to know how profitably management is running the company's operations and how much profit they can afford to withdraw from the business for their own use.

(c)   **Trade contacts**, including suppliers who provide goods to the company on credit and customers who purchase the goods or services provided by the company. **Suppliers** will want to know about the company's ability to pay its debts; **customers** need to know that the company is a secure source of supply and is in no danger of having to close down.

(d)   **Providers of finance to the company**. These might include a bank which allows the company to operate an overdraft, or provides longer-term finance by granting a loan. The bank wants to ensure that the company is able to keep up interest payments, and eventually to repay the amounts advanced.

(e)   **HM Revenue and Customs**, who will want to know about business profits in order to assess the tax payable by the company, and also **any VAT due from/to the company**.

(f)   **Employees of the company**. These should have a right to information about the company's financial situation, because their future careers and the size of their wages and salaries depend on it.

(g)   **Financial analysts and advisers** need information for their clients or audience. For example, stockbrokers need information to advise investors; credit agencies want information to advise potential suppliers of goods to the company; and journalists need information for their reading public.

(h)   **Government and their agencies**. Governments and their agencies are interested in the allocation of resources and therefore in the activities of enterprises. They also require information in order to provide a basis for national statistics.

(i)   **The public**. Enterprises affect members of the public in a variety of ways. For example, they may make a substantial contribution to a local economy by providing employment and using local suppliers. Another important factor is the effect of an enterprise on the environment, for example as regards pollution.

Accounting information is summarised in financial statements to satisfy the **information needs** of these different groups. Not all will be equally satisfied.

4.3 Needs of different users

Managers of a business need the most information, to help them make their planning and control decisions. They obviously have 'special' access to information about the business, because they are able to demand whatever internally produced statements they require. When managers want a large amount of information about the costs and profitability of individual products, or different parts of their business, they can obtain it through a system of cost and management accounting.

Question   Information for managers

Which of the following statements is particularly useful for managers?

A   Financial statements for the last financial year
B   Tax records for the past five years
C   Budgets for the coming financial year
D   Bank statements for the past year

Answer

The correct answer is C. Managers need to look forward and make plans to keep the business profitable. Therefore the most useful information for them would be the budgets for the coming financial year.

In addition to management information, financial statements are prepared (and perhaps published) for the benefit of other user groups, which may demand certain information.

(a)   The **law** provides for the provision of some information. The Companies Acts require every company to publish accounting information for its shareholders; and companies must also file a copy of their accounts with the Registrar of Companies, so that any member of the public who so wishes can go and look at them.

(b)   **HM Revenue and Customs** will receive the information they need to make tax assessments.

(c)   A **bank** might demand a forecast of a company's expected future cash flows as a pre-condition of granting an overdraft.

(d)   The **professional accountancy bodies** have been jointly responsible for issuing **accounting standards** and some standards require companies to publish certain additional information. Accountants, as members of professional bodies, are placed under a strong obligation to ensure that company financial statements conform to the requirements of the standards.

(e)   Some companies provide, voluntarily, specially prepared financial information for issue to their employees. These statements are known as **employee reports**.

Exam focus point

The needs of users can easily be examined by means of a MCQ. For example, you could be given a list of types of information and asked which user group would be most interested in this information.

5 The main elements of financial reports

FAST FORWARD

The two main financial statements are the balance sheet and the profit and loss account.

5.1 Balance sheet

Key term

The **balance sheet** is simply a list of all the assets owned and all the liabilities owed by a business as at a particular date. It is a snapshot of the financial position of the business at a particular moment.

5.1.1 Assets

Key term

An **asset** is something valuable which a business owns or has the use of.

Examples of assets are factories, office buildings, warehouses, delivery vans, lorries, plant and machinery, computer equipment, office furniture, cash and goods held in store awaiting sale to customers.

Some assets are held and used in operations for a long time. An office building is occupied by administrative staff for years. A machine might have a productive life of many years before it wears out. These are called **fixed assets**.

Other assets are held for only a short time. The owner of a newsagent shop, for example, has to sell his newspapers on the same day that he gets them. This is an example of a **current asset**.

5.1.2 Liabilities

Key term

A **liability** is something which is owed to somebody else.

Examples of liabilities are a bank loan or overdraft, amounts owed to a supplier, taxation owed to the government and amounts owed to the owners.

5.1.3 Capital or equity

Key term

Capital is an investment of money in a business to earn profit.

Capital is a special kind of liability. It is the investment that the owner makes and is owed to the owner. In a limited company, capital is also known as equity.

5.1.4 Example of a balance sheet

A balance sheet is called that, because assets will always be equal to liabilities plus capital (or equity). A very simple balance sheet for a sole trader is shown over the page.

XY & Co
BALANCE SHEET AS AT 30 MARCH 20X7

	£	£
Fixed assets		
Freehold premises		50,000
Fixtures and fittings		8,000
Motor vehicles		9,000
		67,000
Current assets		
Stocks	16,000	
Debtors (owed by customers)	500	
Cash	400	
	16,900	
Current liabilities		
Bank overdraft	2,000	
Creditors (owed to suppliers)	5,300	
	7,300	
Net current assets		9,600
		76,600
Capital		
Balance brought forward		75,000
Profit for year		1,600
Balance carried forward		76,600

We will be looking at a balance sheet in a lot more detail later in this Study Text. This example is given simply to illustrate what a balance sheet looks like.

5.2 Profit and loss account

> An **profit and loss account** is a record of income generated and expenditure incurred over a given period. The profit and loss account shows whether the business has had more income than expenditure (a profit) or vice versa (loss).

5.2.1 Revenue and expenses

Revenue is the income for a period (eg sales). The **expenses** are the costs of running the business for the same period.

5.2.2 Form of profit and loss account

The period chosen will depend on the purpose for which the statement is produced. The profit and loss account which forms part of the published annual financial statements of a **limited company** will usually be for the period of a **year**, commencing from the date of the previous year's statements. On the other hand, **management** might want to keep a closer eye on a company's profitability by making up **quarterly or monthly** statements.

A simple profit and loss account for a sole trader is shown below.

A TRADER
PROFIT AND LOSS ACCOUNT FOR THE YEAR ENDED 30 APRIL 20X7

	£
Sales	150,000
Cost of sales	75,000
Gross profit	75,000
Other expenses	64,600
Net profit	10,400

Once again, this example is given purely for illustrative purposes. We will be dealing with a profit and loss account in detail later in this Study Text.

5.3 Purpose of financial statements

Both the balance sheet and the profit and loss account are **summaries of accumulated data**. For example, the profit and loss account shows a figure for income earned from selling goods to customers. This is the total amount of income earned from all the individual sales made during the period. One of the jobs of an accountant is to devise methods of recording such individual transactions, so as to produce summarised financial statements from them.

The balance sheet and the profit and loss account form the basis of the financial statements of most businesses. For limited companies, other information by way of statements and notes may be required by law and/or accounting standards. For example a **cash flow statement** may be required. These are considered in detail later in this Study Text.

Question	Accounting information

The financial statements of a limited company will consist solely of the balance sheet and profit and loss account.

Is this statement correct?

A   True
B   False

Answer

The correct answer is B. As shown above, other statements, such as a cash flow statement, are usually needed.

One of the competences you require to fulfil performance objective 4 of the PER is the ability to prioritise and plan your work to treat objectives, managing conflicting pressures and making best use of time and resources. In the course of your studies for F3, you will be demonstrating this competence.

Chapter Roundup

- **Financial reporting** is a way of recording, analysing and summarising financial data.

- Businesses of whatever size or nature exist to make a **profit**.

- You should be able to distinguish the following:
    - Financial accounting
    - Management accounting

- There are various groups of people who need information about the activities of a business.

- The two main financial statements are the balance sheet and the profit and loss account.

Quick Quiz

1   What is financial reporting?

2   A business entity is owned and run by Alpha, Beta and Gamma.

    What type of business is this an example of?

    A   Sole trader
    B   Partnership
    C   Limited company
    D   Don't know

3   Identify seven user groups who need accounting information.

4   What are the two main financial statements drawn up by accountants?

5   Which of the following is an example of a liability?

    A   Stock
    B   Debtors
    C   Plant and machinery
    D   Loan

Answers to Quick Quiz

1   A way of recording, analysing and summarising financial data.

2   B.   A partnership, as it is owned and run by 3 people.

3   See paragraph 4.2.

4   The profit and loss account and the balance sheet.

5   D.   A loan. The rest are all assets.

Now try the question below from the Exam Question Bank			
Number	**Level**	**Marks**	**Time**
Q1	Examination	2	2 mins

The regulatory framework

Topic list	Syllabus reference
1 The regulatory system	A4(a)
2 The standard setting process	A4(a)-(b)
3 The role of the Stock Exchange	A4(a)
4 Generally accepted accounting practice (GAAP)	A4(a)
5 Accounting standards and choice	A4(b)

Introduction

In this chapter, we introduce the regulatory system run by the Accounting Standards Board (ASB). We are concerned with the **ASB's relationship with other bodies**, and with the way the ASB operates.

You must try to understand and appreciate the contents of this chapter. The examiner is not only interested in whether you can add up; she wants to know whether you can think about a subject which, after all, is your future career. This chapter can and **will be** examined.

Study guide

		Intellectual level
A4	**The regulatory framework**	
(a)	Understand the role of the regulatory system including the roles of the Financial Reporting Council (FRC), the Financial Reporting Review Panel (FRRP), the Accounting Standards Board (ASB), the Urgent Issues Task Force (UITF), and Company Legislation.	1
(b)	Understand the role of Financial Reporting Standards.	1

Exam guide

These ideas are fundamental to your studies and valuable background information. Expect at least one MCQ on the standard setting process or the regulatory system. The examiner is also likely to test you on the different bodies and their relationships. The examiner has highlighted this area as one that is usually answered poorly in the exam.

1 The regulatory system

FAST FORWARD

You should be able to outline the factors which have shaped the development of financial accounting.

1.1 Introduction

Although new to the subject, you may be aware from your reading that there have been considerable upheavals in financial reporting, mainly in response to criticism. The details of the regulatory framework of accounting and the technical aspects of the changes made will be covered later in this text and in your more advanced studies. The purpose of this section is to give a **general picture** of some of the factors which have shaped financial accounting. We will concentrate on the accounts of limited companies because this is the type of organisation whose accounts are most closely regulated by statute or otherwise.

The following factors can be identified.

- Company law
- Accounting concepts and individual judgement
- Accounting standards
- The European Union
- Other international influences
- Generally accepted accounting practice (GAAP)

1.2 Company law

Limited companies are required by law (the Companies Act 1985 or CA 1985) to prepare and publish accounts annually. The form and content of the accounts are regulated primarily by CA 1985, but must also comply with accounting standards.

1.3 Accounting concepts and individual judgement

Financial statements are prepared on the basis of a number of fundamental accounting concepts (or accounting principles as they are called in the Companies Act 1985). Many figures in financial statements are derived from the application of judgement in putting those concepts into practice.

It is clear that different people exercising their judgement on the same facts can arrive at very different conclusions.

Suppose, for example, that an accountancy training firm has an excellent *reputation* amongst students and employers. How would you value this? The firm may have relatively little in the form of assets which you can touch, perhaps a building, desks and chairs. If you simply drew up a balance sheet showing the cost of the assets owned, the business would not seem to be worth much, yet its income earning potential might be high. This is true of many service organisations where the people are among the most valuable assets.

Other examples of areas where the judgement of different people may differ are as follows.

- Valuation of buildings in times of rising property prices.
- Research and development. Is it right to treat this only as an expense? In a sense it is an investment to generate future revenue.
- Accounting for inflation.
- Brands such as 'Jaffa Cakes' or 'Walkman'. Are they assets in the same way that a fork lift truck is an asset?

Working from the same data, different groups of people would produce very different financial statements. If the exercise of judgement is completely unfettered any comparability between the accounts of different organisations will disappear. This will be all the more significant in cases where deliberate manipulation occurs in order to present accounts in the most favourable light.

1.4 Accounting standards

In an attempt to deal with some of the subjectivity, and to achieve comparability between different organisations, **accounting standards** were developed.

1.4.1 The old regime

Between 1970 and 1990 the standards (Statements of Standard Accounting Practice or SSAPs) were devised by the **Accounting Standards Committee**. However, it was felt that these standards were too much concerned with detailed rules in which companies found it all too easy to find loopholes.

1.4.2 The current regime

The Accounting Standards Committee was replaced in 1990 by the **Financial Reporting Council**. Its subsidiary the **Accounting Standards Board** (ASB), issues standards 'concerned with principles rather than fine details'. Its standards are called Financial Reporting Standards (FRSs). However it adopted all existing SSAPs and some of these are still relevant although most have been replaced by FRSs. It is supported in its aim by the Urgent Issues Task Force and the Review Panel.

The **Urgent Issues Task Force (UITF)** is an offshoot of the ASB. Its function is to tackle urgent matters not covered by existing standards and for which, given the urgency, the normal standard setting process would not be practicable.

The **Financial Reporting Review Panel** (FRRP) is concerned with the examination and questioning of departures from accounting standards by large companies.

The standard setting process and its development will be considered in more detail in Section 2 of this chapter.

1.4.3 Accounting Standards and the law

The Companies Act 2006 requires companies to include a note to the accounts stating that the accounts have been prepared in accordance with **applicable accounting standards** or, alternatively, giving details of material departures from those standards, with reasons. The Review Panel and the Secretary of State for

Trade and Industry have the power to apply to the court for revision of the accounts where non-compliance is not justified.

These provisions mean that accounting standards now have the force of law, whereas previously they had no legal standing in statute. In June 1993, Mary Arden QC, in a legal opinion contained in the ASB's *Foreword to Accounting Standards*, stated that courts are more likely than ever to rule that compliance with accounting standards is necessary for accountants to give a 'true and fair' view.

Question	Recap

Without looking:

(a) Why do we need accounting standards?
(b) Who produces them?
(c) Who looks into departures from accounting standards?
(d) Do they have the force of law?

Answer

(a) See Section 1.4
(b) The ASB
(c) The FRRP
(d) Yes

1.5 The European Union

Since the United Kingdom became a member of the European Union (EU) it has been obliged to comply with legal requirements decided on by the EU. It does this by enacting UK laws to implement EU directives. For example, the Companies Act 2006 was enacted in part to implement the provisions of the seventh and eighth directives, which deal with consolidated accounts and auditors. Although your syllabus does not require you to be an expert on EU procedure, you should be aware that the form and content of company accounts can be influenced by international developments.

1.6 Other international influences

One important influence on financial accounting is the **International Accounting Standards Board** (IASB). The forerunner of the IASB was set up in 1973 to work for the improvement and harmonisation of financial reporting. Its members are the professional accounting bodies. The structure of the IASB was reorganised in May 2000.

The objectives of the IASB are:

(a) To **develop**, in the public interest, a single set of high quality, understandable and enforceable **global accounting standards** that require high quality, transparent and comparable information in financial statements and other financial reporting to help participants in the world's capital markets and other users make economic decisions.

(b) To promote the use and **rigorous application** of those standards.

(c) To bring about **convergence of national accounting standards** and International Accounting Standards to high quality solutions.

1.6.1 The use and application of International Financial Reporting Standards (IFRSs)

IFRSs have helped both to improve and to harmonise financial reporting around the world. The standards are used:

- As national requirements, often after a national process
- As the basis for all or some national requirements

- As an international benchmark for those countries which develop their own requirements
- By regulatory authorities for domestic and foreign companies
- By companies themselves

The EU have announced that IFRSs must be used by all listed companies in member states for their consolidated financial statements by from 1 January 2005.

1.7 Generally Accepted Accounting Practice (GAAP)

This term has sprung up in recent years and signifies all the rules, from whatever source, which govern accounting.

Key term

> **GAAP** is a set of rules governing accounting. The rules may derive from:
>
> - Company law (mainly CA 2006)
> - Accounting standards
> - International accounting standards and statutory requirements in other countries (particularly the US)
> - Stock Exchange requirements

GAAP will be considered in more detail in Section 4 of this chapter.

1.8 True and fair view

Company law requires that:

- The balance sheet must give a **true and fair view of the state of affairs** of the company as at the end of the financial year.
- The profit and loss account must give a **true and fair view of the profit or loss** of the company for the financial year.

1.8.1 True and fair 'override'

Key term

> **True and fair view** is not defined in company law or accounting standards. For practical purposes, it can be taken to mean accurate and not misleading.

The Companies Act 2006 states that the directors may depart from any of its provisions if these are inconsistent with the requirement to give a true and fair view. This is commonly referred to as the 'true and fair override'. It has been treated as an important loophole in the law and has been the cause of much argument, and dissatisfaction within the accounting profession.

Question

Forces

List the forces that have shaped financial accounting, stating the effect of each.

Answer

(a) **Company law** requires companies to prepare accounts and regulates their form and content.
(b) **Accounting concepts** are applied by individuals using their **subjective judgement**.
(c) **Accounting standards** help to eliminate subjectivity.
(d) The **European Union** issues directives on accounting matters which we must apply.
(e) **International Financial Reporting Standards** aim to harmonise accounting round the world.
(f) **GAAP** is a collection of rules from various sources, governing accounting.

2 The standard setting process

FAST FORWARD

Limited companies are required by law (the Companies Act 2006 or CA 2006) to **prepare** and **publish accounts annually**. The form and content of the accounts are regulated primarily by CA 2006, but must also comply with accounting standards.

Financial statements are prepared on the basis of a number of fundamental accounting concepts (or accounting principles as they are called in the Companies Act 2006). Many figures in financial statements are derived from the application of judgement in putting those concepts into practice.

It is clear that different people exercising their judgement on the same facts can arrive at very different conclusions. For example, suppose that a business owns a freehold property which it purchased for £100,000.

(a) Some people might argue that no depreciation should be charged on the building because property prices are always rising. The building would appear in the accounts permanently at £100,000.

(b) Others would say that this does not go far enough. If property prices are rising, not only should no depreciation be charged, but the book value of the building should be increased each year by revaluation.

(c) Still others might say that the £100,000 is expenditure incurred by the business and that all expenditure should at some time be charged to the profit and loss account, perhaps by equal annual depreciation charges over the building's useful life.

Working from the same data, these different groups of people would produce very different financial statements. If the exercise of judgement is completely unfettered any comparability between the accounts of different organisations will disappear. This will be all the more significant in cases where deliberate manipulation occurs in order to present accounts in the most favourable light.

Exam focus point

You only need to know the outline of the standard setting process. Concentrate on the roles of the ASB, UITF and FRRP.

2.1 New regime: FRSs

In 1990, however, a new system came into being for producing standards produced for the CCAB in 1988. This proposed that a two tier system should be established. The **Financial Reporting Council**, independent of the profession, now guides the standard setting process. The **Accounting Standards Board** (ASB) issues accounting standards, without the previous requirement to obtain agreement from all CCAB members first.

The ASB is much better staffed and financed than the ASC. The source of this increased finance has been the Stock Exchange, the accountancy bodies and industry.

The ASB has stated its intention to have a small number of standards 'concerned with principles rather than fine details'. This is a change of direction as the ASC's standards were considered unduly prescriptive in the past. If standards lay down detailed rules then it is often possible, by sticking to the letter rather than the spirit of the rules, to get round them.

Although there are considerable difficulties in laying down universally agreed principles, the ASB's approach is to emphasise 'substance over form' – the accountant's traditional approach. New standards issued are no longer called SSAPs but financial reporting standards (FRSs). In time all standards will be replaced by or converted to FRSs.

2.2 Urgent Issues Task Force

An important offshoot of the ASB is an **Urgent Issues Task Force**, whose function is 'to tackle urgent matters not covered by existing standards, and for which, given the urgency, the normal standard-setting process would not be practicable' (Sir Ron Dearing, Chairman of the FRC). This was established in March 1991.

2.3 Financial Reporting Review Panel

The **Review Panel**, chaired by a barrister, is concerned with the examination and questioning of departures from accounting standards by large companies. The Review Panel will be alerted to most cases for investigation by the results of the new CA 1985 requirement that companies must include in the notes to the accounts a statement that they have been prepared in accordance with applicable accounting standards or, alternatively, giving details of material departures from those standards, with reasons.

Although it is expected that most such referrals will be resolved by discussion, the Panel (and the Secretary of State for Trade and Industry) have the power to apply to the court for revision of the accounts, with all costs potentially payable (if the court action is successful) by the company's directors. The auditors may also be disciplined if the audit report on the defective accounts was not qualified with respect to the departure from standards. Revised accounts, whether prepared voluntarily or under duress, will have to be circulated to all persons likely to rely on the previous accounts. The Review Panel was set up in early 1991.

Exam focus point

In the December 2007 exam, there was a 1 mark MCQ on the roles of the ASB and its offshoots. The examiner commented that there was roughly an even split between the two options, suggesting that this area 'is not given adequate attention'. The examiner also commented that she regards this area to be an important part of the F3 syllabus.

2.4 Current accounting standards

The following standards are extant at the date of writing (June 2009). The SSAPs which were in force at the date the ASB was formed have been adopted by the Board. They are gradually being superseded by the new Financial Reporting Standards.

2.4.1 UK accounting standards

Title			Issue date
		Foreword to accounting standards	Jun 93
FRS 1	#	Cash flow statements (revised Oct 96)	Sep 91
FRS 2		Accounting for subsidiary undertakings	Jul 92
FRS 3	#	Reporting financial performance	Oct 92
FRS 5		Reporting the substance of transactions	Apr 94
FRS 6		Acquisitions and mergers	Sep 94
FRS 7		Fair values in acquisition accounting	Sep 94
FRS 8		Related party disclosures	Oct 95
FRS 9		Associates and joint ventures	Nov 97
FRS 10	#	Goodwill and intangible assets	Dec 97
FRS 11		Impairment of fixed assets and goodwill	Jul 98
FRS 12	#	Provisions, contingent liabilities and contingent assets	Sep 98
FRS 15	#	Tangible fixed assets	Feb 99
FRS 16		Current tax	Dec 99
FRS 17		Retirement benefits	Nov 00
FRS 18	#	Accounting policies	Dec 00
FRS 19		Deferred tax	Dec 00
FRS 20		Share-based payment	Apr 04
FRS 21	#	Events after the balance sheet date	May 04
FRS 22		Earnings per share	Dec 04
FRS 23		The effects of changes in foreign exchange rates	Dec 04
FRS 24		Financial reporting in hyperinflationary economies	Dec 04
FRS 25		Financial instruments: disclosure and presentation	Dec 04
FRS 26		Financial instruments: recognition and measurement	Dec 04
FRS 28		Corresponding amounts	Oct 05
FRS 29		Financial instruments: disclosures	Dec 05
FRSSE		Financial reporting standard for smaller entities	Nov 97
SSAP 4		Accounting for government grants	Jul 90
SSAP 5	#	Accounting for value added tax	Apr 74

Title			Issue date
SSAP 9	#	Stocks and long-term contracts	Sep 88
SSAP 13	#	Accounting for research and development	Jan 89
SSAP 19		Accounting for investment properties	Nov 81
SSAP 21		Accounting for leases and hire purchase contracts	Aug 84
SSAP 25		Segmental reporting	Jun 90

Notes

On the Paper F3 syllabus (ie the rest are *not* on the syllabus). The group aspects of FRS 1 and FRS 3 are excluded.

The *Statement of Principles for Financial Reporting* (issued December 1999) is also on your syllabus. It is covered in Chapter 3 of this text.

2.5 Accounting standards and the law

In June 1993, the ASB published its *Foreword to Accounting Standards* in final form. The Foreword contains a legal opinion from Mary Arden QC on the relationship between accounting standards and the Companies Act requirement to show a true and fair view.

Miss Arden considered the changes in the Companies Act which, in her view, strengthen the status of accounting standards. These are the granting of statutory recognition to the existence of standards and the introduction of a procedure whereby the Financial Reporting Review Panel can ask the court to determine whether accounts comply with the true and fair requirement.

'These factors increase the likelihood that the courts will hold that in general compliance with accounting standards is necessary to meet the true and fair requirement.'

Miss Arden added that the improved standard setting process also enhances the status of standards since the standard setting body no longer represents the views of the profession alone. The ASB's rigorous practice of discussion, consultation and investigation in producing its standards is another influencing factor.

3 The role of the Stock Exchange

FAST FORWARD

The Stock Exchange is a market for stocks and shares, and a company whose securities are traded on the main market is known as being 'quoted' as a 'listed' company.

When a share is granted a quotation on The Stock Exchange, it appears on the *Official List* which is published in London for each business day.

In order to receive a listing for its securities, a company must conform with Stock Exchange regulations contained in the **Listing Rules** issued by the Council of The Stock Exchange. The company commits itself to certain procedures and standards, including matters concerning the disclosure of accounting information, which are more extensive than the disclosure requirements of the Companies Acts.

Question

Regulations

To ensure you understand which regulations apply to which type of business, fill in the table below with a 'yes' where compliance is required and 'no' where it is not.

Type of Business	Companies Act	FRSs/ SSAPs	IASs	Stock Exchange Listing Rules
Public Listed Company				
Private Limited Company				
Sole Tradership				

Your table should look like this.

Type of Business	Companies Act	FRSs/ SSAPs	IASs	Stock Exchange Listing Rules
Public Listed Company	YES	YES	NO	YES
Private Limited Company	YES	YES	NO	NO
Sole Tradership	NO	NO	NO	NO

4 Generally accepted accounting practice (GAAP)

FAST FORWARD

GAAP is a term that has sprung up in recent years and it signifies all the rules, from whatever source, which govern accounting.

In the UK this is seen primarily as a combination of:

(a) **Company law** (mainly CA 2006)
(b) **Accounting standards**
(c) **Stock Exchange requirements**

Although those sources are the basis for **UK GAAP**, the concept also includes the effects of non-mandatory sources such as:

(a) **International accounting standards**
(b) **Statutory requirements in other countries**, particularly the US

In the UK, GAAP does not have any statutory or regulatory authority or definition (unlike other countries, such as the US). The term is mentioned rarely in legislation, and only then in fairly limited terms.

The problem of what is 'generally accepted' is not easy to settle, because new practices will obviously not be generally adopted yet. The criteria for a practice being 'generally accepted' will depend on factors such as whether the practice is addressed by UK accounting standards or legislation, or their international equivalents, and whether other companies have adopted the practice. Most importantly perhaps, the question should be whether the practice is consistent with the needs of users and the objectives of financial reporting and whether it is consistent with the 'true and fair' concept.

5 Accounting standards and choice

FAST FORWARD

It is sometimes argued that companies should be given a **choice** in matters of financial reporting on the grounds that accounting standards are detrimental to the quality of such reporting.

There are arguments on both sides.

In favour of accounting standards, the following points can be made.

(a) They reduce or eliminate confusing variations in the methods used to prepare accounts.
(b) They provide a focal point for debate and discussions about accounting practice.
(c) They oblige companies to disclose the accounting policies used in the preparation of accounts.
(d) They are a less rigid alternative to enforcing conformity by means of legislation.
(e) They have obliged companies to disclose more accounting information than they would otherwise have done if accounting standards did not exist. FRS 3 *Reporting financial performance* and FRS 12 *Provisions, contingent liabilities and contingent assets* are examples.

However, the following arguments may be put forward **against** standardisation and in favour of choice.

(a) A set of rules which give backing to one method of preparing accounts might be inappropriate in some circumstances.

(b) Standards may be subject to lobbying or government pressure.

(c) They are not currently based on a conceptual framework of accounting.

(d) There may a trend towards rigidity, and away from flexibility in applying the rules.

Exam focus point

The examiner has indicated that, while Section 5 gives useful background information, you are unlikely to be directly examined on this.

Chapter Roundup

- You should be able to outline the factors which have shaped the development of financial accounting.

- **Limited companies** are required by law (the Companies Act 2006 or CA 2006) to **prepare** and **publish accounts annually**. The form and content of the accounts are regulated primarily by CA 2006, but must also comply with accounting standards.

- The Stock Exchange is a market for stocks and shares, and a company whose securities are traded on the main market is known as being 'quoted' as a 'listed' company.

- GAAP is a term that has sprung up in recent years and it signifies all the rules, from whatever source, which govern accounting.

- It is sometimes argued that companies should be given a **choice** in matters of financial reporting on the grounds that accounting standards are detrimental to the quality of such reporting.

Quick Quiz

1   What are the objectives of the ASB?

    A   To enforce FRSs
    B   To issue FRSs

2   What development at the ASB aids users' interpretation of FRSs?

3   Which of the following arguments is not in favour of accounting standards, but is in favour of accounting choice?

    A   They reduce variations in methods used to produce accounts
    B   They oblige companies to disclose their accounting policies
    C   They are a less rigid alternative to legislation
    D   They may tend towards rigidity in applying the rules

4   What happened in 2005 for listed companies in the EU?

    A   IFRSs to be used for all financial statements
    B   IFRSs to be used for consolidated financial statements

5   The ASB guides the standard setting process. True or false?

Answers to Quick Quiz

1   B   The ASB has no powers of enforcement. The FRRP is the enforcement body.

2   The formation of the Urgent Issues Task Force (UITF)

3   D   The other arguments are all in favour of accounting standards.

4   B   IFRSs to be used in consolidated financial statements.

5   False. The FRC **guides** the standard setting process. The ASB **issues** accounting standards

Now try the question below from the Exam Question Bank			
Number	Level	Marks	Time
Q2	Examination	1	1 min

P
A
R
T

B

The qualitative characteristics of financial information and the fundamental bases of accounting

Accounting conventions

Topic list	Syllabus reference
1 Background	B1(a)
2 Fundamental accounting concepts	B1(a)
3 Other important concepts and conventions	B1(a)
4 The ASB's Statement of Principles	B1(a)–(b)
5 Criticisms of accounting conventions	B1(b)
6 Bases of valuation	B2(a)-(b)
7 Accounting policies (FRS 18)	B2(c)-(d)

Introduction

The purpose of this chapter is to encourage you to think more deeply about the **assumptions** on which financial statements are prepared.

This chapter deals with the accounting conventions which lie behind accounts preparation and which you will meet in Part C in the chapters on bookkeeping.

In Part D, you will see how conventions and assumptions are **put into practice.** You will also deal with certain items which are the subject of accounting standards.

The first part of this chapter deals with two important standards: FRS 18 and the *Statement of principles*. Do not neglect these sections as they contain **very important** basic ideas which underlie the whole of accounting.

In the second half of this chapter, you will consider the bases of valuation of items in the financial statements and FRS 18 on changes in accounting policies.

Study guide

		Intellectual level
B1	**The qualitative characteristics of financial reporting**	
(a)	Define, understand and apply accounting concepts and qualitative characteristics	1
(i)	True and fair view/fair presentation	
(ii)	Going concern	
(iii)	Accruals	
(iv)	Consistency	
(v)	Materiality	
(vi)	Relevance	
(vii)	Reliability	
(viii)	Faithful representation	
(ix)	Substance over form	
(x)	Neutrality	
(xi)	Prudence	
(xii)	Completeness	
(xiii)	Comparability	
(xiv)	Understandability	
(xv)	Business entity concept	
(b)	Understand the balance between qualitative characteristics	1
B2	**Alternative bases used in the preparation of financial information**	
(a)	Identify and explain the main characteristics of alternative valuation bases, eg historical cost, replacement cost, net realisable value, economic value.	1
(b)	Understand the advantages and disadvantages of historical cost accounting	1
(c)	Understand the provisions of Financial Reporting Standards governing financial statements regarding changes in accounting policies	1
(d)	Identify the appropriate accounting treatment if a company changes a material accounting policy	1

Exam guide

This is a very important chapter, which sets the basis of accounting ideas and conventions. Expect questions on all aspects, including the *Statement*. Accounting conventions have been called into question and you may be asked to **question them** yourself in an exam. Pay particular attention to section 5 of this chapter.

Exam focus point

Always **read the question carefully** before answering. Make sure that you understand the requirements and have picked out the main points of the question. Remember that the distractors (wrong options) will include common errors made by students, so always **check your answer** before moving on.

1 Background

Accounting practice recognises a number of concepts.

Accounting practice has developed gradually over a matter of centuries. Many of its procedures are operated automatically by people who have never questioned whether alternative methods exist which are just as valid. However, the procedures in common use imply the acceptance of certain concepts which are by no means self-evident; nor are they the only possible **concepts.** These concepts could be used to build up an accounting framework.

Our next step is to look at some of the more important concepts which are taken for granted in preparing accounts. Originally, a statement of standard accounting practice (SSAP 2 *Disclosure of accounting policies*) described four concepts as *fundamental accounting concepts*: they were **going concern**, **prudence**, **accruals** and **consistency**. These four are also identified as fundamental by the Companies Act 1985, which adds a fifth to the list (the **separate valuation** principle).

In December 2000 FRS 18 *Accounting policies* replaced SSAP 2. FRS 18 emphasises the importance of **going concern** and **accruals** calling them the **bedrock** of financial statements. **Prudence** and **consistency** have been relegated to **'desirable'** elements of financial statements.

Exam focus point

You still need to learn the concepts of prudence and consistency, just put them into the correct context; going concern and accruals are **more** important concepts.

In this chapter we shall single out the following concepts for discussion.

(a)   True and fair view/fair presentation
(b)   Going concern
(c)   Accruals or matching
(d)   Consistency concept
(e)   Prudence
(f)   Materiality
(g)   Substance over form
(h)   Relevance
(i)   Reliability
(j)   Faithful representation
(k)   Neutrality
(l)   Completeness
(m)   Comparability
(n)   Understandability
(o)   Business entity concept

2 Fundamental accounting concepts

FAST FORWARD

Going concern and accruals are the two fundamental accounting concepts as identified by FRS 18 *Accounting policies*.

2.1 The going concern concept

Key term

The **going concern concept** implies that the business will continue in operational existence for the foreseeable future, and that there is no intention to put the company into liquidation or to make drastic cutbacks to the scale of operations.

FRS 18 states that the financial statements **must** be prepared under the going concern basis unless the entity is being (or is going to be) liquidated or if it has ceased (or is about to cease) trading. The directors of a company must also disclose any significant doubts about the company's future if and when they arise.

The main significance of the going concern concept is that the assets of the business should not be valued at their 'break-up' value, which is the amount that they would sell for if they were sold off piecemeal and the business were thus broken up.

2.2 Example: Going concern concept

Emma acquires a T-shirt making machine at a cost of £60,000. The asset has an estimated life of six years, and no residual value. In this case a depreciation cost of £10,000 per annum will be charged.

Using the going concern concept, it is presumed that the business will continue its operations and so the asset will live out its full six years in use. A depreciation charge of £10,000 will be made each year, and the value of the asset in the balance sheet will be its cost less the accumulated amount of depreciation charged to date. After one year, the **net book value** of the asset would therefore be £(60,000 – 10,000) = £50,000, after two years it would be £40,000, after three years £30,000 etc, until it has been written down to a value of 0 after 6 years.

Now suppose that this asset has no other operational use outside the business, and in a forced sale it would only sell for scrap. After one year of operation, its scrap value is, say, £8,000.

The net book value of the asset, applying the going concern concept, is £50,000 after one year, but its immediate sell-off value only £8,000. It can be argued that the asset is over-valued at £50,000 and that it should be written down to £8,000 in the balance sheet and the balance of its cost treated as an expense. However, provided that the going concern concept is valid, so that the asset continues to be used and not sold, it is appropriate to value the asset at its net book value.

Question

Going concern

Now try this example yourself.

A retailer commences business on 1 January and buys a stock of 20 washing machines, each costing £100. During the year he sells 17 machines at £150 each. How should the remaining machines be valued at 31 December if:

(a)   He is forced to close down his business at the end of the year and the remaining machines will realise only £60 each in a forced sale?

(b)   He intends to continue his business into the next year?

Answer

(a)   If the business is to be closed down, the remaining three machines must be valued at the amount they will realise in a forced sale, ie 3 × £60 = £180.

(b)   If the business is regarded as a going concern, the stock unsold at 31 December will be carried forward into the following year, when the cost of the three machines will be matched against the eventual sale proceeds in computing that year's profits. The three machines will therefore appear in the balance sheet at 31 December at cost, 3 × £100 = £300.

2.3 The accruals concept or matching concept

FRS 18 also stipulates that financial statements must be prepared under the accruals concept. This concept is a cornerstone of present day financial statements, so work through this section carefully so that you understand how it is applied during the preparation of accounts.

The **accruals concept** states that revenue and costs must be recognised as they are earned or incurred, not as money is received or paid. They must be matched with one another so far as their relationship can be established or justifiably assumed, and dealt with in the profit and loss account of the period to which they relate.

If Emma makes 20 T-shirts at a cost of £100 and sells them for £200, she makes a profit of £100.

However, if Emma had only sold eighteen T-shirts, it would have been incorrect to charge her profit and loss account with the cost of twenty T-shirts, as she still has two T-shirts in stock. If she intends to sell them in June she is likely to make a profit on the sale. Therefore, only the purchase cost of eighteen T-shirts (£90) should be matched with her sales revenue, leaving her with a profit of £90.

Her balance sheet would therefore look like this.

	£
Assets	
Stock (at cost, ie 2 × £5)	10
Debtors (18 × £10)	180
	190
Liabilities	
Creditors	100
	90
Proprietor's capital (profit for the period)	90

Suppose, Emma had decided to give up selling T-shirts, then the going concern concept would no longer apply and the value of the two T-shirts in the balance sheet would be a break-up valuation rather than cost. Similarly, if the two unsold T-shirts were now unlikely to be sold at more than their cost of £5 each (say, because of damage or a fall in demand) then they should be recorded on the balance sheet at their **net realisable value** (ie the likely eventual sales price less any expenses incurred to make them saleable, eg paint) rather than cost. This shows the application of the prudence concept (see section 3 for details).

In this example, the concepts of going concern and matching are linked. As the business is assumed to be a going concern, it is possible to carry forward the cost of the unsold T-shirts as a charge against profits of the next period.

2.3.1 The accruals concept defined

Essentially, the accruals concept states that, in computing profit, revenue earned must be matched against the expenditure incurred in earning it.

The Companies Act 1985 gives legal recognition to the accruals concept, stating that: 'All income and charges relating to the financial year to which the accounts relate shall be taken into account, without regard to the date of receipt or payment.' This has the effect, as we have seen, of requiring businesses to take credit for sales and purchases when made, rather than when paid for, and also to carry unsold stock forward in the balance sheet rather than to deduct its cost from profit for the period.

3 Other important concepts and conventions

You still need to know these other concepts.

3.1 The prudence concept

Prudence is the inclusion of a degree of caution in the exercise of the judgements needed in making the estimates required under conditions of uncertainty, such that gains and assets are not overstated and losses and liabilities are not understated.

The importance of **prudence** has diminished over time. Prudence is a **desirable quality** of financial statements but **not** a bedrock. The key reason for this change of perspective is that some firms have been over-pessimistic and **over stated provisions** in times of high profits in order to 'profit-smooth'.

You should bear this in mind as you read through the explanation of prudence. On the one hand assets and profits should not be overstated, but a balance must be achieved to prevent the material overstatement of liabilities or losses.

You may have wondered why the three washing machines in Question 1 were stated in the balance sheet at their cost (£100 each) rather than their selling price (£150 each). This is simply an aspect of the prudence concept: to value the machines at £150 would be to anticipate making a profit before the profit had been realised.

The other aspect of the prudence concept is that where a **loss** is foreseen, it **should** be anticipated and taken into account immediately. If a business purchases stock for £1,200 but because of a sudden slump in the market only £900 is likely to be realised when the stock is sold the prudence concept dictates that the stock should be valued at £900. It is not enough to wait until the stock is sold, and then recognise the £300 loss; it must be recognised as soon as it is foreseen.

A profit can be considered to be a **realised profit** when it is in the form of:

- Cash
- Another asset which has a reasonably certain cash value. This includes amounts owing from debtors, provided that there is a reasonable certainty that the debtors will eventually pay up what they owe.

3.2 Example: Prudence concept

A company begins trading on 1 January 20X5 and sells goods worth £100,000 during the year to 31 December. At 31 December there are debts outstanding of £15,000. Of these, the company is now doubtful whether £6,000 will ever be paid.

The company should make an **allowance for debtors** of £6,000. Sales for 20X5 will be shown in the profit and loss account at their full value of £100,000, but the allowance for debtors would be a charge of £6,000. Because there is some uncertainty that the sales will be realised in the form of cash, the prudence concept dictates that the £6,000 should not be included in the profit for the year.

Exam focus point

You should be prepared for an occasional question which tests your ability to recognise a situation which calls for some consideration of the prudence concept. There is no hard-and-fast rule about what 'prudence' is in any particular situation. However, the types of situation in which you might need to discuss prudence and how it should affect the accounts (trading, profit and loss account or balance sheet) are:

- Deciding when revenue should be 'realised' and brought into the trading, profit and loss account (and so deciding when profits are realised)
- Deciding how to put a value to assets in the balance sheet

Attempt your own brief solution to the following question.

 Question

Prudence

It is generally agreed that sales revenue should only be 'realised' and so 'recognised' in the trading, profit and loss account when:

(a) The sale transaction is for a specific quantity of goods at a known price, so that the sales value of the transaction is known for certain.

(b) The sale transaction has been completed, or else it is certain that it will be completed (eg in the case of long-term contract work, when the job is well under way but not yet completed by the end of an accounting period).

(c) The *critical event* in the sale transaction has occurred. The critical event is the event after which:

(i) It becomes virtually certain that cash will eventually be received from the customer.

(ii) Cash is actually received.

Usually, revenue is 'recognised':

(a) When a cash sale is made.

(b) The customer promises to pay on or before a specified future date, and the debt is legally enforceable.

The prudence concept is applied here in the sense that revenue should not be anticipated, and included in the trading, profit and loss account, before it is reasonably certain to 'happen'.

Required

Given that prudence is the main consideration, discuss under what circumstances, if any, revenue might be recognised at the following stages of a sale.

(a) Goods have been acquired by the business which it confidently expects to resell very quickly.

(b) A customer places a firm order for goods.

(c) Goods are delivered to the customer.

(d) The customer is invoiced for goods.

(e) The customer pays for the goods.

(f) The customer's cheque in payment for the goods has been cleared by the bank.

Answer

(a) A sale must never be recognised before the goods have even been ordered by a customer. There is no certainty about the value of the sale, nor when it will take place, even if it is virtually certain that goods will be sold.

(b) A sale must never be recognised when the customer places an order. Even though the order will be for a specific quantity of goods at a specific price, it is not yet certain that the sale transaction will go through. The customer may cancel the order, the supplier might be unable to deliver the goods as ordered or it may be decided that the customer is not a good credit risk.

(c) A sale will be recognised when delivery of the goods is made only when:

(i) The sale is for cash, and so the cash is received at the same time.

(ii) The sale is on credit and the customer accepts delivery (eg by signing a delivery note).

(d) The critical event for a credit sale is usually the despatch of an invoice to the customer. There is then a legally enforceable debt, payable on specified terms, for a completed sale transaction.

(e) The critical event for a cash sale is when delivery takes place and when cash is received; both take place at the same time.

It would be too cautious or 'prudent' to await cash payment for a credit sale transaction before recognising the sale, unless the customer is a high credit risk and there is a serious doubt about his ability or intention to pay.

(f) It would again be over-cautious to wait for clearance of the customer's cheques before recognising sales revenue. Such a precaution would only be justified in cases where there is a very high risk of the bank refusing to honour the cheque.

3.3 The consistency concept

Accounting is not an exact science. There are many areas in which judgement must be exercised in attributing money values to items appearing in accounts. Over the years certain procedures and principles have come to be recognised as good accounting practice, but within these limits there are often various acceptable methods of accounting for similar items.

Key term

> The **consistency concept** states that similar items should be accorded similar accounting treatments.

Part B The qualitative characteristics of financial information and the fundamental bases of accounting | 3: Accounting conventions   33

The consistency concept states that in preparing accounts consistency should be observed in two respects.

(a) Similar items within a single set of accounts should be given similar accounting treatment.

(b) The same treatment should be applied from one period to another in accounting for similar items. This enables valid comparisons to be made from one period to the next (sometimes called the **comparability** concept).

Consistency has been sidelined to a certain extent by FRS 18. FRS 18 is more concerned with the **reliability** of the financial statements. The preparers of financial statements must consider which accounting policy is most appropriate and then apply this policy to give a true and fair view. Changing an accounting policy may contradict the consistency concept. In the next section we look at accounting policies in more detail.

3.4 The business entity concept

Briefly, the concept is that accountants regard a business as a separate entity, distinct from its owners or managers. The concept applies whether the business is a limited company (and so recognised in law as a separate entity) or a sole proprietorship or partnership (in which case the business is not separately recognised by the law.

3.5 The materiality concept

Key term

The **materiality concept**. Only items material in amount or in their nature will affect the true and fair view given by a set of accounts.

An error which is too trivial to affect anyone's understanding of the accounts is referred to as **immaterial**. In preparing accounts it is important to assess what is material and what is not, so that time and money are not wasted in the pursuit of excessive detail.

Determining whether or not an item is material is a **very subjective exercise**. There is no absolute measure of materiality. It is common to apply a convenient rule of thumb (for example to define material items as those with a value greater than 5% of the net profit disclosed by the accounts). However some items disclosed in accounts are regarded as particularly sensitive and even a very small misstatement of such an item would be regarded as material. An example in the accounts of a limited company might be the amount of remuneration paid to directors of the company.

The assessment of an item as material or immaterial may affect its treatment in the accounts. For example, the profit and loss account of a business will show the expenses incurred by the business grouped under suitable captions (heating and lighting expenses, rent and rates expenses etc); but in the case of very small expenses it may be appropriate to lump them together under a caption such as 'sundry expenses', because a more detailed breakdown would be inappropriate for such immaterial amounts.

Attention!

In assessing whether or not an item is material, it is not only the amount of the item which needs to be considered. The context is also important.

3.6 Example: Materiality

(a) If a balance sheet shows fixed assets of £2 million and stocks of £30,000 an error of £20,000 in the depreciation calculations might not be regarded as material, whereas an error of £20,000 in the stock valuation probably would be. In other words, the total of which the erroneous item forms part must be considered.

(b) If a business has a bank loan of £50,000 and a £55,000 balance on bank deposit account, it might well be regarded as a material misstatement if these two amounts were displayed on the balance sheet as 'cash at bank £5,000'. In other words, incorrect presentation may amount to material misstatement even if there is no monetary error.

Question

Would you capitalise the following items in the accounts of a company?

(a)   A box file
(b)   A computer
(c)   A small plastic display stand

Answer

(a)   No. You would write it off to the profit and loss account as an expense.

(b)   Yes. You would capitalise the computer and charge depreciation on it.

(c)   Your answer depends on the size of the company and whether writing off the item has a material effect on its profits. A larger organisation might well write this item off under the heading of advertising expenses, while a small one would capitalise it and depreciate it over time. This is because the item would be material to the small company but not to the large company.

3.7 Objectivity (neutrality)

An accountant must show objectivity in his work. This means he should try to strip his answers of any personal opinion or prejudice and should be as precise and as detailed as the situation warrants. The result of this should be that any number of accountants will give the same answer independently of each other.

Key term

> **Objectivity** means that accountants must be free from bias. They must adopt a neutral stance when analysing accounting data.

In practice, objectivity is difficult. Two accountants faced with the same accounting data may come to different conclusions as to the correct treatment. It was to combat subjectivity that accounting standards were developed.

3.8 The duality concept

Every transaction has two effects. This convention underpins double entry bookkeeping, and you will see it at work in your studies from Chapter 4 onwards.

3.9 Substance over form

Key term

> **Substance over form** means that transactions should be accounted for and presented in accordance with their economic substance, not their legal form.

An example of substance over form is that of assets acquired on hire purchase. Legally the purchaser does not own the asset until the final instalment has been paid. However, the accounting treatment is to record a fixed asset in the accounts at the start of the hire purchase agreement. The substance of the transaction is that the business owns the asset. The same could be said of fixed assets acquired under long-term leases.

3.10 Other qualities

Below are some features that accounting information should have if it is to be useful.

(a)   **Relevance**. The information provided should satisfy the needs of information users. In the case of company accounts, clearly a wide range of information will be needed to satisfy a wide range of users.

(b) **Understandability**. Information may be difficult to understand because it is skimpy or incomplete; but too much detail is also a defect which can cause difficulties of understanding.

(c) **Reliability**. Information will be more reliable if it is independently verified. The law requires that the accounts published by limited companies should be verified by auditors, who must be independent of the company and must hold an approved qualification.

(d) **Completeness**. A company's accounts should present a rounded picture of its economic activities.

(e) **Comparability**. Information should be produced on a consistent basis so that valid comparisons can be made with information from previous periods and with information produced by other sources (for example the accounts of similar companies operating in the same line of business).

(f) **Fair presentation**. Financial statements should **present fairly** the financial position, financial performance and cash flows of an entity. Compliance with FRSs will usually achieve this.

(g) **Faithful representation**. The information gives full details of its effects on the financial statements and is only recognised if its financial effects are certain.

Question
Consistency

Which of the following statements **best** describes the consistency concept?

A   Only material items are disclosed

B   The way an item is presented always remains the same

C   Presentation and classification of items should remain the same unless a change is required by a FRS

Answer

The correct answer is C.

4 The ASB's Statement of Principles

FAST FORWARD

You need to know Chapters 1 to 3 of the ASB statement.

4.1 The search for a conceptual framework

Key term

A **conceptual framework**, is a statement of generally accepted theoretical principles which form the frame of reference for financial reporting. These theoretical principles provide the basis for the development of new reporting standards and the evaluation of those already in existence.

The financial reporting process is concerned with providing information that is useful in decision-making process. Therefore a conceptual framework will form the theoretical basis for determining which events should be accounted for, how they should be measured and how they should be communicated to the user.

Although it is theoretical in nature, a conceptual framework for financial reporting has highly practical final aims.

The need for a conceptual framework is demonstrated by the way UK standards originally developed. Standards were produced in haphazard ways to fight abuses. Had an agreed framework existed, the old ASC could have acted as an architect or designer, rather than a fire-fighter, building accounting rules on the foundation of sound, agreed basic principles.

The lack of a conceptual framework also meant that fundamental principles were tackled more than once in different standards, thereby producing contradictions and inconsistencies in basic concepts, such as those of prudence and matching. This led to ambiguity and it has affected the true and fair concept of financial reporting.

A conceptual framework would also bolster the standard setters against political pressure from various 'lobby groups' and interested parties. Such pressure would only prevail if it was acceptable under the conceptual framework.

Towards the end of its existence, the ASC recognised the IASB's *Framework* on the preparation and presentation of financial statements, as a set of guidelines to help it develop proposals for new standards and revisions to existing standards. This represented a significant shift from the previous approach of developing SSAPs in a haphazard manner as working solutions to practical problems.

The *Framework* deals with:

(a)   The objective of financial statements.

(b)   The qualitative characteristics that determine the usefulness of information in financial statements.

(c)   The definition, recognition and measurement of the elements from which financial statements are constructed.

(d)   Concepts of capital and capital maintenance.

The IASB believes that further international harmonisation of accounting methods can best be promoted by focusing on these four topics since they will then lead to producing financial statements that meet the common needs of most users.

The ASB has already incorporated the IASB's *Framework* into its *Statement of Principles*.

4.1.1 Advantages and disadvantages of a conceptual framework

The advantages arising from using a conceptual framework may be summarised as follows.

(a)   SSAPs were being developed on a 'patchwork quality' basis where a particular accounting problem was recognised by the ASC as having emerged, and resources were then channelled into standardising accounting practice in that area, without regard to whether that particular issue was necessarily the most important issue remaining at that time without standardisation.

(b)   As stated earlier, the development of certain SSAPs (for example SSAP 13) has been subject to considerable political interference from interested parties. Where there is a conflict of interest between user groups on which policies to choose, policies deriving from a conceptual framework will be less open to criticism that the ASC buckled to external pressure.

(c)   Some SSAPs seem to concentrate on the income statement (profit and loss account), some to concentrate on the valuation of net assets (balance sheet). There was no cohesive approach to the financial statements as a whole.

A counter-argument to supporters of a conceptual framework might be as follows.

(a)   Financial statements are intended for a variety of users, and it is not certain that a single conceptual framework can be devised which will suit all users.

(b)   Given the diversity of user requirements, there may be a need for a variety of accounting Standards, each produced for a different purpose (and with different concepts as a basis).

(c)   It is not clear that a conceptual framework will make the task of preparing and then implementing standards any easier than it is now.

Exam focus point

The above sections are for background information only and are unlikely to be examined.

4.2 ASB Statement of Principles

The Accounting Standards Board (ASB) published (in November 1995) an exposure draft of its *Statement of Principles for Financial Reporting.* In March 1999, the text was substantially revised with particular attention being given to the clarity of expression. The *Statement of Principles* was then finalised in December 1999. The statement consists of eight chapters.

(1) The objective of financial statements
(2) The reporting entity
(3) The qualitative characteristics of financial information
(4) The elements of financial statements
(5) Recognition in financial statements
(6) Measurement in financial statements
(7) Presentation of financial information
(8) Accounting for interests in other entities

4.3 What is examinable

The up-to-date Study Guide includes the following as examinable.

- The objectives of financial statements as defined in Chapter 1 of the *Statement of Principles*
- The reporting entity as defined in Chapter 2 of the *Statement of Principles*
- The qualitative characteristics of financial statements in Chapter 3 of the *Statement of Principles*

Exam focus point

> A detailed knowledge of Chapters 4 to 8 of the *Statement of Principles* is not examinable, but students should be aware of their general principles. At the 2009 ACCA Teachers' Conference, the examiner emphasised that students need to be aware of the theoretical aspects of the syllabus eg the *Statement of Principles*.

4.4 Purpose of the Statement of Principles

The following are the main reasons why the ASB developed the *Statement of Principles*.

(a) To assist the ASB by providing a basis for reducing the number of alternative accounting treatments permitted by accounting standards and company law

(b) To provide a framework for the future development of accounting standards

(c) To assist auditors in forming an opinion as to whether financial statements conform with accounting standards

(d) To assist users of accounts in interpreting the information contained in them

(e) To provide guidance in applying accounting standards

(f) To give guidance on areas which are not yet covered by accounting standards

(g) To inform interested parties of the approach taken by the ASB in formulating accounting standards

The role of the *Statement* can thus be summed up as being to provide **consistency, clarity and information**.

4.5 Chapter 1 The objective of financial statements

The main points raised here are as follows.

(a) The objective of financial statements is to provide information about the **financial position, performance** and **financial adaptability** of an enterprise that is useful to a wide range of users for assessing the stewardship of management and for making economic decisions.

(b) It is acknowledged that while all not all the information needs of users can be met by financial statements, there are needs that are common to all users. Financial statements that meet the needs of providers of risk capital to the enterprise will also meet most of the needs of other users that financial statements can satisfy.

Users of financial statements other than investors include the following.

(i) Employees
(ii) Lenders
(iii) Suppliers and other creditors
(iv) Customers
(v) Government and their agencies
(vi) The public

(c) The limitations of financial statements are emphasised as well as the strengths.

(d) All of the components of financial statements (balance sheet, profit and loss account, cash flow statement) are interrelated because they reflect different aspects of the same transactions.

(e) The exposure draft emphasises the ways financial statements provide information about the financial position of an enterprise. The main elements which affect the position of the company are:

(i) The economic resources it controls

(ii) Its financial structure

(iii) Its liquidity and solvency

(iv) Its capacity to adapt to changes in the environment in which it operates (called **financial adaptability**)

The exposure draft discusses the importance of each of these elements and how they are disclosed in the financial statements.

Question
Users of financial statements

Consider the information needs of the users of financial information listed above, including shareholders. (You have covered this in Chapter 1, but see if you can remember them.)

Answer

(a) *Shareholders*

(i) Information is required to help make a decision about buying or selling shares, taking up a rights issue and voting at the Annual General Meeting (AGM).

(ii) The shareholder must have information about the level of dividend, past, present and future and any changes in share price.

(iii) The shareholders will also need to know whether the management has been running the company efficiently.

(iv) As well as the position indicated by the profit and loss account, balance sheet and earnings per share (EPS), the shareholders will want to know about the liquidity position of the company, the company's future prospects, and how the company's shares compare with those of its competitors.

(b) *Employees* need information about the security of employment and future prospects for jobs in the company, and to help with collective pay bargaining.

(c) *Lenders* need information to help them decide whether to lend to a company. They will also need to check that the value of any security remains adequate, that the interest repayments are secure, that the cash is available for redemption at the appropriate time and that any financial restrictions (such as maximum debt/equity ratios) have not been breached. Investors will need information about loans which are traded on the stock market to decide whether to buy or sell them.

(d) *Suppliers* need to know whether the company will be a good customer and pay its debts.

(e) *Customers* need to know whether the company will be able to continue producing and supplying goods.

(f) *Government's* interest in a company may be one of creditor or customer, as well as being specifically concerned with compliance with tax and company law, ability to pay tax and the general contribution of the company to the economy.

(g) The *public* at large would wish to have information for all the reasons mentioned above, but it could be suggested that it would be impossible to provide general purpose accounting information which was specifically designed for the needs of the public.

Part B The qualitative characteristics of financial information and the fundamental bases of accounting | **3: Accounting conventions**

39

4.6 Chapter 2 The reporting entity

This chapter makes the point that it is important that entities that ought to prepare financial statements, in fact do so. The entity must be a cohesive economic unit. It has a determinable boundary and is held to account for all the things it can control.

4.7 Chapter 3 Qualitative characteristics of financial information

A diagrammatic representation is shown below.

(a) Qualitative characteristics that relate to **content** are **relevance** and **reliability**.
(b) Qualitative characteristics that relate to **presentation** are **comparability** and **understandability**.

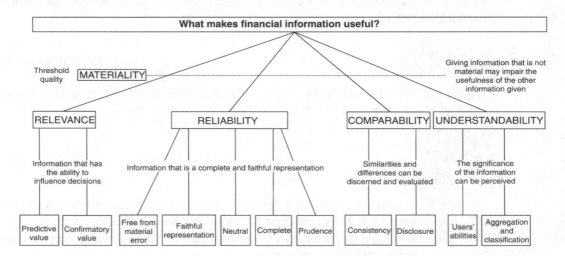

The ASB regards **relevance** and **reliability** as the two primary characteristics of accounting information, and takes the view that **relevance** takes priority. Information that is relevant will enable users to **predict** the outcome of financial decisions (predictive value) and to confirm the corrections or otherwise of financial decisions previously made (confirmatory value).

To be **reliable**, information must be free from error, complete and free from bias (neutral).

Comparability requires **consistent treatment** of similar items and consistent application of accounting policies and measurement bases from one period to the next. Where this is not the case, **disclosure** must be made.

Understandability is limited by the financial knowledge of the user. The ASB refers to 'reasonable knowledge… of accounting', which cannot be presumed in the case of all shareholders. Items should be added together (aggregation) and classified in a manner which makes them as understandable as possible.

4.8 Chapter 4 Elements of financial statements

The elements of financial statements are listed. They are:

(a) Assets
(b) Liabilities
(c) Ownership interest
(d) Gains
(e) Losses
(f) Contributions from owners
(g) Distributions to owners

Any item that does not fall within one of the definitions of elements should not be included in financial statements. The definitions are as follows.

(a) **Assets** are rights or other access to future economic benefits controlled by an entity as a result of past transactions or events.

(b) **Liabilities** are obligations of an entity to transfer economic benefits as a result of past transactions or events.

(c) **Ownership interest** is the residual amount found by deducting all of the entity's liabilities from all of the entity's assets.

(d) **Gains** are increases in ownership interest, other than those relating to contributions from owners.

(e) **Losses** are decreases in ownership interest, other than those relating to distributions to owners.

(f) **Contributions from owners** are increases in ownership interest resulting from investments made by owners in their capacity as owners.

(g) **Distributions to owners** are decreases in ownership interest resulting from transfers made to owners in their capacity as owners.

Question
Asset or liability

Consider the following situations. In each case, do we have an asset or liability within the definitions given by the *Statement of Principles?* Give reasons for your answer.

(a) Pat Ltd has purchased a patent for £20,000. The patent gives the company sole use of a particular manufacturing process which will save £3,000 a year for the next five years.

(b) Baldwin Ltd paid Don Brennan £10,000 to set up a car repair shop, on condition that priority treatment is given to cars from the company's fleet.

(c) Deals on Wheels Ltd provides a warranty with every car sold.

(d) Monty Ltd has signed a contract with a human resources consultant. The terms of the contract are that the consultant is to stay for six months and be paid £3,000 per month.

(e) Rachmann Ltd owns a building which for many years it had let out to students. The building has been declared unsafe by the local council. Not only is it unfit for human habitation, but on more than one occasion slates have fallen off the roof, nearly killing passers-by. To rectify all the damage would cost £300,000; to eliminate the danger to the public would cost £200,000. The building could then be sold for £100,000.

Answer

(a) This is an asset, albeit an intangible one. There is a past event, control and future economic benefit (through cost savings).

(b) This cannot be classified as an asset. Baldwin Ltd has no control over the car repair shop and it is difficult to argue that there are 'future economic benefits'.

(c) This is a liability; the business has taken on an obligation. It would be recognised when the warranty is issued rather than when a claim is made.

(d) As a firm financial commitment, this has all the appearance of a liability. However, as the consultant has not done any work yet, there has been no past event which could give rise to a liability. Similarly, because there has been no past event there is no asset.

(e) The situation is not clear cut. It could be argued that there is a liability, depending on the whether the potential danger to the public arising from the building creates a legal obligation to do the repairs. If there is such a liability, it might be possible to set off the sale proceeds of £100,000 against the cost of essential repairs of £200,000, giving a net obligation to transfer economic benefits of £100,000.

The building is clearly not an asset, because although there is control and there has been a past event, there is no expected access to economic benefit.

4.9 Chapter 5 Recognition in financial statements

This chapter explains what is meant by recognition and discusses the three stages of recognition of assets and liabilities.

(a) Initial recognition
(b) Subsequent remeasurement
(c) Derecognition

The chapter goes on to describe the criteria which determine each of these stages.

4.10 Chapter 6 Measurement in financial statements

This chapter, with its emphasis on current values, is fairly radical and controversial. The following approach is taken.

(a) Initially, when an asset is purchased or a liability incurred, the asset/liability is recorded at the transaction cost, that is historical cost, which at that time is equal to current replacement cost.

(b) An asset/liability may subsequently be 'remeasured'. In a historical cost system, this can involve writing down an asset to its recoverable amount. For a liability, the corresponding treatment would be amendment of the monetary amount to the amount ultimately expected to be paid.

(c) Such re-measurements will, however, only be recognised if there is sufficient evidence that the monetary amount of the asset/liability has changed and the new amount can be reliably measured.

Question	Historical cost

Why might historical cost be considered less relevant to users of accounting statements?

Answer

In times of high inflation, an historic cost only a year old may be hopelessly inadequate to express the current value of an asset.

4.11 Chapter 7 Presentation of financial information

Aspects of this chapter have also given rise to some controversy. The chapter begins by making the general point that financial information is presented in the form of a structured set of financial statements comprising primary statements and supporting notes and, in some cases, supplementary information.

4.11.1 Components of financial statements

The primary financial statements are as follows.

(a) Profit and loss account
(b) Statement of total recognised gains and losses
(c) Balance sheet
(d) Cash flow statement

(a) and (b) are the 'statements of financial performance'.

The notes to the financial statements 'amplify and explore' the primary statements; together they form an 'integrated whole'. Disclosure in the notes does not correct or justify non-disclosure or misrepresentation in the primary financial statements.

'Supplementary information' embraces voluntary disclosures and information which is too subjective for disclosure in the primary financial statement and the notes.

4.12 Chapter 8 Accounting for interests in other entities

Financial statements need to reflect the effect on the reporting entity's financial performance and financial position of its interests in other entities. This involves various measurement, presentation and consolidation issues which are dealt with in this chapter of the *Statement*.

4.13 Summary

The *Statement of Principles* does not have direct effect. It is not an accounting standard with which companies have to comply. Having said that, it is influential and persuasive, especially where there is no specific standard dealing with an issue. The statement should help structure new statements and create a coherent framework, this in turn will prevent controversy and help enhance the reputation of the accounting profession.

5 Criticisms of accounting conventions

FAST FORWARD

It is easy to assume that the accounting conventions with which we are familiar, and which we have been using in this Study Text, are the best ones we could use. However, this is not necessarily the case.

This is potentially a vast topic, so we will confine ourselves to two or three examples.

5.1 Criticisms of the prudence convention

'Prudence' and 'accountant' would appear to go together. Surely this accounting concept is unassailable?

Question
Prudence

Before we go any further, can you remember exactly what prudence is?

Answer

Prudence is, according to Statement of Principles for Financial Reporting the inclusion of a degree of caution in the exercise of the judgements needed in making the estimates required under the conditions of uncertainty, such that gains and assets are not overstated and loses and liabilities are not understated.

An example of the application of the prudence concept is the requirement to value stock at the lower of cost and net realisable value.

This is all very well, but it can lead to problems, of which the following can be identified as the most significant.

(a) **Prudence** most obviously conflicts with the **matching (or accruals)** concept because it requires that the matching of costs and revenues should not take place if there is any doubt about the future recoverability of deferred costs.

(b) **Prudence** also conflicts with the **going concern** concept because it may not be prudent to assume that a business is a going concern (although it is realistic).

(c) **Prudence** makes it difficult to **treat items consistently** because circumstances in one period may require a different treatment from previous periods in order to be prudent.

(d) **Prudence** also undermines several other conventions not recognised as fundamental accounting concepts. For instance, **objectivity** is regarded as important by most users of accounts but prudence (or conservatism as it is sometimes called) implies a subjectivity in coming to accounting judgements. It is also difficult to reconcile prudence with the use of anything other than the **historical cost convention** for valuing assets.

LEARNING MEDIA

Part B The qualitative characteristics of financial information and the fundamental bases of accounting | **3: Accounting conventions** 43

The ASB's *Statement of Principles* places little emphasis on prudence – some critics have said too little – and embraces a system of current value accounting. FRS 18 *Accounting policies* relegates prudence to a **desirable quality** of financial statements. Prudence can result in the smoothing of profits and the deliberate understatement of assets or overstatement of liabilities. Prudence is just one element of reliability.

5.2 Criticisms of the matching concept

Try this question before you go any further.

Question   Matching concept

Can you remember what the matching concept is? A clue: it's the same as the accruals concept.

Answer

Revenue and expenditure are matched under this concept and recorded in the accounts when earned or incurred, rather than on the associated cash movement, provided that it is prudent so to treat them.

This allows most obviously for credit sales, but also results in the identification of stock at the end of each accounting period rather than writing all purchases off to the trading account. Only purchases which result in a sale recorded in the period or are used for promotional or similar purposes should be matched with sales for the period. Therefore, if purchased goods still on hand at the period end are of saleable quality and the company will still be trading in the next period (ie the prudence and going concern concepts are satisfied) then any unsold goods can be treated as current assets and their value can be deducted from purchases and opening stock.

What could possibly be wrong with that? The main criticism relates to the conflict with historical cost accounting.

It can be argued that the matching concept is not applied in historical cost accounting. The matching concept states that revenue earned must be matched against expenditure incurred on earning it. The cost of goods sold in the profit and loss account is normally computed on the basis of their historical cost. However, a continuing business will want to replace stocks sold and will have to do so at ever higher prices. This means that some of the 'profit' shown by the accounts is not profit at all, but must be spent in restoring the assets of the business to their previous level.

It may be argued that the matching concept could be better applied under a system of current cost accounting. This, broadly speaking, values assets at replacement cost. Thus the historical cost profit would be adjusted by the 'cost of sales adjustment' which aims to charge the profit and loss account with the current cost of each item of stock sold at the date of sale.

Other criticisms of the matching concept include the following.

(a)   The nature of the matching process is often **arbitrary**, for example in selecting a depreciation method.

(b)   The matching concept **conflicts with the prudence concept** as indicated in Paragraph 5.3 above.

(c)   The matching concept is about getting the profit and loss account figure right. This is an admirable aim in itself, but it may mean that the **balance sheet contains** rather **arbitrary figures**. For example, when an asset is depreciated, the balance sheet figure is simply the unexpired cost to be allocated to future accounting periods. In other words, it is what is left over after matching has taken place, not in itself a meaningful figure.

Attention!

The *Statement of Principles* places less emphasis on matching than has been the convention, partly because it is **more orientated towards the balance sheet** than the profit and loss account.

5.3 Depreciation of freehold buildings

We will now consider a controversial issue: whether depreciation should be provided on freehold buildings.

It has become common in recent years, particularly in the UK, for companies not to provide any depreciation on freehold buildings. The following points may be made in favour of *not* providing depreciation on freehold buildings.

(a)   The value of the asset is the same or greater at the end of the accounting period than at the beginning. To provide depreciation would therefore be unnecessary, if not misleading.

(b)   The building is well maintained. The cost of this maintenance has already been charged to the profit and loss account. To charge it again would be 'double counting'.

(c)   The value of the building exceeds its cost and if the building were sold the proceeds would be greater than original cost. In other words the net cost of the building, to be allocated over its economic life, is zero.

However, the following points carry greater weight.

(a)   It is irrelevant that the value of the building has not fallen or has risen. The depreciation charge is a means of matching the cost of an asset with the revenue earned over its useful economic life. In charging depreciation no attempt is being made to estimate the current value of an asset.

(b)   Depreciation is charged on other fixed assets used in a business, with the exception of freehold land. SSAP 2 demands **consistent** treatment of items.

(c)   Like other assets, freehold buildings do not last for ever. The accounting treatment should reflect this.

6 Bases of valuation

FAST FORWARD

Items in the financial statements can be valued under a number of bases. For your syllabus, you need to know the following bases.

- Historical cost
- Replacement cost
- Net realisable value
- Economic value

6.1 Historical cost

A basic principle of accounting (some writers include it in the list of fundamental accounting assumptions) is that items are normally stated in accounts at historical cost, ie at the amount which the business paid to acquire them. An important advantage of this procedure is that the objectivity of accounts is maximised: there is usually documentary evidence to prove the amount paid to purchase an asset or pay an expense.

Key term

Historical cost means that transactions are recorded at the cost when they occurred.

In general, accountants prefer to deal with costs, rather than with 'values'. This is because valuations tend to be subjective and to vary according to what the valuation is for.

6.2 Replacement cost

Key term

Replacement cost means the amount needed to replace an items with an identical item.

Example: Replacement cost

XY Ltd bought a machine five years ago for £15,000. It is now worn out and needs replacing. An identical machine can be purchased for £20,000.

      Historical cost is £15,000

      Replacement cost is £20,000

6.3 Net realisable value

Key term

> **Net realisable value** is the expected price less any costs still to be incurred in getting the item ready for sale and then selling it.

Example: Net realisable value

XY Ltd's machine from the example above can be restored to working order at a cost of £5,000. It can then be sold for £10,000. What is its net realisable value?

      Net realisable value = £10,000 – £5,000
                          = £5,000

6.4 Economic value

Key term

> **Economic value** is the value derived from an asset's ability to generate income.

A machine's economic value is the amount of profits it is expected to generate for the remains of its useful life.

Example: Economic value

Suppose XY Ltd buy the new machine for £20,000. It is estimated that the new machine will generate profits of £4,000 per year for its useful life of 8 years. What is its economic value?

      Economic value   = £4,000 × 8
                             = £32,000

6.5 Advantages and disadvantages of historical cost accounting

The **advantage** of historical cost accounting is that the cost is known and can be proved (eg by the invoice). There is no subjectivity or bias in the valuation.

There are a number of **disadvantages** and these usually arise in times of rising prices (inflation). When inflation is low, then historical cost accounting is usually satisfactory. However, when inflation is high the following problems can occur.

6.5.1 Fixed asset values are unrealistic

The most striking example is property. Although some entities have periodically updated the balance sheet values, in general there has been a lack of consistency in the approach adopted and a lack of clarity in the way in which the effects of these changes in value have been expressed.

If fixed assets are retained in the books at their historical cost, **unrealised holding gains are not recognised**. This means that the total holding gain, if any, will be brought into account during the year in which the asset is realised, rather than spread over the period during which it was owned.

There are, in essence, two contradictory points to be considered.

(a)   Although it has long been accepted that a balance sheet prepared under the historical cost concept is an historical record and not a statement of current worth, many people now argue that the balance sheet should at least give an indication of the current value of the company's tangible net assets.

(b) The prudence concept requires that profits should only be recognised when realised in the form either of cash or of other assets, the ultimate cash realisation of which can be assessed with reasonable certainty. It may be argued that recognising unrealised holding gains on fixed assets is contrary to this concept.

On balance, the weight of opinion is now in favour of restating asset values. It is felt that the criticism based on prudence can be met by ensuring that valuations are made as objectively as possible (eg in the case of property, by having independent expert valuations) and by not taking unrealised gains through the profit and loss account, but instead through reserves.

6.5.2 Depreciation is inadequate to finance the replacement of fixed assets

Depreciation is not provided for in order to enforce retention of profits and thus ensure that funds are available for asset replacement. It is intended as a measure of the contribution of fixed assets to the company's activities in the period. However, an incidental effect of providing for depreciation is that not all liquid funds can be paid out to investors and so funds for asset replacement are on hand. What is important is not the replacement of one asset by an identical new one (something that rarely happens) but the replacement of the *operating capability* represented by the old asset.

6.5.3 Holding gains on stocks are included in profit

Another criticism of historical cost depreciation is that it does not fully reflect the value of the asset consumed during the accounting year.

During a period of high inflation the monetary value of stock held may increase significantly while they are being processed. The conventions of historical cost accounting lead to the unrealised part of this holding gain (known as *stock appreciation*) being included in profit for the year.

Exam focus point

> The following example is given to help your understanding of this difficult concept. Exam questions are worth only 1 or 2 marks and so would not be so detailed.

Example: Holding gain

This problem can be illustrated using a simple example. At the beginning of the year a company has 100 units of stock and no other assets. Its trading account for the year is shown below.

TRADING ACCOUNT

	Units	£		Units	£
Opening stock	100	200	Sales (made 31 December)	100	500
Purchases (made 31 December)	100	400			
	200	600			
Closing stock (FIFO basis)	100	400			
	100	200			
Gross profit	–	300			
	100	500		100	500

Apparently the company has made a gross profit of £300. But, at the beginning of the year the company owned 100 units of stock and at the end of the year it owned 100 units of stock and £100 (sales £500 less purchases £400). From this it would seem that a profit of £100 is more reasonable. The remaining £200 is stock appreciation arising as the purchase price increased from £2 to £4.

The criticism can be overcome by using a **capital maintenance concept** based on physical units rather than money values.

6.5.4 Profits (or losses) on holdings of net monetary items are not shown

In periods of inflation the purchasing power, and thus the value, of money falls. It follows that an investment in money will have a lower real value at the end of a period of time than it did at the beginning.

A loss has been incurred. Similarly, the real value of a monetary liability will reduce over a period of time and a gain will be made.

6.5.5 The true effect of inflation on capital maintenance is not shown

To a large extent this follows from the points already mentioned. It is a widely held principle that distributable profits should only be recognised after full allowance has been made for any erosion in the capital value of a business. In historical cost accounts, although capital is maintained in *nominal money terms*, it may not be in *real terms*. In other words, profits may be distributed to the detriment of the long-term viability of the business. This criticism may be made by those who advocate capital maintenance in physical terms.

6.5.6 Comparisons over time are unrealistic

This will tend to an exaggeration of growth. For example, if a company's profit in 1966 was £100,000 and in 1999 £500,000, a shareholder's initial reaction might be that the company had done rather well. If, however, it was then revealed that with £100,000 in 1966 he could buy exactly the same goods as with £500,000 in 1999, the apparent growth would seem less impressive.

7 Accounting policies (FRS 18)

FAST FORWARD

> FRS 18 *Accounting policies* introduces a distinction between **accounting polices** and **accounting estimates**.

The introduction of the *Statement of Principles* had seen a **framework** brought to the standard setting process and a change of **emphasis** in the preparation and regulation of financial statements.

Under FRS 18 there is a distinction between **accounting policies** and **accounting estimates**.

Key terms

An **accounting policy** is concerned with the

- Recognition
- Selection of measurement base and
- Presentation

of assets, liabilities, gains and losses of an entity.

An **accounting estimate** is the method used to establish the monetary value of assets, liabilities, gains and losses using the measurement base selected by the accounting policy.

7.1 Accounting policies

The **most appropriate** accounting policy should be selected in order to give a 'true and fair' view. Two points should be noted about this approach.

- Accounting policies **must conform** to the relevant accounting standards. They can be changed only where a standard **allows** choice.
- Accounting policies should not be chopped and changed on an ad hoc basis. A **balance** must be struck to achieve **consistency** and **reliability**.

A **change in accounting policy** is a change in measurement, presentation or recognition of an item eg a business has written off development expenditure in the past, but now decides to capitalise qualifying development expenditure in the balance sheet.

7.2 Accounting estimates

Accounting estimates involve the use of judgement when applying an accounting policy. The following paragraph gives examples of accounting estimates. The point to note is that a change in accounting estimate does not constitute a change in accounting policy.

7.3 Examples: Accounting estimates

(a) *Depreciation of fixed assets*

   (i) Fixed assets may be depreciated by a number of different methods (by the straight line method, reducing balance method, sum-of-the-digits method, etc).

   (ii) Some fixed assets such as land might not be depreciated at all, because they are not used up.

   (iii) Each method provides a different estimate of depreciation.

   (iv) There remains the more subjective problem of deciding what the expected life of an asset should be, and what its residual value might be, and there is no accounting basis which can rule over this exercise of judgement.

(b) *Research and development expenditure*

   (i) Research expenditure is charged against profit in the period it is incurred. However, development expenditure can be deferred until a later period when the benefits of the development are obtained by the entity.

   (ii) Thus if a company spends £10,000 in 20X5 on developing a new product which is not sold on the market until 20X6, there is a choice of:

      (1) Charging £10,000 against profits in 20X5

      (2) Recording some (or all) of the £10,000 as an asset at the end of 20X5, and charging it against profits in 20X6 (and even 20X7 or later years).

     It depends whether the expenditure is pure research or meets certain conditions so that it can be deferred as development costs (see Chapter 15).

   (iii) There are only two ways of accounting for R & D expenditure. However, there is scope for subjective management decisions about how much of the expenditure should be deferred until later years, and over how many years the costs should be spread.

Question
FRS 18

AB Ltd decides to change its accounting policy following the issue of a new FRS. The FRS includes provisions for accounting for transitional changes.

How should it account for the change in policy?

A   According to FRS 18
B   According to the new FRS

Answer

The correct answer is B. The new FRS includes accounting requirements on the transition.

Chapter Roundup

- Accounting practice recognises a number of concepts.

- Going concern and accruals are the two fundamental accounting concepts as identified by FRS 18 *Accounting policies*.

- You still need to know these other concepts.

- You need to know Chapters 1 and 3 of the ASB statement.

- It is easy to assume that the accounting conventions with which we are familiar, and which we have been using in this Study Text, are the best ones we could use. However, this is not necessarily the case.

- Items in the financial statements can be valued under a number of bases. For your syllabus, you need to know the following bases.
    - Historical cost
    - Replacement cost
    - Net realisable value
    - Economic value

- FRS 18 *Accounting policies* introduces a distinction between **accounting polices** and **accounting estimates**.

Quick Quiz

1 Which FRS deals with accounting assumptions?

2 Which of the following assumptions are included in FRS 18?

    A   Money measurement
    B   Objectivity
    C   Going concern
    D   Business entity

3 Define 'going concern'.

4 What is meant by the prudence concept?

5 Only items which have a monetary value can be included in accounts. Which of the following is a basis of valuation?

    A   Historical cost
    B   Money measurement
    C   Realisation
    D   Business entity

6 Suggest four possible values which might be attributed to an asset in the balance sheet of a business.

7 Making an allowance for debtors is an example of which concept?

    A   Accruals
    B   Going concern
    C   Materiality
    D   Prudence

8 Why is a conceptual framework necessary?

    A   To provide a theoretical basics for financial statements
    B   To provide concepts on which to build a framework

9 Which of the following sections are not included in the ASB's *Statement*?
    A   Users of financial statements
    B   Underlying assumptions
    C   Qualitative characteristics
    D   Concept of capital maintenance

10 What does 'reliability' mean in the context of financial statements?

1   FRS 18 *Accounting policies.*

2   C   Only going concern is included in FRS 18, the others are assumptions and concepts generally used in accountancy, but not mentioned in FRS 18.

3   The assumption that a business will continue in operation for the foreseeable future, without going into liquidation or materially scaling down its operations.

4   Prudence means to be cautious when exercising judgement. In particular profits should not be recognised until realised, but a loss should be recognised as soon as it is foreseen.

5   A   This is the only valuation basis.

6
   - Historical cost
   - Replacement value
   - Net realisable value
   - Economic value

7   D   Prudence

8   A   It forms the theoretical basis for determining what is included in financial statements, how they are measured and how they are communicated.

9   A

10 Free from material error and bias.

Now try the questions below from the Exam Question Bank

Number	Level	Marks	Time
Q3	Examination	2	2 mins
Q4	Examination	2	2 mins
Q5	Examination	2	2 mins
Q6	Examination	2	2 mins

The use of double entry and accounting systems

4

Sources, records and the books of prime entry

Topic list	Syllabus reference
1 The role of source documents	C1(a)-(b), (f)
2 The need for books of prime entry	C2(a)
3 Sales and purchase day books	D1(a)-(b)
4 Cash book	D2(a)
5 Petty cash	D2(b)-(e)

Introduction

From your studies of the first three chapters you should have grasped some important points about the nature and purpose of accounting.

- Most organisations provide products and services in the hope of making a profit for their owners, by receiving payment in money for those goods and services.

- The role of the accounting system is to record these monetary effects and create information about them.

You should also, by now, understand the basic principles underlying the balance sheet and profit and loss account and have an idea of what they look like.

We now turn our attention to the process by which a business transaction works its way through to the financial statements.

It is usual to record a business transaction on a **document**. Such documents include invoices, orders, credit notes and goods received notes, all of which will be discussed in Section 1 of this chapter. In terms of the accounting system these are known as **source documents**. The information on them is processed by the system by, for example, aggregating (adding together) or classifying.

Records of source documents are kept in 'books of prime entry', which, as the name suggests, are the first stage at which a business transaction enters into the accounting system. The various types of books of prime entry are discussed in Sections 2 to 4. We will also look at the treatment of petty cash in Section 5.

In the next chapter we consider what happens to transactions after the books of prime entry stage.

Study guide

			Intellectual level
C1	**Double entry bookkeeping principles including the maintenance of accounting records and sources of information**		
(a)	Identify and explain the function of the main data sources in an accounting system		1
(b)	Outline the contents and purpose of different types of business documentation, including: quotation, sales order, purchase order, goods received note, goods despatched note, invoice, statement, credit note, debit note, remittance advice, receipt		1
(f)	Identify the main types of business transactions, eg sales, purchases, payments, receipts		1
C2	**Ledger accounts, books of prime entry and journals**		
(a)	Identify the main types of ledger accounts and books of prime entry, and understand their nature and function		1
D1	**Sales and purchases**		
(a)	Record sale and purchase transactions in ledger accounts and in day books		1
(b)	Understand and record sales and purchase returns		1
D2	**Cash**		
(a)	Record cash transactions in ledger accounts		1
(b)	Understand the need for a record of petty cash transactions.		1
(c)	Describe the features and operations of petty cash imprest system.		1
(d)	Account for petty cash using imprest and non-imprest methods.		1
(e)	Understand the importance of, and identify controls and security over the petty cash system.		1

Exam guide

These topics are likely to be examined by means of asking which books of prime entry you could use to record a set of transactions.

1 The role of source documents

FAST FORWARD

Business transactions are recorded on **source documents**. Examples include sales and purchase orders, invoices and credit notes.

1.1 Types of source documents

Whenever a business transaction takes place, involving sales or purchases, receiving or paying money, or owing or being owed money, it is usual for the transaction to be recorded on a document. These documents are the source of all the information recorded by a business.

Documents used to record the business transactions in the 'books of account' of the business include the following.

- **Quotation.** A business makes a written offer to a customer to produce or deliver goods or services for a certain amount of money.
- **Sales order**. A customer writes out or signs an order for goods or services he requires.

- **Purchase order**. A business orders from another business goods or services, such as material supplies.
- **Goods received note.** A list of goods that a business has received from a supplier. This is usually prepared by the business's own warehouse or goods receiving area.
- **Goods despatched note.** A list of goods that a business has sent out to a customer.
- **Invoice.** This is discussed further below.
- **Statement.** A document sent out by a supplier to a customer listing all invoices, credit notes and payments received from the customer.
- **Credit note.** A document sent by a supplier to a customer in respect of goods returned or overpayments made by the customer. It is a 'negative' invoice.
- **Debit note.** A document sent by a customer to a supplier in respect of goods returned or an overpayment made. It is a formal request for the supplier to issue a credit note.
- **Remittance advice.** A document sent with a payment, detailing which invoices are being paid and which credit notes offset.
- **Receipt.** A written confirmation that money has been paid. This is usually in respect of cash sales, eg a till receipt from a cash register.

1.2 Invoices

Key term

An **invoice** relates to a sales order or a purchase order.

- When a business sells goods or services on credit to a customer, it sends out an invoice. The details on the invoice should match up with the details on the sales order. The invoice is a request for the customer to pay what he owes.

- When a business buys goods or services on credit it receives an invoice from the supplier. The details on the invoice should match up with the details on the purchase order.

The invoice is primarily a **demand for payment**, but it is used for other purposes as well, as we shall see. Because it has several uses, an invoice is often produced on multi-part stationery, or photocopied, or carbon-copied. The top copy will go to the customer and other copies will be used by various people within the business.

1.2.1 What does an invoice show?

Most invoices are numbered, so that the business can keep track of all the invoices it sends out. Information usually shown on an invoice includes the following.

(a)   Name and address of the seller and the purchaser
(b)   Date of the sale
(c)   Description of what is being sold
(d)   Quantity and unit price of what has been sold (eg 20 pairs of shoes at £25 a pair)
(e)   Details of trade discount, if any (eg 10% reduction in cost if buying over 100 pairs of shoes). We shall look at discounts in a later chapter
(f)   Total amount of the invoice including (in the UK) any details of VAT
(g)   Sometimes, the date by which payment is due, and other terms of sale.

1.2.2 Uses of multi-part invoices

As stated above invoices may be used for different purposes.

- Top copy to customer as a request for payment
- Second copy to accounts department to match to eventual payment
- Third copy to ware house to generate a despatch of goods, as evidenced by a goods despatched note

- Fourth copy stapled to sales order and kept in sales department as a record of sales.

Please note that businesses will design their own invoices and there may be other copies for other departments. Not all businesses will need four part invoices. A very small business may use the customer copy of the invoice as a despatch note as well. In addition, the sales invoice may be stapled to the sales order and both documents passed to the accounts department.

1.3 The credit note

Student Supplies Ltd sent out an invoice to the county council for 450 rulers delivered to the local primary school. The typist accidentally typed in a total of £162.10, instead of £62.10. The county council has been *overcharged* by £100. What is Student Supplies to do?

Alternatively, suppose that when the primary school received the rulers, it found that they had all been broken in the post and that it was going to send them back. Although the county council has received an invoice for £62.10, it has no intention of paying it, because the rulers were useless. Again, what is Student Supplies to do?

The answer is that the supplier (in this case, Student Supplies) sends out a **credit note**. A credit note is sometimes printed in red to distinguish it from an invoice. Otherwise, it will be made out in much the same way as an invoice, but with less detail and 'Credit Note Number' instead of 'Invoice Number'.

Key term

> A **credit note** is a document relating to returned goods or refunds when a customer has been overcharged. It can be regarded as a 'negative invoice'.

1.4 Other documents

The following documents are sometimes used in connection with sales and purchases.

(a) Debit notes
(b) Goods received notes

A **debit note** might be issued to **adjust an invoice** already issued. This is also commonly achieved by issuing a revised invoice after raising a credit or debit note purely for internal purposes (ie to keep the records straight).

More commonly, a debit note is issued to a supplier as a means of formally requesting a credit note.

Goods received notes (GRNs) record a receipt of goods, most commonly in a warehouse. They may be used in addition to suppliers' advice notes. Often the accounts department will require to see the relevant GRN before paying a supplier's invoice. Even where GRNs are not routinely used, the details of a consignment from a supplier which arrives without an advice note must always be recorded.

Question

Complete the blanks

Fill in the blanks.

'Student Supplies Ltd sends out a .... to a credit customer in order to correct an error where a customer has been overcharged on an ....'

Answer

Credit note; invoice.

2 The need for books of prime entry

Books of prime entry record the source documents.

We have seen that in the course of business, source documents are created. The details on these source documents need to be summarised, as otherwise the business might forget to ask for some money, or forget to pay some, or even accidentally pay something twice. In other words, it needs to keep records of source documents – of transactions – so that it can keep tabs on what is going on. Such records are made in **books of prime entry**.

Books of prime entry are books in which we first record transactions.

The main books of prime entry are as follows.

(a)   Sales day book
(b)   Purchase day book
(c)   Sales returns day book
(d)   Purchases returns day book
(e)   Journal (described in the next chapter)
(f)   Cash book
(g)   Petty cash book

It is worth bearing in mind that, for convenience, this chapter describes books of prime entry as if they are actual books. Nowadays, books of prime entry are often not books at all, but rather files hidden in the memory of a computer. However, the principles remain the same whether they are manual or computerised.

You may get a question on books of prime entry, and you also need to know where the entries to the ledger accounts come from and how they are posted.

3 Sales and purchase day books

Day books are the books of prime entry for sales and purchases.

3.1 The sales day book

The **sales day book** is the book of prime entry for credit sales.

The **sales day book** is used to keep a list of all invoices sent out to customers each day. An extract from a sales day book might look like this.

SALES DAY BOOK

Date	Invoice	Customer	Total amount invoiced
20X0			£
Jan 10	247	Jones & Co	105.00
	248	Smith Ltd	86.40
	249	Alex & Co	31.80
	250	Enor College	1,264.60
			1,487.80

Most businesses 'analyse' their sales. For example, suppose that the business sells boots and shoes, and that the sale to Smith was entirely boots, the sale to Alex was entirely shoes, and the other two sales were a mixture of both.

Then the sales day book might look like this.

SALES DAY BOOK

Date 20X0	Invoice	Customer	Total amount invoiced £	Boot sales £	Shoe sales £
Jan 10	247	Jones & Co	105.00	60.00	45.00
	248	Smith Ltd	86.40	86.40	
	249	Alex & Co	31.80		31.80
	250	Enor College	1,264.60	800.30	464.30
			1,487.80	946.70	541.10

This sort of analysis gives the managers of the business useful information which helps them to decide how best to run the business.

3.2 The purchase day book

A business also keeps a record in the purchase day book of all the invoices it receives.

Key term

> The **purchase day book** is the book of prime entry for credit purchases.

An extract from a purchase day book might look like this.

PURCHASE DAY BOOK

Date 20X8	Supplier	Total amount invoiced £	Purchases £	Electricity etc £
Mar 15	Cook & Co	315.00	315.00	
	W Butler	29.40	29.40	
	EEB	116.80		116.80
	Show Fair Ltd	100.00	100.00	
		561.20	444.40	116.80

Points to note:

(a) There is no 'invoice number' column, because the purchase day book records other people's invoices, which have all sorts of different numbers.

(b) Like the sales day book, the purchase day book analyses the invoices which have been sent in. In this example, three of the invoices related to goods which the business intends to re-sell (called simply 'purchases') and the fourth invoice was an electricity bill.

3.3 The sales returns day book

When customers return goods for some reason, the returns are recorded in the sales return day book. An extract from the sales returns day book might look like this:

SALES RETURNS DAY BOOK

Date 20X8	Customer and goods	Amount £
30 April	Owen Plenty	
	3 pairs 'Texas' boots	135.00

Key term

> The **sales returns day book** is the book of prime entry for goods returned by customers.

Not all sales returns day books analyse what goods were returned, but it makes sense to keep as complete a record as possible. Where a business has very few sales returns, it may record a credit note as a negative entry in the sales day book.

3.4 The purchase returns day book

The purchase returns day book is kept to record goods which the business sends back to its suppliers. The business might expect a cash refund and credit note from the supplier.

An extract from the purchase returns day book might look like this:

PURCHASE RETURNS DAY BOOK

Date	Supplier and goods	Amount
20X8		£
29 April	Boxes Ltd	
	300 cardboard boxes	46.60

> **Key term**
>
> The **purchase returns day book** is the book of prime entry for goods returned to suppliers.

Once again, a business with very few purchase returns may record a credit note received as a negative entry in the purchase day book.

4 Cash book

> The cash book is the book of prime entry for the **bank account**.

4.1 The cash book

The cash book is also a day book, which is used to keep a cumulative record of money received and money paid out by the business. The cash book deals with money paid into and out of the business **bank account**. This could be money received on the business premises in notes, coins and cheques. There are also receipts and payments made by bank transfer, standing order, direct debit and, in the case of bank interest and charges, directly by the bank.

Some cash, in notes and coins, is usually kept on the business premises in order to make occasional payments for odd items of expense. This cash is usually accounted for separately in a **petty cash book** (which we will look at shortly).

One side (the left) of the cash book is used to record receipts of cash, and the other side (the right) is used to record payments. The best way to see how the cash book works is to follow through an example. For convenience, we are showing the cash receipts and cash payments sides separately, but they are part of the same book.

> **Key term**
>
> The **cash book** is the book of prime entry for amounts paid into and out of the bank account.

4.2 Example: cash book

At the beginning of 1 September, Robin Plenty had £900 in the bank. During 1 September 20X7, Robin Plenty had the following receipts and payments.

(a)   Cash sale - receipt of £80
(b)   Payment from credit customer Hay £400 less discount allowed £20
(c)   Payment from credit customer Been £720
(d)   Payment from credit customer Seed £150 less discount allowed £10
(e)   Cheque received for cash to provide a short-term loan from Len Dinger £1,800
(f)   Second cash sale - receipts of £150
(g)   Cash received for sale of machine £200
(h)   Payment to supplier Kew £120
(i)   Payment to supplier Hare £310
(j)   Payment of telephone bill £400
(k)   Payment of gas bill £280

(l)   £100 in cash withdrawn from bank for petty cash

(m)   Payment of £1,500 to Hess for new plant and machinery

If you look through these transactions, you will see that seven of them are receipts and six of them are payments.

The receipts part of the cash book for 1 September would look like this.

CASH BOOK (RECEIPTS)

Date 20X7	Narrative	Reference	Total £
1 Sept	Balance b/d*		900
	Cash sale		80
	Debtor: Hay		380
	Debtor: Been		720
	Debtor: Seed		140
	Loan: Len Dinger		1,800
	Cash sale		150
	Sale of fixed asset		200
			4,370
2 Sept	Balance b/d*		1,660

* 'b/d' = brought down (ie brought forward)

Points to note:

(a)   There is space on the right hand side of the cash book so that the receipts can be analysed under various headings - for example, 'receipts from debtors', 'cash sales' and 'other receipts'.

(b)   The cash received in the day amounted to £3,470. Added to the £900 at the start of the day, this comes to £4,370. But this is not, of course, the amount to be carried forward to the next day, because first we have to subtract all the payments made during 1 September.

The payments part of the cash book for 1 September would look like this.

CASH BOOK (PAYMENTS)

Date 20X7	Narrative	Reference	Total £
1 Sept	Creditor: Kew		120
	Creditor: Hare		310
	Telephone		400
	Gas bill		280
	Petty cash		100
	Machinery purchase		1,500
	Balance c/d		1,660
			4,370

As you can see, this is very similar to the receipts part of the cash book. But note the following.

(a)   The analysis on the right would be under headings like 'payments to creditors', 'payments into petty cash', 'wages' and 'other payments'.

(b)   Payments during 1 September totalled £2,710. We know that the total of receipts was £4,370. That means that there is a balance of £4,370 – £2,710 = £1,660 to be 'carried down' to the start of the next day. As you can see this 'balance carried down' is noted at the end of the payments column, so that the receipts and payments totals show the same figure of £4,370 at the end of 1 September. And if you look to the receipts part of this example, you can see that £1,660 has been brought down ready for the next day.

With analysis columns completed, the cash book given in the examples above might look as follows.

CASH BOOK (RECEIPTS SECTION)

Date	Narrative	Total £	Debtors £	Cash sales £	Other £
20X7					
1 Sept	Balance b/d	900			
	Cash sale	80		80	
	Debtor - Hay	380	380		
	Debtor - Been	720	720		
	Debtor - Seed	140	140		
	Loan - Len Dinger	1,800			1,800
	Cash sale	150		150	
	Sale of fixed asset	200			200
		4,370	1,240	230	2,000

CASH BOOK (PAYMENTS SECTION)

Date	Narrative	Total £	Creditors £	Petty cash £	Wages £	Other £
20X7						
1 Sept	Creditor - Kew	120	120			
	Creditor - Hare	310	310			
	Telephone	400				400
	Gas bill	280				280
	Petty cash	100		100		
	Machinery purchase	1,500				1,500
	Balance c/d	1,660				
		4,370	430	100	–	2,180

4.3 Bank statements

Weekly or monthly, a business will receive a **bank statement**. Bank statements should be used to check that the amount shown as a balance in the cash book agrees with the amount on the bank statement, and that no cash has 'gone missing'. This agreement or 'reconciliation' of the cash book with a statement is the subject of a later chapter.

5 Petty cash

FAST FORWARD

Most businesses keep **petty cash** on the premises, which is topped up from the main bank account. Under the **imprest system**, the petty cash is kept at an agreed sum, so that each topping up is equal to the amount paid out in the period.

5.1 What is petty cash?

Most businesses keep a small amount of cash on the premises to make occasional small payments in cash, eg staff refreshments, postage stamps, to pay the office cleaner, taxi fares, etc. This is often called the cash float or **petty cash** account. The cash float can also be the resting place for occasional small receipts, eg cash paid by a visitor to make a phone call, etc.

5.2 Security

As you will appreciate, keeping cash (even in small amounts) on the premises is a security risk. Therefore a petty cash system is usually subject to strict controls.

- Payment is only made in respect of **authorised** claims.
- All claims are supported by **evidence**.

In addition, the business may use the **imprest system** (see Section 5.4 below).

5.2.1 Authorisation

An employee must complete a **petty cash voucher** detailing the expenses claimed. Usually receipts must be attached to the voucher (see below: evidence). The completed voucher then needs to be signed by (say) the employee's manager to **authorise** payment. Some times the petty cashier may be authorised to sign vouchers for small amounts (eg £5 or less) if these are supported by receipts.

5.2.2 Evidence

All petty cash vouchers must have receipts for the expenditure attached, as **evidence** that the employee has really incurred that cost. Sometimes receipts may not be available (eg taxi fares) and the employer may then have systems in place to authorise claims without evidence.

5.3 The petty cash book

A **petty cash book** is a cash book for small payments.

Although the amounts involved are small, petty cash transactions still need to be recorded; otherwise the cash float could be abused for personal expenses or even stolen.

There are usually more payments than receipts, and petty cash must be 'topped up' from time to time with cash from the business bank account. A typical layout follows.

PETTY CASH BOOK

Receipts £	Date 20X7	Narrative	Total £	Milk £	Postage £	Travel £	Other £
250	1 Sept	Bal b/d					
		Milk bill	25	25			
		Postage stamps	5		5		
		Taxi fare	10			10	
		Flowers for sick staff	15				15
		Bal c/d	195				
250			250	25	5	10	15

5.4 Imprest system

Under what is called the **imprest system**, the amount of money in petty cash is kept at an agreed sum or 'float' (say £250). This is called the **imprest amount**. Expense items are recorded on vouchers as they occur, so that at any time:

	£
Cash still held in petty cash	195
Plus voucher payments (25 + 5 + 10 + 15)	55
Must equal the imprest amount	250

The total float is made up regularly (to £250, or whatever the imprest amount is) by means of a cash payment from the bank account into petty cash. The amount of the 'top-up' into petty cash will be the total of the voucher payments since the previous top-up.

The **imprest system** makes a refund of the total paid out in a period.

The June 2008 exam included a question asking students to calculate the imprest amount. Many students did not read the question carefully enough and so arrived at a wrong answer. Make sure you follow the example below, which demonstrates the correct technique.

5.5 Example: petty cash and the imprest system

DEF operates an imprest system for petty cash. During February 20X9, the following petty cash transactions took place.

		£
2.2.X9	Stamps	12.00
3.2.X9	Milk	25.00
8.2.X9	Taxi fare	15.00
17.2.X9	Stamps	5.00
18.2.X9	Received from staff for photocopying	8.00
28.2.X9	Stationery	7.50

The amount remaining in petty cash at the end of the month was £93.50. What is the imprest amount?

A £166.00
B £150.00
C £72.50
D £56.50

The solution is B.

	£	
Opening balance (imprest amount)	150.00	(Balancing figure)
Add: amount received from staff	8.00	
	158.00	
Less: expenditure	(64.50)	(12 + 25 + 15 + 5 + 7.50)
Cash in hand at the end of the month	93.50	

Question

State which books of prime entry the following transactions would be entered into.

(a) Your business pays A Brown (a supplier) £450.00.
(b) You send D Smith (a customer) an invoice for £650.
(c) Your accounts manager asks you for £12 urgently in order to buy some envelopes.
(d) You receive an invoice from A Brown for £300.
(e) You pay D Smith £500.
(f) F Jones (a customer) returns goods to the value of £250.
(g) You return goods to J Green to the value of £504.
(h) F Jones pays you £500.

Answer

(a) Cash book
(b) Sales day book
(c) Petty cash book
(d) Purchases day book
(e) Cash book
(f) Sales returns day book
(g) Purchase returns day book
(h) Cash book

Another book of prime entry is the **journal** which is considered in the next chapter.

- Business transactions are recorded on **source documents**. Examples include sales and purchase orders, invoices and credit notes.

- Books of prime entry record the source documents.

- The main books of prime entry are as follows.

  - Sales day book
  - Purchase day book
  - Sales returns day book
  - Purchases returns day book
  - Journal (described in the next chapter)
  - Cash book
  - Petty cash book

- Day books are the books of prime entry for sales and purchases.

- The cash book is the book of prime entry for the bank account.

- Most businesses keep petty cash on the premises, which is topped up from the main bank account. Under the imprest system, the petty cash is kept at an agreed sum, so that each topping up is equal to the amount paid out in the period.

1   Name four pieces of information normally shown on an invoice.

2   Which of the following is not a book of prime entry.

    A   Sales invoice
    B   Purchase day book
    C   Sales day book
    D   Journal

3   Which of the following is a source document for petty cash.

    A   Purchase invoice
    B   Quotation
    C   Sales invoice
    D   Receipt and claim form

4   What is the purchase returns day book used to record?

    A   Supplier's invoices
    B   Customer's invoices
    C   Details of goods returned to suppliers
    D   Details of goods returned by customers

5   What is the difference between the cash book and the petty cash book?

6   Petty cash is controlled under an imprest system. The imprest amount is £100. During a period, payments totalling £53 have been made. How much needs to be reimbursed at the end of the period to restore petty cash to the imprest account?

    A   £100
    B   £53
    C   £47
    D   £50

7   All petty cash claims are automatically paid from petty cash.

    Is this statement:

    A   True
    B   False

1   **Four** from the following
    - Invoice number
    - Seller's name and address
    - Purchaser's name and address
    - Date of sale
    - Description of goods or services
    - Quantity and unit price
    - Trade discount (if any)
    - Total amount, including sales tax (if any)
    - Any special terms

2   A   Sales invoice is a source document

3   D   The claim form and receipt form the source document for the petty cash system.

4   C   Supplier's invoices (A) are recorded in the purchase day book, customer's invoices (B) are recorded in the sales day book and goods returned by customers (D) are recorded in the sales returns day book.

5   The cash book records amounts paid into or out of the bank account. The petty cash book records payments of small amounts of cash.

6   B   Under the imprest system, a reimbursement is made of the amount of the vouchers (or payments made) for the period.

7   B   Only **authorised** and **evidenced** petty cash claims are paid out of petty cash.

Now try the questions below from the Exam Question Bank

Number	Level	Marks	Time
Q7	Examination	2	2 mins
Q8	Examination	1	1 min

Ledger accounts and double entry

Topic list	Syllabus reference
1 Why do we need ledger accounts?	C1(e)
2 The nominal ledger	C1(e), C2(a), C3(a)
3 The accounting equation	C1(d), D8(a)
4 Double entry bookkeeping	C1(c)
5 The journal	C2(b)-(c)
6 Day book analysis	D1(a)-(b), D2(a)
7 The imprest system	D2(d)
8 The sales and purchase ledgers	D1(a), D1(b), D8(a)

Introduction

In the previous chapter we saw how to organise transactions into lists (ie entered into books of prime entry). It is not easy, however, to see how a business is doing from the information scattered throughout these books of prime entry. The lists need to be summarised. This is **ledger accounting**, which we look at in Sections 1 and 2.

The summary is produced in the nominal ledger by a process you may have heard of known as **double entry bookkeeping**. This is the cornerstone of accounts preparation and is surprisingly simple, once you have grasped the rules. We will look at the essentials in Sections 3 and 4.

In Section 5, we will deal with the final book of prime entry: **the journal**.

We will then look in detail at posting transactions from the day books to the ledgers in Sections 6 and 7.

Finally, we will consider how to deal with credit transactions in Section 8.

Study guide

		Intellectual level
C1	**Double entry bookkeeping principles including the maintenance of accounting records and sources of information**	
(c)	Understand and apply the concept of double entry accounting and the duality concept	1
(d)	Understand and apply the accounting equation	1
(e)	Understand how the accounting system contributes to providing useful accounting information and complies with organisational policies and deadlines	1
C2	**Ledger accounts, books of prime entry and journals**	
(a)	Identify the main types of ledger accounts and books of prime entry and understand their nature and function	1
(b)	Understand and illustrate the uses of journals and the posting of journal entries into ledger accounts	1
(c)	Identify correct journals from given narrative	1
C3	**Accounting systems and the impact of information technology on financial reporting**	
(a)	Understand the basic function and form of accounting records in a typical manual system	1
D1	**Sales and purchases**	
(a)	Record sales and purchase transactions in ledger accounts and in day books	1
(b)	Understand and record sales and purchase returns	1
D2	**Cash**	
(a)	Record cash transactions in ledger accounts	1
(d)	Account for petty cash using imprest and non-imprest methods	1
D8	**Debtors and creditors**	
(a)	Explain and identify examples of debtors and creditors	1

Exam guide

This chapter is the fundamental background for all accounting. It is, therefore, **extremely important** and is highly likely to be examined.

1 Why do we need ledger accounts?

FAST FORWARD

Ledger accounts are a summary of the books of prime entry.

In earlier chapters we saw how a profit and loss account and balance sheet are presented. We have also seen, by means of the accounting equation and the business equation, that it would be possible to prepare a statement of the affairs of a business at any time we like, and that a profit and loss account and a balance sheet could be drawn up on any date, relating to any period of time.

A business is continually making transactions (eg buying and selling and) we do not want to prepare a profit and loss account and a balance sheet on completion of every individual transaction. To do so would be a time-consuming and cumbersome administrative task.

It is common sense that a business should keep a record of the transactions that it makes, the assets it acquires and liabilities it incurs. When the time comes to prepare a profit and loss account and a balance sheet, the relevant information can be taken from those records.

The **records of transactions, assets and liabilities** should be:

(a) **Dated** and in **chronological order**, so that transactions can be related to a particular period of time.
(b) Built up in **cumulative totals**. For example, a business may build up the total of its sales:

    (i)   Day by day (eg total sales on Monday, total sales on Tuesday)
    (ii)   Week by week
    (iii) Month by month
    (iv) Year by year

We have already seen the first step in this process, which is to list all the transactions in various books of prime entry. Now we must turn our attention to the method used to summarise these records: **ledger accounting** and **double entry**.

This system of summarising information speeds up the provision of useful information to managers and so helps managers to keep to organisational deadlines (eg provision of monthly profit figures for management purposes).

2 The nominal ledger

Key term

> The **nominal ledger** is an accounting record which summarises the financial affairs of a business.

2.1 What is the nominal ledger?

The nominal ledger is sometimes called the **'general ledger'**. The information contained in the books of prime entry (see Chapter 4) is **summarised** and **posted** to accounts in the nominal ledger.

It contains details of assets, liabilities and capital, income and expenditure and so profit and loss. It consists of a large number of different accounts, each account having its own purpose or 'name' and an identity or code.

There may be various subdivisions, whether for convenience, ease of handling, confidentiality, security, or to meet the needs of computer software design. For example, the ledger may be split alphabetically, with different clerks responsible for sections A-F, G-M, N-R and S-Z. This can help to stop fraud, as there would have to be collusion between the different section clerks.

Examples of accounts in the nominal ledger include the following.

(a) Plant and machinery at cost (fixed asset)
(b) Motor vehicles at cost (fixed asset)
(c) Plant and machinery, provision for depreciation (liability)
(d) Motor vehicles, provision for depreciation (liability)
(e) Proprietor's capital (liability)
(f) Stocks – raw materials (current asset)
(g) Stocks – finished goods (current asset)
(h) Total debtors (current asset)
(i) Total creditors (current liability)
(j) Wages and salaries (expense item)
(k) Rent and rates (expense item)
(l) Advertising expenses (expense item)
(m) Bank charges (expense item)
(n) Motor expenses (expense item)
(o) Telephone expenses (expense item)
(p) Sales (income or revenue item)
(q) Total cash or bank overdraft (current asset or liability)

In the financial statements, the revenue and expenditure accounts will help to form the profit and loss account; while the asset and liability accounts go into the balance sheet.

2.2 The format of a ledger account

If a ledger account were to be kept in an actual book rather than as a computer record, it might look like this:

ADVERTISING EXPENSES

Date	Narrative	Reference	£	Date	Narrative	Reference	£
20X6							
15 April	JFK Agency for quarter to 31 March	PL 348	2,500				

For the rest of this chapter, we will assume that a manual system is being used in order to illustrate fully the workings of the ledger accounts. However, a computerised system performs the same functions, although the actual ledger accounts may be 'hidden' inside the computer!

There are two sides to the account, and an account heading on top, and so it is convenient to think in terms of 'T' accounts.

(a) On top of the account is its name.

(b) There is a left hand side, or **debit side**.

(c) There is a right hand side, or **credit side**.

NAME OF ACCOUNT

DEBIT SIDE	£	CREDIT SIDE	£

3 The accounting equation

FAST FORWARD

The assets of a business must be equal to the liabilities (accounting equation).

We will start by showing how to account for a business's transactions from the time that trading first begins. We will use an example to illustrate the 'accounting equation', ie the rule that the assets of a business will at all times equal its liabilities. This is also known as **the balance sheet equation**.

3.1 Example: the accounting equation

Courtney Spice starts a business. The business begins by owning the cash that Courtney put into it, £2,500. The business is a separate entity in accounting terms and so it owes the money to Courtney as **capital**.

Key term

In accounting, **capital** is an investment of money (funds) with the intention of earning a return. A business proprietor invests capital with the intention of earning profit. As long as that money is invested, accountants will treat the capital as money owed to the proprietor by the business.

When Courtney Spice sets up her business:

Capital invested	=	£2,500
Cash	=	£2,500

Capital invested is a form of liability, because it is an amount owed by the business to its owner(s). Adapting this to the idea that liabilities and assets are always equal amounts, we can state the accounting equation as follows.

Assets		=	Capital		+	Liabilities

For Courtney Spice, as at 1 July 20X6:

£2,500 (cash)	=	£2,500	+	£0

3.2 Example continued

Courtney Spice uses some of the money invested to purchase a market stall from Noel Jarvis, who is retiring from his fruit and vegetables business. The cost of the stall is £1,800.

She also purchases some herbs and spices from a trader in the Albert Square wholesale market, at a cost of £650.

This leaves £50 in cash, after paying for the stall and goods for resale, out of the original £2,500. Courtney kept £30 in the bank and drew out £20 in small change to use as a float. She was now ready for her first day of market trading on 3 July 20X6.

The assets and liabilities of the business have now altered, and at 3 July, before trading begins, the state of her business is as follows.

Assets	£	=	Capital		+	Liabilities
Stall	1,800	=	£2,500		+	£0
Herbs and spices	650					
Cash at bank	30					
Cash in hand	20					
	2,500					

The stall and the herbs and spices are physical items, but they must be given a money value. This money value is usually what they cost the business (called **historical cost** in accounting terms).

3.3 Profit introduced into the accounting equation

Let us now suppose that on 3 July Courtney has a very successful day. She is able to sell all of her herbs and spices, for £900. All of her sales are for cash.

Since Courtney has sold goods costing £650 to earn revenue of £900, we can say that she has **earned a profit of £250 on the day's trading.**

Profits belong to the owners of a business. In this case, the £250 belongs to Courtney Spice. However, so long as the business retains the profits, and does not pay anything out to its owners, the **retained profits** are accounted for as an addition to the proprietor's capital.

Assets		=	Capital		+	Liabilities
	£			£		
Stall	1,800		Original investment	2,500		
Herbs and spices	0					
Cash in hand and at bank						
(30+20+900)	950		Retained profit	250		
	2,750	=		2,750	+	£0

We can re-arrange the accounting equation to help us to calculate the capital balance.

Assets – liabilities	=	Capital, which is the same as
Net assets	=	Capital

At the beginning and then at the end of 3 July 20X6 Courtney Spice's financial position was as follows.

		Net Assets	Capital
(a)	At the beginning of the day:	£(2,500 – 0) = £2,500 =	£2,500
(b)	At the end of the day:	£(2,750 – 0) = £2,750 =	£2,750

There has been an increase of £250 in net assets, which is the amount of profits earned during the day.

3.4 Drawings

Key term

> **Drawings** are amounts of money taken out of a business by its owner.

Since Courtney Spice has made a profit of £250 from her first day's work, she might well feel fully justified in drawing some of the profits out of the business. After all, business owners, like everyone else, need income for living expenses. We will suppose that Courtney decides to pay herself £180, in 'wages'.

The payment of £180 is probably regarded by Courtney as a fair reward for her day's work, and she might think of the sum as being in the nature of wages. However, the £180 is not an expense to be deducted before the figure of net profit is arrived at. In other words, it would be incorrect to calculate the net profit earned by the business as follows.

	£
Profit on sale of herbs and spices etc	250
Less 'wages' paid to Courtney	180
Net profit earned by business (incorrect)	70

This is because any amounts paid by a business to its proprietor are treated by accountants as withdrawals of profit (the usual term is **appropriations of profit**), and not as expenses incurred by the business. In the case of Courtney's business, the true position is that the net profit earned is the £250 surplus on sale of flowers.

	£
Net profit earned by business	250
Less profit withdrawn by Courtney	180
Net profit retained in the business	70

Profits are capital as long as they are retained in the business. Once they are **appropriated**, the business suffers a reduction in capital.

The drawings are taken in cash, and so the business loses £180 of its cash assets. After the drawings have been made, the accounting equation would be restated.

(a)

Assets	£	=	Capital	£	+	Liabilities
Stall	1,800		Original investment	2,500		
Herbs and spices	0		Retained profit	70		
Cash (950-180)	770					
	2,570			2,570	+	£0

(b) Alternatively

	Net assets		Capital
	£(2,570 – 0) =		£2,570

The increase in net assets since trading operations began is now only £(2,570 – 2,500) = £70, which is the amount of the retained profits.

Question

Capital

Which of the following is correct?

A   Capital = assets + liabilities
B   Capital = liabilities – assets
C   Capital = assets – liabilities
D   Capital + assets = liabilities

Answer

The correct answer is C. As assets = liabilities + capital, then capital = assets – liabilities

3.5 The business equation

FAST FORWARD

The business equation gives a definition of profits earned.

The preceding example has attempted to show that the amount of profit earned can be related to the increase in the net assets of the business, and the drawings of profits by the proprietor.

Formula to learn

Profit (P) = Increase in net assets (I) + drawings (D) − capital introduced (C_i)

In our example of Courtney Spice's business on 3 July 20X6, after drawings have been taken:

Profit   = £ 70 + £180 − £0
         = £250

3.6 Example continued

The next market day is on 10 July, and Courtney gets ready by purchasing more herbs and spices for cash, at a cost of £740. She was not feeling well, however, because of a heavy cold, and so she decided to accept the offer of help for the day from her cousin Bianca. Bianca would be paid a wage of £40 at the end of the day.

Trading on 10 July was again very brisk, and Courtney and Bianca sold all their goods for £1,100 cash. Courtney paid Bianca her wage of £40 and drew out £200 for herself.

Required

(a)   State the accounting equation before trading began on 10 July.

(b)   State the accounting equation at the end of 10 July, after paying Bianca:

    (i)   But before drawings are taken out.
    (ii)   After drawings have been made.

(c)   State the business equation to compute profits earned on 10 July.

You are reminded that the accounting equation for the business at the end of transactions for 3 July is given in Paragraph 3.4.

Solution

(a)   After the purchase of the goods for £740.

Assets		=	Capital	+	Liabilities
	£				
Stall	1,800				
Goods	740				
Cash (770 − 740)	30				
	2,570	=	£ 2,570	+	£0

(b)   (i)   On 10 July, all the goods are sold for £1,100 cash, and Bianca is paid £40. The profit for the day is £320.

	£	£
Sales		1,100
Less cost of goods sold	740	
Bianca's wage	40	
		780
Profit		320

	Assets		=	Capital		+	Liabilities
		£			£		£
Stall	1,800			At beginning of 10 July	2,570		
Goods	0			Profits earned on 10 July	320		
Cash							
(30+ 1,100 – 40)	1,090						
	2,890		=		2,890	+	£0

(ii)   After Courtney has taken drawings of £200 in cash, retained profits will be only £(320 - 200) = £120.

	Assets		=	Capital		+	Liabilities
		£			£		£
Stall	1,800			At beginning of 10 July	2,570		
Goods	0			Retained profits for 10 July	120		
Cash							
(1,090 – 200)	890						
	2,690		=		2,690	+	£0

(c)   The increase in net assets on 10 July, after drawings have been taken, is as follows.

	£
Net assets at end of 10 July	2,690
Net assets at beginning of 10 July	2,570
Increase in net assets	120

The business equation is:

$$P = I + D - C_i$$
$$= £120 + £200 - £0$$
$$= £320$$

This confirms the calculation of profit made in b(i).

Tutorial note. It is very important that you understand the principles described so far. Do not read on until you are confident that you understand the solution to this example.

3.7 Creditors and debtors

FAST FORWARD

Creditors are liabilities. Debtors are assets.

Key term

A **creditor** is a person to whom a business owes money.

A **trade creditor** is a person to whom a business owes money for debts incurred in the course of trading operations. In an examination question, this term might refer to debts still outstanding which arise from the purchase from suppliers of materials, components or goods for resale.

A business does not always pay immediately for goods or services it buys. It is a common business practice to make purchases on credit, with a promise to pay within 30 days, or two months or three months of the date of the bill or 'invoice' for the goods. For example, if A buys goods costing £2,000 on credit from B, B might send A an invoice for £2,000, dated say 1 March, with credit terms that payment must be made within 30 days. If A then delays payment until 31 March, B will be a creditor of A between 1 and 31 March, for £2,000.

A creditor is a **liability** of a business.

Key term

Just as a business might buy goods on credit, so too might it sell goods to customers on credit. A customer who buys goods without paying cash for them straight away is a **debtor**.

For example, suppose that C sells goods on credit to D for £6,000 on terms that the debt must be settled within two months of the invoice date 1 October. If D does not pay the £6,000 until 30 November, D will be a debtor of C for £6,000 from 1 October until 30 November.

A debtor is an asset of a business. When the debt is finally paid, the debtor 'disappears' as an asset, to be replaced by 'cash at bank and in hand'.

3.8 Example continued

The example of Courtney Spice's market stall will be continued further, by looking at the consequences of the following transactions in the week to 17 July 20X6. (See Paragraph 3.6 (b)(ii) for the situation as at the end of 10 July.)

(a)   Courtney Spice realises that she is going to need more money in the business and so she makes the following arrangements.

   (i)   She invests immediately a further £250 of her own capital.

   (ii)   She persuades her Uncle Felix to lend her £500 immediately. Uncle Felix tells her that she can repay the loan whenever she likes, but in the meantime, she must pay him interest of £5 per week each week at the end of the market day. They agree that it will probably be quite a long time before the loan is eventually repaid.

(b)   She is very pleased with the progress of her business, and decides that she can afford to buy a second hand van to pick up herbs and spices from her supplier and bring them to her stall in the market. She finds a car dealer, Laurie Loader, who agrees to sell her a van on credit for £700. Courtney agrees to pay for the van after 30 days' trial use.

(c)   During the week before the next market day (which is on 17 July), Courtney's Uncle Grant telephones her to ask whether she would be interested in selling him some spice racks and herb chopping boards as presents for his friends. Courtney tells him that she will look for a supplier. After some investigations, she buys what Uncle Grant has asked for, paying £300 in cash to the supplier. Uncle Grant accepts delivery of the goods and agrees to pay £350 to Courtney for them, but he asks if she can wait until the end of the month for payment. Courtney agrees.

(d)   The next market day approaches, and Courtney buys herbs and spices costing £800. Of these purchases £750 are paid in cash, with the remaining £50 on seven days' credit. Courtney decides to use Bianca's services again as an assistant on market day, at an agreed wage of £40.

(e)   For the third market day running, on 17 July, Courtney succeeds in selling all her goods earning revenue of £1,250 (all in cash). She decides to take out drawings of £240 for her week's work. She also pays Bianca £40 in cash. She decides to make the interest payment to her Uncle Felix the next time she sees him.

(f)   We shall ignore any van expenses for the week, for the sake of relative simplicity.

Required

(a)   State the accounting equation:

   (i)   After Courtney and Uncle Felix have put more money into the business and after the purchase of the van.

   (ii)   After the sale of goods to Uncle Grant.

   (iii)   After the purchase of goods for the weekly market.

   (iv)   At the end of the day's trading on 17 July, and after drawings have been appropriated out of profit.

(b)   State the business equation showing profit earned during the week ended 17 July.

Question	Formula

Before you look through the solution, can you state the formula for the business equation?

Solution

There are a number of different transactions to account for here. This solution deals with them one at a time in chronological order. (In practice, it would be possible to do one set of calculations which combines the results of all the transactions, but we shall defer such 'shortcut' methods until later.)

(a)　(i)　*The addition of Courtney's extra capital and Uncle Felix's loan*

An investment analyst might define the loan of Uncle Felix as a capital investment on the grounds that it will probably be for the long term. Uncle Felix is not the owner of the business, however, even though he has made an investment of a loan in it. He would only become an owner if Courtney offered him a partnership in the business, and she has not done so. To the business, Uncle Felix is a long-term creditor, and it is more appropriate to define his investment as a liability of the business and not as business capital.

The accounting equation after £(250 + 500) = £750 cash is put into the business will be:

Assets	£	=	Capital	£	+	Liabilities	£
Stall	1,800		As at end of 10 July	2,690		Loan	500
Goods	0		Additional capital put in	250			
Cash (890+750)	1,640						
	3,440	=		2,940	=		500

The purchase of the van (cost £700) is on credit.

Assets	£	=	Capital	£	+	Liabilities	£
Stall	1,800		As at end of 10 July	2,690		Loan	500
Van	700		Additional capital	250		Creditor	700
Cash	1,640						
	4,140	=		2,940	+		1,200

(ii)　*The sale of goods to Uncle Grant on credit (£350) which cost the business £300 (cash paid)*

Assets	£	=	Capital	£	+	Liabilities	£
Stall	1,800		As at end of 10 July	2,690		Loan	500
Van	700		Additional capital	250		Creditor	700
Debtors	350		Profit on sale to				
Cash(1,640 – 300)	1,340		Uncle Grant	50			
	4,190	=		2,990	+		1,200

(iii)　*After the purchase of goods for the weekly market (£750 paid in cash and £50 of purchases on credit)*

Assets	£	=	Capital	£	+	Liabilities	£
Stall	1,800		As at end of 10 July	2,690		Loan	500
Van	700					Creditor for van	700
Goods	800		Additional capital	250		Creditor for goods	50
Debtors	350		Profit on sale to				
Cash (1,340 – 750)	590		Uncle Grant	50			
	4,240	=		2,990	+		1,250

(iv)　*After market trading on 17 July*

Sales of goods costing £800 earned revenues of £1,250. Bianca's wages were £40 (paid), Uncle Felix's interest charge is £5 (not paid yet) and drawings out of profits were £240 (paid). The profit for 17 July may be calculated as follows, taking the full £5 of interest as a cost on that day.

	£	£
Sales		1,250
Cost of goods sold	800	
Wages	40	
Interest	5	
		845
Profit earned on 17 July		405
Profit on sale of goods to Uncle Grant		50
Profit for the week		455
Drawings appropriated out of profits		240
Retained profit		215

Assets		=	Capital		+	Liabilities	
	£			£			£
Stall	1,800		As at end of 10 July	2,690		Loan	500
Van	700		Additional capital	250		Creditor for van	700
Stocks	0					Creditor for goods	50
Debtors	350						
Cash (590+ 1,250 – 40 – 240)	1,560		Profits retained	215		Creditor for interest payment	5
	4,410	=		3,155	+		1,255

(b)   The increase in the net assets of the business during the week was as follows.

	£
Net assets as at the end of 17 July £(4,410 – 1,255)	3,155
Net assets as at the end of 10 July (as above)	2,690
Increase in net assets	465

The business equation for the week ended 17 July is as follows.

(Remember that extra capital of £250 was invested by the proprietor.)

$$P = I + D - Ci$$
$$= £465 + £240 - £250$$
$$= £455$$

This confirms the calculation of profit above in (a)(iv).

In the example above, we have 'matched' the income earned with the expenses incurred in earning it. So in part (a)(iv), we included all the costs of the goods sold of £800, even though £50 had not yet been paid in cash. Also the interest of £5 was deducted from income, even though it had not yet been paid. This is known as the **matching convention**.

Although the accounting and business equation are unlikely to be directly examined, you will probably need to use the principles in answering a multiple choice question.

Question

Calculate the profit for the year ended 31 December 20X1 from the following information.

	1 January 20X1		31 December 20X1	
	£	£	£	£
Assets				
Property	20,000		20,000	
Machinery	6,000		9,000	
Debtors	4,000		8,000	
Cash	1,000		1,500	
		31,000		38,500
Liabilities				
Overdraft	6,000		9,000	
Creditors	5,000		3,000	
		(11,000)		(12,000)
Net assets		20,000		26,500
Drawings during the year				£4,500
Additional capital introduced by the proprietor during the year				£5,000

Answer

The increase in net assets during the year was £(26,500 - 20,000) = £6,500.

$P = I + D - C_i$
$= £6,500 + £4,500 - £5,000$
$= £6,000$

4 Double entry bookkeeping

FAST FORWARD
Double entry bookkeeping is the method used to transfer our weekly/monthly totals from our books of prime entry into the nominal ledger.

4.1 Dual effect (duality concept)

Central to this process is the idea that every transaction has two effects, the **dual effect**. This feature is not something peculiar to businesses. If you were to purchase a car for £1,000 cash for instance, you would be affected in two ways.

(a)   You own a car worth £1,000.
(b)   You have £1,000 less cash.

If instead you got a bank loan to make the purchase:

(a)   You own a car worth £1,000.
(b)   You owe the bank £1,000.

A month later if you pay a garage £50 to have the exhaust replaced:

(a)   You have £50 less cash.
(b)   You have incurred a repairs expense of £50.

Ledger accounts, with their debit and credit side, are kept in a way which allows the two-sided nature of business transactions to be recorded. This system of accounting is known as the **'double entry'** system of bookkeeping, so called because **every transaction is recorded twice** in the accounts.

4.2 The rules of double entry bookkeeping

A debit entry will:

- increase an asset
- decrease a liability
- increase an expense

A credit entry will:

- decrease an asset
- increase a liability
- increase income

The basic rule which must always be observed is that **every financial transaction gives rise to two accounting entries, one a debit and the other a credit**. The total value of debit entries in the nominal ledger is therefore always equal at any time to the total value of credit entries. Which account receives the credit entry and which receives the debit depends on the nature of the transaction.

Key terms

- An **increase** in an **expense** (eg a purchase of stationery) or an **increase in an asset** (eg a purchase of office furniture) is a **debit**.
- An **increase** in **income** (eg a sale) or an **increase in a liability** (eg buying goods on credit) is a **credit**.
- A **decrease** in an **asset** (eg making a cash payment) is a **credit**.
- A **decrease** in a **liability** (eg paying a creditor) is a **debit**.

This can be illustrated by the 'T' accounts below.

ASSET				LIABILITY	
DEBIT	CREDIT			DEBIT	CREDIT
Increase	Decrease			Decrease	Increase

CAPITAL	
DEBIT	CREDIT
Decrease	Increase

Income increases profit, which increases capital, so:

INCOME				EXPENSES	
DEBIT	CREDIT			DEBIT	CREDIT
Decrease	Increase			Increase	Decrease

Have a go at the question below before you learn about this topic in detail.

Question | Double entry

Complete the following table relating to the transactions of a bookshop. (The first two are done for you.)

(a) Purchase of books on credit

(i)	creditors increase	CREDIT	creditors	(increase in liability)
(ii)	purchases expense increases	DEBIT	purchases	(item of expense)

(b)   Purchase of cash register

    (i)   own a cash register   DEBIT   cash register   (increase in asset)
    (ii)   cash at bank decreases   CREDIT   cash at bank   (decrease in asset)

(c)   Payment received from a debtor

    (i)   debtors decrease
    (ii)   cash at bank increases

(d)   Purchase of van

    (i)   own a van
    (ii)   cash at bank decreases

Answer

(c)   Payment received from a debtor

    (i)   debtors decrease   CREDIT   debtors   (decrease in asset)
    (ii)   cash at bank increases   DEBIT   cash at bank   (increase in asset)

(d)   Purchase of van

    (i)   own a van   DEBIT   van   (increases in asset)
    (ii)   cash at bank decreases   CREDIT   cash at bank   (decrease in asset)

How did you get on? Students coming to the subject for the first time often have difficulty in knowing where to begin. A good starting point is the cash account, ie the nominal ledger account in which receipts and payments of cash are recorded. (This is different to the *cash book* which is a book of prime entry and the totals are posted to the *cash account*). The rule to remember about the cash account is as follows.

(a)   A cash **payment** is a **credit** entry in the cash account. Here the **asset is decreasing**. Cash may be paid out, for example, to pay an expense (such as rates) or to purchase an asset (such as a machine). The matching debit entry is therefore made in the appropriate expense account or asset account.

(b)   A cash **receipt** is a **debit** entry in the cash account. Here the **asset is increasing**. Cash might be received, for example, by a retailer who makes a cash sale. The credit entry would then be made in the sales account.

This is the opposite way round to the entries on a bank statement. Can you think why?

Cash at bank is an asset in your hands as the **bank owes you** the money. From the **bank's point of view it is a liability**. The bank owes you the balance on your account. This is a creditor and so a positive balance is a credit balance on your bank statement.

Key term

> **Double entry bookkeeping** is the method by which a business records financial transactions. An account is maintained for every supplier, customer, asset, liability, and income and expense. Every transaction is recorded twice so that for every *debit* there is an equal, corresponding *credit*.

4.3 Example: double entry for cash transactions

In the cash book of a business, the following transactions have been recorded.

(a)   A cash sale (ie a receipt) of £2
(b)   Payment of a rent bill totalling £150
(c)   Buying some goods for cash at £100
(d)   Buying some shelves for cash at £200

How would these four transactions be posted to the ledger accounts? For that matter, which ledger accounts should they be posted to? Don't forget that each transaction will be posted twice, in accordance with the rule of double entry.

Solution

(a) The two sides of the transaction are:

(i) Cash is received (debit entry in the cash account).
(ii) Sales increase by £2 (credit entry in the sales account).

CASH AT BANK ACCOUNT

	£		£
Sales a/c	2		

SALES ACCOUNT

	£		£
		Cash at bank a/c	2

(Note how the entry in the cash account is cross-referenced to the sales account and vice-versa. This enables a person looking at one of the accounts to trace where the other half of the double entry can be found.)

(b) The two sides of the transaction are:

(i) Cash is paid (credit entry in the cash account).
(ii) Rent expense increases by £150 (debit entry in the rent account).

CASH AT BANK ACCOUNT

	£		£
		Rent a/c	150

RENT ACCOUNT

	£		£
Cash at bank a/c	150		

(c) The two sides of the transaction are:

(i) Cash is paid (credit entry in the cash account).
(ii) Purchases increase by £100 (debit entry in the purchases account).

CASH AT BANK ACCOUNT

	£		£
		Purchases a/c	100

PURCHASES ACCOUNT

	£		£
Cash at bank a/c	100		

(d) The two sides of the transaction are:

(i) Cash is paid (credit entry in the cash at bank account).
(ii) Assets – in this case, shelves – increase by £200 (debit entry in shelves account).

CASH AT BANK ACCOUNT

	£		£
		Shelves a/c	200

SHELVES (ASSET) ACCOUNT

	£		£
Cash at bank a/c	200		

If all four of these transactions related to the same business, the cash at bank account of that business would end up looking as follows.

CASH AT BANK ACCOUNT

	£		£
Sales a/c	2	Rent a/c	150
		Purchases a/c	100
		Shelves a/c	200

4.4 Credit transactions

FAST FORWARD Some accounts in the nominal ledger represent the total of very many smaller balances. For example, the **total debtors account** represents all the balances owed by individual customers of the business while the **total creditors account** represents all money owed by the business to its suppliers.

Not all transactions are settled immediately in cash. A business might purchase goods or fixed assets from its suppliers on credit terms, so that the suppliers would be creditors of the business until settlement was made in cash. Equally, the business might grant credit terms to its customers who would then be debtors of the business. Clearly no entries can be made in the cash book when a credit transaction occurs, because initially no cash has been received or paid. Where then can the details of the transactions be entered?

The solution to this problem is to use **debtors and creditors accounts**. When a business acquires goods or services on credit, the credit entry is made in an account designated 'creditors' instead of in the cash account. The debit entry is made in the appropriate expense or asset account, exactly as in the case of cash transactions. Similarly, when a sale is made to a credit customer the entries made are a debit to the total debtors account (instead of cash account) and a credit to sales account.

4.5 Example: Credit transactions

Recorded in the sales day book and the purchase day book are the following transactions.

(a) The business sells goods on credit to a customer Mr A for £2,000.
(b) The business buys goods on credit from a supplier B Ltd for £100.

How and where are these transactions posted in the ledger accounts?

Solution

(a)

TOTAL DEBTORS ACCOUNT

	£		£
Sales a/c	2,000		

SALES ACCOUNT

	£		£
		Debtors account	2,000

(b)

TOTAL CREDITORS ACCOUNT

	£		£
		Purchases a/c	100

PURCHASES ACCOUNT

	£		£
Creditors a/c	100		

4.6 When cash is paid to creditors or by debtors

What happens when a credit transaction is eventually settled in cash? Suppose that, in the example above, the business paid £100 to B Ltd one month after the goods were acquired. The two sides of this new transaction are:

(a)   Cash is paid (credit entry in the cash account)
(b)   The amount owing to creditors is reduced (debit entry in the creditors account).

CASH AT BANK ACCOUNT

	£		£
		Creditors a/c (B Ltd)	100

TOTAL CREDITORS ACCOUNT

	£		£
Cash at bank a/c	100		

If we now bring together the two parts of this example, the original purchase of goods on credit and the eventual settlement in cash, we find that the accounts appear as follows.

CASH AT BANK ACCOUNT

	£		£
		Creditors a/c	100

PURCHASES ACCOUNT

	£		£
Creditors a/c	100		

TOTAL CREDITORS ACCOUNT

	£		£
Cash at bank a/c	100	Purchases a/c	100

The two entries in the creditors account cancel each other out, indicating that no money is owing to creditors any more. We are left with a credit entry of £100 in the cash account and a debit entry of £100 in the purchases account. These are exactly the entries which would have been made to record a *cash* purchase of £100 (compare example above). This is what we would expect: after the business has paid off its creditors it is in exactly the position of a business which has made cash purchases of £100, and the accounting records reflect this similarity.

Similar reasoning applies when a customer settles his debt. In the example above when Mr A pays his debt of £2,000 the two sides of the transaction are:

(a)   Cash is received (debit entry in the cash at bank account)
(b)   The amount owed by debtors is reduced (credit entry in the debtors account).

CASH AT BANK ACCOUNT

	£		£
Debtors a/c	2,000		

TOTAL DEBTORS ACCOUNT

	£		£
		Cash at bank a/c	2,000

The accounts recording this sale to, and payment by, Mr A now appear as follows.

CASH AT BANK ACCOUNT

	£		£
Debtors a/c	2,000		

SALES ACCOUNT

	£		£
		Debtors a/c	2,000

TOTAL DEBTORS ACCOUNT

	£		£
Sales a/c	2,000	Cash at bank a/c	2,000

The two entries in the debtors account cancel each other out; while the entries in the cash account and sales account reflect the same position as if the sale had been made for cash (see above).

Now try the following questions.

Question

Debit and credit entries

See if you can identify the debit and credit entries in the following transactions.

(a)   Bought a machine on credit from A, cost £8,000.
(b)   Bought goods on credit from B, cost £500.
(c)   Sold goods on credit to C, value £1,200.
(d)   Paid D (a creditor) £300.
(e)   Collected £180 from E, a debtor.
(f)   Paid wages £4,000.
(g)   Received rent bill of £700 from landlord G.
(h)   Paid rent of £700 to landlord G.
(i)   Paid insurance premium £90.
(j)   Received a credit note for £450 from supplier H.
(k)   Sent out a credit note for £200 to customer I.

Answer

			£	£
(a)	DEBIT	Machine account (fixed asset)	8,000	
	CREDIT	Creditors		8,000
(b)	DEBIT	Purchases account	500	
	CREDIT	Creditors		500
(c)	DEBIT	Debtors	1,200	
	CREDIT	Sales		1,200
(d)	DEBIT	Creditors	300	
	CREDIT	Cash at bank		300
(e)	DEBIT	Cash at bank	180	
	CREDIT	Debtors		180
(f)	DEBIT	Wages account	4,000	
	CREDIT	Cash at bank		4,000
(g)	DEBIT	Rent account	700	
	CREDIT	Creditors		700
(h)	DEBIT	Creditors	700	
	CREDIT	Cash at bank		700

(i)	DEBIT	Insurance costs	90	
	CREDIT	Cash at bank		90
(j)	DEBIT	Creditors	450	
	CREDIT	Purchase returns		450
(k)	DEBIT	Sales returns	200	
	CREDIT	Debtors		200

Question   Ledger entries

See now whether you can record the ledger entries for the following transactions. Ron Knuckle set up a business selling keep fit equipment, trading under the name of Buy Your Biceps Shop. He put £7,000 of his own money into a business bank account (transaction A) and in his first period of trading, the following transactions occurred.

		£

Transaction		£
B	Paid rent of shop for the period	3,500
C	Purchased equipment (stocks) on credit	5,000
D	Raised loan from bank	1,000
E	Purchase of shop fittings (for cash)	2,000
F	Sales of equipment: cash	10,000
G	Sales of equipment: on credit	2,500
H	Payments to trade creditors	5,000
I	Payments from debtors	2,500
J	Interest on loan (paid)	100
K	Other expenses (all paid in cash)	1,900
L	Drawings	1,500

All stocks purchased during the period was sold, and so there were no closing stocks of equipment.

Try to do as much of this exercise as you can by yourself before reading the solution.

Answer

Clearly, there should be an account for cash, debtors, creditors, purchases, a shop fittings account, sales, a loan account and a proprietor's capital account. It is also useful to keep a separate **drawings account** until the end of each accounting period. Other accounts should be set up as they seem appropriate and in this exercise, accounts for rent, bank interest and other expenses would seem appropriate.

It has been suggested to you that the cash account is a good place to start, if possible. You should notice that cash transactions include the initial input of capital by Ron Knuckle, subsequent drawings, the payment of rent, the loan from the bank, the interest, some cash sales and cash purchases, and payments to creditors and by debtors. (The transactions are identified below by their reference, to help you to find them.)

CASH AT BANK

	£		£
Capital – Ron Knuckle (A)	7,000	Rent (B)	3,500
Bank loan (D)	1,000	Shop fittings (E)	2,000
Sales (F)	10,000	Trade creditors (H)	5,000
Debtors (I)	2,500	Bank loan interest (J)	100
		Incidental expenses (K)	1,900
		Drawings (L)	1,500

CAPITAL (RON KNUCKLE)

	£		£
		Cash at bank (A)	7,000

BANK LOAN

	£		£
		Cash at bank (D)	1,000

PURCHASES

	£		£
Trade creditors (C)	5,000		

TRADE CREDITORS

	£		£
Cash at bank (H)	5,000	Purchases (C)	5,000

RENT

	£		£
Cash at bank (B)	3,500		

FIXED ASSETS

	£		£
Cash at bank (E)	2,000		

SALES

	£		£
		Cash at bank (F)	10,000
		Debtors (G)	2,500

DEBTORS

	£		£
Sales (G)	2,500	Cash at bank (I)	2,500

BANK LOAN INTEREST

	£		£
Cash at bank (J)	100		

OTHER EXPENSES

	£		£
Cash at bank (K)	1,900		

DRAWINGS ACCOUNT

	£		£
Cash at bank (L)	1,500		

(a) If you want to make sure that this solution is complete, you should go through the transactions A to L and tick off each of them twice in the ledger accounts, once as a debit and once as a credit. When you have finished, all transactions in the 'T' account should be ticked, with only totals left over.

(b) In fact, there is an easier way to check that the solution to this sort of problem does 'balance' properly, which we will meet in the next chapter.

(c) On asset and liability accounts, the debit or credit balance represents the amount of the asset or liability outstanding at the period end. For example, on the cash account, debits exceed credits by

£6,500 and so there is a debit balance of cash in hand of £6,500. On the capital account, there is a credit balance of £7,000 and so the business owes Ron £7,000.

(d)   The balances on the revenue and expenses accounts represent the total of each revenue or expense for the period. For example, sales for the period total £12,500.

5 The journal

FAST FORWARD

You should remember that one of the books of prime entry from the previous chapter was the **journal**.

Key term

The **journal** keeps a record of unusual movement between accounts. It is used to record any double entries made which do not arise from the other books of prime entry. For example, journal entries are made when errors are discovered and need to be corrected.

5.1 Format

Whatever type of transaction is being recorded, the **format of a journal entry** is:

Date	Debit	Credit
	£	£
Account to be debited	X	
Account to be credited		X
(Narrative to explain the transaction)		

(Remember: in due course, the ledger accounts will be written up to include the transactions listed in the journal.)

A **narrative explanation** must accompany each journal entry. It is required for audit and control, to indicate the purpose and authority of every transaction which is not first recorded in a book of prime entry.

Exam focus point

An examination question might ask you to 'journalise' transactions which would not in practice be recorded in the journal at all. If you are faced with such a problem, you should simply record the debit and credit entries for every transaction you can recognise, giving some supporting narrative to each transaction.

5.2 Examples: journal entries

The following is a summary of the transactions of 'Hair by Fiona' hairdressing business of which Fiona is the sole proprietor.

1 January	Put in cash of £2,000 as capital
	Purchased brushes and combs for cash £50
	Purchased hair driers from Gilroy Ltd on credit £150
30 January	Paid three months rent to 31 March £300
	Collected and paid in takings £600
31 January	Gave Mrs Sullivan a perm, highlights etc on credit £80

Show the transactions by means of journal entries.

Solution

JOURNAL

			£	£
1 January	DEBIT	Cash at bank	2,000	
	CREDIT	Fiona Middleton − capital account		2,000
		Initial capital introduced		
1 January	DEBIT	Brushes and combs account	50	
	CREDIT	Cash at bank		50
		The purchase for cash of brushes and combs as fixed assets		
1 January	DEBIT	Hair dryer account	150	
	CREDIT	Sundry creditors account *		150
		The purchase on credit of hair driers as fixed assets		
30 January	DEBIT	Rent account	300	
	CREDIT	Cash at bank		300
		The payment of rent to 31 March		
30 January	DEBIT	Cash at bank	600	
	CREDIT	Sales (or takings account)		600
		Cash takings		
31 January	DEBIT	Debtors account	80	
	CREDIT	Sales account (or takings account)		80
		The provision of a hair-do on credit		

* *Note.* Creditors who have supplied fixed assets are included amongst sundry creditors, as distinct from creditors who have supplied raw materials or goods for resale, who are trade creditors. It is quite common to have separate 'total creditors' accounts, one for trade creditors and another for sundry other creditors.

5.3 General entries and the correction of errors

Journals can be used to adjust figures at the end of the accounting period. For example, debenture interest paid on the last day of the accounting period.

	Debit	Credit
31 December 20X6		
Interest expense	800	
Interest payable		800

Being interest paid to debenture holders

The journal is most commonly used to record corrections to errors that have been made in writing up the nominal ledger accounts. Errors corrected by the journal must be **capable of correction by means of a double entry** in the ledger accounts. In other words the error must not have caused total debits and total credits to be unequal. Special rules, covered in a later chapter, apply when errors are made which break the rule of double entry.

There are several types of error which can occur.

Errors may occur because an invoice has accidentally been posted to the wrong account. For example, the fee for stationery has been posted to the computer supplies account.

The journal to correct this would be

	Debit	Credit
31 December 20X6		
Stationery	800	
Computer supplies		800

Being invoice posted to the wrong account

Another common error is to transpose the figures and post the wrong amount. This will be correct as follows:

		Debit	Credit
31 December 20X6			
Sales		121	
Debtors			121

Being incorrect figure posted to sales

Errors are looked at in detail in Chapter 16 along with the method of using journal entries to correct them.

6 Day book analysis

FAST FORWARD

> Entries in the day books are totalled and analysed before posting to the nominal ledger.

6.1 Sales day book

In the previous chapter, we used the following example of four transactions entered into the sales day book.

SALES DAY BOOK

Date 20X0	Invoice	Customer	Total amount invoiced £	Boot sales £	Shoe sales
Jan 10	247	Jones & Co	105.00	60.00	45.00
	248	Smith Ltd	86.40	86.40	
	249	Alex & Co	31.80		31.80
	250	Enor College	1,264.60	800.30	464.30
			1,487.80	946.70	541.10

We have already seen that in theory these transactions are posted to the ledger accounts as follows.

DEBIT	Total debtors account	£1,487.80	
CREDIT	Sales account		£1,487.80

However a total sales account is not very informative, particularly if the business sells lots of different products. So, using our example, the business might open up a 'sale of shoes' account and a 'sale of boots' account, then at the end of the day, the ledger account postings are:

		£	£
DEBIT	Debtors account	1,487.80	
CREDIT	Sale of shoes account		541.10
	Sale of boots account		946.70

That is why the analysis of sales is kept. Exactly the same reasoning lies behind the analyses kept in other books of prime entry.

6.2 Sales returns day book

We will now look at the sales returns day book in Chapter 4.

SALES RETURNS DAY BOOK

Date 20X8	Credit note	Customer and goods	Amount £
30 April	CR008	Owen Plenty 3 pairs 'Texas' boots	135.00

This will be posted as follows.

		£	£
DEBIT	Sales returns – boots	135.00	
CREDIT	Trade debtors		135.00

6.3 Purchase day book and purchases returns day book

The purchase day book and purchases returns day book in Chapter 4 can be posted in a similar way.

6.3.1 Purchases

		£	£
DEBIT	Purchases	444.40	
	Electricity	116.80	
CREDIT	Trade creditors		561.20

6.3.2 Purchase return

		£	£
DEBIT	Trade creditors	46.60	
CREDIT	Purchases returns		46.60

7 The imprest system

In the last chapter, we saw how the petty cash book was used to operate the imprest system. It is now time to see how the **double entry** works.

A business starts off a cash float on 1.3.20X7 with £250. This will be a payment from cash at bank to petty cash, ie:

DEBIT	Petty cash	£250	
CREDIT	Cash at bank		£250

Five payments were made out of petty cash during March 20X7. The petty cash book might look as follows.

				Payments	
Receipts	Date	Narrative	Total	Postage	Travel
£			£	£	£
250.00	1.3.X7	Cash			
	2.3.X7	Stamps	12.00	12.00	
	8.3.X7	Stamps	10.00	10.00	
	19.3.X7	Travel	16.00		16.00
	23.3.X7	Travel	5.00		5.00
	28.3.X7	Stamps	11.50	11.50	
250.00			54.50	33.50	21.00

At the end of each month (or at any other suitable interval) the total credits in the petty cash book are **posted** to ledger accounts. For March 20X7, £33.50 would be debited to postage account, and £21.00 to travel account. The total expenditure of £54.50 is credited to the petty cash account. The cash float would need to be topped up by a payment of £54.50 from the main cash book, ie:

		£	£
DEBIT	Petty cash	54.50	
CREDIT	Cash		54.50

So the rules of double entry have been satisfied, and the petty cash book for the month of March 20X7 will look like this.

Receipts £	Date	Narrative	Total £	Payments Postage £	Travel £
250.00	1.3.X7	Cash			
	2.3.X7	Stamps	12.00	12.00	
	8.3.X7	Stamps	10.00	10.00	
	19.3.X7	Travel	16.00		16.00
	23.3.X7	Travel	5.00		5.00
	28.3.X7	Stamps	11.50	11.50	
	31.3.X7	Balance c/d	195.50		
250.00			250.00	33.50	21.00
195.50	1.4.X7	Balance b/d			
54.50	1.4.X7	Cash			

As you can see, the cash float is back up to £250 on 1.4.X7, ready for more payments to be made.

The petty cash account in the ledger will appear as follows.

PETTY CASH

		£			£
1.3.X7	Cash	250.00	31.3.X7	Payments	54.50
1.4.X7	Cash	54.50	1.4.X7	Balance c/d	250.00
		304.50			304.50
1.4.X7	Balance b/d	250.00			

Question   Imprest system

Summit Glazing operates an imprest petty cash system. The imprest amount is £150.00. At the end of the period the totals of the four analysis columns in the petty cash book were as follows.

	£
Column 1	23.12
Column 2	6.74
Column 3	12.90
Column 4	28.50

How much cash is required to restore the imprest amount?

Answer

£71.26. This is the total amount of cash that has been used.

8 The sales and purchase ledgers

FAST FORWARD

The sales and purchase ledgers contain the personal accounts of individual debtors and creditors. They do not normally form part of the double entry system.

8.1 Impersonal accounts and personal accounts

The accounts in the nominal ledger (ledger accounts) relate to types of income, expense, asset, liability – rent, rates, sales, total debtors, total creditors etc – rather than to the person to whom the money is paid or from whom it is received. They are therefore called **impersonal** accounts. However, there is also a need for **personal** accounts, most commonly for debtors and creditors, and these are contained in the sales ledger and purchase ledger.

8.2 The sales ledger

The sales day book provides a chronological record of invoices sent out by a business to credit customers. For many businesses, this might involve very large numbers of invoices per day or per week. The same customer might appear in several different places in the sales day book, for purchases he has made on credit at different times. So at any point in time, a customer may owe money on several unpaid invoices.

In addition to keeping a chronological record of invoices, a business should also keep a record of how much money each individual credit customer owes, and what this total debt consists of. The need for a **personal account for each customer** is a practical one.

(a)   A customer might telephone, and ask how much he currently owes. Staff must be able to tell him.

(b)   It is a common practice to send out statements to credit customers at the end of each month, showing how much they still owe, and itemising new invoices sent out and payments received during the month.

(c)   The managers of the business will want to keep a check on the credit position of an individual customer, and to ensure that no customer is exceeding his credit limit by purchasing more goods.

(d)   Most important is the need to match payments received against debts owed. If a customer makes a payment, the business must be able to set off the payment against the customer's debt and establish how much he still owes on balance.

Key term

> The **sales ledger** is a ledger for customers' personal accounts.

Sales ledger accounts are written up as follows.

(a)   When entries are made in the sales day book (invoices sent out), they are subsequently also made in the **debit side** of the relevant customer account in the sales ledger.

(b)   Similarly, when entries are made in the cash book (payments received), or in the sales returns day book, they are also made in the **credit side** of the relevant customer account.

Here is an example of how a sales ledger account is laid out.

ENOR COLLEGE

A/c no: SL 9

		£			£
	Balance b/f	250.00			
10.1.X0	Sales – SDB 48				
	(invoice no 250)	1,264.60		Balance c/d	1,514.60
		1,514.60			1,514.60
11.1.X0	Balance b/d	1,514.60			

The debit side of this personal account, then, shows amounts owed by Enor College. When Enor pays some of the money it owes it will be entered into the cash book (receipts) and subsequently 'posted' to the credit side of the personal account. For example, if the college paid £250 on 10.1.20X0, it would appear as follows.

A/c no: SL 9

	£			£
Balance b/f	250.00	10.1.X0	Cash	250.00
10.1.X0 Sales – SDB 48				
(invoice no 250)	1,264.60		Balance c/d	1,264.60
	1,514.60			1,514.60
11.1.X0 Balance b/d	1,264.60			

The opening balance owed by Enor College on 11.1.X0 is now £1,264.60 instead of £1,514.60, because of the £250 receipt which came in on 10.1.X0.

8.3 The purchase ledger (bought ledger)

The purchase ledger, like the sales ledger, consists of a number of personal accounts. These are separate accounts for **each individual supplier**, and they enable a business to keep a continuous record of how much it owes each supplier at any time.

> The **purchase ledger** is a ledger for suppliers' personal accounts.

After entries are made in the purchase day book, cash book, or purchase returns day book – ie after entries are made in the books of prime entry – they are also made in the relevant supplier account in the purchase ledger. Again we say that the entries in the purchase day book are **posted** to the suppliers' personal accounts in the purchase ledger.

Here is an example of how a purchase ledger account is laid out.

COOK & CO

A/c no: PL 31

	£		£
Balance c/d	515.00	Balance b/f	200.00
		15 Mar 20X8	
		Invoice received	
		PDB 37	315.00
	515.00		515.00
		16 March 20X8	
		Balance b/d	515.00

The credit side of this personal account, then, shows amounts owing to Cook & Co. If the business paid Cook & Co some money, it would be entered into the cash book (payments) and subsequently be posted to the debit side of the personal account. For example, if the business paid Cook & Co £100 on 15 March 20X8, it would appear as follows:

COOK & CO

A/c no: PL 31

		£			£
15.3.X8	Cash	100.00		Balance b/f	200.00
			15.3.X8	Invoice received	
	Balance c/d	415.00	PDB 37		315.00
		515.00			515.00
			16.3.X8	Balance b/d	415.00

The opening balance owed to Cook & Co on 16.3.X8 is now £415.00 instead of £515.00 because of the £100 payment made during 15.3.X8.

The remainder of the balance b/f of £100.00 (£200.00 b/f less payment of £100.00) is in dispute and Cook and Co send the business a credit note for £100.00 on 17.3.X8.

COOK & CO

A/c no: PL 31

		£			£
17.3.X8	Credit note received	100.00	16.3.X8	Balance b/f	415.00
	Balance c/d	315.00			
		415.00			415.00
			17.3.X8	Balance b/d	315.00

The business now owes Cook & Co the amount of the invoice received on 15.3.X8.

Important

> Please note that, in a manual system, the account is not 'balanced off' after each transaction. It is more likely to be done once a month. However, we have done this to show the effect of the transactions.

Chapter Roundup

- Ledger accounts are a summary of the books of prime entry.

- The assets of a business must be equal to the liabilities (accounting equation).

- The business equation gives a definition of profits earned.

- Creditors are liabilities. Debtors are assets.

- **Double entry bookkeeping** is the method used to transfer our weekly/monthly totals from our books of prime entry into the nominal ledger.

- A debit entry will:
    - increase an asset
    - decrease a liability
    - increase an expense

- A credit entry will:
    - decrease an asset
    - increase a liability
    - increase income

- Some accounts in the nominal ledger represent the total of very many smaller balances. For example, the **total debtors account** represents all the balances owed by individual customers of the business while the **total creditors account** represents all money owed by the business to its suppliers.

- You should remember that one of the books of prime entry from the previous chapter was the **journal**.

- Entries in the day books are totalled and analysed before posting to the nominal ledger.

- In the last chapter, we saw how the petty cash book was used to operate the impress system. It is now time to see how the **double entry** works.

- The sales and purchase ledgers contain the personal accounts of individual debtors and creditors. They do not normally form part of the double entry system.

1   What is the double entry to record a cash sale of £50?

2   What is the double entry to record a credit sale of £50?

    A   Debit cash £50, credit sales £50
    B   Debit debtors £50, credit sales £50
    C   Debit sales £50, credit debtors £50
    D   Debit sales £50, credit cash £50

3   What is the double entry to record a purchase of office chairs for £1,000?

    A   Debit fixed assets £1,000, credit cash £1,000
    B   Debit cash £1,000, credit purchases £1,000

4   What is the double entry to record a credit sale of £500 to A?

    A   Debit debtors £500, credit sales £500
    B   Debit sales ledger (A's account) £500, credit sales £500

5   Name one reason for making a journal entry.

6   Individual customer accounts are kept in which ledger?

    A   General ledger
    B   Total debtors
    C   Sales ledger
    D   Nominal ledger

			£	£
1	DEBIT	Cash a/c	50	
	CREDIT	Sales a/c		50

2 B

3 A

4 A The sales ledger is a memorandum account and not part of the double entry system.

5 Most commonly to correct an error, although it can be used to make any entry that is not recorded in a book of prime entry (eg prepayments, accrued expenses, depreciation).

6 C The sales ledger contains the individual customer accounts. The general ledger (A) and nominal ledger (D) are different names for the same ledger. This contains the total debtors account (B) which is the **total** of all the individual customer accounts.

Now try the question below from the Exam Question Bank

Number	Level	Marks	Time
Q9	Examination	1	1 min

From trial balance to financial statements

Topic list	Syllabus reference
1 The trial balance	C2(d), E1(a)-(d)
2 The trading and profit and loss account	A3(a)
3 The balance sheet	A3(a)
4 Balancing accounts and preparing financial statements	C2(d), A3(a)

Introduction

In the previous chapter you learned the principles of double entry and how to post to the ledger accounts. The next step in our progress towards the financial statements is the **trial balance**.

Before transferring the relevant balances at the year end to the profit and loss account and putting closing balances carried forward into the balance sheet, it is usual to test the accuracy of double entry bookkeeping records by preparing a trial balance. This is done by taking all the balances on every account. Because of the self-balancing nature of the system of double entry the **total of the debit balances will be exactly equal to the total of the credit balances**.

In very straightforward circumstances, where no complications arise and where the records are complete, it is possible to prepare accounts directly from a trial balance. This is covered in Section 4.

Study guide

		Intellectual level
A3	**The main elements of financial reports**	
(a)	Understand and identify the purpose of each of the main financial statements	1
C2	**Ledger accounts, books of prime entry and journals**	
(d)	Illustrate how to balance and close a ledger account	1
E1	**Trial balance**	
(a)	Identify the purpose of a trial balance	1
(b)	Extract ledger balances into a trial balance	1
(c)	Prepare extracts of an opening trial balance	1
(d)	Identify and understand the limitations of a trial balance	1

Exam guide

Exam questions at all levels in financial accounting sometimes involve preparation of final accounts from trial balance. Last but not least, you may end up having to do it in 'real life'.

1 The trial balance

FAST FORWARD

A trial balance is a means of checking that the total debits equal total credits.

You have a list of transactions, and has asked you to post them to the relevant ledger accounts. You do it as quickly as possible and find that you have a little time left over at the end of the examination. How do you check that you have posted all the debit and credit entries properly?

There is no foolproof method, but a technique which shows up the more obvious mistakes is to prepare a **trial balance.**

Key term

A **trial balance** is a list of ledger balances shown in debit and credit columns.

1.1 The first step

Before you draw up a trial balance, you must have a collection of ledger accounts. For the sake of convenience, we will use the accounts of Ron Knuckle, which we drew up in the previous chapter.

CASH AT BANK

	£		£
Capital: Ron Knuckle	7,000	Rent	3,500
Bank loan	1,000	Shop fittings	2,000
Sales	10,000	Trade creditors	5,000
Debtors	2,500	Bank loan interest	100
		Other expenses	1,900
		Drawings	1,500

CAPITAL (RON KNUCKLE)

	£		£
		Cash at bank	7,000

BANK LOAN

	£		£
		Cash at bank	1,000

PURCHASES

	£		£
Trade creditors	5,000		

TRADE CREDITORS

	£		£
Cash at bank	5,000	Purchases	5,000

RENT

	£		£
Cash at bank	3,500		

SHOP FITTINGS

	£		£
Cash at bank	2,000		

SALES

	£		£
		Cash at bank	10,000
		Debtors	2,500

DEBTORS

	£		£
Sales	2,500	Cash at bank	2,500

BANK LOAN INTEREST

	£		£
Cash at bank	100		

OTHER EXPENSES

	£		£
Cash at bank	1,900		

DRAWINGS

	£		£
Cash at bank	1,500		

The next step is to 'balance' each account.

1.2 Balancing ledger accounts

At the end of an accounting period, a **balance is struck** on each account in turn. This means that all the debits on the account are totalled and so are all the credits. **If the total debits exceed the total credits there is said to be a debit balance on the account; if the credits exceed the debits then the account has a credit balance.**

In our simple example, there is very little balancing to do.

(a)   Both the trade creditors account and the debtors account balance off to zero.
(b)   The cash at bank account has a debit balance of £6,500.
(c)   The total on the sales account is £12,500, which is a credit balance.

CASH AT BANK

	£		£
Capital: Ron Knuckle	7,000	Rent	3,500
Bank loan	1,000	Shop fittings	2,000
Sales	10,000	Trade creditors	5,000
Debtors	2,500	Bank loan interest	100
		Other expenses	1,900
		Drawings	1,500
			14,000
		Balancing figure – the amount of cash left over after payments have been made	6,500
	20,500		20,500

CREDITORS

	£		£
Cash at bank	5,000	Purchases	5,000

SALES

	£		£
		Cash at bank	10,000
		Debtors	2,500
			12,500

DEBTORS

	£		£
Sales	2,500	Cash at bank	2,500

Otherwise, the accounts have only one entry each, so there is no totalling to do to arrive at the balance on each account.

1.3 Collecting the balances

If the basic principle of double entry has been correctly applied throughout the period it will be found that the credit balances equal the debit balances in total. This can be illustrated by collecting together the balances on Ron Knuckle's accounts.

	Debit £	Credit £
Cash at bank	6,500	
Capital		7,000
Bank loan		1,000
Purchases	5,000	
Trade creditors	–	–
Rent	3,500	
Shop fittings	2,000	
Sales		12,500
Debtors	–	–
Bank loan interest	100	
Other expenses	1,900	
Drawings	1,500	
	20,500	20,500

This list of balances is called the **trial balance**. It does not matter in what order the various accounts are listed. It is just a method used to test the accuracy of the double entry bookkeeping.

1.4 What if the trial balance shows unequal debit and credit balances?

If the two columns of the trial balance are not equal, there must be an error in recording the transactions in the accounts. A trial balance, however, will not disclose the following types of errors.

(a) The **complete omission** of a transaction, because neither a debit nor a credit is made.

(b) The posting of a debit or credit to the correct side of the ledger, but to a **wrong account**.

(c) **Compensating errors** (eg an error of £100 is exactly cancelled by another £100 error elsewhere).

(d) **Errors of principle**, eg cash received from debtors being debited to the debtors account and credited to cash instead of the other way round.

1.5 Example: trial balance

As at 30.3.20X7, your business has the following balances on its ledger accounts.

Accounts	Balance £
Bank loan	12,000
Cash at bank	11,700
Capital	13,000
Rates	1,880
Trade creditors	11,200
Purchases	12,400
Sales	14,600
Sundry creditors	1,620
Debtors	12,000
Bank loan interest	1,400
Other expenses	11,020
Vehicles	2,020

During the year the business made the following transactions.

(a) Bought materials for £1,000, half for cash and half on credit.

(b) Made £1,040 sales, £800 of which was for credit.

(c) Paid wages to shop assistants of £260 in cash.

You are required to draw up a trial balance showing the balances as at the end of 31.3.X7.

Solution

First it is necessary to put the original balances into a trial balance – ie decide which are debit and which are credit balances.

Account	Dr £	Cr £
Bank loan (liability = credit)		12,000
Cash at bank (asset = debit)	11,700	
Capital (credit)		13,000
Rates (expense = debit)	1,880	
Trade creditors (liability = credit)		11,200
Purchases (expense = debit)	12,400	
Sales (income = credit)		14,600
Sundry creditors (liability = credit)		1,620
Debtors (asset = debit)	12,000	
Bank loan interest (expense = debit)	1,400	
Other expenses (expense = debit)	11,020	
Vehicles (asset = debit)	2,020	
	52,420	52,420

Now we must take account of the effects of the three transactions which took place on 31.3.X7.

			£	£
(a)	DEBIT	Purchases	1,000	
	CREDIT	Cash at bank		500
		Trade creditors		500
(b)	DEBIT	Cash at bank	240	
		Debtors	800	
	CREDIT	Sales		1,040
(c)	DEBIT	Other expenses	260	
	CREDIT	Cash at bank		260

When these figures are included in the trial balance, it becomes:

Account	Dr £	Cr £
Bank loan		12,000
Cash at bank (11,700 + 240 – 500 – 260)	11,180	
Capital		13,000
Rates	1,880	
Trade creditors		11,700
Purchases	13,400	
Sales		15,640
Sundry creditors		1,620
Debtors	12,800	
Bank loan interest	1,400	
Other expenses	11,280	
Vehicles	2,020	
	53,960	53,960

Before moving on, try this question to make sure you have understood the basics.

Question	List of balances

Here is a list of balances. Arrange them into debit and credit columns as in a trial balance.

LIST OF BALANCES AS AT 31 JULY 20X2

		£
Cash at bank		215
Bank		96
Capital		250
Rent		30
Carriage		23
Creditors:	B Jackson	130
	G Mitchell	186
	D Wickes	64
Debtors	D Cotton	129
	C Beale	26
Purchases		459
Sales		348

TRIAL BALANCE AS AT 31 JULY 20X2

	Dr £	Cr £
Cash at bank	215	
Bank	96	
Capital		250
Rent	30	
Carriage	23	
Creditors – B Jackson		130
– G Mitchell		186
– D Wickes		64
Debtors – D Cotton	129	
– C Beale	26	
Purchases	459	
Sales		348
	978	978

2 The trading and profit and loss account

FAST FORWARD

This time, the trading and profit and loss account is a new ledger account, not the financial statement.

The first step in the process of preparing the financial statements is to open up another ledger account, called the **trading and profit and loss account**. In it a business summarises its results for the period by gathering together all the ledger account balances relating to income and expenses. This account is still part of the double entry system, so the basic rule of double entry still applies: every debit must have an equal and opposite credit entry.

This trading, profit and loss account we have opened up is **not** the financial statement we are aiming for, even though it has the same name. The difference between the two is not very great, because they contain the same information. However, the financial statement lays it out differently and may be much less detailed.

So what do we do with this new ledger account? The first step is to look through the ledger accounts and identify which ones relate to income and expenses. In the case of Ron Knuckle, the income and expense accounts consist of purchases, rent, sales, bank loan interest, and other expenses.

The balances on these accounts are transferred to the new trading, profit and loss account. For example, the balance on the purchases account is £5,000 DR. To balance this to zero, we write in £5,000 CR. But to comply with the rule of double entry, there has to be a debit entry somewhere, so we write £5,000 DR in the trading, profit and loss account. Now the balance on the purchases account has been moved to the trading, profit and loss account.

If we do the same thing with all the income and expense accounts of Ron Knuckle, the result is as follows.

PURCHASES

	£		£
Trade creditors	5,000	Trading and P & L a/c	5,000

RENT

	£		£
Cash at bank	3,500	Trading and P & L a/c	3,500

SALES

	£		£
Trading and P & L a/c	12,500	Cash at bank	10,000
		Debtors	2,500
	12,500		12,500

BANK LOAN INTEREST

	£		£
Cash at bank	100	Trading and P & L a/c	100

OTHER EXPENSES

	£		£
Cash at bank	1,900	Trading and P & L a/c	1,900

TRADING AND PROFIT AND LOSS ACCOUNT

	£		£
Purchases	5,000	Sales	12,500
Rent	3,500		
Bank loan interest	100		
Other expenses	1,900		

(Note that the trading and profit and loss account has not yet been balanced off but we will return to that later.)

If you look at the items we have gathered together in the trading, profit and loss account, they should strike a chord in your memory. They are the same items that we need to draw up the trading, profit and loss account in the form of a financial statement. With a little rearrangement they could be presented as follows.

RON KNUCKLE: TRADING AND PROFIT AND LOSS ACCOUNT

		£	£
Sales	⎫ Trading account		12,500
Cost of sales (= purchases in this case)	⎬		(5,000)
Gross profit	⎭		7,500
Expenses			
Rent	⎫ Profit and loss account	3,500	
Bank loan interest	⎬	100	
Other expenses	⎭	1,900	
			(5,500)
Net profit			2,000

3 The balance sheet

FAST FORWARD

The remaining ledger accounts form the balance sheet.

Look back at the ledger accounts of Ron Knuckle. Now that we have dealt with those relating to income and expenses, which ones are left? The answer is that we still have to find out what to do with cash, capital, bank loan, trade creditors, shop fittings, debtors and the drawings account.

Are these the only ledger accounts left? No: don't forget there is still the last one we opened up, called the **trading and profit and loss account**. The balance on this account represents the profit earned by the business, and if you go through the arithmetic, you will find that it has a credit balance – a profit – of £2,000. (Not surprisingly, this is the figure that is shown in the trading profit and loss account financial statement.)

These remaining accounts must also be balanced and ruled off, but since they represent assets and liabilities of the business (not income and expenses) their balances are not transferred to the trading profit and loss account. Instead they are **carried forward** in the books of the business. This means that they become opening balances for the next accounting period and indicate the value of the assets and liabilities at the end of one period and the beginning of the next.

The conventional method of ruling off a ledger account at the end of an accounting period is illustrated by the bank loan account in Ron Knuckle's books.

BANK LOAN ACCOUNT

	£		£
Balance carried forward (c/f)	1,000	Cash at bank	1,000
		Balance brought forward (b/f)	1,000

Ron Knuckle therefore begins the new accounting period with a credit balance of £1,000 on this account. A **credit balance brought forward** denotes a **liability**. An **asset** would be represented by a **debit balance brought forward**.

One further point is worth noting before we move on to complete this example. You will remember that a proprietor's capital comprises any cash introduced by him, plus any profits made by the business, less any drawings made by him. At the stage we have now reached these three elements are contained in different ledger accounts: cash introduced of £7,000 appears in the capital account; drawings of £1,500 appear in the drawings account; and the profit made by the business is represented by the £2,000 credit balance on the trading profit and loss account. It is convenient to gather together all these amounts into one **capital account**, in the same way as we earlier gathered together income and expense accounts into one trading and profit and loss account.

If we go ahead and gather the three amounts together, the results are as follows.

DRAWINGS

	£		£
Cash at bank	1,500	Capital a/c	1,500

TRADING AND PROFIT AND LOSS ACCOUNT

	£		£
Purchases	5,000	Sales	12,500
Rent	3,500		
Bank loan interest	100		
Other expenses	1,900		
Capital a/c	2,000		
	12,500		12,500

CAPITAL

	£		£
Drawings	1,500	Cash at bank	7,000
Balance c/f	7,500	Trading and P & L a/c	2,000
	9,000		9,000
		Balance b/f	7,500

A re-arrangement of these balances will complete Ron Knuckle's simple balance sheet:

RON KNUCKLE
BALANCE SHEET AT END OF FIRST TRADING PERIOD

	£	£
Fixed assets		
Shop fittings		2,000
Current assets		
Cash	6,500	
Current liabilities		
Bank loan	(1,000)	
Net current assets		5,500
Net assets		7,500
Proprietor's capital		7,500

When a balance sheet is drawn up for an accounting period which is not the first one, then it ought to show the capital at the start of the accounting period and the capital at the end of the accounting period. This will be illustrated in the next example.

4 Balancing accounts and preparing financial statements

You can now prepare basic financial statements.

The question which follows is **by far the most important in this text so far**. It uses all the accounting steps from entering up ledger accounts to preparing the financial statements. It is very important that you try the question by yourself: if you do not, you will be missing out a vital part of this Text.

Exam focus point

At the 2009 ACCA Teachers' Conference, the examiner emphasised the need to practise full length questions in order to fully understand the techniques involved.

Question   **Financial statements**

A business is established with capital of £2,000, and this amount is paid into a business bank account by the proprietor. During the first year's trading, the following transactions occurred:

	£
Purchases of goods for resale, on credit	4,300
Payments to trade creditors	3,600
Sales, all on credit	5,800
Payments from debtors	3,200
Fixed assets purchased for cash	1,500
Other expenses, all paid in cash	900

The bank has provided an overdraft facility of up to £3,000.

Prepare the ledger accounts, a trading and profit and loss account for the year and a balance sheet as at the end of the year.

Answer

The first thing to do is to open ledger accounts so that the transactions can be entered up. The relevant accounts which we need for this example are: cash; capital; trade creditors; purchases; fixed assets; sales and debtors; other expenses.

The next step is to work out the double entry bookkeeping for each transaction. Normally you would write them straight into the accounts, but to make this example easier to follow, they are first listed below.

(a)	Establishing business (£2,000)	DR	Cash;	CR	Capital
(b)	Purchases (£4,300)	DR	Purchases;	CR	Creditors
(c)	Payments to creditors (£3,600)	DR	Creditors;	CR	Cash
(d)	Sales (£5,800)	DR	Debtors;	CR	Sales
(e)	Payments by debtors (£3,200)	DR	Cash;	CR	Debtors
(f)	Fixed assets (£1,500)	DR	Fixed assets;	CR	Cash
(g)	Other (cash) expenses (£900)	DR	Other expenses;	CR	Cash

So far, the ledger accounts will look like this.

CASH AT BANK

	£		£
Capital	2,000	Creditors	3,600
		Fixed assets	1,500
Debtors	3,200	Other expenses	900

CAPITAL

	£		£
		Cash	2,000

CREDITORS

	£		£
Cash at bank	3,600	Purchases	4,300

PURCHASES

	£		£
Creditors	4,300		

FIXED ASSETS

	£		£
Cash at bank	1,500		

SALES

	£		£
		Debtors	5,800

DEBTORS

	£		£
Sales	5,800	Cash at bank	3,200

OTHER EXPENSES

	£		£
Cash at bank	900		

The next thing to do is to balance all these accounts. It is at this stage that you could, if you wanted to, draw up a trial balance to make sure the double entries are accurate. There is not very much point in this simple example, but if you did draw up a trial balance, it would look like this.

	Dr £	Cr £
Cash at bank		800
Capital		2,000
Creditors		700
Purchases	4,300	
Fixed assets	1,500	
Sales		5,800
Debtors	2,600	
Other expenses	900	
	9,300	9,300

After balancing the accounts, the trading and profit and loss account should be opened. Into it should be transferred all the balances relating to income and expenses (ie purchases, other expenses, and sales). At this point, the ledger accounts will be:

CASH AT BANK

	£		£
Capital	2,000	Trade creditors	3,600
Debtors	3,200	Fixed assets	1,500
Balance c/f	800	Other expenses	900
	6,000		6,000
		Balance b/f	800*

* A credit balance b/f means that this cash item is a liability, not an asset. This indicates a bank overdraft of £800, with cash income of £5,200 falling short of payments of £6,000 by this amount.

CAPITAL

	£		£
Balance c/f	2,600	Cash at bank	2,000
		P & L a/c	600
	2,600		2,600

TRADE CREDITORS

	£		£
Cash at bank	3,600	Purchases	4,300
Balance c/f	700		
	4,300		4,300
		Balance b/f	700

PURCHASES ACCOUNT

	£		£
Trade creditors	4,300	Trading a/c	4,300

FIXED ASSETS

	£		£
Cash at bank	1,500	Balance c/f	1,500
Balance b/f	1,500		

SALES

	£		£
Trading a/c	5,800	Debtors	5,800

DEBTORS

	£		£
Sales	5,800	Cash at bank	3,200
		Balance c/f	2,600
	5,800		5,800
Balance b/f	2,600		

OTHER EXPENSES

	£		£
Cash at bank	900	P & L a/c	900

TRADING AND PROFIT AND LOSS ACCOUNT

	£		£
Purchases account	4,300	Sales	5,800
Gross profit c/f	1,500		
	5,800		5,800
Other expenses	900	Gross profit b/f	1,500
Net profit (transferred to capital account)	600		
	1,500		1,500

So the trading and profit and loss account financial statement will be:

TRADING PROFIT AND LOSS ACCOUNT
FOR THE ACCOUNTING PERIOD

	£
Sales	5,800
Cost of sales (purchases)	(4,300)
Gross profit	1,500
Expenses	900
Net profit	600

Listing and then rearranging the balances on the ledger accounts gives the balance sheet as:

BALANCE SHEET AS AT THE END OF THE PERIOD

	£	£
Fixed assets		1,500
Current assets		
Debtors	2,600	
Current liabilities		
Bank overdraft	800	
Trade creditors	700	
	1,500	
Net current assets		1,100
		2,600
Capital		
At start of period		2,000
Net profit for period		600
At end of period		2,600

The above example is highly detailed. This detail is given to help you to work through the example properly. You may wish to do things this way yourself until you get more practised in accounting techniques and are confident enough to take short cuts.

The techniques are worth practising as you may well get a MCQ requiring you to calculate a figure for the profit and loss account or balance sheet from a trial balance.

Question
Opening trial balance

Alpha has the following opening balances on its ledger accounts.

	£
Fixtures	5,000
Debtors	2,000
Bank account	1,000
Loan	3,000

(a)   What is the total assets figure?

    A   £6,000
    B   £5,000
    C   £8,000
    D   £3,000

(b)   What is the opening figure for capital?

    A   £6,000
    B   £5,000
    C   £8,000
    D   £3,000

Answer

(a)   C   Assets = 5,000 + 2,000 + 1,000
                = 8,000

(b)   B   Capital = assets – liabilities
                 = (5,000 + 2,000 + 1,000) – 3,000
                 = 5,000

Chapter Roundup

- A trial balance is a means of checking that the total debits equal total credits.
- This time, the trading and profit and loss account is a new ledger account, not the financial statement.
- The remaining ledger accounts form the balance sheet.
- You can now prepare basic financial statements.

Quick Quiz

1   What is the purpose of a trial balance?

2   A trial balance may still balance if some of the balances are wrong.

    Is this statement correct?

    A   Yes
    B   No

3   In a period, sales are £140,000, purchases £75,000 and other expenses £25,000. What is the figure for net profit to be transferred to the capital account?

    A   £40,000
    B   £65,000
    C   £75,000
    D   £140,000

4   The balance on an expense account will go to the P&L account. However, the balance on a liability account is written off to capital.

    Is this statement correct?

    A   Yes
    B   No

5   The balance brought down on the bank account is a debit figure. This means that the balance is overdrawn. True or false?

1   To test the accuracy of the double entry bookkeeping.

2   A   See Section 1.4.

3   A

TRADING, PROFIT AND LOSS ACCOUNT

	£		£
Purchases	75,000	Sales	140,000
Gross profit c/d	65,000		
	140,000		140,000
Other expenses	25,000	Gross profit b/d	65,000
Net profit – to capital a/c	40,000		
	65,000		65,000

B is the **gross** profit figure, while C is the figure for purchases and D sales.

4   B   When an expense account is balanced off, the balance is transferred to the income and expense account. When a liability account is balanced off, the balance is carried forward to the next accounting period.

5   False. A debit balance brought down is an asset and means that the bank account is **not** overdrawn.

Now try the question below from the Exam Question Bank

Number	Level	Marks	Time
Q10	Examination	2	2 mins

P
A
R
T

D

Recording transactions and events

Value Added Tax

Topic list	Syllabus reference
1 The nature of VAT and how it is collected	D1(c)-(d)
2 Accounting for VAT	D1(d)

Introduction

Many business transactions involve **VAT (value added tax)**. Invoices and bills show any VAT charged separately.

VAT is charged on the supply of goods and services. It is an **indirect tax**, and is also called a sales tax under international accounting standards.

Section 1 explains how VAT works.

Section 2 deals with the accounting treatment of VAT. If you understand the principle behind the tax and how it is collected, you will understand the accounting treatment.

Study guide

		Intellectual level
D1	**Sales and purchases**	
(c)	Understand the general principles of the operation of Value Added Tax (VAT)	1
(d)	Calculate VAT on transactions and record the consequent accounting entries	1

Exam guide

This topic could well be examined as part of another topic eg whether VAT needs to be included when accounting for fixed assets. Be prepared for a range of rates to be used in the exam.

1 The nature of VAT and how it is collected

Value Added Tax is an indirect tax levied on the sale of goods and services. It is currently administered by HM Revenue and Customs (HMRC).

1.1 How is VAT levied?

VAT is a cumulative tax, collected at various stages of a product's life. In the illustrative example below, a manufacturer of a television buys materials and components and then sells the television to a wholesaler, who in turn sells it to a retailer, who then sells it to a customer. It is assumed that the rate for VAT is 17.5% on all items. All the other figures are for illustration only.

1.2 Example

			Price net of VAT £	VAT 17.5% £	Total price £
(a)	(i)	Manufacturer purchases raw materials and components	40	7	47
	(ii)	Manufacturer sells the completed television to a wholesaler	200	35	235
		The manufacturer hands over to HMRC		28	
(b)	(i)	Wholesaler purchases television for	200	35	235
	(ii)	Wholesaler sells television to a retailer	320	56	376
		Wholesaler hands over to HMRC		21	
(c)	(i)	Retailer purchases television for	320	56	376
	(ii)	Retailer sells television	480	84	564
		Retailer hands over to HMRC		28	
(d)		Customer purchases television for	480	84	564

The total tax of £84 is borne by the ultimate consumer. However, the tax is handed over to the authorities in stages. If we assume that the VAT of £7 on the initial supplies to the manufacturer is paid by the supplier, HMRC would collect the VAT as follows.

	£
Supplier of materials and components	7
Manufacturer	28
Wholesaler	21
Retailer	28
Total VAT paid	84

1.3 Input and output VAT

VAT charged on goods and services sold by a business is referred to as **output VAT**. VAT paid on goods and services 'bought in' by a business is referred to as **input VAT**.

If output VAT exceeds input VAT, the business pays the difference in tax to the authorities. If output VAT is less than input VAT in a period, HMRC will refund the difference to the business.

The example above assumes that the supplier, manufacturer, wholesaler and retailer are all VAT-registered traders.

A VAT-registered trader must carry out the following tasks.

(a) Charge VAT on the goods and services sold at the rate prescribed by the government. This is output VAT.

(b) Pay VAT on goods and services purchased from other businesses. This is input VAT.

(c) Pay to Customs and Excise the difference between the VAT collected on sales and the VAT paid to suppliers for purchases. Payments are made at quarterly intervals.

1.4 Irrecoverable VAT

There are some circumstances in which traders are not allowed to reclaim VAT paid on their inputs. In these cases the trader must bear the cost of VAT and account for it accordingly. Three such cases need to be considered.

(a) Non-registered persons
(b) Registered persons carrying on exempted activities
(c) Non-deductible inputs

VAT has been temporarily reduced to 15% until 31 December 2009, when it will return to 17.5%.

The examiner has indicated that various rates will be used in the exam, so read each question carefully.

Where VAT is not recoverable, for any of the reasons described above, it must be regarded as part of the cost of the items purchased and included in the P&L charge or in the balance sheet as appropriate.

1.5 Relief for irrecoverable debts

Relief is available for VAT on irrecoverable debts if the debt is over six months old (measured from the date of the supply) and has been written off in the creditor's accounts. Where a supplier of goods or services has accounted for VAT on the supply and the customer does not pay, the supplier may claim a refund of VAT on the amount unpaid.

If the customer later pays all or part of the amount owed, a corresponding part of the VAT repaid must be paid back to HMRC.

2 Accounting for VAT

Registered businesses charge output VAT on sales and suffer input VAT on purchases. VAT does not affect the profit and loss account, but is simply being collected on behalf of HMRC to whom a quarterly payment is made.

SSAP 5 *Accounting for Value Added Tax* requires that sales should be stated net of VAT and that purchases should be stated net of recoverable VAT.

2.1 Profit and loss account

A business does not make any profit out of the VAT it charges. It therefore follows that its profit and loss account figures should not include VAT. For example, if a business sells goods for £600 + VAT £105, ie for £705 total price, the sales account should only record the £600 excluding VAT. The accounting entries to record the sale would be as follows.

DEBIT	Cash or debtors	£705	
CREDIT	Sales		£600
CREDIT	VAT creditor (output VAT)		£105

(a)   If input VAT is recoverable, the cost of purchases should exclude the VAT and be recorded net of tax. For example, if a business purchases goods on credit for £400 + VAT £70, the transaction would be recorded as follows.

DEBIT	Purchases	£400	
DEBIT	VAT creditor (input VAT recoverable)	£70	
CREDIT	Creditors		£470

(b)   If the input VAT is not recoverable, the cost of purchases must include the tax, because it is the business itself which must bear the cost of the tax.

Exam focus point

	Purchases	*Sales*
P&L account	Irrecoverable input VAT: include Recoverable input VAT: exclude	Exclude VAT

2.2 VAT in the cash book, sales day book and purchase day book

When a business makes a credit sale the total amount invoiced, including VAT, will be recorded in the sales day book. The analysis columns will then separate the VAT from the sales income of the business as follows.

		Sales	
Date	*Total*	*income*	*VAT*
	£	£	£
A Detter and Sons	235	200	35

When a business is invoiced by a supplier the total amount payable, including VAT, will be recorded in the purchase day book. The analysis columns will then separate the recoverable input VAT from the net purchase cost to the business as follows.

Date	*Total*	*Purchase*	*VAT*
	£	£	£
A Splier (Merchants)	188	160	28

When debtors pay what they owe, or creditors are paid, there is **no need to show** the VAT in an analysis column of the cash book, because input and output VAT arise when the sale is made, not when the debt is settled.

However, VAT charged on **cash sales** or VAT paid on **cash purchases** will be analysed in a separate column of the cash book. This is because output VAT has just arisen from the cash sale and must be credited to the VAT creditor in the ledger accounts. Similarly input VAT paid on cash purchases, having just arisen, must be debited to the VAT creditor.

For example, the receipts side of a cash book might be written up as follows.

Date	Narrative	Total	Sales ledger	Cash sales	Output VAT on cash sales
		£	£	£	£
	A Detter & Sons	235	235		
	Owen	660	660		
	Cash sales	329		280	49
	Newgate Merchants	184	184		
	Cash sales	94		80	14
		1,502	1,079	360	63

The payments side of a cash book might be written up as follows.

Date	Narrative	Total	Purchase ledger	Cash purchases and sundry items	Input VAT on cash purchases
		£	£	£	£
	A Splier (Merchants)	188	188		
	Telephone bill paid	141		120	21
	Cash purchase of stationery	47		40	7
	VAT paid to HMRC	1,400		1,400	
		1,776	188	1,560	28

Question

Are trade debtors and trade creditors shown in the accounts inclusive of VAT or exclusive of VAT?

Answer

They are shown **inclusive** of VAT, as the balance sheet must reflect the total amount due from debtors and due to creditors.

Exam focus point

A small element of VAT is quite likely in questions. It is worth spending a bit of time ensuring that you understand the logic behind the way VAT is accounted for, rather than trying to learn the rules by rote. This will ensure that even if you forget the rules, you will be able to work out what should be done.

2.3 Creditor for VAT

FAST FORWARD

An outstanding creditor for VAT will appear as a current liability in the balance sheet.

The VAT paid to the authorities each quarter is the difference between recoverable input VAT on purchases and output VAT on sales. For example, if a business is invoiced for input VAT of £8,000 and charges VAT of £15,000 on its credit sales and VAT of £2,000 on its cash sales, the VAT creditor account would be as follows.

VAT CREDITOR

	£		£
Creditors (input VAT)	8,000	Debtors (output VAT invoiced)	15,000
Cash (payment to authorities)	9,000	Cash (output VAT on cash sales)	2,000
	17,000		17,000

Payments to the authorities do not coincide with the end of the accounting period of a business, and so at the balance sheet date there will be a balance on the VAT creditor account. If this balance is for an amount payable to the authorities, the outstanding creditor for VAT will appear as a current liability in the balance sheet.

Occasionally, a business will be owed money back by the authorities, and in such a situation, the VAT refund owed by the authorities would be a current asset in the balance sheet.

Question

A business in its first period of trading charges £4,000 of VAT on its sales and suffers £3,500 of VAT on its purchases which include £250 VAT on business entertaining. Prepare the VAT creditor account.

Answer

VAT CREDITOR ACCOUNT

	£		£
Creditors (3,500 – 250)	3,250	Debtors	4,000
Balance c/d (owed to HMRC)	750		
	4,000		4,000
		Balance b/d	750

Attention!

The amount of VAT charged is affected by discounts. However, we will deal with this at the same time as discounts in Chapter 14.

The main points

(a) Credit sales

(i) Include VAT in sales day book; show it separately

(ii) Include gross receipts from debtors in cashbook; no need to show VAT separately

(iii) Exclude VAT element from P&L account

(iv) Credit VAT creditor with output VAT element of debtors invoiced

(c) Cash sales

(i) Include gross receipts in cashbook; show VAT separately

(ii) Exclude VAT element from P&L account

(iii) Credit VAT creditor with output VAT element of cash sales

(b) Credit purchases

(i) Include VAT in purchases day book; show it separately

(ii) Include gross payments in cashbook; no need to show VAT separately

(iii) Exclude recoverable VAT from P&L account

(iv) Include irrecoverable VAT in P&L account

(v) Debit VAT creditor with recoverable input VAT element of credit purchases

(d) Cash purchases

(i) Include gross payments in cashbook: show VAT separately

(ii) Exclude recoverable VAT from P&L account

(iii) Include irrecoverable VAT in P&L account

(iv) Debit VAT creditor with recoverable input VAT element of cash purchases

In VAT questions, remember to check the tax rate used. It may not be 17.5%! If you are required to calculate VAT, the rate will always be given.

Chapter Roundup

- **Value Added Tax** is an indirect tax levied on the sale of goods and services. It is currently administered by HM Revenue and Customs (HMRC).

- If output VAT exceeds input VAT, the business pays the difference in tax to the authorities. If output VAT is less than input VAT in a period, HMRC will refund the difference to the business.

- Where VAT is not recoverable, for any of the reasons described above, it must be regarded as part of the cost of the items purchased and included in the I/S charge or in the balance sheet as appropriate.

- Registered businesses charge output VAT on sales and suffer input VAT on purchases. VAT does not affect the profit and loss account, but is simply being collected on behalf of HMRC to whom a quarterly payment is made.

- An outstanding creditor for VAT will appear as a current liability in the balance sheet.

Quick Quiz

1   Value Added Tax is:

   A   A direct tax levied on sales of goods and services
   B   An indirect tax levied on the sales of goods and services
   C   Administered by the Treasury
   D   Charged by businesses on taxable supplies

2   VAT is due on all sales.

   Is this statement correct?

   A   Yes
   B   No

3   When VAT is not recoverable on the cost of a motor car, it should be treated in which of the following ways?

   A   Deducted from the cost of the asset capitalised
   B   Included in the cost of the asset capitalised
   C   Deducted from output tax for the period
   D   Written off to P&L as an expense

4   Purchases of goods costing £500 subject to VAT at 17.5% occur. Which of the following correctly records the **credit purchase**?

A	Dr	Purchases	£500.00	
	Dr	VAT	£87.50	
	Cr	Creditors		£587.50
B	Dr	Purchases	£587.50	
	Cr	Creditors		£587.50
C	Dr	Purchases	£412.50	
	Dr	VAT	£87.50	
	Cr	Creditors		£500.00
D	Dr	Purchases	£500.00	
	Cr	VAT		£87.50
	Cr	Creditors		£412.50

5   A business purchases goods valued at £400. VAT is charged at 17.5%. The double entry to record the purchase is:

DEBIT _____ £_____

DEBIT _____ £_____

CREDIT _____ £_____

6   Fill in the blanks.

Input VAT is _____,

output VAT is _____.

7   When a cash sale is made for £117.50 (including VAT at 17.5%) the entries made are:

DEBIT _____ account £_____

CREDIT _____ account £_____

CREDIT _____ account £_____

8   When a cash purchase of £117.50 is made (including VAT at 17.5%) the entries are:

A	Debit	Purchases	117.50	
	Credit	Cash		117.50
B	Debit	Purchases	100.00	
	Debit	VAT	17.50	
	Credit	Cash		117.50
C	Debit	Cash	100.00	
	Debit	VAT	17.50	
	Credit	Purchases		117.50
D	Debit	Cash	117.50	
	Credit	Purchases		117.50

9   The VAT paid to HMRC each quarter is the difference between _____

_____ and _____

_____.

1 B   Correct
   A   Incorrect, the consumer has a choice as to whether or not to consume so VAT is only chargeable when this choice is exercised.
   C   Incorrect, VAT is administrated by HMRC.
   D   Only VAT registered traders can charge VAT.

2 B   VAT is only due on **taxable** outputs.

3 B   Correct the balance sheet value will therefore include VAT and the depreciation charge will rise accordingly
   A   Incorrect, it must be added.
   C   Incorrect.
   D   Incorrect, the motor car is a fixed asset not an expense, VAT will form part of the depreciable amount of the asset.

4 A   Correct, recoverable input tax is debited to the VAT a/c and the purchases account is debited net of VAT.
   B   Incorrect, the VAT has not been reclaimed.
   C   Incorrect, the £500 is subject to VAT.
   D   Incorrect, reversal of the VAT transaction has occurred.

5 DEBIT: PURCHASES   £400
              VAT   £70
   CREDIT: CASH or CREDITORS   £470

6 Input VAT is VAT suffered on goods and services brought by a business, output VAT is the VAT collected on sales.

7 DEBIT   Cash account   £117.50
   CREDIT   Sales account   £100.00
   CREDIT   VAT account   £17.50

8 B

9 The VAT paid to HMRC each quarter is the difference between output VAT collected on sales and input VAT suffered on purchases and expenses.

Now try the question below from the Exam Question Bank

Number	Level	Marks	Time
Q11	Examination	2	2 mins

Accounting for stock

Topic list	Syllabus reference
1 Cost of goods sold	D3(a)
2 Accounting for opening and closing stocks	D3(a), (b)
3 Stocktaking	D3(f)
4 Valuing stocks	D3(c), (g), (i)
5 Statutory regulations and SSAP 9 requirements	D3(d), (e), (h)

Introduction

Stock is one of the most important assets in a company's balance sheet. As we have seen, it also affects the profit and loss account.

So far you have come across stock in the preparation of a simple balance sheet. Here we will look at the calculation of the cost of goods sold. This chapter also explores the **difficulties of valuing stock**.

This is the first time (although by no means the last) that you will be required to consider the impact of the relevant accounting standard and statutory rules on the valuation and presentation of an item in the accounts.

Study guide

		Intellectual level
D3	**Stock**	
(a)	Recognise the need for adjustments for stock in preparing financial statements	1
(b)	Record opening and closing stock	1
(c)	Identify the alternative methods of valuing stock	1
(d)	Understand and apply the ASB requirements for valuing stock	1
(e)	Recognise which costs should be included in valuing stock	1
(f)	Understand the use of continuous and period end stock records	1
(g)	Calculate the value of closing stock using FIFO (first in, first out) and AVCO (average cost)	1
(h)	Understand the impact of accounting concepts on the valuation of stock	1
(i)	Identify the impact of stock valuation methods on profit and on assets	1

Exam guide

You will definitely be examined on stocks. You might have to calculate closing stock or cost of sales.

1 Cost of goods sold

FAST FORWARD You must learn the formula for **cost of goods sold**: Opening stock + purchases – closing stock.

1.1 Unsold goods in stock at the end of an accounting period

Goods might be unsold at the end of an accounting period and so still be **held in stock** at the end of the period. The purchase cost of these goods should not be included therefore in the cost of sales of the period.

1.2 Example: Closing stock

Perry P Louis, trading as the Umbrella Shop, ends his financial year on 30 September each year. On 1 October 20X4 he had no goods in stock. During the year to 30 September 20X5, he purchased 30,000 umbrellas costing £60,000 from umbrella wholesalers and suppliers. He resold the umbrellas for £5 each, and sales for the year amounted to £100,000 (20,000 umbrellas). At 30 September there were 10,000 unsold umbrellas left in stock, valued at £2 each.

What was Perry P Louis's gross profit for the year?

Solution

Perry P Louis purchased 30,000 umbrellas, but only sold 20,000. Purchase costs of £60,000 and sales of £100,000 do not represent the same quantity of goods.

The gross profit for the year should be calculated by 'matching' the sales value of the 20,000 umbrellas sold with the cost of those 20,000 umbrellas. The cost of sales in this example is therefore the cost of purchases minus the cost of goods in stock at the year end.

	£	£
Sales (20,000 units)		100,000
Purchases (30,000 units)	60,000	
Less closing stock (10,000 units @ £2)	20,000	
Cost of sales (20,000 units)		40,000
Gross profit		60,000

1.3 Example continued

The Umbrella Shop's next accounting year runs from 1 October 20X5 to 30 September 20X6. During the course of this year, Perry P Louis purchased 40,000 umbrellas at a total cost of £95,000. During the year he sold 45,000 umbrellas for £230,000. At 30 September 20X6 he had 5,000 umbrellas left in stock, which had cost £12,000.

What was his gross profit for the year?

Solution

In this accounting year, he purchased 40,000 umbrellas to add to the 10,000 he already had in stock at the start of the year. He sold 45,000, leaving 5,000 umbrellas in stock at the year end. Once again, gross profit should be calculated by matching the value of 45,000 units of sales with the cost of those 45,000 units.

The cost of sales is the value of the 10,000 umbrellas in stock at the beginning of the year, plus the cost of the 40,000 umbrellas purchased, less the value of the 5,000 umbrellas in stock at the year end.

	£	£
Sales (45,000 units)		230,000
Opening stock (10,000 units) *	20,000	
Add purchases (40,000 units)	95,000	
	115,000	
Less closing stock (5,000 units)	12,000	
Cost of sales (45,000 units)		103,000
Gross profit		127,000

*Taken from the closing stock value of the previous accounting year, see paragraph 1.2.

1.4 The cost of goods sold

The cost of goods sold is found by applying the following formula.

Formula to
learn

	£
Opening stock value	X
Add cost of purchases (or, in the case of a manufacturing company, the cost of production)	X
	X
Less closing stock value	(X)
Equals cost of goods sold	X

In other words, to match 'sales' and the 'cost of goods sold', it is necessary to adjust the cost of goods manufactured or purchased to allow for increases or reduction in stock levels during the period.

Hopefully you will agree that the 'formula' above is logical. You should learn it, because it is fundamental among the principles of accounting.

Test your knowledge of the formula with the following example.

1.5 Example: Cost of goods sold and variations in stock levels

On 1 January 20X6, the Grand Union Food Stores had goods in stock valued at £6,000. During 20X6 its proprietor, who ran the shop, purchased supplies costing £50,000. Sales turnover for the year to 31 December 20X6 amounted to £80,000. The cost of goods in stock at 31 December 20X6 was £12,500.

Calculate the gross profit for the year.

Solution

GRAND UNION FOOD STORES
TRADING ACCOUNT FOR THE YEAR ENDED 31 DECEMBER 20X6

	£	£
Sales		80,000
Opening stocks	6,000	
Add purchases	50,000	
	56,000	
Less closing stocks	12,500	
Cost of goods sold		43,500
Gross profit		36,500

1.6 The cost of carriage inwards and outwards

'Carriage' refers to the **cost of transporting purchased goods** from the supplier to the premises of the business which has bought them. Someone has to pay for these delivery costs: sometimes the supplier pays, and sometimes the purchaser pays. When the purchaser pays, the cost to the purchaser is carriage inwards (**into** the business). When the supplier pays, the cost to the supplier is known as carriage outwards (**out of** the business).

The **cost of carriage inwards** is usually added to the **cost of purchases**, and is therefore included in the **trading account**.

The **cost of carriage outwards** is a **selling and distribution expense** in the **profit and loss account**.

1.7 Example: Carriage inwards and carriage outwards

Gwyn Tring, trading as Clickety Clocks, imports and resells cuckoo clocks and grandfather clocks. He must pay for the costs of delivering the clocks from his supplier in Switzerland to his shop in Wales.

He resells the clocks to other traders throughout the country, paying the costs of carriage for the consignments from his business premises to his customers.

On 1 July 20X5, he had clocks in stock valued at £17,000. During the year to 30 June 20X6 he purchased more clocks at a cost of £75,000. Carriage inwards amounted to £2,000. Sales for the year were £162,100. Other expenses of the business amounted to £56,000 excluding carriage outwards which cost £2,500. Gwyn Tring took drawings of £20,000 from the business during the course of the year. The value of the goods in stock at the year end was £15,400.

Required

Prepare the trading, profit and loss account of Clickety Clocks for the year ended 30 June 20X6.

Solution

CLICKETY CLOCKS
TRADING, PROFIT AND LOSS ACCOUNT FOR THE YEAR ENDED 30 JUNE 20X6

	£	£
Sales		162,100
Opening stock	17,000	
Purchases	75,000	
Carriage inwards	2,000	
	94,000	
Less closing stock	15,400	
Cost of goods sold		78,600
Gross profit		83,500
Carriage outwards	2,500	
Other expenses	56,000	
		58,500
Net profit (transferred to capital account)		25,000

1.8 Goods written off or written down

A trader might be unable to sell all the goods that he purchases, because a number of things might happen to the goods before they can be sold. For example:

(a)   Goods might be lost or stolen.

(b)   Goods might be damaged, and so become worthless. Such damaged goods might be thrown away.

(c)   Goods might become obsolete or out of fashion. These might have to be thrown away, or possibly sold off at a very low price in a clearance sale.

When goods are **lost, stolen or thrown away** as worthless, the business will make a loss on those goods because their **'sales value' will be nil**.

Similarly, when goods lose value because they have become **obsolete** or out of fashion, the business will **make a loss** if their clearance sales value is less than their cost. For example, if goods which originally cost £500 are now obsolete and could only be sold for £150, the business would suffer a loss of £350.

If, at the end of an accounting period, a business still has goods in stock which are either worthless or worth less than their original cost, the value of the stocks should be **written down** to:

(a)   Nothing, if they are worthless.

(b)   Or their net realisable value, if this is less than their original cost.

This means that the loss will be reported as soon as the loss is foreseen, even if the goods have not yet been thrown away or sold off at a cheap price. This is an application of another concept – the prudence concept – which we will look at in a later chapter.

The costs of stock written off or written down should not usually cause any problems in calculating the gross profit of a business, because the cost of goods sold will include the cost of stocks written off or written down, as the following example shows.

1.9 Example: Stocks written off and written down

Lucas Wagg, trading as Fairlock Fashions, ends his financial year on 31 March. At 1 April 20X5 he had goods in stock valued at £8,800. During the year to 31 March 20X6, he purchased goods costing £48,000. Fashion goods which cost £2,100 were still held in stock at 31 March 20X6, and Lucas Wagg believes that these could only now be sold at a sale price of £400. The goods still held in stock at 31 March 20X6 (including the fashion goods) had an original purchase cost of £7,600. Sales for the year were £81,400.

Required

Calculate the gross profit of Fairlock Fashions for the year ended 31 March 20X6.

Solution

Initial calculation of closing stock values:

STOCK COUNT

	At cost £	Realisable value £	Amount written down £
Fashion goods	2,100	400	1,700
Other goods (balancing figure)	5,500	5,500	
	7,600	5,900	1,700

FAIRLOCK FASHIONS
TRADING ACCOUNT FOR THE YEAR ENDED 31 MARCH 20X6

	£	£
Sales		81,400
Value of opening stock	8,800	
Purchases	48,000	
	56,800	
Less closing stock	5,900	
Cost of goods sold		50,900
Gross profit		30,500

Question **Gross profit**

Gross profit for 20X7 can be calculated from

A   purchases for 20X7, plus stock at 31 December 20X7, less stock at 1 January 20X7
B   purchases for 20X7, less stock at 31 December 20X7, plus stock at 1 January 20X7
C   cost of goods sold during 20X7, plus sales during 20X7
D   net profit for 20X7, plus expenses for 20X7

Answer

The correct answer is D. Gross profit less expenses = net profit. Therefore net profit plus expenses = gross profit.

2 Accounting for opening and closing stocks

FAST FORWARD

> **Opening stocks** brought forward in the stock account are transferred to the trading account, and so at the end of the accounting year the balance on the stock account ceases to be the opening stock value b/f and becomes instead the closing stock value c/f.

In Section 1, we saw that in order to calculate **gross profit** it is necessary to work out the **cost of goods sold**, and in order to calculate the cost of goods sold it is necessary to have values for the **opening stock** (ie stock in hand at the beginning of the accounting period) and **closing stock** (ie stock in hand at the end of the accounting period).

You should remember, in fact, that the trading part of a profit and loss account includes:

	£
Opening stock	X
Plus purchases	X
Less closing stock	(X)
Equals cost of goods sold	X

However, just writing down this formula hides three basic problems.

(a) How do you manage to get a **precise count** of stock in hand at any one time?
(b) Even once it has been counted, how do you **value** the stock?
(c) Assuming the stock is given a value, how does the **double entry** bookkeeping for stock work?

The purpose of this chapter is to answer all three of these questions. In order to make the presentation a little easier to follow, it is convenient to take the last one first.

2.1 Ledger accounting for stocks

FAST FORWARD

> The value of **closing stock** is accounted for in the nominal ledger by debiting a stock account and crediting the trading account at the end of an accounting period. Stock will therefore have a debit balance at the end of a period, and this balance will be shown in the balance sheet as a current asset.

It has already been shown that purchases are introduced to the trading account by means of the double entry:

DEBIT	Trading account	£X
CREDIT	Purchases account	£X

But what about opening and closing stocks? How are their values accounted for in the double entry bookkeeping system? The answer is that a **stock account** must be kept. This stock account is only ever used at the end of an accounting period, when the business counts up and values the stock in hand, in a stocktake.

(a) When a stock-take is made, the business will have a value for its closing stock, and the double entry is:

DEBIT	Stock account (closing stock value)	£X
CREDIT	Trading account	£X

However, rather than show the closing stock as a 'plus' value in the trading account (eg by adding it to sales) it is usual to show it as a 'minus' figure in arriving at cost of sales. This is illustrated in paragraph 1 above. The debit balance on stock account represents an asset, which will be shown as part of current assets in the balance sheet.

(b) Closing stock at the end of one period becomes opening stock at the start of the next period. The stock account remains unchanged until the end of the next period, when the value of opening stock is taken to the trading account; ie

DEBIT	Trading account	£X
CREDIT	Stock account (value of opening stock)	£X

Partly as an example of how this ledger accounting for stocks works, and partly as revision of ledger accounting in general, try the following question. It is an example from an earlier part of this text which has had a closing stocks figure included.

Question
Closing stock

A business is established with capital of £2,000 and this amount is paid into a business bank account by the proprietor. During the first year's trading, the following transactions occurred.

	£
Purchases of goods for resale, on credit	4,300
Payments to trade creditors	3,600
Sales, all on credit	4,000
Payments from debtors	3,200
Fixed assets purchased for cash	1,500
Other expenses, all paid in cash	900

The bank has provided an overdraft facility of up to £3,000.

All 'other expenses' relate to the current year.

Closing stocks of goods are valued at £1,800. (Because this is the first year of the business, there are no opening stocks.)

Ignore depreciation and drawings.

Required

Prepare the ledger accounts, a trading, profit and loss account for the year and a balance sheet as at the end of the year.

Answer

CASH

	£		£
Capital	2,000	Trade creditors	3,600
Debtors	3,200	Fixed assets	1,500
Balance c/f	800	Other expenses	900
	6,000		6,000
		Balance b/f	800

CAPITAL

	£		£
Balance c/f	2,600	Cash	2,000
		P & L a/c	600
	2,600		2,600
		Balance b/f	2,600

TRADE CREDITORS

	£		£
Cash	3,600	Purchases	4,300
Balance c/f	700		
	4,300		4,300
		Balance b/f	700

PURCHASES ACCOUNT

	£		£
Trade creditors	4,300	Trading a/c	4,300

FIXED ASSETS

	£		£
Cash	1,500	Balance c/f	1,500
Balance b/f	1,500		

SALES

	£		£
Trading a/c	4,000	Debtors	4,000

DEBTORS

	£		£
Sales	4,000	Cash	3,200
		Balance c/f	800
	4,000		4,000
Balance b/f	800		

OTHER EXPENSES

	£		£
Cash	900	P & L a/c	900

TRADING AND PROFIT AND LOSS ACCOUNT

	£		£
Purchases account	4,300	Sales	4,000
Gross profit c/f	1,500	Closing stock (stock account)	1,800
	5,800		5,800
Other expenses	900	Gross profit b/f	1,500
Net profit (transferred to capital account)	600		
	1,500		1,500

STOCK ACCOUNT

	£		£
Trading account (closing stock)	1,800	Balance c/f (balance sheet)	1,800

BALANCE SHEET AS AT THE END OF THE PERIOD

	£	£
Fixed assets		1,500
Current assets		
Goods in stock	1,800	
Debtors	800	
	2,600	
Current liabilities		
Bank overdraft	800	
Trade creditors	700	
	1,500	
Net current assets		1,100
		2,600

	£
Capital	
At start of period	2,000
Profit for period	600
	2,600

So if we can establish the value of stocks on hand, the above paragraphs and exercise show us how to account for that value. That takes care of one of the problems noted in the introduction of this chapter. But now another of those problems becomes apparent – how do we establish the value of stocks on hand? The first step must be to establish **how much stock is held**.

3 Stocktaking

FAST FORWARD A stocktake is a means of physically counting the stock still held.

Business trading is a continuous activity, but accounting statements must be drawn up at a particular date. In preparing a balance sheet it is necessary to 'freeze' the activity of a business so as to determine its assets and liabilities at a given moment. This includes establishing the quantities of stocks on hand, which can create problems.

A business buys stocks continually during its trading operations and either sells the goods onwards to customers or incorporates them as raw materials in manufactured products. This constant movement of stocks makes it difficult to establish what exactly is held at any precise moment.

In simple cases, when a business holds easily counted and relatively small amounts of stock, quantities of stocks on hand at the balance sheet date can be determined by physically counting them in a **stocktake**.

The continuous nature of trading activity may cause a problem in that stock movements will not necessarily cease during the time that the physical stocktake is in progress. Two possible solutions are:

(a)   to **close down** the business while the count takes place; or
(b)   to keep **detailed records** of stock movements during the course of the stocktake.

Closing down the business for a short period for a stocktake (eg over a weekend or at Christmas) is considerably **easier** than trying to keep detailed records of stock movements during a stocktake. So most businesses prefer that method unless they happen to keep detailed records of stock movements anyway (for example, because they wish to keep strict control on stock movements).

In more complicated cases, where a business holds considerable quantities of varied stock, an alternative approach to establishing stock quantities is to maintain **continuous stock records**. This means that a card is kept for every item of stock, showing receipts and issues from the stores, and a running total. A few stock items are counted each day to make sure their record cards are correct – this is called a 'continuous' stocktake because it is spread out over the year rather than completed in one stocktake at a designated time.

One obstacle is overcome once a business has established how much stock is on hand. But another of the problems noted in the introduction immediately raises its head. What **value** should the business place on those stocks?

4 Valuing stocks

FAST FORWARD The **value** of stock is calculated at the lower of **cost** and **net realisable value** for each separate item or group of items. **Cost** can be arrived at by using **FIFO** or **AVCO**.

4.1 The basic rule

There are **several methods** which, in theory, might be used for the valuation of stock items.

(a)   Stocks might be valued at their **expected selling price**.
(b)   Stocks might be valued at their expected selling price, less any costs still to be incurred in getting them ready for sale and then selling them. This amount is referred to as the **net realisable value** (NRV) of the stocks.
(c)   Stocks might be valued at their **historical cost** (ie the cost at which they were originally bought).
(d)   Stocks might be valued at the amount it would cost to replace them. This amount is referred to as the **current replacement cost** of stocks.

Current replacement costs are not used in the type of accounts dealt with in this syllabus.

4.1.1 Selling price

The use of selling prices in stock valuation is **ruled out** because this would create a profit for the business before the stock has been sold.

A simple example might help to explain this. Suppose that a trader buys two items of stock, each costing £100. He can sell them for £140 each, but in the accounting period we shall consider, he has only sold one of them. The other is closing stock in hand.

Since only one item has been sold, you might think it is common sense that profit ought to be £40. But if closing stock is valued at selling price, profit would be £80 – ie profit would be taken on the closing stock as well.

	£	£
Sales		140
Opening stock		
Purchases (2 × 100)	200	
	200	
Less closing stock (at selling price)	140	
Cost of sale		60
Profit		80

This would contradict the accounting concept of prudence – ie to claim a profit before the item has actually been sold.

4.1.2 NRV

The same objection **usually** applies to the use of NRV in stock valuation. Say that the item purchased for £100 requires £5 of further expenditure in getting it ready for sale and then selling it (eg £5 of processing costs and distribution costs). If its expected selling price is £140, its NRV is £(140-5) = £135. To value it at £135 in the balance sheet would still be to anticipate a £35 profit.

We are left with **historical cost** as the normal basis of stock valuation. **The only time when historical cost is not used is in the exceptional cases where the prudence concept requires a lower value to be used.**

Staying with the above example, suppose that the market in this kind of product suddenly slumps and the item's expected selling price is only £90. The item's NRV is then £(90 – 5) = £85 and the business has in effect made a loss of £15 (£100 – £85). The prudence concept requires that losses should be recognised as soon as they are foreseen. This can be achieved by valuing the stock item in the balance sheet at its NRV of £85.

4.1.3 Lower of cost and NRV

The argument developed above suggests that the rule to follow is that stocks should be valued at cost, or if lower, net realisable value. The accounting treatment of stock is governed by an accounting standard, SSAP 9 *Stocks and long-term contracts*. You will recall that accounting standards have been developed to remove subjectivity and to enhance comparability of financial statements. SSAP 9 states that **stock should be valued at the lower of cost and net realisable value**. This is an important rule and one which you should learn by heart.

Rule to learn

> Stocks should be valued at the lower of cost and net realisable value.

4.2 Applying the basic valuation rule

If a business has many stock items on hand the comparison of cost and NRV should theoretically be carried out for each item separately. It is not sufficient to compare the total cost of all stock items with their total NRV. An example will show why.

Suppose a company has four items of stock on hand at the end of its accounting period. Their cost and NRVs are as follows:

Stock item	Cost £	NRV £	Lower of cost/NRV £
1	27	32	27
2	14	8	8
3	43	55	43
4	29	40	29
	113	135	107

It would be incorrect to compare total costs (£113) with total NRV (£135) and to state stocks at £113 in the balance sheet. The company can foresee a loss of £6 on item 2 and this should be recognised. If the four items are taken together in total the loss on item 2 is masked by the anticipated profits on the other items. By performing the cost/NRV comparison for each item separately the prudent valuation of £107 can be derived. This is the value which should appear in the balance sheet.

However, for a company with large amounts of stock this procedure may be impracticable. In this case it is acceptable to group similar items into categories and perform the comparison of cost and NRV category by category, rather than item by item.

Question

From the following figures, calculate the figure for stock valuation:

(a) Category by category
(b) Item by item

Stock at 31 December 20X7			
Item	**Categories**	**Cost**	**Net realisable value**
1	A	560	660
2	A	880	740
3	A	780	960
4	B	340	500
5	B	420	620
6	C	800	700
7	C	1,720	1,200
8	D	1,140	1,320
9	D	1,540	1,980

Answer

(a) Category by category:

£

A Lower of (560 + 880 + 780) or (660 + 740 + 960)
   ie 2,220 or 2,360 2,220

B Lower of (340 + 420) or (500 + 620)
   ie 760 or 1,120 760

C Lower of (860 + 1,720) or (700 + 1,200)
   ie 2,520 or 1,900 1,900

D Lower of (1,140 + 1,540) or (1,320 + 1,980)
   ie 2,680 or 3,300 2,680
   7,560

(b) Item by item: 560 + 740 + 780 + 340 + 420 + 700 + 1,200 + 1,140 + 1,540 = £7,420

So have we now solved the problem of how a business should value its stocks? It seems that all the business has to do is to choose the lower of cost and net realisable value. This is true as far as it goes, but there is one further problem, perhaps not so easy to foresee: for a given item of stock, **what was** the **cost**?

4.3 Determining the purchase cost

Stock may be **raw materials** or components bought from suppliers, **finished goods** which have been made by the business but not yet sold, or work in the process of production, but only part-completed (this type of stock is called **work in progress** or WIP). It will simplify matters, however, if we think about the historical cost of purchased raw materials and components, which ought to be their purchase price.

A business may be continually purchasing consignments of a particular component. As each consignment is received from suppliers they are stored in the appropriate bin or on the appropriate shelf or pallet, where they will be mingled with previous consignments. When the storekeeper issues components to production he will simply pull out from the bin the nearest components to hand, which may have arrived in the latest consignment or in an earlier consignment or in several different consignments. Our concern is to devise a pricing technique, a rule of thumb which we can use to attribute a cost to each of the components issued from stores.

There are two main techniques which you need to know for your syllabus.

Key terms

> (a) **FIFO (first in, first out).** Using this technique, we assume that components are used in the order in which they are received from suppliers. The components issued are deemed to have formed part of the oldest consignment still unused and are costed accordingly.
>
> (b) **Average cost (AVCO).** As purchase prices change with each new consignment, the average price of components in the bin is constantly changed. Each component in the bin at any moment is assumed to have been purchased at the average price of all components in the bin at that moment.

If you are preparing **financial accounts** you would normally expect to use FIFO or AVCO for the balance sheet valuation of stock. You should note that the term FIFO refers to **pricing techniques** only. The actual components can be used in any order. LIFO (last in, first out) is not used in financial statements.

To illustrate the various pricing methods, the following transactions will be used in each case:

TRANSACTIONS DURING MAY 20X3

	Quantity Units	Unit cost £	Total cost £	Market value per unit date of transactions £
Opening balance 1 May	100	2.00	200	
Receipts 3 May	400	2.10	840	2.11
Issues 4 May	200			2.11
Receipts 9 May	300	2.12	636	2.15
Issues 11 May	400			2.20
Receipts 18 May	100	2.40	240	2.35
Issues 20 May	100			2.35
Closing balance 31 May	200			2.38
			1,916	

Receipts mean goods are received into store and issues represent the issue of goods from store.

The problem is to put a valuation on:

(a)   The issues of materials
(b)   The closing stock

How would issues and closing stock be valued using:

(a)   FIFO?
(b)   Average cost?

4.4 FIFO (first in, first out)

FIFO assumes that materials are **issued out of stock in the order in which they were delivered into stock**, ie issues are priced at the cost of the earliest delivery remaining in stock.

The cost of issues and closing stock value in the example, using FIFO would be as follows (note that o/s stands for opening stock).

Date of issue	Quantity Units	Value issued £	Cost of issues £	£
4 May	200	100 o/s at £2	200	
		100 at £2.10	210	
				410
11 May	400	300 at £2.10	630	
		100 at £2.12	212	
				842
20 May	100	100 at £2.12	212	
				1,464
Closing stock value	200	100 at £2.12	212	
		100 at £2.40	240	
				452
				1,916

Note that the cost of materials issued plus the value of closing stock equals the cost of purchases plus the value of opening stock (£1,916).

4.5 Average cost

There are various ways in which average costs may be used in pricing stock issues. The most common (cumulative weighted average pricing) is illustrated below.

The **cumulative weighted average pricing method** calculates a weighted average price for all units in stock. Issues are priced at this average cost, and the balance of stock remaining would have the same unit valuation.

A new weighted average price is calculated whenever a new delivery of materials into store is received. This is the key feature of cumulative weighted average pricing.

In our example, issue costs and closing stock values would be as follows.

Date	Received Units	Issued Units	Balance Units	Total stock value £	Unit cost £	Price of issue £
Opening stock			100	200	2.00	
3 May	400			840	2.10	
			500	1,040	2.08 *	
4 May		200		(416)	2.08 **	416
			300	624	2.08	
9 May	300			636	2.12	
			600	1,260	2.10 *	
11 May		400		(840)	2.10 **	840
			200	420	2.10	
18 May	100			240	2.40	
			300	660	2.20 *	
20 May		100		(220)	2.20 **	220
						1,476
Closing stock value			200	440	2.20	440
						1,916

* A new unit cost of stock is calculated whenever a new receipt of materials occurs.

** Whenever stocks are issued, the unit value of the items issued is the current weighted average cost per unit at the time of the issue.

For this method too, the cost of materials issued plus the value of closing stock equals the cost of purchases plus the value of opening stock (£1,916).

4.6 Stock valuations and profit

In the previous descriptions of FIFO and average cost, the example used raw materials as an illustration. Each method of valuation produced different costs both of closing stocks and also of material issues. Since raw material costs affect the cost of production, and the cost of production works through eventually into the cost of sales, it follows that different methods of stock valuation will provide different profit figures. An example may help to illustrate this point.

4.7 Example: Stock valuations and profit

On 1 November 20X2 a company held 300 units of finished goods item No 9639 in stock. These were valued at £12 each. During November 20X2 three batches of finished goods were received into store from the production department as follows:

Date	Units received	Production cost per unit
10 November	400	£12.50
20 November	400	£14
25 November	400	£15

Goods sold out of stock during November were as follows:

Date	Units sold	Sale price per unit
14 November	500	£20
21 November	500	£20
28 November	100	£20

What was the profit from selling stock item 9639 in November 20X2, applying the following principles of stock valuation:

(a)   FIFO
(b)   Cumulative weighted average costing (AVCO)?

Ignore administration, sales and distribution costs.

Solution

(a)   FIFO

Date	Issue costs	Issue cost Total £	Closing stock £
14 November	300 units × £12 plus		
	200 units × £12.50	6,100	
21 November	200 units × £12.50 plus		
	300 units × £14	6,700	
28 November	100 units × £14	1,400	
Closing stock	400 units × £15		6,000
		14,200	6,000

(b)   Cumulative weighted average costs (AVCO):

		Unit cost £	Balance in stock £	Total cost of issues £	Closing stock £
1 November	Opening stock 300	12.000	3,600		
10 November	400	12.500	5,000		
	700	12.286	8,600		
14 November	500	12.286	6,143	6,143	
	200	12.286	2,457		
20 November	400	14.000	5,600		
	600	13.428	8,057		
21 November	500	13.428	6,714	6,714	
	100	13.428	1,343		
25 November	400	15.000	6,000		
	500	14.686	7,343		
28 November	100	14.686	1,469	1,469	
30 November	400	14.686	5,874	14,326	5,874

Summary: profit

	FIFO £	AVCO £
Opening stock	3,600	3,600
Cost of production	16,600	16,600
	20,200	20,200
Closing stock	6,000	5,874
Cost of sales	14,200	14,326
Sales (1,100 × £20)	22,000	22,000
Profit	7,800	7,674

Different stock valuations have produced different cost of sales figures, and therefore different profits. In our example opening stock values are the same, therefore the difference in the amount of profit under each method is the same as the difference in the valuations of closing stock.

The profit differences are only temporary. In our example, the opening stock in December 20X2 will be £6,000 or £5,874, depending on the stock valuation used. Different opening stock values will affect the cost of sales and profits in December, so that in the long run inequalities in costs of sales each month will even themselves out.

Question	FIFO

A firm has the following transactions with its product R.

Year 1
Opening stock: nil
Buys 10 units at £300 per unit
Buys 12 units at £250 per unit
Sells 8 units at £400 per unit
Buys 6 units at £200 per unit
Sells 12 units at £400 per unit

Year 2
Buys 10 units at £200 per unit
Sells 5 units at £400 per unit
Buys 12 units at £150 per unit
Sells 25 units at £400 per unit

Using FIFO, calculate the following on an item by item basis for both year 1 and year 2.

(i)   The closing stock
(ii) The sales
(iii) The cost of sales
(iv) The gross profit

Answer

Year 1

Purchases (units)	Sales (units)	Balance (units)	Stock value £	Unit cost £	Cost of sales £	Sales £
10		10	3,000	300		
12			3,000	250		
		22	6,000			
	8		(2,400)		2,400	3,200
		14	3,600			
6			1,200	200		
		20	4,800			
	12		(3,100)*		3,100	4,800
		8	1,700		5,500	8,000

* 2 @ £300 + 10 @ £250 = £3,100

Year 2

Purchases (units)	Sales (units)	Balance (units)	Stock value £	Unit cost £	Cost of sales £	Sales £
B/f		8	1,700			
10			2,000	200		
		18	3,700			
	5		(1,100)*		1,100	2,000
		13	2,600			
12		25	1,800	150		
			4,400			
25			(4,400)**		4,400	10,000
		0	0		5,500	12,000

* 2 @ £250 + 3 @ £200 = £1,100
** 13 @ £200 + 12 @ £150 = £4,400

Trading account
Year 1

	£	£
Sales		8,000
Opening stock	0	
Purchases	7,200	
	7,200	
Closing stock	1,700	
Cost of sales		5,500
Gross profit		2,500

Year 2	£	£
Sales		12,000
Opening stock	1,700	
Purchases	3,800	
	5,500	
Closing stock	0	
Cost of sales		5,500
Gross profit		6,500

5 Statutory regulations and SSAP 9 requirements

Stock should be valued at the lower of cost and net realisable value.

5.1 Introduction

In most businesses the value put on stock is an important factor in the determination of profit. Stock valuation is, however, a highly subjective exercise and consequently there is a wide variety of different methods used in practice.

The **statutory regulations** (now embodied in the CA 2006) and SSAP 9 requirements have been developed to achieve greater uniformity in the valuation methods used and in the disclosure in financial statements prepared under the historical cost convention.

SSAP 9 defines stocks and work in progress as:

(a) Goods or other assets purchased for resale
(b) Consumable stores
(c) Raw materials and components purchased for incorporation into products for sale
(d) Products and services in intermediate stages of completion
(e) Long-term contract balances
(f) Finished goods

In published accounts, the Companies Act 2006 requires that these stock categories should be grouped and disclosed under the following headings:

(a) Raw materials and consumables (ie (c) and (b) above)
(b) Work in progress (ie (d) and (e) above)
(c) Finished goods and goods for resale (ie (f) and (a) above)
(d) Payments on account. This is presumably intended to cover the case of a company which has paid for stock items but not yet received them into stock

A distinction is also made in SSAP 9 between:

(a) Stocks and work in progress other than long-term contract work in progress
(b) Long-term contract work in progress.

Long-term contracts are outside the scope of your Paper F3 studies.

5.2 Determination of the cost of stock

To determine profit, **costs should be matched with related revenues**. Since the cost of unsold stock and work in progress at the end of an accounting period has been incurred in the expectation of future sales revenue, it is appropriate to carry these costs forward in the balance sheet, and to charge them against the profits of the period in which the future sales revenue is eventually earned.

SSAP9 requires stock to be valued 'at cost, or, if lower, at net realisable value.'

The **comparison** of cost and net realisable value should be made **separately** for **each** item of stock, but if this is impracticable, **similar categories** of stock item can be grouped together.

This valuation principle has now been given legislative backing by the CA 2006, which requires that the amount to be included in the balance sheet in respect of any current asset (including stocks) is the lower of its purchase price or production cost, and its net realisable value.

5.3 Definitions

The SSAP 9 definition of NRV is as follows.

> *'Net realisable value*: the actual or estimated selling price (net of trade but before settlement discounts) less:
>
> (a)   All further costs to completion.
> (b)   All costs to be incurred in marketing, selling and distributing.'

The cost of stocks is harder to determine. SSAP 9 states:

> 'Cost is… that expenditure which has been incurred in the normal course of business in bringing the product or service to its present location and condition. This expenditure should include, in addition to the cost of purchase, such costs of conversion as are appropriate to that location and condition.
>
> Cost of purchase comprises purchase price including import duties, transport and handling costs and any other directly attributable costs, less trade discounts, rebates and subsidies.
>
> Cost of conversion comprises:
>
> (a)   Costs which are specifically attributable to units of production, eg direct labour, direct expenses and sub-contracted work.
>
> (b)   Production overheads.
>
> (c)   Other overheads, if any, attributable in the particular circumstances of the business to bringing the product or service to its present location and condition.'

5.4 Determination of cost

The CA 2006 also allows (but, unlike SSAP 9, does not require) the inclusion of production overheads in the valuation of stock.

Two further points to note concern the determination of cost of purchase (purchase price in CA 2006 terminology) and attributable production overhead.

SSAP 9 states the following general principle regarding **cost of purchase**:

> 'The methods used in allocating costs to stocks need to be selected with a view to providing the fairest possible approximation to the expenditure actually incurred.'

The appendix to SSAP9 states that methods such as base stock and LIFO do not generally satisfy the principle, though it is worth noting that LIFO is, with FIFO and weighted average price, one of the methods specifically permitted by the CA 2006. The Act merely requires that the chosen method should be one which, in the directors' opinion, is appropriate to the company.

When **allocating production overheads to the valuation of stock** care must be taken to exclude all abnormal overheads such as exceptional spoilage, idle capacity and other losses which are avoidable under normal conditions. Refer again to the SSAP 9 definition of cost quoted above which allows only 'expenditure incurred in the normal course of business'.

The appendix to SSAP 9 provides practical guidelines on the valuation of stocks and work in progress. A detailed discussion of these is outside the scope of your F3 syllabus. It is relevant to note, however, that in the UK, the **HM Revenue and Customs** accepts FIFO, average cost and (in the case of many retailing companies) 'selling price less normal gross profit margin' as stock valuation methods in arriving at taxable profit.

Question

Hudson Ltd specialises in retailing one product. The firm purchases its stock from a regional wholesaler and sells through a catalogue. Details of Hudson Ltd's purchases and sales for the three month period 1 January to 31 March 20X7 are as follows.

Purchases

Date	Quantity in units	Price per unit £
14 January	280	24
30 January	160	24
15 February	300	25
3 March	150	26
29 March	240	26

Sales

Date	Quantity in units	Price per unit £
22 January	170	60
4 February	140	60
18 February	90	63
26 February	70	64
4 March	110	64
19 March	200	66
30 March	80	66

Note. Hudson Ltd had no stock in hand at 1 January 20X7.

Required

(a) Record the company's stock movements for the period 1 January to 31 March by the preparation of a stores card applying FIFO

(b) Prepare the firm's trading account for the three month period applying FIFO

(c) Note how SSAP 9 affects the valuation of a company's stock in trade.

Answer

(a)

		Quantity Movement	Quantity Balance	Movement Unit cost £	Movement Total value £
14 Jan	Receipt	280	280	24	6,720
22 Jan	Issue	(170)	110	24	(4,080)
30 Jan	Receipt	160	270	24	3,840
4 Feb	Issue	(140)	130	24	(3,360)
15 Feb	Receipt	300	430	25	7,500
18 Feb	Issue	(90)	340	24	(2,160)
				40 24	
26 Feb	Issue	(70)	270	30 25	(1,710)
3 Mar	Receipt	150	420	26	3,900
4 Mar	Issue	(110)	310	25	(2,750)
				160 25	
19 Mar	Issue	(200)	110	40 26	(5,040)
29 Mar	Receipt	240	350	26	6,240
30 Mar	Issue	(80)	270	26	(2,080)
			Total receipts		28,200
			Total issues		21,180
					7,020

(b)   HUDSON
TRADING ACCOUNT FOR THE 3 MONTH PERIOD TO 31 MARCH 20X7

	£	£
Sales		54,270
Opening stock	–	
Purchases	28,200	
	28,200	
Closing stock	7,020	
Cost of sales		21,180
Gross profit		33,090

Workings: Sales 1 Jan to 31 Mar X5

	Units	Selling price	
		£	£
22 Jan	170	60	10,200
4 Feb	140	60	8,400
18 Feb	90	63	5,670
26 Feb	70	64	4,480
4 Mar	110	64	7,040
19 Mar	200	66	13,200
30 Mar	80	66	5,280
			54,270

(c)   SSAP 9 states that stocks should be stated at the lower of cost and net realisable value. Cost is defined as the expenditure which has been incurred in the normal course of business in bringing the product or service to its present location and condition. Net realisable value is the actual or estimated selling price less all further costs to be incurred in realising the stock.

5.5 Net realisable value (NRV)

As a general rule assets should not be carried at amounts greater than those expected to be realised from their sale or use. In the case of stocks this amount could fall below cost when items are **damaged or become obsolete**, or where the **costs to completion have increased** in order to make the sale.

In fact we can identify the principal situations in which **NRV is likely to be less than cost.**

(a)   An **increase in costs** or a **fall in selling price**
(b)   A **physical deterioration** in the condition of stock
(c)   **Obsolescence** of products
(d)   A decision as part of the company's marketing strategy to manufacture and sell products at a **loss**
(e)   **Errors in production or purchasing**

A write down of stocks would normally take place on an item by item basis, but similar or related items may be **grouped together**. This grouping together is acceptable for, say, items in the same product line, but it is not acceptable to write down inventories based on a whole classification (eg finished goods) or a whole business.

The assessment of NRV should take place **at the same time** as estimates are made of selling price, using the most reliable information available. Fluctuations of price or cost should be taken into account if they relate directly to **events after the reporting period,** which confirm conditions existing at the end of the period.

The reasons why stock is held must also be taken into account. Some stock, for example, may be held to satisfy a firm contract and its NRV will therefore be the **contract price**. Any additional stock of the same type held at the period end will, in contrast, be assessed according to general sales prices when NRV is estimated.

Net realisable value must be reassessed at the end of each period and compared again with cost. If the NRV has risen for stocks held over the end of more than one period, then the previous write down must be

reversed to the extent that the stock is then valued at the lower of cost and the new NRV. This may be possible when selling prices have fallen in the past and then risen again.

On occasion a write down to NRV may be of such size, incidence or nature that it must be **disclosed separately**.

5.6 Recognition as an expense

The following treatment is required **when stock are sold**.

(a)   The **carrying amount** is recognised as an expense in the period in which the related revenue is recognised

(b)   The amount of any **write-down of stocks** to NRV and all losses of stocks are recognised as an expense in the period the write-down or loss occurs

(c)   The amount of any **reversal of any write-down of stocks**, arising from an increase in NRV, is recognised as a reduction in the amount of stocks recognised as an expense in the period in which the reversal occurs

Chapter Roundup

- You must learn the formula for **cost of goods sold**: Opening stock + purchases – closing stock.

- **Opening stocks** brought forward in the stock account are transferred to the trading account, and so at the end of the accounting year the balance on the stock account ceases to be the opening stock value b/f and becomes instead the closing stock value c/f.

- The value of **closing stock** is accounted for in the nominal ledger by debiting a stock account and crediting the trading account at the end of an accounting period. Stock will therefore have a debit balance at the end of a period, and this balance will be shown in the balance sheet as a current asset.

- A stocktake is a means of physically counting the stock still held.

- The **value** of stock is calculated at the lower of **cost** and **net realisable value** for each separate item or group of items. **Cost** can be arrived at by using **FIFO** or **AVCO**.

- Stock should be valued at the lower of cost and net realisable value.

1   When is a stock account used?

2   How is closing stock incorporated in the financial statements?

    A   Debit: P&L   Credit: balance sheet
    B   Debit: balance sheet   Credit: P&L

3   What is 'continuous' stocktaking?

4   An item of stock was purchased for £10. However, due to a fall in demand, its selling price will be only £8. In addition further costs will be incurred prior to sale of £1. What is the net realisable value?

    A   £7
    B   £8
    C   £10
    D   £11

5   Why is stock not valued at expected selling price?

6   When valuing stock at historical cost, the following methods are available.

    (1)   FIFO
    (2)   AVCO
    (3)   LIFO
    (4)   Standard cost

    Which methods are allowable under SSAP 9?

    A   (1), (2), (3)
    B   (1), (2), (3), (4)
    C   (1) only
    D   (1), (2) and (4)

7   What is included in the cost of purchase of stock according to SSAP 9?

    A   Purchase price less trade discount
    B   Purchase price plus transport costs less trade discount
    C   Purchase price less import duties less trade discount
    D   Purchase price plus import duties plus transport costs less trade discount

8   What type of costs should be recognised as an expense, not as part of the cost of stock?

9   What are the most likely situations when the NRV of stock fall below cost?

1   Only at the end of an accounting period.

2   B   DEBIT: Stock in hand (balance sheet)
           CREDIT: Closing stock (trading account)

3   A card is kept for every item of stock. It shows receipts and issues, with a running total. A few stock items are counted each day to test that the cards are correct.

4   A   Net realisable value is selling price (£8) less further costs to sale (£1), ie £7.

5   Mainly because this would result in the business taking a profit before the goods have been sold.

6   D   Only FIFO, AVCO and standard costing are allowed.

7   D   Purchase price **plus** import duties (and other taxes) **plus** transport costs **less** trade discount.

8   Costs arising outside the normal course of business.

9   • Increase in costs or a fall in selling price
     • Physical deterioration of stock
     • Obsolescence
     • Marketing strategy
     • Errors in production or purchasing

Now try the questions below from the Exam Question Bank

Number	Level	Marks	Time
Q12	Examination	2	2 mins
Q13	Examination	2	2 mins

Tangible fixed assets

Topic list	Syllabus reference
1 Capital and revenue expenditure	D4(a)-(d)
2 Depreciation	D5(a)-(g)
3 Fixed asset disposals	D4(e), (f)
4 Fixed assets: Statutory requirements	D4(i)
5 FRS 15 Tangible fixed assets	D4(i)
6 Revaluations	D4(g), D4(h), D5(e)
7 The fixed assets register	D4(j)
8 Worked example	D4(a)-(i), D5(a)-(g)

Introduction

We start by looking at capital and revenue expenditure.

You should by now be familiar with the distinction between **fixed and current assets**, a fixed asset being one bought for ongoing use in the business. If you are unsure of this, look back to Chapter 1 to refresh your memory.

Fixed assets might be held and used by a business for a number of years, but they wear out or lose their usefulness in the course of time. Nearly every tangible fixed asset has a **limited** life. The process by which this is recognised in the accounts is **depreciation**, and this is discussed in Section 2.

Section 3 deals with **disposals** of fixed assets. A profit may arise on the sale of a fixed asset if too much depreciation has been charged.

Section 4 deals with the statutory requirements relating to fixed assets. Fixed assets are the subject of a *financial reporting standard* (FRS 15), which you will need to know for your exam. The standard is fairly straightforward and is discussed in Section 5.

Occasionally, particularly in the case of land or buildings, the market value of a fixed asset will rise with time. The asset may then be **revalued**. The accounting treatment of revaluations and the effect on depreciation are considered in Section 6.

Section 7 looks at how organisations record their fixed assets.

You are now ready to prepare the accounts of a sole trader! Section 8 shows you how.

Study guide

		Intellectual level
D4	**Tangible fixed assets**	
(a)	Define fixed assets	1
(b)	Recognise the difference between current and fixed assets	1
(c)	Explain the differences between capital and revenue items	1
(d)	Classify expenditure as capital or revenue expenditure	1
(e)	Prepare ledger entries to record the acquisition and disposal of fixed assets	1
(f)	Calculate and record profits or losses on disposal of fixed assets in the profit and loss account including part exchange transactions	1
(g)	Record the revaluation of a fixed asset in ledger accounts, the balance sheet and in the statement of total recognised gains and losses	1
(h)	Calculate the profit or loss on disposal of a revalued asset	1
(i)	Illustrate how fixed asset balances and movements are disclosed in financial statements	1
(j)	Explain the purpose and function of a fixed asset register	1
D5	**Depreciation**	1
(a)	Understand and explain the purpose of depreciation	1
(b)	Calculate the charge for depreciation using straight line and reducing balance methods	1
(c)	Identify the circumstances where different methods of depreciation would be appropriate	1
(d)	Illustrate how depreciation expense and accumulated depreciation are recorder in ledger accounts	1
(e)	Calculate depreciation on a revalued fixed asset including the transfer of excess depreciation between the revaluation reserve and accumulated profits	1
(f)	Calculate the adjustments to depreciation necessary if changes are made in the estimated useful life and/or residual value of a fixed asset	2
(g)	Record depreciation in the profit and loss account and balance sheet	1

Exam guide

This is a key subject area. You will need to calculate depreciation and perhaps the profit or loss on disposal of a fixed asset. You also need to understand the main points of FRS 15 *Tangible fixed assets* well enough to answer a question on its application.

1 Capital and revenue expenditure

FAST FORWARD

Capital expenditure is expenditure which results in the **acquisition of fixed assets**.

Revenue expenditure is expenditure incurred for the **purpose of the trade** or to **maintain fixed assets**.

You need to be familiar with an important distinction, the distinction between **capital and revenue expenditure**.

1.1 Definitions

> **Capital expenditure** is expenditure which results in the acquisition of fixed assets, or an improvement in their earning capacity.
>
> (a) Capital expenditure is not charged as an expense in the profit and loss account, although a depreciation charge will usually be made to write off the capital expenditure gradually over time. Depreciation charges are expenses in the profit and loss account.
>
> (b) Capital expenditure on fixed assets results in the appearance of a fixed asset in the balance sheet of the business.
>
> **Revenue expenditure** is expenditure which is incurred for either of the following reasons.
>
> (a) For the purpose of the trade of the business. This includes expenditure classified as selling and distribution expenses, administration expenses and finance charges.
>
> (b) To maintain the existing earning capacity of fixed assets.

Revenue expenditure is charged to the profit and loss account of a period, if it relates to the trading activity and sales of that particular period. For example, a business buys ten widgets for £200 (£20 each) and sells eight of them during an accounting period. It has two widgets left at the end of the period. The full £200 is revenue expenditure but only £160 is a cost of goods sold during the period. The remaining £40 (cost of two units) will be included in the balance sheet as a current asset valued at £40.

A business purchases a building for £30,000. It then adds an extension to the building at a cost of £10,000. The building needs to have a few broken windows mended, its floors polished and some missing roof tiles replaced. These cleaning and maintenance jobs cost £900.

In this example, the original purchase (£30,000) and the cost of the extension (£10,000) are capital expenditure, because they are incurred to acquire and then improve a fixed asset. The other costs of £900 are revenue expenditure, because these merely maintain the building and thus the 'earning capacity' of the building.

1.2 Capital income and revenue income

Capital income is the proceeds from the sale of non-trading assets (ie proceeds from the sale of fixed assets, including fixed asset investments). The profits (or losses) from the sale of fixed assets are included in the profit and loss account of a business, for the accounting period in which the sale takes place.

Revenue income is income derived from the following sources.

(a) The sale of trading assets or provision of services
(b) Interest and dividends received from investments held by the business

1.3 Capital transactions

The categorisation of capital and revenue items given above does not mention raising additional capital from the owner(s) of the business, or raising and repaying loans. These are transactions which:

(a) Add to the cash assets of the business, thereby creating a corresponding liability (capital or loan).
(b) When a loan is repaid, reduce the liabilities (loan) and the assets (cash) of the business.

None of these transactions would be reported through the profit and loss account.

1.4 Why is the distinction between capital and revenue items important?

Revenue expenditure results from the purchase of goods and services that will:

(a) Be used fully in the accounting period in which they are purchased, and so be a cost or expense in the trading, profit and loss account.

(b)   Result in a current asset as at the end of the accounting period because the goods or services have not yet been consumed or made use of. The current asset would be shown in the balance sheet and is not yet a cost or expense in the trading, profit and loss account.

Capital expenditure results in the **purchase or improvement** of fixed assets, which are assets that will provide benefits to the business in more than one accounting period, and which are not acquired with a view to being resold in the normal course of trade. The cost of purchased fixed assets is not charged in full to the trading, profit and loss account of the period in which the purchase occurs. Instead, the fixed asset is gradually depreciated over a number of accounting periods.

Since revenue items and capital items are accounted for in different ways, the correct and consistent calculation of profit for any accounting period depends on the correct and consistent classification of items as revenue or capital.

This may seem rather confusing at the moment, but things will become clearer in the next few chapters. In the meantime just get used to the terminology. These words appear in the accounts standards themselves, as we will see.

Question   Capital or revenue

State whether each of the following items should be classified as 'capital' or 'revenue' expenditure or income for the purpose of preparing the trading, profit and loss account and the balance sheet of the business.

(a)   The purchase of leasehold premises.
(b)   The annual depreciation of leasehold premises.
(c)   Solicitors' fees in connection with the purchase of leasehold premises.
(d)   The costs of adding extra storage capacity to a mainframe computer used by the business.
(e)   Computer repairs and maintenance costs.
(f)   Profit on the sale of an office building.
(g)   Revenue from sales by credit card.
(h)   The cost of new machinery.
(i)   Customs duty charged on the machinery when imported into the country.
(j)   The 'carriage' costs of transporting the new machinery from the supplier's factory to the premises of the business purchasing the machinery.
(k)   The cost of installing the new machinery in the premises of the business.
(l)   The wages of the machine operators.

Answer

(a)   Capital expenditure.
(b)   Depreciation of a fixed asset is a revenue expenditure.
(c)   The legal fees associated with the purchase of a property may be added to the purchase price and classified as capital expenditure. The cost of the leasehold premises in the balance sheet of the business will then include the legal fees.
(d)   Capital expenditure (enhancing an existing fixed asset).
(e)   Revenue expenditure.
(f)   Capital income (net of the costs of sale).
(g)   Revenue income.
(h)   Capital expenditure.
(i)   If customs duties are borne by the purchaser of the fixed asset, they may be added to the cost of the machinery and classified as capital expenditure.
(j)   Similarly, if carriage costs are paid for by the purchaser of the fixed asset, they may be included in the cost of the fixed asset and classified as capital expenditure.

(k)   Installation costs of a fixed asset are also added to the fixed asset's cost and classified as capital expenditure.

(l)   Revenue expenditure.

2 Depreciation

A fixed asset is acquired for use within a business with a view to earning profits. Its life extends over more than one accounting period, and so it earns profits over more than one period. In contrast, a current asset is used and replaced many times within the period eg stock is sold and replaced, debtors increase with sales and decrease with payments received.

With the exception of land held on freehold or very long leasehold, every fixed asset eventually wears out over time. Machines, cars and other vehicles, fixtures and fittings, and even buildings do not last for ever. When a business acquires a fixed asset, it will have some idea about how long its useful life will be, and it might decide:

(a)   To keep on using the fixed asset until it becomes completely worn out, useless, and worthless.

(b)   To sell off the fixed asset at the end of its useful life, either by selling it as a second-hand item or as scrap.

Since a fixed asset has a cost, and a limited useful life, and its value eventually declines, it follows that a charge should be made in the trading, profit and loss account to reflect the use that is made of the asset by the business. This charge is called **depreciation**.

2.1 Definition of depreciation

Suppose that a business buys a machine for £40,000. Its expected life is four years, and at the end of that time it is expected to be worthless.

Since the fixed asset is used to make profits for four years, it would be reasonable to charge the cost of the asset over those four years (perhaps by charging £10,000 per annum) so that at the end of the four years the total cost of £40,000 would have been charged against profits.

Indeed, one way of defining depreciation is to describe it as **a means of spreading the cost of a fixed asset over its useful life**, and so matching the cost against the full period during which it earns profits for the business. Depreciation charges are an example of the application of the accruals (or matching) concept to calculate profits.

Depreciation has two important aspects.

(a)   Depreciation is a **measure of the wearing out** or depletion of a fixed asset through use, time or obsolescence.

(b)   Depreciation charges should be **spread fairly** over a fixed asset's life, and so allocated to the accounting periods which are expected to benefit (ie make profits) from the asset's use.

The total charge for depreciation: the depreciable amount

The total amount to be charged over the life of a fixed asset ('the depreciable amount') is usually its cost less any expected 'residual' sales value or disposal value at the end of the asset's life.

(a)   A fixed asset costing £20,000, which has an expected life of five years and an expected residual value of nil, should be depreciated by £20,000 in total over the five year period.

(b)   A fixed asset costing £20,000, which has an expected life of five years and an expected residual value of £3,000, should be depreciated by £17,000 in total over the five years.

2.2 Depreciation in the accounts of a business

When a fixed asset is depreciated, two things must be accounted for.

(a)   The **charge for depreciation** is a **cost or expense** of the accounting period. Depreciation is an expense in the profit and loss account.

(b)   At the same time, the fixed asset is wearing out and diminishing in value. So the value of the fixed asset in the balance sheet must be reduced by the amount of depreciation charged. The balance sheet value of the fixed asset will be its **'net book value'**, which is the value after depreciation in the books of account of the business.

The amount of depreciation will build up (or 'accumulate') over time, as more depreciation is charged in each successive accounting period. This accumulated depreciation is a 'provision' because it provides for the fall in value in use of the fixed asset. The term 'provision for depreciation' means the 'accumulated depreciation' of a fixed asset.

For example, if a fixed asset costing £40,000 has an expected life of four years and an estimated residual value of nil, it might be depreciated by £10,000 per annum.

	Depreciation charge for the year (P & L a/c) (A)	Accumulated depreciation at end of year (B)	Cost of the asset (C)	Net book value at end of year (C-B)
	£	£	£	£
At beginning of its life	–	–	40,000	40,000
Year 1	10,000	10,000	40,000	30,000
Year 2	10,000	20,000	40,000	20,000
Year 3	10,000	30,000	40,000	10,000
Year 4	10,000	40,000	40,000	0

So each year, £10,000 depreciation is charged as an expense in the profit and loss account. Also each year, the net book value (NBV) recorded in the balance sheet reduces by £10,000 until the NBV reaches the residual value (nil in this case).

2.3 Methods of depreciation

There are several different methods of depreciation. Of these, the ones you need to know about are:
- Straight line method
- Reducing balance method

2.4 The straight line method

This is the most commonly used method of all. The total depreciable amount is charged in equal instalments to each accounting period over the expected useful life of the asset. So the net book value of the fixed asset declines at a steady rate, or in a 'straight line' over time.

The annual depreciation charge is calculated as:

$$\frac{\text{Cost of asset minus residual value}}{\text{Expected useful life of the asset}}$$

2.5 Example: straight line depreciation

(a)   A fixed asset costing £20,000 with an estimated life of 10 years and no residual value would be depreciated at the rate of:

$$\frac{£20,000}{10 \text{ years}} = £2,000 \text{ per annum}$$

(b)   A fixed asset costing £60,000 has an estimated life of 5 years and a residual value of £7,000. The annual depreciation charge using the straight line method would be:

$$\frac{£(60,000 - 7,000)}{5 \text{ years}} = £10,600 \text{ per annum}$$

The net book value of the fixed asset would be:

	After 1 year £	After 2 years £	After 3 years £	After 4 years £	After 5 years £
Cost of the asset	60,000	60,000	60,000	60,000	60,000
Accumulated depreciation	10,600	21,200	31,800	42,400	53,000
Net book value	49,400	38,800	28,200	17,600	7,000*

* ie its estimated residual value.

Since the depreciation charge per annum is the same amount every year with the straight line method, it is often convenient to state that depreciation is charged at the rate of x per cent per annum on the cost of the asset. In the example above, the depreciation charge per annum is 10% of cost (ie 10% of £20,000 = £2,000).

Examination questions often describe straight line depreciation in this way.

The straight line method of depreciation is a fair allocation of the total depreciable amount between the different accounting periods, provided the business enjoys equal benefits from the use of the asset in every period throughout its life. An example of this could be shelving (fixtures and fittings) used in the accounts department.

2.5.1 Assets acquired in the middle of an accounting period

A business can purchase new fixed assets at any time during the course of an accounting period. So it might seem fair to charge a reduced amount for depreciation in the period when the purchase occurs.

2.5.2 Example: assets acquired in the middle of an accounting period

A business which has an accounting year which runs from 1 January to 31 December purchases a new fixed asset on 1 April 20X1, at a cost of £24,000. The expected life of the asset is 4 years, and its residual value is nil. What should be the depreciation charge for 20X1?

Solution

The annual depreciation charge will be $\dfrac{24,000}{4 \text{ years}} = £6,000$ per annum

However, since the asset was acquired on 1 April 20X1, the business has only benefited from the use of the asset for 9 months instead of a full 12 months. It would therefore seem fair to charge depreciation in 20X1 of only

9/12 × £6,000 = £4,500

Exam focus point

If an examination question gives you the purchase or disposal date of a fixed asset, part way through an accounting period, you should assume that depreciation is calculated as a 'part-year' amount, unless told to the contrary in the question.

In practice, many businesses ignore the niceties of part-year depreciation, and charge a full year's depreciation on fixed assets in the year of their purchase and/or disposal, regardless of the time of year they were acquired.

2.6 The reducing balance method

The **reducing balance method** of depreciation calculates the depreciation charge as a fixed percentage of the net book value of the asset, as at the end of the accounting period.

For example, a business purchases a fixed asset at a cost of £10,000. Its expected useful life is 3 years and its estimated residual value is £2,160. The business wishes to use the reducing balance method to depreciate the asset, and calculates that the rate of depreciation should be 40% of the reducing balance (NBV) of the asset. (The method of deciding that 40% is a suitable annual percentage is a problem of mathematics, not financial accounting, and is not described here.)

The total depreciable amount is £(10,000 – 2,160) = £7,840.

The depreciation charge per annum and the net book value of the asset as at the end of each year will be as follows:

	NBV £	Accumulated depreciation £	
Asset at cost	10,000		
Depreciation in year 1 (40% × £10,000)	4,000	4,000	
Net book value at end of year 1	6,000		
Depreciation in year 2			
(40% × £6,000)	2,400	6,400	(4,000 + 2,400)
Net book value at end of year 2	3,600		
Depreciation in year 3 (40% × £3,600)	1,440	7,840	(6,400 + 1,440)
Net book value at end of year 3	2,160		

With the reducing balance method, the annual charge for depreciation is higher in the earlier years of the asset's life, and lower in the later years. In the example above, the annual charges for years 1, 2 and 3 are £4,000, £2,400 and £1,440 respectively. The reducing balance method, therefore, is used when it is considered fair to allocate a greater proportion of the total depreciable amount to the earlier years and a lower proportion to later years, on the assumption that the benefits obtained by the business from using the asset decline over time. An example of this could be machinery in a factory, where productivity falls as the machine gets older.

2.7 Applying a depreciation method consistently

It is up to the business concerned to decide which method of depreciation to apply to its fixed assets. Once that decision has been made, however, it should not be changed - the chosen method of depreciation should be applied **consistently from year to year**. This is an instance of the consistency concept, which we looked at in Chapter 3.

Similarly, it is up to the business to decide what a sensible life span for a fixed asset should be. Again, once that life span has been chosen, it should not be changed unless something unexpected happens to the fixed asset.

It is permissible for a business to depreciate different categories of fixed assets in different ways. For example, if a business owns three cars, then each car would normally be depreciated in the same way (eg by the straight line method); but another category of fixed asset, say, photocopiers, can be depreciated using a different method (eg by the reducing balance method).

 Question   **Depreciation methods**

A lorry bought for a business cost £17,000. It is expected to last for five years and then be sold for scrap for £2,000.

Required

Work out the depreciation to be charged each year under:

(a)   The straight line method
(b)   The reducing balance method (using a rate of 35%)

(a)   Under the straight line method, depreciation for each of the five years is: $\dfrac{£17{,}000 - £2{,}000}{5} =$
£3,000 pa (5 × £3,000 = £15,000).

(b)   Under the reducing balance method, depreciation for each of the five years is:

Year	Depreciation		£
1	35% × £17,000	=	5,950
2	35% × (£17,000 − £5,950) = 35% × £11,050	=	3,868
3	35% × (£11,050 − £3,868) = 35% × £7,182	=	2,514
4	35% × (£7,182 − £2,514) = 35% × £4,668	=	1,634
5	Balance to bring book value down to £2,000 = £4,668 − £1,634 − 2,000	=	1,034
			15,000

2.8 Change in method of depreciation

Having made the above comments about consistency, the depreciation method should be reviewed for appropriateness. If there are any changes in the expected pattern of use of the asset (and hence economic benefit), then the method used should be changed. In such cases, the remaining net book value is depreciated under the new method, ie only current and future periods are affected; the change is not retrospective.

2.9 Example: Change in method of depreciation

Jakob Ltd purchased an asset for £100,000 on 1.1.X1. It had an estimated useful life of 5 years and it was depreciated using the reducing balance method at a rate of 40%. On 1.1.X3 it was decided to change the method to straight line.

Show the depreciation charge for each year (to 31 December) of the asset's life.

Solution

Year		Depreciation charge £	Aggregate depreciation £
20X1	£100,000 × 40%	40,000	40,000
20X2	£60,000 × 40%	24,000	64,000
20X3	$\dfrac{£100{,}000 - £64{,}000}{3}$	12,000	76,000
20X4		12,000	88,000
20X5		12,000	100,000

2.10 A fall in the value of a fixed asset

When the 'market' value of a fixed asset falls so that it is worth less than the amount of its net book value, and the fall in value is expected to be **permanent**, the asset should be **written down to its new low market value**. The charge in the profit and loss account for the permanent diminution in the value of the asset during the accounting period should then be:

	£
Net book value at the beginning of the period	X
Less: new reduced value	(X)
Equals: the charge for the diminution in the asset's value in the period.	X

2.11 Example: Fall in asset value

A business purchased a leasehold property on 1 January 20X1 at a cost of £100,000. The lease has a 20 year life. After 5 years' use, on 1 January 20X6, the business decides that since property prices have fallen sharply, the leasehold is now worth only £60,000, and that the value of the asset should be reduced in the accounts of the business.

The leasehold was being depreciated at the rate of 5% per annum on cost.

Before the asset is reduced in value, the annual depreciation charge is:

$$\frac{£100,000}{20 \text{ years}} = £5,000 \text{ per annum } (= 5\% \text{ of } £100,000)$$

After 5 years, the accumulated depreciation would be £25,000, and the net book value of the leasehold £75,000, which is £15,000 more than the new asset value. This £15,000 should be written off as a charge for depreciation or fall in the asset's value in year 5, so that the total charge in year 5 is:

	£
Net book value of the leasehold after 4 years (£100,000 - 20,000)	80,000
Revised asset value at end of year 5	60,000
Charge against profit in year 5	20,000

An alternative method of calculation is:

	£
'Normal' depreciation charge per annum	5,000
Further fall in value, from net book value at end of year 5 to revised value	15,000
Charge against profit in year 5	20,000

The leasehold has a further 15 years to run, and its value is now £60,000. From year 6 to year 20, the annual charge for depreciation will be:

$$\frac{£60,000}{15 \text{ years}} = £4,000 \text{ per annum}$$

2.12 Change in expected life of an asset

The depreciation charge on a fixed asset depends not only on the cost (or value) of the asset and its estimated residual value, but also on its **estimated useful life**.

A business purchased a fixed asset costing £12,000 with an estimated life of four years and no residual value. If it used the straight line method of depreciation, it would make an annual provision of 25% of £12,000 = £3,000.

Now what would happen if the business decided after two years that the useful life of the asset has been underestimated, and it still had five more years in use to come (making its total life seven years)?

For the first two years, the asset was depreciated by £3,000 per annum, so that its net book value after two years is £(12,000 − 6,000) = £6,000. If the remaining life of the asset is now revised to five more years, the remaining amount to be depreciated (£6,000) is spread over the remaining life, giving an annual depreciation charge for the final five years of:

$$\frac{\text{Net book value at time of life readjustment, minus residual value}}{\text{New estimate of remaining useful life}}$$

$$= \frac{£6,000}{5 \text{ years}} = £1,200 \text{ per annum}$$

Formula to learn

$$\text{New depreciation} = \frac{\text{NBV less residual value}}{\text{Revised useful life}}$$

The same formula is used if there is a **revision of residual value**.

In the above example, the business also decides that the fixed asset will have a residual value of £1,000 at the end of the five years. The new depreciation is calculated as follows:

$$\text{New depreciation} = \frac{\text{NBV less new residual value}}{\text{Revised useful life}}$$

$$= \frac{£6,000 - £1,000}{5}$$

$$= £1,000 \text{ per annum}$$

2.13 Depreciation is not a cash expense

Depreciation spreads the cost of a fixed asset (less its estimated residual value) over the asset's life. The cash payment for the fixed asset will be made when, or soon after, the asset is purchased. Therefore, annual depreciation of the asset in subsequent years is **not a cash expense**.

For example, a business purchased some shop fittings for £6,000 on 1 July 20X5 and paid for them in cash on that date.

Subsequently, depreciation may be charged at £600 pa for ten years. So each year £600 is deducted from profits and the net book value of the fittings goes down, but no actual cash is being paid. The cash was all paid on 1 July 20X5. So annual depreciation is not a cash expense, but rather an allocation of the original cost to later years.

2.14 Accumulated depreciation

Accumulated **depreciation** is the amount set aside as a charge for the wearing out of fixed assets.

There are two basic aspects of accumulated depreciation to remember:

(a)   A depreciation charge is made in the profit and loss account in each accounting period for every depreciable fixed asset. Nearly all fixed assets are depreciable, the most important exceptions being freehold land and long-term investments.

(b)   The total accumulated depreciation on a fixed asset builds up as the asset gets older. The depreciation accumulates until the fixed asset is fully depreciated.

The ledger accounting entries for depreciation are as follows.

(a)   There is an accumulated depreciation account for each separate category of fixed assets, for example, plant and machinery, land and buildings, fixtures and fittings.

(b)   The depreciation charge for an accounting period is a charge against profit. It is an increase in the accumulated depreciation and is accounted for as follows:

DEBIT   P & L account (depreciation expense)
CREDIT   Accumulated depreciation account

with the depreciation charge for the period.

(c)   The balance on the account is the **total accumulated depreciation**. This is always a credit balance brought forward in the ledger account for depreciation.

(d)   The fixed asset accounts are unaffected by depreciation. Fixed assets are recorded in these accounts at cost (or, if they are revalued, at their revalued amount).

(e)   In the balance sheet of the business, the total balance on the accumulated depreciation account is set against the value of fixed asset accounts (ie fixed assets at cost or revalued amount) to derive the net book value of the fixed assets.

2.15 Example: Accumulated depreciation

Brian Box set up his own computer software business on 1 March 20X6. He purchased a computer system on credit from a manufacturer, at a cost of £16,000. The system has an expected life of three years and a residual value of £2,500. Using the straight line method of depreciation, the fixed asset account, provision for depreciation account and P & L account (extract) and balance sheet (extract) would be as follows, for each of the next three years ended 28 February 20X7, 20X8 and 20X9.

FIXED ASSET – COMPUTER EQUIPMENT

	Date		£	Date		£
(a)	1.3.X6	Creditor	16,000	28.2.X7	Balance c/f	16,000
(b)	1.3.X7	Balance b/f	16,000	28.2.X8	Balance c/f	16,000
(c)	1.3.X8	Balance b/f	16,000	28.2.X9	Balance c/f	16,000
(d)	1.3.X9	Balance b/f	16,000			

In theory, the fixed asset has completed its expected useful life. However, until it is sold off or scrapped, the asset will still appear in the balance sheet at cost (less accumulated depreciation) and it should remain in the ledger account for computer equipment until it is eventually disposed of.

ACCUMULATED DEPRECIATION

	Date		£	Date		£
(a)	28.2.X7	Balance c/f	4,500	28.2.X7	P & L account	4,500
(b)	28.2.X8	Balance c/f	9,000	1.3.X7	Balance b/f	4,500
				28.2.X8	P & L account	4,500
			9,000			9,000
(c)	28.2.X9	Balance c/f	13,500	1.3.X8	Balance b/f	9,000
				28.2.X9	P & L account	4,500
			13,500			13,500
				1 Mar 20X9 Balance b/f		13,500

The annual depreciation charge is $\dfrac{(£16,000 - 2,500)}{3 \text{ years}}$ = £4,500 pa

At the end of three years, the asset is fully depreciated down to its residual value. If it continues to be used by Brian Box, it will not be depreciated any further (unless its estimated residual value is reduced).

P & L ACCOUNT (EXTRACT)

	Date		£
(a)	28 Feb 20X7	Accumulated depreciation	4,500
(b)	28 Feb 20X8	Accumulated depreciation	4,500
(c)	28 Feb 20X9	Accumulated depreciation	4,500

BALANCE SHEET (EXTRACT) AS AT 28 FEBRUARY

	20X7	20X8	20X9
	£	£	£
Computer equipment at cost	16,000	16,000	16,000
Less accumulated depreciation	4,500	9,000	13,500
Net book value	11,500	7,000	2,500

2.16 Example: provision for depreciation with assets acquired part-way through the year

Brian Box prospers in his computer software business, and before long he purchases a car for himself, and later for his chief assistant Bill Ockhead. Relevant data is as follows:

	Date of purchase	Cost	Estimated life	Estimated residual value
Brian Box car	1 June 20X6	£20,000	3 years	£2,000
Bill Ockhead car	1 June 20X7	£8,000	3 years	£2,000

The straight line method of depreciation is to be used.

Prepare the motor vehicles account and accumulated depreciation of motor vehicle account for the years to 28 February 20X7 and 20X8. (You should allow for the part-year's use of a car in computing the annual charge for depreciation.)

Calculate the net book value of the motor vehicles as at 28 February 20X8.

Solution

(a) (i) Brian Box car   Annual depreciation $\dfrac{£(20,000-2,000)}{3 \text{ years}}$ =   £6,000 pa

Monthly depreciation £500

Depreciation	1 June-20X6 - 28 February 20X7 (9 months)	£4,500
	1 March 20X7 - 28 February 20X8	£6,000

(ii) Bill Ockhead car   Annual depreciation $\dfrac{£(8,000-2,000)}{3 \text{ years}}$ =   £2,000 pa

Depreciation	1 June 20X7 - 28 February 20X8 (9 months)	£1,500

(b)

MOTOR VEHICLES

Date		£	Date		£
1 Jun 20X6	Creditors (or cash) (car purchase)	20,000	28 Feb 20X7	Balance c/f	20,000
1 Mar 20X7	Balance b/f	20,000			
1 Jun 20X7	Creditors (or cash) (car purchase)	8,000	28 Feb 20X8	Balance c/f	28,000
		28,000			28,000
1 Mar 20X8	Balance b/f	28,000			

ACCUMULATED DEPRECIATION OF MOTOR VEHICLES

Date		£	Date		£
28 Feb 20X7	Balance c/f	4,500	28 Feb 20X7	P & L account	4,500
			1 Mar 20X7	Balance b/f	4,500
28 Feb 20X8	Balance c/f	12,000	28 Feb 20X8	P & L account (6,000+1,500)	7,500
		12,000			12,000
			1 March 20X8	Balance b/f	12,000

BALANCE SHEET (WORKINGS) AS AT 28 FEBRUARY 20X8

	Brian Box car		Bill Ockhead car		Total
	£	£	£	£	£
Asset at cost		20,000		8,000	28,000
Accumulated depreciation: Year to:					
28 Feb 20X7	4,500		–		
28 Feb 20X8	6,000		1,500		
		10,500		1,500	12,000
Net book value		9,500		6,500	16,000

3 Fixed asset disposals

FAST FORWARD

When a fixed asset is **sold**, there is likely to be a **profit or loss on disposal**. This is the difference between the net sale price of the asset and its net book value at the time of disposal.

3.1 The disposal of fixed assets

A business may sell off a fixed asset long before its useful life has ended, eg to get more a more up to date model.

Whenever a business sells something, it makes a profit or a loss. So when fixed assets are disposed of, there is a profit or loss on disposal. This is a **capital gain** or a **capital loss**.

These gains or losses are reported in the profit and loss account of the business (and not as a trading profit in the trading account). They are commonly referred to as **'profit on disposal of fixed assets'** or **'loss on disposal'**.

Examination questions on the disposal of fixed assets usually ask for ledger accounts to be prepared, showing the entries in the accounts to record the disposal. But before we look at the ledger accounting for disposing of assets, we had better look at the principles behind calculating the profit (or loss) on disposing of assets.

3.2 The principles behind calculating the profit or loss on disposal

The profit or loss on the disposal of a fixed asset is the difference between:

(a)   The net book value of the asset at the time of its sale.
(b)   Its net sale price, which is the price minus any costs of making the sale.

A profit is made when the sale price exceeds the net book value, and a loss is made when the sale price is less than the net book value.

3.3 Example: Disposal of a fixed asset

A business purchased a fixed asset on 1 January 20X1 for £25,000. It had an estimated life of six years and an estimated residual value of £7,000. The asset was eventually sold after three years on 1 January 20X4 to another trader who paid £17,500 for it.

What was the profit or loss on disposal, assuming that the business uses the straight line method for depreciation?

Solution

$$\text{Annual depreciation} = \frac{£(25,000 - 7,000)}{6 \text{ years}}$$

$$= £3,000 \text{ per annum}$$

	£
Cost of asset	25,000
Less accumulated depreciation (three years)	9,000
Net book value at date of disposal	16,000
Sale price	17,500
Profit on disposal	1,500

This profit will be shown in the profit and loss account of the business, where it will be an item of other income added to the gross profit brought down from the trading account, as shown below.

	£
Gross profit	30,000
Profit on disposal of fixed assets	1,500
	31,500
Expenses	21,500
Net profit	10,000

3.4 Second example: disposal of a fixed asset

A business purchased a machine on 1 July 20X1 at a cost of £35,000. The machine had an estimated residual value of £3,000 and a life of eight years. The machine was sold for £18,600 on 31 December 20X4, the last day of the accounting year of the business. To make the sale, the business had to incur dismantling costs and costs of transporting the machine to the buyer's premises. These amounted to £1,200.

The business uses the straight line method of depreciation. What was the profit or loss on disposal of the machine?

Solution

$$\text{Annual depreciation } \frac{£(35,000 - 3,000)}{8 \text{ years}} = £4,000 \text{ per annum}$$

It is assumed that in 20X1 only one-half year's depreciation was charged, because the asset was purchased six months into the year.

	£	£
Fixed asset at cost		35,000
Depreciation in 20X1 (6 months)	2,000	
20X2, 20X3 and 20X4 (3 years)	12,000	
Accumulated depreciation		14,000
Net book value at date of disposal		21,000
Sale price	18,600	
Costs incurred in making the sale	(1,200)	
Net sale price		17,400
Loss on disposal		(3,600)

This loss will be shown as an expense in the profit and loss account of the business. It is a capital loss, not a trading loss, and it should not therefore be shown in the trading account.

Profit and loss account (extract)		£
Gross profit		30,000
Expenses	21,500	
Loss on sale of fixed assets	3,600	25,100
Net profit		4,900

3.5 The disposal of fixed assets: ledger accounting entries

A profit on disposal is an item of 'other income' in the P & L account, and a loss on disposal is an item of expense in the P & L account.

It is customary in ledger accounting to record the disposal of fixed assets in a **disposal of fixed assets** account.

(a)   The profit or loss on disposal is the difference between:

(i)   The sale price of the asset (if any).
(ii)   The net book value of the asset at the time of sale.

(b)   The relevant items which must appear in the disposal of fixed assets account are therefore:

(i)   The value of the asset (at cost, or revalued amount*).
(ii)   The accumulated depreciation up to the date of sale.
(iii)   The sale price of the asset.

*To simplify the explanation of the rules, we will assume now that the fixed assets disposed of are valued at cost.

(c) The ledger accounting entries are:

(i) DEBIT   Disposal of fixed asset account
     CREDIT Fixed asset account

With the cost of the asset disposed of.

(ii) DEBIT   Provision for depreciation account (or accumulated depreciation account)
     CREDIT Disposal of fixed asset account

With the accumulated depreciation on the asset as at the date of sale.

(iii) DEBIT   Debtor account or cash book
      CREDIT Disposal of fixed asset account

With the sale price of the asset. The sale is therefore not recorded in a sales account, but in the disposal of fixed asset account itself.

(iv) The balance on the disposal account is the profit or loss on disposal and the corresponding double entry is recorded in the P & L account itself.

Exam focus point

Calculation of profit or loss on disposal is likely to come up in an exam.

3.6 Example: Disposal of assets: ledger accounting entries

A business has £110,000 worth of machinery at cost. Its policy is to make a provision for depreciation at 20% per annum straight line. The total provision now stands at £70,000. The business now sells for £19,000 a machine which it purchased exactly two years ago for £30,000.

Show the relevant ledger entries.

Solution

PLANT AND MACHINERY ACCOUNT

	£		£
Balance b/f	110,000	Plant disposals account	30,000
		Balance c/f	80,000
	110,000		110,000
Balance b/f	80,000		

PLANT AND MACHINERY ACCUMULATED DEPRECIATION

	£		£
Plant disposals (20% of £30,000 for 2 years)	12,000	Balance b/f	70,000
Balance c/f	58,000		
	70,000		70,000
		Balance b/f	58,000

PLANT DISPOSALS

	£		£
Plant and machinery account	30,000	Accumulated depreciation	12,000
Profit and loss a/c (profit on sale)	1,000	Cash	19,000
	31,000		31,000

Check:

	£
Asset at cost	30,000
Accumulated depreciation at time of sale	12,000
Net book value at time of sale	18,000
Sale price	19,000
Profit on sale	1,000

3.7 Example continued: Part exchange

Taking the example above assume that, instead of the machine being sold for £19,000, it was exchanged for a new machine costing £60,000, a credit of £19,000 being received upon exchange. In other words £19,000 is the trade-in price of the old machine. Now what are the relevant ledger account entries?

Solution

PLANT AND MACHINERY ACCOUNT

	£		£
Balance b/f	110,000	Plant disposal	30,000
Cash (60,000 - 19,000)	41,000	Balance c/f	140,000
Plant disposals	19,000		
	170,000		170,000
Balance b/f	140,000		

The new asset is recorded in the fixed asset account at cost £(41,000 + 19,000) = £60,000.

PLANT AND MACHINERY ACCUMULATED DEPRECIATION

	£		£
Plant disposals (20% of £30,000 for 2 years)	12,000	Balance b/f	70,000
Balance c/f	58,000		
	70,000		70,000
		Balance b/f	58,000

PLANT DISPOSALS

	£		£
Plant and machinery	30,000	Accumulate depreciation	12,000
Profit transferred to P & L	1,000	Plant and machinery	19,000
	31,000		31,000

A business purchased two widget-making machines on 1 January 20X5 at a cost of £15,000 each. Each had an estimated life of five years and a nil residual value. The straight line method of depreciation is used.

Owing to an unforeseen slump in market demand for widgets, the business decided to reduce its output of widgets, and switch to making other products instead. On 31 March 20X7, one widget-making machine was sold (on credit) to a buyer for £8,000.

Later in the year, however, it was decided to abandon production of widgets altogether, and the second machine was sold on 1 December 20X7 for £2,500 cash.

Prepare the machinery account, provision for depreciation of machinery account and disposal of machinery account for the accounting year to 31 December 20X7.

Answer

MACHINERY ACCOUNT

20X7		£	20X7		£
1 Jan	Balance b/f	30,000	31 Mar	Disposal of machinery account	15,000
			1 Dec	Disposal of machinery account	15,000
		30,000			30,000

PROVISION FOR DEPRECIATION OF MACHINERY

		£			£
20X7			*20X7*		
31 Mar	Disposal of machinery account*	6,750	1 Jan	Balance b/f	12,000
1 Dec	Disposal of machinery account**	8,750	31 Dec	P & L account***	3,500
		15,500			15,500

*   Depreciation at date of disposal £6,000 + £750
**   Depreciation at date of disposal £6,000 + £2,750
***   Depreciation charge for the year = £750 + £2,750

DISPOSAL OF MACHINERY

		£			£
20X7			*20X7*		
31 Mar	Machinery account	15,000	31 Mar	Debtor account (sale price)	8,000
			31 Mar	Provision for depreciation	6,750
1 Dec	Machinery	15,000	1 Dec	Cash (sale price)	2,500
			1 Dec	Provision for depreciation	8,750
			31 Dec	P & L account (loss on disposal)	4,000
		30,000			30,000

You should be able to calculate that there was a loss on the first disposal of £250, and on the second disposal of £3,750, giving a total loss of £4,000.

Workings

1   At 1 January 20X7, accumulated depreciation on the machines will be 2 machines × 2 years × $\frac{£15,000}{5}$ per machine pa = £12,000, or £6,000 per machine

2   Monthly depreciation is $\frac{£3,000}{12}$ = £250 per machine per month

3   The machines are disposed of in 20X7.

   (a)   On 31 March - after 3 months of the year.
          Depreciation for the year on the machine = 3 months × £250 = £750.

   (b)   On 1 December - after 11 months of the year.
          Depreciation for the year on the machine = 11 months × £250 = £2,750

4 Fixed assets: Statutory requirements

This section acts as an introduction to the Companies Act requirements for all fixed assets.

4.1 Statutory provisions relating to all fixed assets

The standard balance sheet format of CA 2006 divides fixed assets into three categories:

(a)   **Intangible assets**
(b)   **Tangible assets**
(c)   **Investments**

Companies Act requirements in regard to fixed assets may be considered under two headings.

(a)   **Valuation:** the amounts at which fixed assets should be stated in the balance sheet.

(b)   **Disclosure:** the information which should be disclosed in the accounts as to valuation of fixed assets and as to movements on fixed asset accounts during the year.

4.2 Valuation of fixed assets

Where an asset is **purchased**, its cost is simply the **purchase price plus any expenses incidental to its acquisition.**

From your studies of double entry in Chapter 5 you should remember that the entries to record an acquisition are:

DEBIT   Fixed asset – cost   £X
CREDIT   Cash (or creditor)   £X

Where an asset is **produced by a company for its own use**, its 'production cost' **must** include the cost of **raw materials, consumables** and **other attributable direct costs** (such as labour). Production cost may additionally include a reasonable proportion of indirect costs, together with the interest on any capital borrowed to finance production of the asset.

The 'cost' of any fixed asset having a limited economic life, whether purchase price or production cost, must be reduced by provisions for depreciation calculated to write off the cost, less any residual value, systematically over the period of the asset's useful life. This very general requirement is supplemented by the more detailed provisions of FRS 15 *Tangible fixed assets*.

Provision for a permanent reduction in value (now called impairment) of a fixed asset must be made in the profit and loss account and the asset should be disclosed at the reduced amount in the balance sheet. Any such provision should be disclosed on the face of the profit and loss account or by way of note. Where a provision becomes no longer necessary, because the conditions giving rise to it have altered, it should be written back, and again disclosure should be made.

4.3 Fixed assets valuation: alternative accounting rules

Although the Companies Act 2006 maintains historical cost principles as the normal basis for the preparation of accounts, **alternative bases** allowing for revaluations and current cost accounting are permitted provided that:

(a)   The items affected and the basis of valuation are disclosed in a note to the accounts.

(b)   The historical cost in the current and previous years is separately disclosed in the balance sheet or in a note to the accounts. Alternatively, the difference between the revalued amount and historical cost may be disclosed.

Using the **alternative accounting rules** the appropriate value of any fixed asset (its current cost or market value), rather than its purchase price or production cost, may be included in the balance sheet.

Where appropriate, depreciation may be provided on the basis of the new valuation(s), such depreciation being referred to in the Companies Act 2006 as the 'adjusted amount' of depreciation. For profit and loss account purposes it is acceptable under the Companies Act to calculate (and disclose) depreciation in respect of any such fixed asset on the basis of historical cost. If the 'historical cost amount' rather than the 'adjusted amount' of depreciation were to be used in the profit and loss account, the difference between the two would be shown separately in the profit and loss account or in a note to the accounts.

(However, FRS 15 (see below) specifically states that depreciation must be charged on the revalued amount and that the *whole* charge must be taken to the profit and loss account.)

4.4 Revaluation reserve

Where the value of any fixed asset is determined by using the alternative accounting rules the amount of profit or loss arising must be credited or (as the case may be) debited to a separate reserve, the revaluation reserve. The calculation of the relevant amounts should be based on the written down values of the assets prior to revaluation.

The revaluation reserve must be reduced to the extent that the amounts standing to the credit of the reserves are, in the opinion of the directors of the company, no longer necessary for the purposes of the accounting policies adopted by the company. However, an amount may only be transferred from the reserve to the profit and loss account if either:

(a)   The amount in question was previously charged to that account

(b)   It represents realised profit (for example on disposal of a fixed asset).

The **only other** transfer possible from the revaluation reserve is on capitalisation, that is, when a bonus issue is made.

The amount of a revaluation reserve must be shown under a separate sub-heading on the balance sheet. However, the reserve need not necessarily be called a 'revaluation reserve'.

4.5 Fixed assets: disclosure

Notes to the accounts must show, for each class of fixed assets, an analysis of the movements on both costs and depreciation provisions.

The following format (with notional figures) is commonly used to disclose fixed assets movements.

	Total £	Land and buildings £	Plant and machinery £
Cost or valuation			
At 1 January 20X4	50,000	40,000	10,000
Revaluation surplus	12,000	12,000	–
Additions in year	4,000	–	4,000
Disposals in year	(1,000)	–	(1,000)
At 31 December 20X4	65,000	52,000	13,000
Depreciation			
At 1 January 20X4	16,000	10,000	6,000
Charge for year	4,000	1,000	3,000
Elimination on revaluation	–	(10,000)	–
Eliminated on disposals	(500)	–	(500)
At 31 December 20X4	9,500	1,000	8,500
Net book value			
At 31 December 20X4	55,500	51,000	4,500
At 1 January 20X4	34,000	30,000	4,000

Where any fixed assets of a company (other than listed investments) are included in the accounts at an alternative accounting valuation, the following information must also be given.

(a)   The years (so far as they are known to the directors) in which the assets were severally valued and the several values

(b)   In the case of assets that have been valued during the financial period, the names of the persons who valued them or particulars of their qualifications for doing so and (whichever is stated) the bases of valuation used by them.

A note to the accounts must classify land and buildings under the headings of:

(a)   Freehold property

(b)   Leasehold property, distinguishing between:

(i) Long leaseholds, in which the unexpired term of the lease at the balance sheet date is not less than 50 years.

(ii) Short leaseholds which are all leaseholds other than long leaseholds.

5 FRS 15 Tangible fixed assets

FAST FORWARD ▶▶

FRS 15 *Tangible fixed assets* was published in February 1999. It goes into a lot more detail than the Companies Act.

5.1 Objective

FRS 15 deals with accounting for the initial measurement, valuation and depreciation of tangible fixed assets. It also sets out the information that should be disclosed to enable readers to understand the impact of the accounting policies adopted in relation to these issues.

5.2 Initial measurement

A tangible fixed asset should **initially be measured at cost**.

Key term

> **Cost** is purchase price and any costs directly attributable to bringing the asset into working condition for its intended use.

Examples of directly attributable costs are:

- **Acquisition costs**, eg stamp duty, import duties
- Cost of **site preparation** and clearance
- Initial **delivery and handling** costs
- **Installation** costs
- **Professional fees** eg legal fees
- The estimated cost of **dismantling and removing** the asset and restoring the site, to the extent that it is recognised as a provision under FRS 12 *Provisions, contingent liabilities and contingent assets* (discussed in Chapter 13).

Any abnormal costs, such as those arising from design error, industrial disputes or idle capacity are not directly attributable costs and therefore should not be capitalised as part of the cost of the asset.

5.2.1 Finance costs

The **capitalisation of finance costs**, including interest, is **optional**. However, if an entity does capitalise finance costs they must do so **consistently**.

All finance costs that are **directly attributable** to the construction of a tangible fixed asset should be capitalised as part of the cost of the asset.

Key term

> **Directly attributable finance costs** are those that would have been avoided if there had been no expenditure on the asset.

If finance costs are capitalised, capitalisation should start when:

- Finance costs are being incurred
- Expenditure on the asset is being incurred
- Activities necessary to get the asset ready for use are in progress

Capitalisation of finance costs should cease when the asset is ready for use.

5.3 Subsequent expenditure

Subsequent expenditure on a tangible fixed asset should only be capitalised in the following three circumstances.

(a) It enhances the economic benefits over and above those previously estimated. An example might be modifications made to a piece of machinery that increases its capacity or useful life.

(b) A component of an asset that has been treated separately for depreciation purposes (because it has a substantially different useful economic life from the rest of the asset) has been restored or replaced.

(c) It relates to a major inspection or overhaul that restores economic benefits that have been consumed and reflected in the depreciation charge.

Question | Examples

Can you think of examples for (b) and (c) above?

Answer

(b) A factory building may require a new roof every 10 years, whereas the factory itself may have a useful economic life of 50 years. In this case the roof will be treated as a separate asset and depreciated over 10 years and the expenditure incurred in replacing the roof will be accounted for as an addition and the carrying amount of the replaced asset removed from the balance sheet.

(c) An aircraft may be required by law to be overhauled every three years. Unless the overhaul is carried out the aircraft will not be licensed to fly. The entity will reflect the need to overhaul the aircraft by depreciating an amount equivalent to the estimated cost of the overhaul over the three year period. The cost of the overhaul will then be capitalised because it restores the economic value of the aircraft.

5.4 Valuation

FRS 15 supplements and clarifies the rules on revaluation of fixed assets which the Companies Act allows. Revaluation is discussed in the next section.

5.5 Depreciation

As noted earlier, the Companies Act 2006 requires that all fixed assets having a limited economic life should be depreciated. FRS 15 gives a useful discussion of the purpose of depreciation and supplements the statutory requirements in important ways.

Key term

> **Depreciation** is defined in FRS 15 as the measure of the cost or revalued amount of the economic benefits of the tangible fixed asset that have been consumed during the period. Consumption includes the wearing out, using up or other reduction in the useful economic life of a tangible fixed asset, whether arising from use, effluxion of time or obsolescence through either changes in technology or demand for the goods and services produced by the asset.

This definition covers the amortisation of assets with a pre-determined life, such as a leasehold, and the depletion of wasting assets such as mines.

The need to depreciate fixed assets arises from the accruals concept. If money is expended in purchasing an asset then the amount expended must at some time be charged against profits. If the asset is one which contributes to an enterprise's revenue over a number of accounting periods it would be inappropriate to charge any single period (for example the period in which the asset was acquired) with the whole of the expenditure. Instead, some method must be found of spreading the cost of the asset over its useful economic life.

This view of depreciation as a process of **allocation** of the cost of an asset over several accounting periods is the view adopted by FRS 15. It is worth mentioning here two common **misconceptions** about the purpose and effects of depreciation.

(a)   It is sometimes thought that the net book value (NBV) of an asset is equal to its net realisable value and that the object of charging depreciation is to reflect the fall in value of an asset over its life. This misconception is the basis of a common, but incorrect, argument which says that freehold properties (say) need not be depreciated in times when property values are rising. It is true that historical cost balance sheets often give a misleading impression when a property's NBV is much below its market value, but in such a case it is open to a business to incorporate a revaluation into its books, or even to prepare its accounts on the current cost convention. This is a separate problem from that of allocating the property's cost over successive accounting periods.

(b)   Another misconception is that depreciation is provided so that an asset can be replaced at the end of its useful life. This is not the case.

(i)   If there is no intention of replacing the asset, it could then be argued that there is no need to provide for any depreciation at all.

(ii)   If prices are rising, the replacement cost of the asset will exceed the amount of depreciation provided.

FRS 15 contains **no detailed guidance** on the calculation of depreciation or the suitability of the various depreciation methods, merely stating the following two **general principles**.

'The depreciable amount of a tangible fixed asset should be allocated on a **systematic** basis over its useful economic life. The depreciation method used should reflect as fairly as possible the pattern in which the asset's economic benefits are consumed by the entity. The depreciation charge for each period should be recognised as an expense in the profit and loss account unless it is permitted to be included in the carrying amount of another asset.'

'A variety of methods can be used to allocate the depreciable amount of a tangible fixed asset on a systematic basis over its useful economic life. The method chosen should result in a **depreciation charge throughout the asset's useful** economic life and not just towards the end of its useful economic life or when the asset is falling in value.'

We will therefore consider first the factors affecting depreciation and then proceed to an analysis of the main depreciation methods available.

5.6 Factors affecting depreciation

FRS 15 states that the following factors need to be considered in determining the useful economic life, residual value and depreciation method of an asset.

(a)   The **expected usage** of the asset by the entity, assessed by reference to the asset's expected capacity or physical output

(b)   The **expected physical deterioration** of the asset through use or effluxion of time; this will depend upon the repair and maintenance programme of the entity both when the asset is in use and when it is idle

(c)   **Economic or technological obsolescence**, for example arising from changes or improvements in production, or a change in the market demand for the product or service output of that asset

(d)   **Legal or similar limits** on the use of the asset, such as the expiry dates of related leases

If it becomes clear that the **original estimate** of an asset's useful life was **incorrect**, it should be **revised**. Normally, no adjustment should be made in respect of the depreciation charged in previous years; instead the remaining net book value of the asset should be depreciated over the new estimate of its remaining useful life. If future results could be materially distorted, the adjustment to accumulated depreciation should be recognised in the accounts in accordance with FRS 3 (usually as an exceptional item). FRS 3 is discussed in a later chapter of this Study Text.

5.7 Methods of depreciation

The **cost of an asset less its residual value is known as the depreciable amount** of the asset. For example, if plant has a five year expected life and the anticipated capital costs are:

	£
Purchase cost	19,000
Delivery	1,500
Installation by own employees	2,700
	23,200

While the residual value at the end of the fifth year is expected to be £3,200, the depreciable amount would be £20,000. Any repair and maintenance costs incurred during the period are written off as running costs in the year in which they are incurred.

However, if major improvements are made to an asset, thereby increasing its expected life, the depreciable amount should be adjusted. For example, if at the beginning of year 3, £11,000 was spent on technological improvements to the plant so prolonging its expected life by three years (with a residual value of £1,200 at the end of the eighth year), the depreciable amount would be adjusted.

	£
Original depreciable amount	20,000
Less amount already depreciated (say 2 × £4,000)	8,000
	12,000
Add fall in residual value £(3,200 – 1,200)	2,000
	14,000
Add further capital expenditure	11,000
New depreciable amount	25,000

The new depreciable amount would be written off over the remaining useful life of the asset, 6 years.

There are a number of different methods of calculating the depreciation charge for an accounting period, each giving a different result. The most common are:

- Straight line method
- Reducing balance method
- Sum of digits method
- Machine hour method
- Revaluation

The **straight line method** is the simplest and the most commonly used in practice. The **reducing balance** and **sum of digits** methods are accelerated methods which lead to a higher charge in earlier years. Since repair and maintenance costs tend to increase as assets grow older these methods lead to a more even allocation of total fixed asset costs (depreciation plus maintenance).

The **machine hour method** is suited to assets which depreciate primarily through use rather than through passing of time. Such assets might include mines and quarries, which are subject to gradual exhaustion of the minerals that they contain, and also delivery lorries, which may be argued to depreciate in accordance with the number of miles travelled.

Neither the CA nor FRS 15 prescribes which method should be used. **Management** must **exercise its judgement**. Furthermore, FRS 15 states:

> 'The useful economic life of a tangible fixed asset should be **reviewed at the end of each reporting period** and revised if expectations are significantly different from previous estimates. If a useful economic life is revised, the carrying amount of the tangible fixed asset at the date of revision should be **depreciated over the revised remaining useful economic life**.'

FRS 15 also states that a **change from one method** of providing depreciation **to another** is permissible only on the grounds that the new method will give a **fairer presentation** of the results and of the financial position. Such a change does **not**, however, constitute a **change of accounting policy**; the carrying amount of the tangible fixed asset is depreciated using the revised method over the remaining useful economic life, beginning in the period in which the change is made.

Tangible fixed assets other than non depreciable land, should be **reviewed for impairment** at the end of the reporting period where:

- No depreciation is charged on the grounds that it would immaterial
- The estimated remaining useful economic life exceeds 50 years.

The review should be in accordance with FRS 11 *Impairment of fixed assets and goodwill* (this is not within the scope of Paper F3).

Many companies carry fixed assets in their balance sheets at revalued amounts, particularly in the case of freehold buildings. When this is done, the **depreciation charge** should be calculated **on the basis of the revalued amount** (not the original cost), in spite of the alternative accounting rules in CA 2006.

Where the tangible fixed asset comprises two or more major components with substantially different useful economic lives, each component should be accounted for separately for depreciation purposes and depreciated over its individual useful economic life.

You still need to charge depreciation if there is subsequent expenditure on a tangible fixed asset that maintains or enhances the previously assessed standard of performance of the asset.

5.8 Disclosure requirements of FRS 15

The following information should be disclosed separately in the financial statements for each class of tangible fixed assets.

(a) The depreciation methods used
(b) The useful economic lives or the depreciation rates used
(c) Total depreciation charged for the period
(d) Where material, the financial effect of a change during the period in either the estimate of useful economic lives or the estimate of residual values
(e) The cost or revalued amount at the beginning of the financial period and at the balance sheet date
(f) The cumulative amount of provisions for depreciation or impairment at the beginning of the financial period and at the balance sheet date
(g) A reconciliation of the movements, separately disclosing additions, disposals, revaluations, transfers, depreciation, impairment losses, and reversals of past impairment losses written back in the financial period
(h) The net carrying amount at the beginning of the financial period and at the balance sheet date

Where there has been a change in the depreciation method used, the effect, if material, should be disclosed in the period of change. The reason for the change should also be disclosed.

Question

FRS 15

The Furrow Manufacturing Company has recently purchased a machine for £256,000 and expects to use it for three years at the end of which period it will be sold as scrap for £4,000.

REQUIREMENTS:
(a) Calculate in respect of each of the three years the annual depreciation charge using each of the following methods:

   (i) Straight line
   (ii) Reducing balance (at 75% per annum).

(b) Suppose that the Furrow Manufacturing Company adopted the reducing balance method and depreciated the machine for one year; then at the end of the following year the company decided to change from the reducing balance method to the straight line method. Indicate how the machine should appear in the balance sheet at the end of its second year (including any notes relating thereto) assuming that all the original estimates had proved accurate, and bearing in mind the requirements of FRS 15.

Answer

(a)   The depreciable amount of the machine is £(256,000 – 4,000) = £252,000

  (i)   The annual depreciation charge $\dfrac{£252,000}{3} = £84,000$

  (ii)   The annual depreciation charge is as follows.

		NBV £'000	Charge for year £'000
Year 1:	cost	256	
	depreciation (75%)	(192)	192
	net book value	64	
Year 2:	depreciation (75%)	(48)	48
	net book value	16	
Year 3:	depreciation (75%)	(12)	12
	net book value	4	
			252

(b)   FRS 15 states that if the depreciation method is changed it is unnecessary to adjust amounts charged in previous years. Instead, the new method is simply applied to the unamortised cost of the asset over its remaining useful life.

At the end of year 1, the machine's net book value (after one year's depreciation on the reducing balance method) is £64,000 (see part (a)). For year 2, it is decided to use the straight line method over the remaining two years of useful life. The charge for depreciation in year 2 will therefore be £30,000 ((£64,000 – £4,000) ÷ 2) and the asset's net book value at the end of year 2 will be £34,000.

FURROW MANUFACTURING COMPANY
BALANCE SHEET AT END OF YEAR 2 (EXTRACT)

		£
Fixed assets		
Tangible assets		
Plant and machinery:	cost	256,000
	depreciation	(222,000)
		34,000

Question

Annette Book is the financial controller of a medium-sized publishing company. The managing director, Eddie Torial, is a man of sound literary judgement and marketing instinct, but has no accountancy training. Annette has received from him the following note.

'I understand that we have to provide "depreciation" on all our fixed assets except land. This is going to come out of our profit, so there has to be a reason for it. Could you answer the following questions?'

(a)   Why do we provide depreciation?
(b)   What exactly is net book value? (I think I know roughly what it is.)
(c)   Why do we sometimes use the reducing balance method and not the straight line method?

Required

Write Annette's reply to Eddie, addressing each of the above queries.

Answer

To:	Eddie Torial
	Managing Director
From:	Annette Book
Date:	5 March 1997
Subject:	Depreciation

(a)   The accounts of a business try to recognise that the cost of a fixed asset is gradually consumed as the asset wears out. This is done by gradually writing off the asset's cost in the profit and loss account over several accounting periods. This process is known as depreciation, and is an example of the matching concept. FRS 15 *Tangible fixed assets* requires that depreciation should be allocated to charge against income a fair proportion of cost or valuation of the asset to each accounting period expected to benefit from its use.

With regard to the matching principle, it is fair that the profits should be reduced by the depreciation charge; this is not an arbitrary exercise. Depreciation is not, as is sometime supposed, an attempt to set aside funds to purchase new fixed assets when required. Depreciation is not generally provided on freehold land because it does not 'wear out' (unless it is held for mining etc).

(b)   In simple terms the net book value of an asset is the cost of an asset less the 'accumulated depreciation', that is all depreciation charged so far. It should be emphasised that the main purpose of charging depreciation is to ensure that profits are fairly reported. Thus depreciation is concerned with the profit and loss account rather than the balance sheet. In consequence the net book value figure in the balance sheet can be quite arbitrary. In particular, it does not necessarily bear any relation to the market value of an asset and is of little use for planning and decision making.

An obvious example of the disparity between net book value and market value is found in the case of buildings, which may be worth more than ten times as much as their net book value.

(c)   The reducing balance method of depreciation is used instead of the straight line method when it is considered fair to allocate a greater proportion of the total depreciable amount to the earlier years and a lower proportion to the later years on the assumption that the benefits obtained by the business from using the asset decline over time.

In favour of this method it may be argued that it links the depreciation charge to the costs of maintaining and running the asset. In the early years these costs are low and the depreciation charge is high, while in later years this is reversed.

---

xam focus
int

Student Accountant contains a two part article on *Property, plant and equipment and tangible fixed assets* in its 30 May 2007 and 1 August 2007 editions. These are worth reading.

6 Revaluations

AST FORWARD

When a fixed asset is **revalued**, depreciation is charged on the **revalued amount**.

For freehold property which is in operational use, the principle laid down in FRS 15 is that since **buildings have a finite useful life**, a part of their **cost must be charged against profit each year,** in order to be consistent with the accruals concept.

Although **freehold land does not normally require a provision for depreciation** (unless it is subject to depletion, for example where mineral resources are extracted) **buildings on that land have a limited life** which may be affected by technological and environmental changes. **Buildings should therefore be depreciated.**

Where there is a freehold property this means that the land element in its cost will not be depreciated, but the building element of cost must be depreciated.

As previously discussed, a property's NBV may be well below its market value. A business may, therefore, decide to revalue the property to its market value. When a property is revalued, depreciation should be charged to write off the new valuation over the estimated remaining useful life of the building (see paragraph 4.3).

The gain on revaluation can not go to the profit and loss account, as it has not been realised. Instead, it is recognised in the statement of total recognised gains and losses (see Chapter 21). From here, the 'gain' is transferred to a revaluation reserve.

6.1 Example: Revaluation of a freehold building

A freehold building is purchased on 1 January 20X4 for £20,000. Its estimated useful life is 20 years and it is depreciated at the rate of £1,000 per annum in each of the years ending 31 December 20X4 and 20X5. On 1 January 20X6 a professional valuer estimates the value of the building at £54,000.

On the assumption that the revaluation is to be incorporated into the books of account, and that the original estimate of useful life was correct, show the relevant ledger accounts for the period 1 January 20X4 to 31 December 20X6.

Solution

FREEHOLD BUILDING AT COST

		£			£
1.1.X4	Purchase	20,000	31.12.X4	Balance c/d	20,000
1.1.X5	Balance b/d	20,000	31.12.X5	Balance c/d	20,000
1.1.X6	Balance b/d	20,000			
	Revaluation	34,000	31.12.X6	Balance c/d	54,000
		54,000			54,000

DEPRECIATION ON FREEHOLD BUILDINGS

		£			£
31.12.X4	Balance c/d	1,000	31.12.X4	P & L account	1,000
			1.1.X5	Balance b/d	1,000
31.12.X5	Balance c/d	2,000	31.12.X5	P & L account	1,000
		2,000			2,000
1.1.X6	Revaluation	2,000	1.1.X6	Balance b/d	2,000
			31.12.X6	P & L account	
31.12.X6	Balance c/d	3,000		(£54,000/18 years)	3,000
		5,000			5,000

REVALUATION RESERVE

		£			£
			1.1.X6	Freehold building	34,000
31.12.X6	Balance c/d	36,000		Dep'n on freehold	2,000
		36,000			36,000

Note that the revaluation surplus is the difference between valuation (£54,000) and net book value at the time of revaluation (£20,000 – £2,000 = £18,000). The revalued amount, £54,000, must then be depreciated over the asset's remaining estimated useful life of 18 years, ie £3,000 per annum.

Balance sheet as at 31.12.X6 (extracts)

(a) **Revaluation**

		£
Fixed assets		
Freehold buildings	– valuation	54,000
	– accumulated depreciation	(3,000)
	– NBV	51,000
Capital and reserves		
Revaluation reserves		36,000

(b) **If revaluation had not taken place**

		£
Fixed assets		
Freehold buildings	– cost	20,000
	– accumulated depreciation (3 years)	(3,000)
	– NBV	17,000

Note that the balance sheet under (a) is effectively £15,000 (£51,000 – £36,000), compared to £17,000 under (b). This difference of £2,000 is due to the increased depreciation after the revaluation (old rate of depreciation £1,000 pa, new rate £3,000 pa).

6.2 FRS 15 rules

An entity may adopt a policy of **revaluing tangible fixed assets**. Where this policy is adopted **it must be applied consistently** to all assets of the same class.

> A **class of fixed assets** is 'a category of tangible fixed assets having a similar nature, function or use in the business of an entity'. (FRS 15)

Where an asset is revalued its carrying amount should be its **current value** as at the balance sheet date, current value being the **lower of replacement cost and recoverable amount**.

To achieve the above, the standard states that a **full valuation** should be carried out **at least every five years** with an **interim valuation in year 3**. If it is likely that there has been a material change in value, interim valuations in years 1, 2 and 4 should also be carried out.

A full valuation should be conducted by either a **qualified external valuer** or a **qualified internal valuer**, provided that the valuation has been subject to review by a qualified external valuer. An interim valuation may be carried out by either an external or internal valuer.

For certain types of assets (other than properties) eg company cars, there may be an active second hand market for the asset or appropriate indices may exist, so that the directors can establish the asset's value with reasonable reliability and therefore avoid the need to use the services of a qualified valuer.

> For your exam, you should be able to apply the FRS 15 rules. Practically, you only need to know how to treat revaluations in the ledger accounts, how to set up a revaluation reserve and how to calculate revised depreciation.

6.3 Example: disposal of a revalued asset

Returning to the case of the revalued asset in 6.1 above, suppose that the property is sold for £75,000 on 1 January 20X7. What is the profit on disposal?

Solution

FREEHOLD BUILDING AT COST

	£		£
Balance b/d	54,000	Disposal account	54,000

DEPRECIATION ON FREEHOLD BUILDINGS

	£		£
Disposal account	3,000	Balance b/d	3,000

REVALUATION RESERVE

	£		£
Disposal account	36,000	Balance b/d	36,000

DISPOSAL ACCOUNT

	£		£
Building – cost	54,000	Cash	75,000
Profit on disposal	60,000	Depreciation	3,000
		Revaluation reserve	36,000
	114,000		114,000

Ignoring the revaluation:

	£
Original cost of building	20,000
Depreciation (£2,000 + £3,000)	(5,000)
Net book value	15,000
Sale proceeds	75,000
Profit on disposal	60,000

6.4 Revaluation downwards

After some years, it may become apparent that the building is overvalued and needs to be revalued downwards

Using the example above five years later, the land is still valued at £75,000 but the building is now valued at £25,000.

BUILDING COST

	£		£
Balance b/f	75,000	Revaluation reserve	50,000
		Bal c/f	25,000

BUILDING-ACCUMULATED DEPRECIATION

	£		£
Revaluation reserve	15,000	Balance b/f (5 × £3,000)	15,000

LAND COST

	£		£
Balance b/f	75,000	Balance c/f	75,000

REVALUATION RESERVE

	£		£
Cost	50,000	Balance b/f	105,000
Bal c/f	70,000	Excess depreciation	15,000
	120,000	(accumulated depreciation)	120,000

7 The fixed assets register

An **asset register** is used to record all fixed assets and is an **internal check** on the accuracy of the nominal ledger.

Nearly all organisations keep a fixed assets register. This is a listing of all fixed assets owned by the organisation, broken down perhaps by department, location or asset type.

A fixed assets register is maintained primarily for internal purposes. It shows an organisation's investment in capital equipment. A fixed asset register is also part of the **internal control system**. Fixed assets registers are sometimes called **real accounts.**

7.1 Data kept in a fixed assets register

Details about each fixed asset include the following.

- The internal reference number (for physical identification purposes)
- Manufacturer's serial number (for maintenance purposes)
- Description of asset
- Location of asset
- Department which 'owns' asset
- Purchase date (for calculation of depreciation)
- Cost
- Depreciation method and estimated useful life (for calculation of depreciation)
- Net book value (or written down value)

The following events give rise to entries in a fixed asset register.

- Purchase of an asset
- Sale of an asset
- Loss or destruction of an asset
- Transfer of assets between departments
- Revision of estimated useful life of an asset
- Scrapping of an asset
- Revaluation of an asset

'Outputs' from a fixed assets register include the following.

- Reconciliations of NBV to the nominal ledger
- Depreciation charges posted to the nominal ledger
- Physical verification/audit purposes

7.2 Layout of fixed assets register

The layout of a fixed assets register (and the degree of detail included) depends on the organisation in question. With a hand written fixed asset register, the details are usually recorded in columns spread across two facing pages. The column headings reflect the details outlined in Section 7.1 above. For the layout of a computerised fixed asset register, see Section 7.4.

7.3 Control

It is important, for external reporting (ie the audit) and for internal purposes, that there are controls over fixed assets. The fixed assets register has already been mentioned. Four further points should be made in this context.

(a)   **Purchase** of fixed assets must be authorised and must only be made by a responsible official. The purchaser should obtain several quotations. The person authorising the expenditure should not be the person using the asset.

(b)   Procedures should exist and be enforced for **disposal** of fixed assets to ensure that the sales proceeds are not misappropriated.

(c)   The fixed assets register must reconcile with the nominal ledger.

(d)   The fixed assets register must reconcile with the physical presence of capital items.

7.3.1 The fixed assets register and the nominal ledger

The fixed assets register is not part of the double entry and is there for **memorandum** and **control** purposes.

The fixed assets register must be reconciled to the nominal ledger to make sure that all additions, disposals and depreciation charges have been posted. For example, the total of all the 'cost' figures in the register for motor vehicles should equal the balance on the 'motor vehicles cost' account in the nominal ledger. The same goes for accumulated depreciation.

7.3.2 The fixed assets register and the physical assets

It is possible that the fixed assets register may not reconcile with the fixed assets actually present. This may be for the following reasons.

- Asset has been stolen or damaged, which has not been noticed or recorded
- Excessive wear and tear or obsolescence has not been recorded
- New assets not yet recorded in the register because it has not been kept up to date
- Errors made in entering details in the register
- Improvement and modifications have not been recorded in the register

Therefore it is important that the company physically inspects all the items in the fixed assets register and keeps the fixed assets register up to date.

The nature of the inspection will vary between organisations. A large company could inspect 25% of assets by value each year, aiming to cover all categories every five years. A small company may inspect all its fixed assets very quickly, although this 'inspection' may not be formally recorded.

7.3.3 Dealing with discrepancies

As mentioned above, some assets may require an adjustment in their expected life due to excessive wear and tear or damage. The proper person must authorise any change to estimates of the life of an asset. The accounts department will need a copy of the authorised changes to make the right adjustments in the journal, the register and the ledger.

When discrepancies are discovered, it may be possible to resolve them by updating the fixed assets register and/or nominal ledger. It may not be possible for the person who discovers the discrepancy to resolve it himself. For example, if a fixed asset has to be revalued downwards due to wear and tear or obsolescence, it should be authorised by his superior.

7.4 Example: Extract from a computerised fixed assets register

Most fixed assets registers will be computerised. Below is an extract from a fixed asset register showing one item as it might appear when the details are printed out.

FASSET HOLDINGS PLC

	Asset Code: 938	Next depreciation: 539.36
A	Description:	1 × Seisha Laser printer YCA40809
B	Date of purchase:	25/05/X6
C	Cost:	1618.25
D	Accumulated depreciation:	584.35
E	Depreciation %:	33.33%
F	Depreciation type:	straight line
G	Date of disposal:	NOT SET
H	Sale proceeds:	0.00
I	Accumulated depreciation amount:	55Q O/EQPT DEP CHARGE
J	Depreciation expense account:	34F DEPN O/EQPT
K	Depreciation period:	standard
L	Comments:	electronic office
M	Residual value:	0.00
N	Cost account:	65C O/E ADDITIONS

8 Worked example

You have already had practice at preparing a profit and loss account and balance sheet from a simple trial balance. Now see if you can do the same thing but at a more advanced level, taking account of adjustments for depreciation and stock . Have a go at the following question.

Exam focus point

At the 2009 ACCA Teachers' Conference, the examiner recommended working full length questions not only to become familiar with the techniques involved, but also as a good grounding for future studies at F7.

Question

Kevin Webster

The following trial balance was extracted from the ledger of Kevin Webster, a sole trader, as at 31 May 20X1, the end of his financial year.

KEVIN WEBSTER
TRIAL BALANCE AS AT 31 MAY 20X1

	Dr £	Cr £
Property, at cost	120,000	
Equipment, at cost	80,000	
Provisions for depreciation (as at 1 June 20X0)		
– on property		20,000
– on equipment		38,000
Purchases	250,000	
Sales		402,200
Stock, as at 1 June 20X0	50,000	
Returns out (purchase returns)		15,000
Wages and salaries	58,800	
Selling expenses	22,600	
Loan interest	5,100	
Other operating expenses	17,700	
Trade creditors		36,000
Trade debtors	38,000	
Cash on hand	300	
Bank	1,300	
Drawings	24,000	
17% long-term loan		30,000
Capital, as at 1 June 20X0		126,600
	667,800	667,800

The following additional information as at 31 May 20X1 is available.

(a)   Stock as at the close of business has been valued at cost at £42,000.

(b)   Depreciation for the year ended 31 May 20X1 has still to be provided for as follows:
Property: 1.5% per annum using the straight line method
Equipment: 25% per annum using the reducing balance method

Required

Prepare Kevin Webster's profit & loss account for the year ended 31 May 20X1 and his balance sheet as at that date.

Answer

KEVIN WEBSTER
TRADING AND PROFIT AND LOSS ACCOUNT FOR THE YEAR ENDED 31 MAY 20X1

	£	£
Sales		402,200
Cost of sales		
Opening stock	50,000	
Purchases	250,000	
Purchases returns	(15,000)	
	285,000	
Closing stock	42,000	
		243,000
Gross profit		159,200
Expenses		
Wages and salaries	58,800	
Selling expenses	22,600	
Loan interest	5,100	
Depreciation (W1)	12,300	
Other operating expenses	17,700	
		116,500
Net profit for the year		42,700

KEVIN WEBSTER
BALANCE SHEET AS AT 31 MAY 20X1

	£	£
Fixed assets		
Property: cost	120,000	
accumulated depreciation (W1)	21,800	
		98,200
Equipment: cost	80,000	
accumulated depreciation (W1)	48,500	
		31,500
		129,700
Current assets		
Stock	42,000	
Trade debtors	38,000	
Bank	1,300	
Cash in hand	300	
	81,600	
Current liabilities		
Trade creditors	36,000	
Net current assets		45,600
		175,300
Long-term liabilities		
17% loan		30,000
		145,300
Capital		
Capital		
Balance at 1 June 20X0		126,600
Net profit for the year		42,700
Drawings		(24,000)
Balance at 31 May 20X1		145,300

Working

1	*Depreciation*	
	Property	£
	Opening provision	20,000
	Provision for the year (1.5% × 120,000)	1,800
	Closing provision	21,800
	Equipment	
	Opening provision	38,000
	Provision for the year (25% × 42,000)	10,500
	Closing provision	48,500
	Change to P+L (1,800 + 10,500)	12,300

Chapter Roundup

- **Capital expenditure** is expenditure which results in the acquisition of fixed assets.

  Revenue expenditure is expenditure incurred for the purpose of the trade or to maintain fixed assets.

- This section is a detailed look at depreciation and how it is calculated. Depreciation is also discussed in Section 5 when we will see how FRS 15 affects the use of depreciation.

- When a fixed asset is **sold**, there is likely to be a **profit or loss on disposal**. This is the difference between the net sale price of the asset and its net book value at the time of disposal.

- This section acts as an introduction to the Companies Act requirements for all fixed assets.

- FRS 15 *Tangible fixed assets* was published in February 1999. It goes into a lot more detail than the Companies Act.

- When a fixed asset is **revalued**, depreciation is charged on the **revalued amount**.

- An **asset register** is used to record all fixed assets and is an **internal check** on the accuracy of the nominal ledger.

1   Which of the following statements regarding fixed asset accounting is correct?

    A   All fixed assets should be revalued each year.

    B   Fixed assets may be revalued at the discretion of management. Once revaluation has occurred it must be repeated regularly for all fixed assets in a class.

    C   Management can choose which fixed assets in a class of fixed assets should be revalued.

    D   Fixed assets should be revalued to reflect rising prices.

2   Which of the following statements regarding depreciation is correct?

    A   All fixed assets must be depreciated.

    B   Straight line depreciation is usually the most appropriate method of depreciation.

    C   A change in the chosen depreciation method is a change in accounting policy which should be disclosed.

    D   Depreciation charges must be based upon the depreciable amount.

3   What is an asset's net book value?

    A   Its cost less annual depreciation
    B   Its cost less accumulated depreciation
    C   Its net realisable value
    D   Its replacement value

4   Give two common depreciation methods.

5   A fixed asset (cost £10,000, depreciation £7,500) is given in part exchange for a new asset costing £20,500. The agreed trade-in value was £3,500. The profit and loss account will include?

    A   A loss on disposal £1,000
    B   A profit on disposal £1,000
    C   A loss on purchase of a new asset £3,500
    D   A profit on disposal £3,500

6   What details about a fixed asset might be included in an assets register?

7   Why might the assets register not reconcile with the fixed assets accounts?

    A   Asset stolen or damaged
    B   New asset, not yet recorded in the ledger
    C   Errors in the ledger
    D   All of the above

Answers to Quick Quiz

1 B Correct.
   A Fixed assets may be revalued, there is no requirement to do so in FRS 15.
   C Incorrect, all fixed assets in a class must be revalued.
   D Incorrect, fixed assets may be reduced in value as well as being increased.

2 D Correct.
   A Incorrect, some fixed assets are not depreciated eg land.
   B Incorrect, management should choose the most appropriate method.
   C Incorrect, a method change is not a change in accounting policy.

3 B Its cost less accumulated depreciation.

4 Straight-line and reducing balance.

5 B

		£
Net book value at disposal		2,500
Trade-in allowance		3,500
Profit		1,000

6 • Date of purchase
   • Description
   • Original cost
   • Depreciation rate and method
   • Accumulated depreciation to date
   • Date and amount of any revaluation

7 D Other reasons include an asset that is obsolete and so scrapped or improvements not yet recorded in the register.

Now try the questions below from the Exam Question Bank

Number	Level	Marks	Time
Q14	Examination	2	2 mins
Q15	Examination	2	2 mins
Q16	Examination	2	2 mins
Q17	Examination	1	1 min

10

Intangible fixed assets

Topic list	Syllabus reference
1 Intangible assets	D6(a)-(b)
2 Research and development costs	D6(c)-(f)

Introduction

Intangible fixed assets are fixed assets which have a value to the business because they have been paid for, but which do not have any physical substance. The most significant of such intangible assets are **research** and **deferred development costs**.

In many companies, especially those which produce food or 'scientific' products such as medicines or 'high technology' products, the expenditure on **research and development** is considerable. When R & D is a large item of cost its accounting treatment may have a significant influence on the profits of a business and its balance sheet valuation. Because of this attempts have been made to standardise the treatment, and these are discussed in this chapter.

Study guide

		Intellectual level
D6	**Intangible fixed assets and amortisation**	
(a)	Recognise the difference between tangible and intangible fixed assets	1
(b)	Identify types of intangible assets	1
(c)	Identify the definition and treatment of 'research costs' and 'development costs' in accordance with FRSs	1
(d)	Calculate amounts to be capitalised on development expenditure or to be expensed from given information	1
(e)	Explain the purpose of amortisation	1
(f)	Calculate and account for the charge for amortisation	1

Exam guide

Calculations of R&D expenses are highly likely to be examined. Be prepared for a question asking you to apply the standard to a given situation.

Exam focus point

At the 2009 ACCA Teachers' Conference, the examiner highlighted intangible fixed assets as one of the areas that are consistently answered badly in the exam.

1 Intangible assets

1.1 Intangible assets

'Intangible assets' means assets that literally cannot be touched, as opposed to tangible assets (such as plant and machinery) which have a physical existence. Intangible assets include goodwill (which we will meet in Chapter 19), intellectual rights (eg patents, performing rights and authorship rights), as well as research and development costs.

1.2 Accounting treatment

Intangible assets are usually capitalised in the accounts and amortised (another word for depreciation but referring specifically to intangible assets). Amortisation is intended to write off the asset over its economic life (under the accruals concept).

1.3 Example: patent

A business buys a patent for £50,000. It expects to use the patent for the next ten years, after which it will be valueless. Amortisation is calculated in the same way as for tangible assets:

$$\frac{\text{Cost} - \text{residual value}}{\text{Estimated useful life}}$$

In this case, amortisation will be £5,000 per annum (50,000/10).

2 Research and development costs

FAST FORWARD

Expenditure on **research** must always be written off in the period in which it is incurred.

Development costs are also usually written off. However, if the criteria laid down by SSAP 13 are satisfied, development expenditure can be capitalised as an **intangible asset**. If it has a **finite useful life**, it should then be amortised over that life.

2.1 Introduction to R & D

Large companies may spend significant amounts of money on **research and development** (R & D) activities. These amounts must be credited to cash and debited to an account for research and development expenditure. The accounting problem is how to treat the debit balance on R & D account at the balance sheet date.

There are two possibilities.

(a) The debit balance may be classified as an **expense** and transferred to the profit and loss account. This is referred to as 'writing off' the expenditure.

(b) The debit balance may be classified as an **asset** and included in the balance sheet. This is referred to as 'capitalising' or 'carrying forward' or 'deferring' the expenditure.

The argument for writing off R & D expenditure is that it is an expense just like rates or wages and its accounting treatment should be the same.

The argument for carrying forward R & D expenditure is based on the accruals concept. If R & D activity eventually leads to new or improved products which generate revenue, the costs should be carried forward to be matched against that revenue in future accounting periods.

R & D expenditure is the subject of an accounting standard, SSAP 13 *Accounting for research and development*. SSAP 13 defines research and development expenditure as falling into one or more of the following categories.

(a) **Pure research** is original research to obtain new scientific or technical knowledge or understanding. There is no clear commercial end in view and such research work does not have a practical application. Companies and other business entities might carry out this type of research in the hope that it will provide new knowledge which can subsequently be exploited.

(b) **Applied research** is original research work which also seeks to obtain new scientific or technical knowledge, but which has a specific practical aim or application (eg research on improvements in the effectiveness of medicines). Applied research may develop from 'pioneering' pure research, but many companies have full-time research teams working on applied research projects.

(c) **Development** is the use of existing scientific and technical knowledge to produce new (or substantially improved) products or systems, prior to starting commercial production operations.

2.2 How do we distinguish these categories?

The dividing line between each of these categories will often be indistinct in practice, and some expenditure might be classified as research or as development. It may be even more difficult to distinguish development costs from production costs. For example, if a prototype model of a new product is developed and then sold to a customer, the costs of the prototype will include both development and production expenditure.

SSAP 13 states that although there may be practical difficulties in isolating research costs and development costs, there is a difference of principle in the method of accounting for each type of expenditure.

(a) (i) Expenditure on pure and applied research is usually a continuing operation which is necessary to ensure a company's survival.

(ii)   One accounting period does not gain more than any other from such work, and it is therefore appropriate that **research costs** should be **written off** as they are incurred (ie in the year of expenditure).

(iii)   This conforms with CA 1985, which seems not to envisage the capitalisation of research expenditure in any circumstances.

(b) (i)   The development of new and improved products is different, because development expenditure is incurred with a particular commercial aim in view and in the reasonable expectation of earning profits or reducing costs.

(ii)   In these circumstances it is appropriate that development costs should be deferred (capitalised) and matched against the future revenues.

Exam focus point

If you are in a hurry, or revising, just read the SECTOR mnemonic below.

SSAP 13 attempts to restrict indiscriminate deferrals of development expenditure and states that development costs may only be deferred to future periods, when the following criteria are met.

(a)   There must be a clearly defined development project, and the related expenditure on this project is separately identifiable.

(b)   The expected outcome of the project must have been assessed, and there should be reasonable certainty that it is both

(i)   Technically feasible
(ii)   Commercially viable, having regard to market conditions, competition, public opinion and consumer and environmental legislation

(c)   The eventual profits from the developed product or system should reasonably be expected to cover the past and future development costs.

(d)   The company should have adequate resources to complete the development project.

If *any* of these conditions are not satisfied the development costs should be written off in the year of expenditure.

The following mnemonic may be helpful. Remember: SECTOR.

S	Separately defined project
E	Expenditure separately identifiable
C	Commercially viable
T	Technically feasible
O	Overall profit expected
R	Resources exist to complete project

Where development expenditure is deferred to future periods, its **amortisation should begin with the commencement of production**, and should then be written off over the period in which the product is expected to be sold. Deferred development expenditure should be reviewed at the end of every accounting period. If the conditions which justified the deferral of the expenditure no longer apply or are considered doubtful, the deferred expenditure, to the extent that it is now considered to be irrecoverable, should be written off.

Development expenditure once written off can now be reinstated, if the uncertainties which had led to its being written off no longer apply. This was not permitted by the original SSAP 13, but it has been amended because the CA 1985 does permit the reinstatement of costs previously written off.

2.3 Examples of R & D items

Examples given by SSAP 13 (revised) of activities that would normally be **included** in R & D are:

(a) Experimental, theoretical or other work aimed at the discovery of new knowledge or the advancement of existing knowledge.

(b) Searching for applications of that knowledge.

(c) Formulation and design of possible applications for such work.

(d) Testing in search for, or evaluation of, product, service or process alternatives.

(e) Design, construction and testing of pre-production prototypes and models and development batches.

(f) Design of products, services, processes or systems involving new technology or substantially improving those already produced or installed.

(g) Construction and operation of pilot plants.

2.4 Examples of non R & D items

Examples of activities that would normally be **excluded** from research and development include:

(a) Testing and analysis either of equipment or product for purposes of quality or quantity control.

(b) Periodic alterations to existing products, services or processes even though these may represent some improvement.

(c) Operational research not tied to a specific research and development activity.

(d) Cost of corrective action in connection with break-downs during commercial production.

(e) Legal and administrative work in connection with patent applications, records and litigation and the sale or licensing of patents.

(f) Activity, including design and construction engineering, relating to the construction, relocation, rearrangement or start-up of facilities or equipment other than facilities or equipment whose sole use is for a particular research and development project.

(g) Market research.

Under the revised SSAP 13, a company can still defer the expenditure under the accruals concept (if it is prudent so to do) but it must be disclosed entirely separately from deferred development expenditure.

2.5 Examples of items excluded from SSAP 13

The above provisions of SSAP 13 do not extend to the following cases.

(a) Expenditure on tangible fixed assets acquired or constructed to provide facilities for research and/or development activities should be capitalised and depreciated over their useful lives in the usual way. However, the depreciation may be capitalised as part of deferred development expenditure if the development work for which the assets are used meets the criteria given above.

(b) Expenditure incurred in locating mineral deposits in extractive industries is outside the scope of SSAP 13.

(c) Expenditure incurred where there is a firm contract to:

(i) Carry out development work on behalf of third parties on such terms that the related expenditure is to be fully reimbursed.

(ii) Develop and manufacture at an agreed price which has been calculated to reimburse expenditure on development as well as on manufacture.

Is not to be treated as deferred development expenditure.

Any such expenditure which has not been reimbursed at the balance sheet date should be included in work in progress.

(a)   Tank Top Ltd has purchased a tank for £50,000. The purpose of the tank is to investigate the possibility of growing food under water. What would be the appropriate accounting treatment for this item as per SSAP 13?

(b)   Applying the accounting concepts of accruals, prudence and consistency to the requirements of SSAP 13, discuss whether there is any conflict between these concepts and SSAP 13.

Answer

(a)   SSAP 13 states that expenditure on tangible fixed assets acquired or constructed to provide facilities for research and/or development activities should be capitalised and depreciated over their useful lives in the usual way. The depreciation may be capitalised as part of deferred development expenditure if the development work for which the assets are used meets the criteria given in the SSAP. However, since the tank is for pure research, this does not apply.

(b)   The argument for carrying forward development expenditure is based on the accruals concept. If R&D activity eventually leads to new or improved products which generate revenue, the costs should be carried forward to be matched against that revenue in future accounting periods.

However, it could be argued that SSAP 13 conflicts with the prudence concept. Research and development projects have considerable risk. For prudence to prevail, all such costs should be expensed rather than capitalised in advance of the known success of the project. SSAP 13 is, however, prudent in defining the criteria for capitalisation very narrowly.

There is a clear conflict between SSAP 13 and the consistency concept in that companies have a choice between immediate write off and capitalisation. While some consistency is achieved through the requirement to apply the policy of deferral (if adopted) to all development projects that meet the criteria, it is certainly possible for a company to change from a policy of writing off to one of deferral. It is also apparent that different companies may treat the same type of expenditure in different ways. Possibly the choice of treatment may be influenced by the wish to present the results in a favourable light, rather than to give a true and fair view.

Exam focus point

There is an article on research and development in the *Student Accountant* dated 7 September 2007. You are recommended to read this article.

2.6 Disclosure requirements

The Companies Act 1985 does not require disclosure of the total amount of R & D expenditure during an accounting period, but SSAP 13 (revised) requires that all large companies (defined below) should disclose this total, distinguishing between current year expenditure and amortisation of deferred development expenditure.

SSAP 13 (revised) requires the following companies to disclose R & D expenditure.

(a)   All public companies

(b)   All special category companies (ie banking and insurance companies)

(c)   All holding companies with a plc or special category company as a subsidiary

(d)   All companies who satisfy the criteria, multiplied by 10, for defining a medium-sized company (see para 2.17 for details)

Part (d) means that a private company will be exempted if it is not itself (and does not control) a special category company and it meets two of the following criteria:

- turnover ≤ £228 million
- total assets (*before* deduction of current or long-term liabilities) ≤ £114 million
- ≤ 2,500 employees

These are the new criteria for financial years ending on or after 30 January 2004.

Where deferred development costs are included in a company's balance sheet the following information must be given in the notes to the accounts:

(a) Movements on deferred development expenditure, and the amount brought forward and carried forward at the beginning and end of the period.

(b) The accounting policy used to account for R & D expenditure should be clearly explained.

Question

R&D disclosure

Y Ltd is a research company which specialises in developing new materials and manufacturing processes for the furniture industry. The company receives payments from a variety of manufacturers, which pay for the right to use the company's patented fabrics and processes.

Research and development costs for the year ended 30 September 20X5 can be analysed as follows.

	£
Expenditure on continuing research projects	1,420,000
Amortisation of development expenditure capitalised in earlier years	240,000

New projects started during the year:

Project A	280,000

New flame-proof padding. Expected to cost a total of £800,000 to develop. Expected total revenue £2,000,000 once work completed - probably late 20X6

Project B	150,000

New colour-fast dye. Expected to cost a total of £3,000,000 to complete. Future revenues are likely to exceed £5,000,000. The completion date is uncertain because external funding will have to be obtained before research work can be completed.

Project C	110,000

Investigation of new adhesive recently developed in aerospace industry. If this proves effective then Y Ltd may well generate significant income because it will be used in place of existing adhesives.

	2,200,000

The company has a policy of capitalising all development expenditure where permitted by SSAP 13. The NRV of deferred development expenditure at 30 September 20X5 is £2,400,000, excluding any capitalisation needed for Projects A, B and C.

Explain how the three research projects A, B and C will be dealt with in Y Ltd's profit and loss account and balance sheet.

In each case, explain your proposed treatment in terms of SSAP 13 and, where relevant, in terms of the fundamental accounting assumptions of going concern and accruals, and the prudence concept.

Answer

Project A

This project meets the SECTOR criteria for SSAP 13 for development expenditure to be recognised as an asset. These are as follows.

(a) The product or process is clearly defined and the costs attributable to the product or process can be separately identified and measured reliably.

(b) The project is commercially feasible.

(c) The technical feasibility of the product or process can be demonstrated.

(d) An overall profit is expected.

(e) Adequate resources exist, or their availability can be demonstrated, to complete the project and market or use the product or process.

The capitalisation development costs in a company which is a going concern means that these are accrued in order that they can be matched against the income they are expected to generate.

Hence the costs of £280,000 incurred to date should be transferred from research and development costs to capitalised development expenditure and carried forward until revenues are generated; they should then be matched with those revenues.

Project B

Whilst this project meets most of the criteria discussed above which would enable the costs to be carried forward it fails on the requirements that 'adequate resources exist, or their availability can be demonstrated, to complete the project.

Hence it would be prudent to write off these costs. Once funding is obtained the situation can then be reassessed and these and future costs may be capitalised. In this case the prudence concept overrides the accruals assumption.

Project C

This is a research project according to SSAP 13, ie original and planned investigation undertaken with the prospect of gaining new scientific or technical knowledge or understanding.

There is no certainty as to its ultimate success or commercial viability and therefore it cannot be considered to be a development project. SSAP 13 therefore requires that costs be written off as incurred. Once again, prudence overrides the accruals assumption.

The disclosure in the accounts is as follows.

Profit and loss account (extract)

	£
R&D expenditure (1,420,000 + 150,000 + 110,000)	1,680,000
Amortisation of deferred development expenditure	240,000

Balance sheet (extract)

	£
Deferred development expenditure (2,400,000 + 280,000)	2,680,000

Chapter Roundup

- Expenditure on **research** must always be written off in the period in which it is incurred.

  Development costs are also usually written off. However, if the criteria laid down by SSAP 13 are satisfied, development expenditure can be capitalised as an **intangible asset**. If it has a **finite useful life**, it should then be amortised over that life.

Quick Quiz

1   What is the required accounting treatment for expenditure on research?

    A   Write off as an expense in the period it is incurred
    B   Capitalise and carry forward as an asset

2   Which of the following items is an intangible asset?

    A   Land
    B   Patents
    C   Buildings
    D   Van

3   Research expenditure is incurred in the application of knowledge for the production of new products.

    Is this statement

    A   True
    B   False

4   XY Ltd has development expenditure of £500,000. Its policy is to amortise development expenditure at 2% per annum. Accumulated amortisation brought forward is £20,000. What is the charge in the profit and loss account for the year's amortisation?

    A   £10,000
    B   £400
    C   £20,000
    D   £9,600

5   Given the facts in 4 above, what is the amount shown in the balance sheet for development expenditure?

    A   £500,000
    B   £480,000
    C   £470,000
    D   £490,000

Answers to Quick Quiz

1   A   Research expenditure is always written off as it is incurred.

2   B   All the others are tangible assets.

3   B   False. This is a definition of development expenditure.

4   A $2\% \times £500,000 = £10,000$.

5   C   Deferred development expenditure b/f is £480,000 (cost £500,000 – accumulated depreciation £20,000), then deduct annual depreciation of £10,000 to give figure c/f of £470,000.

Now try the question below from the Exam Question Bank

Number	Level	Marks	Time
Q18	Examination	2	2 mins

11

Accruals
and prepayments

Introduction

In Chapter 8, we looked at the adjustments which may need to be made to the
cost of goods sold. This chapter deals with the adjustments which may need to
be made to the **expenses**.

Study guide

		Intellectual level
D7	**Accruals and prepayments**	
(a)	Understand how the matching concept applies to accruals and prepayments	1
(b)	Identify and calculate the adjustments needed for accruals and prepayments in preparing financial statements	1
(c)	Illustrate the process of adjusting for accruals and prepayments in preparing financial statements	1
(d)	Prepare the journal entries and ledger entries for the creation of an accrual or prepayment	1
(e)	Understand and identify the impact on profit and net assets of accruals and prepayments	1

Exam guide

These topics are very important and you are bound to have a question including the calculation of or adjustment for accruals and prepayments.

1 Accruals and prepayments

FAST FORWARD

Accrued expenses (**accruals**) are expenses which relate to an accounting period but have not been paid for. They are shown in the balance sheet as a liability.

Prepaid expenses (**prepayments**) are expenses which have already been paid but relate to a future accounting period. They are shown in the balance sheet as an asset.

1.1 Introduction

It has already been stated that the gross profit for a period should be calculated by **matching** sales and the cost of goods sold. In the same way, the net profit for a period should be calculated by charging the expenses which relate to that period. For example, in preparing the profit and loss account of a business for a period of, say, six months, it would be appropriate to charge six months' expenses for rent and rates, insurance costs and telephone costs etc.

Expenses might not be paid for during the period to which they relate. For example, if a business rents a shop for £20,000 per annum, it might pay the full annual rent on, say, 1 April each year. Now if we were to calculate the profit of the business for the first six months of the year 20X7, the correct charge for rent in the profit and loss account would be £10,000 even though the rent payment would be £20,000 in that period. Similarly, the rent charge in a profit and loss account for the business in the second six months of the year would be £10,000, even though no rent payment would be made in that six month period.

Key terms

Accruals or accrued expenses are expenses which are charged against the profit for a particular period, even though they have not yet been paid for.

Prepayments are payments which have been made in one accounting period, but should not be charged against profit until a later period, because they relate to that later period.

Accruals and prepayments might seem difficult at first, but the following examples might help to clarify the principle involved, that expenses should be matched against the period to which they relate.

1.2 Example: Accruals

Horace Goodrunning, trading as Goodrunning Motor Spares, ends his financial year on 28 February each year. His telephone was installed on 1 April 20X6 and he receives his telephone account quarterly at the end of each quarter. He pays it promptly as soon as it is received. On the basis of the following data, you are required to calculate the telephone expense to be charged to the profit and loss account for the year ended 28 February 20X7.

Goodrunning Motor Spares - telephone expense for the three months ended:

	£
30.6.20X6	23.50
30.9.20X6	27.20
31.12.20X6	33.40
31.3.20X7	36.00

Solution

The telephone expenses for the year ended 28 February 20X7 are:

	£
1 March - 31 March 20X6 (no telephone)	0.00
1 April - 30 June 20X6	23.50
1 July - 30 September 20X6	27.20
1 October - 31 December 20X6	33.40
1 January - 28 February 20X7 (two months)	24.00
	108.10

The charge for the period 1 January - 28 February 20X7 is two-thirds of the quarterly charge received on 31 March. As at 28 February 20X7, no telephone bill has been received for the quarter, because it is not due for another month. However, it would be inappropriate to ignore the telephone expenses for January and February, and so an accrued charge of £24 should be made, being two-thirds of the quarter's bill of £36.

The accrued charge will also appear in the balance sheet of the business as at 28 February 20X7, as a current liability.

Question   **Ratsnuffer**

Ratsnuffer is a business dealing in pest control. Its owner, Roy Dent, employs a team of eight who were paid £12,000 per annum each in the year to 31 December 20X5. At the start of 20X6 he raised salaries by 10% to £13,200 per annum each.

On 1 July 20X6, he hired a trainee at a salary of £8,400 per annum.

He pays his work force on the first working day of every month, one month in arrears, so that his employees receive their salary for January on the first working day in February, etc.

Required

(a)   Calculate the cost of salaries which would be charged in the profit and loss account of Ratsnuffer for the year ended 31 December 20X6.

(b)   Calculate the amount actually paid in salaries during the year (ie the amount of cash received by the work force).

(c)   State the amount of accrued charges for salaries which would appear in the balance sheet of Ratsnuffer as at 31 December 20X6.

Answer

(a)   *Salaries cost in the profit and loss account*

	£
Cost of 8 employees for a full year at £13,200 each	105,600
Cost of trainee for a half year	4,200
	109,800

(b)   *Salaries actually paid in 20X6*

	£
December 20X5 salaries paid in January (8 employees × £1,000 per month)	8,000
Salaries of 8 employees for January - November 20X6 paid in February – December	
(8 employees × £1,100 per month × 11 months)	96,800
Salaries of trainee (for July - November paid in August - December	
20X6: 5 months × £700 per month)	3,500
Salaries actually paid	108,300

(c)   *Accrued salaries costs as at 31 December 20X6*
         (ie costs charged in the P & L account, but not yet paid)

	£
8 employees x 1 month x £1,100 per month	8,800
1 trainee x 1 month x £700 per month	700
	9,500

(d)   *Summary*

	£
Accrued wages costs as at 31 December 20X5	8,000
Add salaries cost for 20X6 (P & L account)	109,800
	117,800
Less salaries paid	108,300
Equals accrued wages costs as at 31 December 20X6	9,500

1.3 Example: Prepayments

The Square Wheels Garage pays fire insurance annually in advance on 1 June each year. The firm's financial year end is 28 February. From the following record of insurance payments you are required to calculate the charge to profit and loss for the financial year to 28 February 20X8.

Insurance paid

	£
1.6.20X6	600
1.6.20X7	700

Insurance cost for:

		£
(a)	The 3 months, 1 March - 31 May 20X7 (3/12 × £600)	150
(b)	The 9 months, 1 June 20X7 - 28 February 20X8 (9/12 × £700)	525
Insurance cost for the year, charged to the P & L account		675

At 28 February 20X8 there is a prepayment for fire insurance, covering the period 1 March - 31 May 20X8. This insurance premium was paid on 1 June 20X7, but only nine months worth of the full annual cost is chargeable to the accounting period ended 28 February 20X8. The prepayment of (3/12 × £700) £175 as at 28 February 20X8 will appear as a current asset in the balance sheet of the Square Wheels Garage as at that date.

In the same way, there was a prepayment of (3/12 × £600) £150 in the balance sheet one year earlier as at 28 February 20X7.

Summary	£
Prepaid insurance premiums as at 28 February 20X7	150
Add insurance premiums paid 1 June 20X7	700
	850
Less insurance costs charged to the P & L account for the year ended 28 February 20X8	675
Equals prepaid insurance premiums as at 28 February 20X8	175

Question

Photocopier rental

The Batley Print Shop rents a photocopying machine from a supplier for which it makes a quarterly payment as follows:

(a)   three months rental in advance;
(b)   a further charge of 2 pence per copy made during the quarter just ended.

The rental agreement began on 1 August 20X4 and the first six quarterly bills were as follows.

Bills dated and received	Rental	Costs of copies taken	Total
	£	£	£
1 August 20X4	2,100	0	2,100
1 November 20X4	2,100	1,500	3,600
1 February 20X5	2,100	1,400	3,500
1 May 20X5	2,100	1,800	3,900
1 August 20X5	2,700	1,650	4,350
1 November 20X5	2,700	1,950	4,650

The bills are paid promptly, as soon as they are received.

(a)   Calculate the charge for photocopying expenses for the year to 31 August 20X4 and the amount of prepayments and/or accrued charges as at that date.

(b)   Calculate the charge for photocopying expenses for the following year to 31 August 20X5, and the amount of prepayments and/or accrued charges as at that date.

Answer

(a)   *Year to 31 August 20X4*   £

One months' rental (1/3 × £2,100) *	700
Accrued copying charges (1/3 × £1,500) **	500
Photocopying expense (P & L account)	1,200

*   From the quarterly bill dated 1 August 20X4
**   From the quarterly bill dated 1 November 20X4

There is a prepayment for 2 months' rental (£1,400) as at 31 August 20X4.

(b)   *Year to 31 August 20X5*

	£	£
Rental from 1 September 20X4 - 31 July 20X5 (11 months at £2,100 per quarter or £700 per month)		7,700
Rental from 1 August - 31 August 20X5 (1/3 × £2,700)		900
Rental charge for the year		8,600
Copying charges:		
1 September - 31 October 20X4 (2/3 × £1,500)	1,000	
1 November 20X4 - 31 January 20X5	1,400	
1 February - 30 April 20X5	1,800	
1 May - 31 July 20X5	1,650	
Accrued charges for August 20X5 (1/3 × £1,950)	650	
		6,500
Total photocopying expenses (P & L account)		15,100

There is a prepayment for 2 months' rental (£1,800) as at 31 August 20X5.

	Rental charges £	Copying costs £
Prepayments as at 31.8.20X4	1,400	
Accrued charges as at 31.8.20X4		(500)
Bills received during the year		
1 November 20X4	2,100	1,500
1 February 20X5	2,100	1,400
1 May 20X5	2,100	1,800
1 August 20X5	2,700	1,650
Prepayment as at 31.8.20X5	(1,800)	
Accrued charges as at 31.8.20X5		650
Charge to the P & L account for the year	8,600	6,500
Balance sheet items as at 31 August 20X5		
Prepaid rental (current asset)	1,800	
Accrued copying charges (current liability)		650

> **Exam focus point**
>
> You will almost certainly have to deal with accruals and prepayments in the exam. Make sure you understand the logic, then you will be able to do whatever question comes up.

1.4 Further example: Accruals

Suppose that Willie Woggle opens a shop on 1 May 20X6 to sell hiking and camping equipment. The rent of the shop is £12,000 per annum, payable quarterly in arrears (with the first payment on 31 July 20X6). Willie decides that his accounting period should end on 31 December each year.

The rent account as at 31 December 20X6 will record only two rental payments (on 31 July and 31 October) and there will be two months' accrued rental expenses for November and December 20X6, (£2,000) since the next rental payment is not due until 31 January 20X7.

The charge to the P & L account for the period to 31 December 20X6 will be for 8 months' rent (May-December inclusive) and so it follows that the total rental cost should be £8,000.

So far, the rent account appears as follows.

RENT ACCOUNT

		£			£
20X6			*20X6*		
31 July	Cash	3,000			
31 Oct	Cash	3,000	31 Dec	P & L account	8,000

To complete the picture, the accruals of £2,000 have to be put in, not only to balance the account, but also to have an opening balance of £2,000 ready for next year. So the accrued rent of £2,000 is debited to the rent account as a balance to be carried down, and credited to the rent account as a balance brought down.

RENT ACCOUNT

		£			£
20X6			*20X6*		
31 July	Cash *	3,000			
31 Oct	Cash *	3,000			
31 Dec	Balance c/f (accruals)	2,000	31 Dec	P & L account	8,000
		8,000			8,000
			20X7		
			1 Jan	Balance b/f	2,000

* The corresponding credit entry would be cash if rent is paid without the need for an invoice - eg with payment by standing order or direct debit at the bank. If there is always an invoice where rent becomes payable, the double entry would be:

DEBIT   Rent account   £2,000
CREDIT   Creditors   £2,000

Then when the rent is paid, the ledger entries would be:

DEBIT   Creditors   £2,000
CREDIT   Cash   £2,000

The rent account for the **next** year to 31 December 20X7, assuming no increase in rent in that year, would be as follows.

RENT ACCOUNT

20X7		£	20X7		£
31 Jan	Cash	3,000	1 Jan	Balance b/f	2,000
30 Apr	Cash	3,000			
31 Jul	Cash	3,000			
31 Oct	Cash	3,000			
31 Dec	Balance c/f (accruals)	2,000	31 Dec	P & L account	12,000
		14,000			14,000
			20X8		
			1 Jan	Balance b/f	2,000

Here you will see that, for a full year, a full twelve months' rental charges are taken as an expense to the P & L account.

1.5 Further example: Prepayments of income

Terry Trunk commences business as a landscape gardener on 1 September 20X5. He immediately decides to join his local trade association, the Confederation of Luton Gardeners, for which the annual membership subscription is £180, payable annually in advance. He paid this amount on 1 September. The Confederation's accounting period ends on 30 June each year.

In the first period to 30 June 20X6 (10 months), a full year's membership will have been paid, but only ten twelfths of the subscription should be charged to the period (ie $10/12 \times £180 = £150$). There is a prepayment of two months of membership subscription – ie $2/12 \times £180 = £30$.

The prepayment is recognised in the Confederation's ledger account for subscriptions. For simplicity, only Terry's subscription is shown. This is done by using the balance carried down/brought down technique.

DEBIT   Subscriptions account with prepayment as a balance c/f   £30
CREDIT   Subscriptions account with the same balance b/f   £30

The remaining expenses in the subscriptions account should then be taken to the P & L account. The balance on the account will appear as a current liability (prepaid subscriptions) in the balance sheet as at 30 June 20X6.

SUBSCRIPTIONS ACCOUNT

20X6		£	20X5		£
30 Jun	P & L account	150	1 Sept	Cash	180
30 Jun	Balance c/f (prepayment)	30			
		180			180
			20X6		
			1 Jul	Balance b/f	30

The subscription account for the next year, assuming no increase in the annual charge and that Terry Trunk remains a member of the association, will be:

SUBSCRIPTIONS ACCOUNT

			£				£
20X7				*20X6*			
30 Jun	P & L account		180	1 Jul	Balance b/f		30
30 Jun	Balance c/f			1 Sep	Cash		180
	(prepayment)		30				
			210				210
				20X67			
				1 Jul	Balance b/f		30

Again, we see here for a full accounting year, the charge to the P & L account is for a full year's subscriptions. Remember that the prepaid subscription brought forward is, theoretically, repayable to Terry if he ceases to be a member. Therefore it is a liability.

1.6 Effect on profit and net assets

You may find the following table a useful summary of the effects of accruals and prepayments.

	Effect on income/expenses	Effect on profits	Effect on assets/liabilities
Accruals	Increases expenses	Reduces profit	Increases liabilities
Prepayments	Reduces expenses	Increases profit	Increases assets
Prepayments of income	Reduces income	Reduces profit	Increases liabilities

Question	The Umbrella Shop

The Umbrella Shop has the following trial balance as at 30 September 20X8.

	£	£
Sales		156,000
Purchases	65,000	
Land & buildings – net book value at 30.9.X8	125,000	
Plant & machinery – net book value at 30.9.X8	75,000	
Stock at 1.10.X7	10,000	
Cash at bank	12,000	
Trade debtors	54,000	
Trade creditors		40,000
Selling expenses	10,000	
Cash in hand	2,000	
Administration expenses	15,000	
Finance expenses	5,000	
Carriage inwards	1,000	
Carriage outwards	2,000	
Capital account at 1.10.X7		180,000
	376,000	376,000

The following information is available:

(a) Closing stock at 30.9.X8 is £13,000, after writing off damaged goods of £2,000.

(b) Included in administration expenses is machinery rental of £6,000 covering the year to 31 December 20X8.

(c) A late invoice for £12,000 covering rent for the year ended 30 June 20X9 has not been included in the trial balance.

Prepare a trading and profit and loss account and balance sheet for the year ended 30 September 20X8.

Answer

THE UMBRELLA SHOP
TRADING AND PROFIT AND LOSS ACCOUNT FOR THE YEAR END 30 SEPTEMBER 20X8

	£	£
Sales		156,000
Opening stock	10,000	
Purchases	65,000	
Carriage inwards	1,000	
	76,000	
Closing stock (W1)	13,000	
Cost of goods sold		63,000
Gross profit		93,000
Selling expenses	10,000	
Carriage outwards	2,000	
Administration expenses (W2)	16,500	
Finance expenses	5,000	33,500
Net profit for the period		59,500

THE UMBRELLA SHOP
BALANCE SHEET AS AT 30 SEPTEMBER 20X8

	£	£
Fixed assets		
Land & buildings		125,000
Plant & machinery		75,000
		200,000
Current assets		
Stock (W1)	13,000	
Trade debtors	54,000	
Prepayments (W4)	1,500	
Cash at bank and in hand	14,000	
	82,500	
Current liabilities	40,000	
Trade creditor	3,000	
Accruals (W3)	43,000	
Net current assets		39,500
		239,500
Capital		
Proprietor's capital		
Balance brought forward		180,000
Profit for the period		59,500
Balance carried forward		239,500

Workings

1   *Closing stock*

As the figure of £13,000 is **after** writing off damaged goods, no further adjustments are necessary. Remember that you are effectively crediting closing stock to the trading account of the profit and loss account and the corresponding debit is to the balance sheet.

2 *Administration expenses*

	£
Per trial balance	15,000
Add: accrual (W3)	3,000
	18,000
Less: prepayment (W4)	(1,500)
	16,500

3 *Accrual*

	£
Rent for year to 30 June 20X9	12,000
Accrual for period to 30 September 20X8 ($^3/_{12} \times £12,000$)	3,000

4 *Prepayment*

	£
Machinery rental for the year to 31 December 20X8	6,000
Prepayment for period 1 October to 31 December 20X8 ($^3/_{12} \times £6,000$)	1,500

Chapter Roundup

- **Accrued expenses (accruals)** are expenses which relate to an accounting period but have not been paid for. They are shown in the balance sheet as a liability.

  Prepaid expenses (prepayments) are expenses which have already been paid but relate to a future accounting period. They are shown in the balance sheet as an asset.

1   How is the cost of goods sold calculated?

    A   Opening stock + purchases + closing stock
    B   Opening stock + closing stock – purchases
    C   Opening stock + purchases – closing stock
    D   Closing stock + purchases – closing stock

2   Electricity paid during the year is £14,000. There was an opening accrual b/f of £500. A bill for the quarter ended 31 January 20X7 was £900. What is the electricity charge in the profit and loss account for the year ended 31 December 20X6?

    A   £14,000
    B   £14,100
    C   £13,900
    D   £14,400

3   If a business has paid rent of £1,000 for the year to 31 March 20X9, what is the prepayment in the accounts for the year to 31 December 20X8?

    A   £250
    B   £750

4   What is the correct journal for an electricity prepayment of £500?

    A   Debit: prepayment   £500
                Credit: expense   £500

    B   Debit: expense   £500
                Credit: prepayment   £500

5   An accrual is an expense charged against profit for a period, even though it has not yet been paid or invoiced.

    Is this statement:

    A   True
    B   False

1   C

2   B

ELECTRICITY

	£		£
Cash	14,000	Accrual b/f	500
Accrual c/f (2/3 × 900)	600	Profit and loss account	14,100
	14,600		14,600

3   A $^3/_{12} \times £1,000 = £250$

4   A   A prepayment needs to reduce the expense and set up an asset in the balance sheet.

5   A   True.

Now try the questions below from the Exam Question Bank

Number	Level	Marks	Time
Q19	Examination	2	2 mins
Q20	Examination	2	2 mins

Irrecoverable debts and allowances

Topic list	Syllabus reference
1 Irrecoverable debts	D8(b)-(f)
2 Allowances for debtors	D8(g)-(i)
3 Accounting for irrecoverable debts and allowances	D8(e)-(g), (h)-(i)

Introduction

In this chapter we move closer to our goal of preparing the financial statements. We look at the adjustments which need to be made in respect of credit sales and purchases:

- **Irrecoverable debts**
- **Allowances for debtors**

Important note:

In past exam papers you will see reference to 'allowance for doubtful debts'. ACCA announced that this terminology would no longer be used, starting from the December 2005 sitting. The December 2005 exam referred to 'debtors allowances' or 'allowance for debtors' and that is the terminology used in this text.

In addition, 'bad debts' are now usually referred to as 'irrecoverable debts' (although you may see both terms used in the exam).

Study guide

		Intellectual level
D8	**Debtors and creditors**	
(b)	Identify the benefits and costs of offering credit facilities to customers	1
(c)	Understand the purpose of an aged debtors analysis	1
(d)	Understand the purpose of credit limits	1
(e)	Prepare the bookkeeping entries to write off a bad (irrecoverable) debt	1
(f)	Record a bad (irrecoverable) debt recovered	1
(g)	Identify the impact of bad (irrecoverable) debts on the profit and loss account and on the balance sheet	1
(h)	Prepare the bookkeeping entries to create and adjust an allowance for debtors	1
(i)	Illustrate how to include movements in the allowance for debtors in the profit and loss account and how the closing balance of the allowance should appear in the balance sheet	1

Exam guide

This topic is particularly suitable for MCQs. Such questions will nearly always involve an adjustment for irrecoverable debts and/or allowances for debtors.

1 Irrecoverable debts

FAST FORWARD

> Irrecoverable debts are specific debts owed to a business which it decides are never going to be paid. They are written off as an expense in the profit and loss account.

1.1 Introduction

Very few businesses expect to be paid immediately in cash, unless they are retail businesses on the high street. Most businesses buy and sell to one another on credit terms. This has the **benefit** of allowing businesses to keep trading without having to provide cash 'up front'. So a business will allow credit terms to customers and receive credit terms from its suppliers. Ideally a business wants to receive money from its customers as quickly as possible, but delay paying its suppliers for as long as possible. This can lead to problems.

Most businesses aim to control such problems by means of **credit control**. A customer will be given a **credit limit**, which cannot be exceeded (compare an overdraft limit or a credit card limit). If an order would take the account over its credit limit, it will not be filled until a payment is received.

Another tool in **credit control** is the **aged debtors analysis**. This shows how long invoices have been outstanding and may indicate that a customer is unable to pay. Most credit controllers will have a system for chasing up payment of late outstanding invoices.

Customers who buy goods on credit might fail to pay for them, perhaps out of dishonesty or perhaps because they have gone bankrupt and cannot pay. Customers in another country might be prevented from paying by the unexpected introduction of foreign exchange control restrictions by their country's government during the credit period. Therefore the **costs** of offering credit facilities to customers can include:

(a) Interest costs of an overdraft, if customers do not pay promptly
(b) Costs of trying to obtain payment
(c) Court costs

For one reason or another, a business might decide to give up expecting payment and to write the debt off.

An **irrecoverable debt** is a debt which is not expected to be repaid.

1.2 Writing off irrecoverable debts

When a business decides that a particular debt is unlikely ever to be repaid, the amount of the debt should be **'written off'** as an expense in the profit and loss account.

DR   Irrecoverable debt
CR   Debtors control (total debtors) account

For example, if Alfred's Mini-Cab Service sends an invoice for £300 to a customer who subsequently does a 'moonlight flit' from his office premises, never to be seen or heard of again, the debt of £300 must be written off. It might seem sensible to record the business transaction as:

Sales £(300 – 300) = £0.

However, irrecoverable debts written off are accounted for as follows.

(a) **Sales** are shown at their invoice value in the **trading account**. The sale has been made, and gross profit should be earned. The subsequent failure to collect the debt is a separate matter, which is reported in the P & L account.

(b) Irrecoverable debts written off are shown as an expense in the profit and loss account.

In our example of Alfred's Mini-Cab Service:

	£
Sale (in the trading account)	300
Irrecoverable debt written off (expense in the P & L account)	300
Net profit on this transaction	0

Obviously, when a debt is written off, the value of the debtor as a current asset falls to zero. If the debt is expected to be uncollectable, its **'net realisable value'** is nil, and so it has a zero balance sheet value.

Double entry

		£	£
DEBIT	Irrecoverable debt	300	
CREDIT	Debtors account		300

1.3 Irrecoverable debts written off and subsequently paid

An irrecoverable debt which has been written off might occasionally be unexpectedly paid. Regardless of when the payment is received, the accounting entries are as follows.

Double entry

		£	£
DEBIT	Cash account	X	
CREDIT	Irrecoverable debts		X

For example, a trading, profit and loss account for the Blacksmith's Forge for the year to 31 December 20X5 could be prepared as shown below from the following information.

	£
Stocks of goods in hand, 1 January 20X5	6,000
Purchases of goods	122,000
Stocks of goods in hand, 31 December 20X5	8,000
Cash sales	100,000
Credit sales	70,000
Discounts allowed	1,200
Discounts received	5,000
Irrecoverable debts written off	9,000
Debts paid in 20X5 which were previously written off as irrecoverable in 20X4 (ie irrecoverable debts received)	2,000
Other expenses	31,800

BLACKSMITH'S FORGE
TRADING, PROFIT AND LOSS ACCOUNT FOR THE YEAR ENDED 31.12.20X5

	£	£
Sales		170,000
Opening stock	6,000	
Purchases	122,000	
	128,000	
Less closing stock	8,000	
Cost of goods sold		120,000
Gross profit		50,000
Add: discounts received		5,000
		55,000
Expenses		
Discounts allowed	1,200	
Irrecoverable debts written off (9,000 – 2,000)	7,000	
Other expenses	31,800	
		40,000
Net profit		15,000

2 Allowances for debtors

FAST FORWARD

Allowances for debtors may be **specific** (an allowance against a particular debtor) or simply a percentage allowance based on past experience of irrecoverable debts. An increase in the allowance for debtors is shown as an expense in the profit and loss account.

Trade debtors in the balance sheet are shown **net** of any debtors allowance.

When irrecoverable debts are written off, specific debts owed to the business are identified as unlikely ever to be collected.

However, because of the risks involved in selling goods on credit, it might be accepted that a certain percentage of outstanding debts at any time are unlikely to be collected. But although it might be estimated that, say, 5% of debts will turn out bad, the business will not know until later which specific debts are bad.

A business commences operations on 1 July 20X4, and in the twelve months to 30 June 20X5 makes sales of £300,000 (all on credit) and writes off irrecoverable debts amounting to £6,000. Cash received from customers during the year is £244,000, so that at 30 June 20X5, the business has outstanding debtors of £50,000.

	£
Credit sales during the year	300,000
Add debtors at 1 July 20X4	0
Total debts owed to the business	300,000
Less cash received from credit customers	244,000
	56,000
Less irrecoverable debts written off	6,000
Debtors outstanding at 30 June 20X5	50,000

Now, some of these outstanding debts might turn out to be irrecoverable. The business does not know on 30 June 20X5 which specific debts in the total £50,000 owed will be bad, but it might guess (from experience perhaps) that 5% of debts will eventually be found to be irrecoverable.

When a business expects irrecoverable debts amongst its current debtors, but does not yet know which specific debts will be bad, it can make a **general allowance for debtors**.

Key term

A **general allowance for debtors** is an estimate of the percentage of debts which are not expected to be paid, based on prior experience.

An allowance for debtors provides for future irrecoverable debts, as a prudent precaution by the business. The business will be more likely to avoid claiming profits which subsequently fail to materialise because some debts turn out to be irrecoverable.

(a) When an allowance is first made, the amount of this initial allowance is charged as an expense in the profit and loss account of the business, for the period in which the allowance is created.

(b) When an allowance already exists, but is subsequently increased in size, the amount of the **increase** in allowance is charged as an **expense** in the profit and loss account, for the period in which the increased allowance is made.

(c) When an allowance already exists, but is subsequently reduced in size, the amount of the **decrease** in allowance is recorded as an item of **'income'** in the profit and loss account, for the period in which the reduction in allowance is made.

xam focus oint

In an exam you will often be required to calculate the increase or decrease in the allowance for debtors.

The balance sheet, as well as the profit and loss account of a business, must be adjusted to show an allowance for debtors.

ttention!

The value of debtors in the balance sheet must be shown after deducting the allowance for debtors.

This is because the net realisable value of all the debtors of the business is estimated to be less than their 'sales value'. After all, this is the reason for making the allowance in the first place. The net realisable value of debtors is the total value of debtors minus the allowance for debtors. Such an allowance is an example of the **prudence concept**, discussed in detail in Chapter 3.

In the example above the newly created allowance for debtors at 30 June 20X5 will be 5% of £50,000 = £2,500. This means that although total debtors are £50,000, eventual payment of only £47,500 is expected.

(a) In the P & L account, the newly created allowance of £2,500 will be shown as an expense.
(b) In the balance sheet, debtors will be shown as:

	£
Total debtors at 30 June 20X5	50,000
Less allowance for debtors	2,500
	47,500

Double entry

		£	£
DEBIT	Allowance for debtors (P&L)	2,500	
CREDIT	Allowance for debtors (B/S)		2,500

2.1 Example: Allowance for debtors

Corin Flakes owns and runs the Aerobic Health Foods Shop in Dundee. He commenced trading on 1 January 20X1, selling health foods to customers, most of whom make use of a credit facility that Corin offers. (Customers are allowed to purchase up to £200 of goods on credit but must repay a certain proportion of their outstanding debt every month.)

This credit system gives rise to a large number of bad debts, and Corin Flake's results for his first three years of operations are as follows.

Year to 31 December 20X1
Gross profit	£27,000
Irrecoverable debts written off	£8,000
Debts owed by customers as at 31 December 20X1	£40,000
Allowance for debtors	2½% of outstanding debtors
Other expenses	£20,000

Year to 31 December 20X2
Gross profit	£45,000
Irrecoverable debts written off	£10,000
Debts owed by customers as at 31 December 20X2	£50,000
Allowance for debtors	2½% of outstanding debtors
Other expenses	£28,750

Year to 31 December 20X3
Gross profit	£60,000
Irrecoverable debts written off	£11,000
Debts owed by customers as at 31 December 20X3	£30,000
Allowance for debtors	3% of outstanding debtors
Other expenses	£32,850

Required

For each of these three years, prepare the profit and loss account of the business, and state the value of debtors appearing in the balance sheet as at 31 December.

Solution

AEROBIC HEALTH FOOD SHOP
PROFIT AND LOSS ACCOUNTS FOR THE YEARS ENDED 31 DECEMBER

	20X1		*20X2*		*20X3*	
	£	£	£	£	£	£
Gross profit		27,000		45,000		60,000
Sundry income : reduction in allowance for debtors*						350
						60,350
Expenses:						
Irrecoverable debts written off	8,000		10,000		11,000	
Increase in allowance for debtors*	1,000		250		–	
Other expenses	20,000		28,750		32,850	
		29,000		39,000		43,850
Net(loss)/profit		(2,000)		6,000		16,500

*At 1 January 20X1 when Corin began trading the allowance for debtors was nil. At 31 December 20X1 the allowance required was 2½% of £40,000 = £1,000. The increase in the allowance is therefore £1,000. At 31 December 20X2 the allowance required was 2½% of £50,000 = £1,250. The 20X1 allowance must therefore be increased by £250. At 31 December 20X3 the allowance required is 3% × £30,000 = £900. The 20X2 allowance is therefore reduced by £350.

VALUE OF DEBTORS IN THE BALANCE SHEET

	As at 31.12.20X1	*As at 31.12.20X2*	*As at 31.12.20X3*
	£	£	£
Total value of debtors	40,000	50,000	30,000
Less allowance for debtors	1,000	1,250	900
Balance sheet value	39,000	48,750	29,100

You should now try to use what you have learned to attempt a solution to the following exercise, which involves preparing a trading, profit and loss account and balance sheet.

The financial affairs of Newbegin Tools prior to the commencement of trading were as follows.

NEWBEGIN TOOLS
BALANCE SHEET AS AT 1 AUGUST 20X5

	£	£
Fixed assets		
Motor vehicle	2,000	
Shop fittings	3,000	
		5,000
Current assets		
Stocks	12,000	
Cash	1,000	
	13,000	
Current liabilities		
Bank overdraft	2,000	
Trade creditors	4,000	
	6,000	
Net current assets		7,000
		12,000
Financed by		
Capital		12,000

At the end of six months the business had made the following transactions.

(a) Goods were purchased on credit at a gross amount of £9,800. Payments made to creditors totalled £7,600.

(b) Closing stocks of goods were valued at £5,450.

(c) Cash sales and credit sales together totalled £27,250.

(d) Outstanding debtors' balances at 31 January 20X6 amounted to £3,250 of which £250 were to be written off.

(e) An allowance for debtors is to be made amounting to 2% of the remaining outstanding debtors.

(f) Cash payments were made in respect of the following expenses.

		£
(i)	Stationery, postage and wrapping	500
(ii)	Telephone charges	200
(iii)	Electricity	600
(iv)	Cleaning and refreshments	150

(g) Cash drawings by the proprietor, Alf Newbegin, amounted to £6,000.

(h) The outstanding overdraft balance as at 1 August 20X5 was paid off. Interest charges and bank charges on the overdraft amounted to £40.

Alf Newbegin knew the balance of cash on hand at 31 January 20X6 but he wanted to know if the business had made a profit for the six months that it had been trading, and so he asked his friend, Harry Oldhand, if he could tell him.

Prepare the trading, profit and loss account of Newbegin Tools for the six months to 31 January 20X6 and a balance sheet as at that date.

The trading, profit and loss account should be fairly straightforward.

NEWBEGIN TOOLS
TRADING AND PROFIT AND LOSS ACCOUNT
FOR THE SIX MONTHS ENDED 31 JANUARY 20X6

	£	£
Sales		27,250
Opening stocks	12,000	
Purchases	9,800	
	21,800	
Less closing stocks	5,450	
Cost of goods sold		16,350
Gross profit		10,900
Electricity (note (a))	600	
Stationery, postage and wrapping	500	
Irrecoverable debts written off	250	
Allowance for debtors (note (b))	60	
Telephone charges	200	
Cleaning and refreshments	150	
Interest and bank charges	40	
		1,800
Net profit		9,100

Notes

(a)   Expenses are grouped into sales and distribution expenses (here assumed to be electricity, stationery and postage, bad debts and provision for doubtful debts) administration expenses (here assumed to be telephone charges and cleaning) and finance charges.

(b)   2% of £3,000 = £60.

The preparation of a balance sheet is not so easy, because we must calculate the value of creditors and cash in hand.

(a)   *Creditors as at 31 January 20X6*

The amount owing to creditors is the sum of the amount owing at the beginning of the period, plus the cost of purchases during the period, less the payments already made for purchases. (What is still owed is the total amount of costs incurred less payments already made.)

	£
Creditors as at 1 August 20X5	4,000
Add purchases during the period	9,800
	13,800
Less payments to creditors during the period	(7,600)
	6,200

(b)   *Cash at bank and in hand at 31 January 20X6*

This too requires a fairly lengthy calculation. You need to identify cash payments received and cash payments made.

(i)   *Cash received from sales*

	£
Total sales in the period	27,250
Add debtors as at 1 August 20X5	0
	27,250
Less unpaid debts as at 31 January 20X6	3,250
Cash received	24,000

	(ii)	Cash paid	£
		Trade creditors	7,600
		Stationery, postage and wrapping	500
		Telephone charges	200
		Electricity	600
		Cleaning and refreshments	150
		Bank charges and interest	40
		Bank overdraft repaid	2,000
		Drawings by proprietor	6,000
			17,090

Note. It is easy to forget some of these payments, especially drawings.

	(iii)		£
		Cash in hand at 1 August 20X5	1,000
		Cash received in the period	24,000
			25,000
		Cash paid in the period	(17,090)
		Cash at bank and in hand as at 31 January 20X6	7,910

(c) When irrecoverable debts are written off, the value of outstanding debtors must be reduced by the amount written off. This is because the debtors are no longer expected to pay, and it would be misleading and absurd to show them in the balance sheet as current assets of the business for which cash payment is expected within one year. Debtors in the balance sheet will be valued at £3,000 less the allowance for debtors of £60 – ie at £2,940.

(d) Fixed assets should be depreciated. However, in this exercise depreciation has been ignored.

NEWBEGIN TOOLS
BALANCE SHEET AS AT 31 JANUARY 20X6

	£	£
Fixed assets		
Motor vehicles	2,000	
Shop fittings	3,000	
		5,000
Current assets		
Stocks	5,450	
Debtors	2,940	
Cash	7,910	
	16,300	
Current liabilities		
Trade creditors	(6,200)	
Net current assets		10,100
		15,100
Capital		
Capital at 1 August 20X5		12,000
Net profit for the period		9,100
		21,500
Less drawings		6,000
Capital at 31 January 20X6		15,100

The bank overdraft has now been repaid and is therefore not shown.

3 Accounting for irrecoverable debts and allowances

This section summarises the double entry required for writing off irrecoverable debts and setting up allowances.

3.1 Irrecoverable debts written off: ledger accounting entries

For irrecoverable debts written off, there is a irrecoverable debts account. The double-entry bookkeeping is fairly straightforward, but there are two separate transactions to record.

(a)   When it is decided that a particular debt will not be paid, the customer is no longer called an outstanding debtor, and becomes a irrecoverable debt. We therefore:

DEBIT   Irrecoverable debts account (expense)
CREDIT   Debtors account

(b)   At the end of the accounting period, the balance on the irrecoverable debts account is transferred to the P & L ledger account (like all other expense accounts):

DEBIT   P & L account
CREDIT   Irrecoverable debts account.

However, where an irrecoverable debt is subsequently recovered, the accounting entries will be as follows.

DEBIT   Cash account
CREDIT   Irrecoverable debts account (expense)

3.2 Example: Irrecoverable debts written off

At 1 October 20X5 a business had total outstanding debts of £8,600. During the year to 30 September 20X6:

(a)   Credit sales amounted to £44,000.
(b)   Payments from various debtors amounted to £49,000.
(c)   Two debts, for £180 and £420, were declared irrecoverable and the customers are no longer purchasing goods from the company. These are to be written off.

Required

Prepare the debtors account and the irrecoverable debts account for the year.

Solution

DEBTORS

	£		£
Opening balance b/f	8,600	Cash	49,000
Sales	44,000	Irrecoverable debts	180
		Irrecoverable debts	420
		Closing balance c/f	3,000
	52,600		52,600
Opening balance b/f	3,000		

IRRECOVERABLE DEBTS

	£		£
Debtors	180	P & L a/c: irrecoverable debts written off	600
Debtors	420		
	600		600

In the sales ledger, personal accounts of the customers whose debts are irrecoverable will be taken off the ledger. The business should then take steps to ensure that it does not sell goods on credit to those customers again.

3.3 Allowance for debtors: Ledger accounting entries

FAST FORWARD

Only the **movement** on the debtors allowance is debited or credited to irrecoverable debts in the profit and loss account.

An allowance for debtors is rather different. A business might know from past experience that, say 2% of debtors' balances are unlikely to be collected. It would then be considered prudent to make a general allowance of 2%. It may be that no particular customers are regarded as suspect and so it is not possible to write off any individual customer balances as irrecoverable debts. The procedure is then to leave the total debtors balances completely untouched, but to open up an allowance account by the following entries:

DEBIT   Irrecoverable debts (expense)
CREDIT   allowance for debtors (balance sheet)

ttention!

When preparing a balance sheet, the credit balance on the allowance account is deducted from the total debit balances in the debtors ledger.

In subsequent years, adjustments may be needed to the amount of the allowance. The procedure to be followed then is as follows.

(a)   Calculate the new allowance required.

(b)   Compare it with the existing balance on the allowance account (ie the balance b/f from the previous accounting period).

(c)   Calculate increase or decrease required.

  (i)   If a higher allowance is required now:

    CREDIT   Allowance for debtors
    DEBIT   P & L account

    with the amount of the increase.

  (ii)   If a lower allowance is needed now than before:

    DEBIT   Allowance for debtors
    CREDIT   P & L account

    with the amount of the decrease.

3.4 Example: Accounting entries for allowing for debtors

Alex Gullible has total debtors' balances outstanding at 31 December 20X2 of £28,000. He believes that about 1% of these balances will not be collected and wishes to make an appropriate allowance. Before now, he has not made any allowance for debtors at all.

On 31 December 20X3 his debtors balances amount to £40,000. His experience during the year has convinced him that an allowance of 5% should be made.

What accounting entries should Alex make on 31 December 20X2 and 31 December 20X3, and what figures for debtors will appear in his balance sheets as at those dates?

Solution

At 31 December 20X2

Allowance required   = 1% × £28,000
                       = £280

Alex will make the following entries:

DEBIT   P & L account   £280
CREDIT   Allowance for debtors   £280

In the balance sheet debtors will appear as follows under current assets.

	£
Sales ledger balances	28,000
Less allowance for debtors	280
	27,720

At 31 December 20X3

Following the procedure described above, Alex will calculate as follows.

	£
Allowance required now (5% × £40,000)	2,000
Existing allowance	(280)
∴ Additional allowance required	1,720

He will make the following entries:

DEBIT	P & L account (doubtful debts)	£1,720	
CREDIT	Allowance for debtors		£1,720

The allowance account will by now appear as follows.

ALLOWANCE FOR DEBTORS

20X2		£	20X2		£
31 Dec	Balance c/f	280	31 Dec	P & L account	280
20X3			20X3		
31 Dec	Balance c/f	2,000	1 Jan	Balance b/f	280
			31 Dec	P & L account	1,720
		2,000			2,000
			20X4		
			1 Jan	Balance b/f	2,000

For the balance sheet debtors will be valued as follows.

	£
Sales ledger balances	40,000
Less allowance for debtors	2,000
	38,000

In practice, it is unnecessary to show the total debtors balances and the allowance as separate items in the balance sheet. A balance sheet would normally show only the net figure (£27,720 in 20X2, £38,000 in 20X3).

Now try the following question on allowance for debtors for yourself.

Question
Allowance for debtors

Horace Goodrunning fears that his business will suffer an increase in defaulting debtors in the future and so he decides to make an allowance for debtors of 2% of outstanding debtors at the balance sheet date from 28 February 20X6. On 28 February 20X8, Horace decides that the allowance has been over-estimated and he reduces it to 1% of outstanding debtors. Outstanding debtors balances at the various balance sheet dates are as follows.

	£
28.2.20X6	15,200
28.2.20X7	17,100
28.2.20X8	21,400

You are required to show extracts from the following accounts for each of the three years above.

(a) Debtors
(b) Allowance for debtors
(c) Profit and loss

Show how debtors would appear in the balance sheet at the end of each year.

The entries for the three years are denoted by (a), (b) and (c) in each account.

DEBTORS (EXTRACT)

			£
(a)	28.2.20X6	Balance	15,200
(b)	28.2.20X7	Balance	17,100
(c)	28.2.20X8	Balance	21,400

ALLOWANCE FOR DEBTORS

			£			£
(a)	28.2.20X6	Balance c/f (2% of 15,200)	304	28.2.20X6	Profit and loss	304
			304			304
(b)	28.2.20X7	Balance c/f (2% of 17,100)	342	1.3.20X6	Balance b/f	304
				28.2.20X7	Profit and loss (note (i))	38
			342			342
(c)	28.2.20X8	Profit and loss (note (ii))	128	1.3.20X7	Balance b/f	342
	28.2.20X8	Balance c/f (1% of 21,400)	214			
			342			342
				1.3.20X8	Balance b/f	214

PROFIT AND LOSS (EXTRACT)

		£			£
28.2.20X6	Allowance for debtors	304			
28.2.20X7	Allowance for debtors	38			
			28.2.20X8	Allowance for debtors	128

Notes

(i)   The increase in the allowance is £(342 – 304) = £38
(ii) The decrease in the allowance is £(342 – 214) = £128

We calculate the net debtors figure for inclusion in the balance sheet as follows.

	20X6 £	20X7 £	20X8 £
Current assets			
Debtors	15,200	17,100	21,400
Less allowance for debtors	304	342	214
Balance sheet debtors	14,896	16,758	21,186

Exam focus point

> There was a question on irrecoverable debts and the allowance for debtors in December 2008. The examiner commented that this was one of the questions that was answered particularly badly. A similar question is shown below to demonstrate the correct technique.

3.5 Example: combined entries

Fatima's debtors at 31 May 20X7 were £723,800. The balance on the allowance for debtors account at 1 June 20X6 was £15,250. Fatima has decided to change the allowance for debtors to 1.5% of debtors at 31 May 20X7.

On 14 May 20X7 Fatima received £540 in final settlement of a debt written off during the year ended 31 May 20X6.

What total amount should be recognised for debtors in the profit and loss account for the year ended 31 May 20X7?

Solution

The exam question gave four options for 2 marks. However we will concentrate on calculating the correct answer.

First note the requirement's wording 'recognised for debtors in the profit and loss account'. This means that the examiner wants to know the total charge (or recovery) in respect of irrecoverable debts and the allowance for debtors.

Secondly consider the allowance for debtors.

	£
Closing provision required (723,800 × 1.5%)	10,857
Opening provision	(15,250)
Reduction needed	(4,393)

Thirdly, the amount received of £540 had already been written off the previous year and now needs to be credited to irrecoverable debts.

Total credit to profit and loss = 540 + 4,393
= 4,933

Chapter Roundup

- Irrecoverable debts are specific debts owed to a business which it decides are never going to be paid. They are written off as an expense in the profit and loss account.

- Allowances for debtors may be specific (an allowance against a particular debtor) or simply a percentage allowance based on past experience of irrecoverable debts. An increase in the allowance for debtors is shown as an expense in the profit and loss account.

  Trade debtors in the balance sheet are shown net of any debtors allowance.

- This section summarises the double entry required for writing off irrecoverable debts and setting up allowances.

- Only the **movement** on the debtors allowance is debited or credited to irrecoverable debts in the profit and loss account.

Quick Quiz

1   An irrecoverable debt arises in which of the following situations?

    A   A customer pays part of the account
    B   An invoice is in dispute
    C   The customer goes bankrupt
    D   The invoice is not yet due for payment

2   Irrecoverable debts are £5,000. Trade debtors at the year end are £120,000. If an allowance for debtors of 5% is required, what is the entry for irrecoverable debts and allowance for debtors in the profit and loss account?

    A   £5,000
    B   £11,000
    C   £6,000
    D   £10,750

3   An allowance for debtors of 2% is required. Trade debtors at the period end are £200,000 and the allowable for debtors brought forward from the previous period is £2,000. What movement is required this year?

    A   Increase by £4,000
    B   Decrease by £4,000
    C   Increase by £2,000
    D   Decrease by £2,000

4   If a debtors allowance is increased, what is the effect on the profit and loss account?

    A   Reduction in expenses
    B   Increase in expenses

5   What is the double entry to record an irrecoverable debt written off?

    A   Debit: expenses   Credit: trade debtors
    B   Debit: trade debtors   Credit: expenses

Answers to Quick Quiz

1   C

2   B   £5,000 + (5% × 120,000)

3   C   2% of £200,000 = £4,000. Therefore the allowable needs to be increased by £2,000.

4   B   The increase in the allowance is charged as an expense in the profit and loss account.

5   A   DEBIT   Irrecoverable debts account (expenses)
            CREDIT   Trade debtors

Now try the question below from the Exam Question Bank

Number	Level	Marks	Time
Q21	Examination	2	2 mins

Provisions and contingencies

Topic list	Syllabus reference
1 FRS 12 Provisions, contingent liabilities and contingent assets	D9(a)-(f)

Introduction

You are required here to consider accounting issues which are the subject of a financial reporting standard (FRS 12).

FRS 12 is an important standard that you will meet again later in your studies. At this stage, you need to understand the basic definitions and whether an item needs to be disclosed in the financial statements.

Study guide

Exam guide

These are extremely important topics that will feature in your future studies and so are highly likely to be examined.

Exam focus point

> At the 2009 ACCA Teachers' Conference, the examiner highlighted areas that are consistently answered badly in the exam. Provisions are one of those areas, so make sure you study this chapter closely.

1 FRS 12 Provisions, contingent liabilities and contingent assets

FAST FORWARD

> Financial statements must include **all the information necessary for an understanding of the company's financial position**. Provisions, contingent liabilities and contingent assets are 'uncertainties' that must be accounted for consistently if they are to achieve this understanding.

FRS 12 *Provisions, contingent liabilities and contingent assets* aims to ensure that appropriate **recognition** and **measurement** are applied to provisions, contingent liabilities and contingent assets and that **sufficient information** is disclosed in the **notes** to the financial statements to enable users to understand their nature, timing and amount.

1.1 Provisions

You will be familiar with provisions for depreciation and allowance for debtors from your earlier studies. The sorts of provisions addressed by FRS 12 are, however, rather different.

Before FRS 12, there was no accounting standard dealing with provisions. Companies wanting to show their results in the most favourable light used to make large **'one off' provisions** in years where a high level of underlying profits was generated. These provisions, often known as **'big bath'** provisions, were then available to shield expenditure in future years when perhaps the underlying profits were not as good.

In other words, **provisions were used for profit smoothing**. Profit smoothing is misleading.

Points to note

> **The key aim of FRS 12 is to ensure that** provisions are made only where there are valid grounds for them.

FRS 12 views a provision as a **liability**.

A **provision** is a **liability** of uncertain timing or amount.

A **liability** is an obligation of an entity to transfer economic benefits as a result of past transactions or events. (FRS 12)

The FRS distinguishes provisions from other liabilities such as trade creditors and accruals. This is on the basis that for a provision there is **uncertainty** about the timing or amount of the future expenditure. Whilst uncertainty is clearly present in the case of certain accruals the uncertainty is generally much less than for provisions.

A provision is accounted for as follows:

DEBIT   Expense account
CREDIT   Provision account

1.1.1 Example of provisions

A business has been told by its lawyers that it is likely to have to pay £10,000 damages for a product that failed. The business duly set up a provision at 31 December 20X7. However the following year, the lawyers found that damages were more likely to be £50,000.

How is the provision treated in the accounts at:

(a)   31 December 20X7?
(b)   31 December 20X8?

(a)   The business needs to set up a provision as follows.

DEBIT: Damages   (P&L)   £10,000
CREDIT: Provision   (B/S)   £10,000

EXTRACT FROM PROFIT AND LOSS ACCOUNT

	£
Expenses:	
Provision for damages	10,000

EXTRACT FROM BALANCE SHEET

	£
Long-term liabilities	
Provision for damages	10,000

(b)   The business needs to increase the provision.

DEBIT: Damages   (P&L)   £40,000
CREDIT: Provision   (B/S)   £40,000

Do not forget that the provision account has already got a balance bought forward of £10,000, so that we only need to account for the **increase** in the provision.

EXTRACT FROM PROFIT AND LOSS ACCOUNT

	£
Expenses:	
Provision for damages	40,000

EXTRACT FROM BALANCE SHEET

	£
Long-term liabilities	
Provision for damages	50,000

1.1.2 Legal and constructive obligation

A provision is set up when there is a legal and constructive obligation. This means that the business is obliged to pay an amount as a result of this obligation. Examples include warranties, guarantees and sales returns.

Warranties are given on new items , for example cars, that they will be repaired free of charge if something goes wrong during an initial period of ownership, for example two years. Extended warranties may be granted on payment of a premium.

Guarantees may be given to a bank to help another company in a group to obtain a loan.

Sales returns may arise on a regular basis and it may be prudent to make a provision to cover these.

1.1.3 Example of sales returns

Apple Co has noticed that sales returns average 5% of sales during a year. It has decided to make a provision for these sales returns. During the year ended 30 April 20X8, sales are £500,000 and sales for the year ended 30 April 20X9 are projected to be £750,000. Set up a provision as at 30 April 20X8.

Solution

The provision is to be set up to meet **future** liabilities. It is likely that any returns for the year ended 30 April 20X8 have already been made. Therefore the provision must be based on projected sales for the following year ie 5% × £750,000 (£37,500).

1.2 Recognition

FRS 12 states that a provision should be **recognised** as a liability in the financial statements when:

- An entity has a **present obligation** (legal or constructive) as a result of a past event
- It is probable that a **transfer of economic benefits** will be required to settle the obligation
- A **reliable estimate** can be made of the obligation

1.2.1 Meaning of obligation

It is fairly clear what a legal obligation is. However, you may not know what a **constructive obligation** is.

Key term

> FRS 12 defines a **constructive obligation** as
>
> 'An obligation that derives from an entity's actions where:
>
> - By an established pattern of past practice, published policies or a sufficiently specific current statement the entity has indicated to other parties that it will accept certain responsibilities.
> - As a result, the entity has created a valid expectation on the part of those other parties that it will discharge those responsibilities.

 Question

Provision

In which of the following circumstances might a provision be recognised?

(a) On 13 December 20X9 the board of an entity decided to close down a division. The accounting date of the company is 31 December. Before 31 December 20X9 the decision was not communicated to any of those affected and no other steps were taken to implement the decision.

(b) The board agreed a detailed closure plan on 20 December 20X9 and details were given to customers and employees.

(c) A company is obliged to incur clean up costs for environmental damage (that has already been caused).

(d) A company intends to carry out future expenditure to operate in a particular way in the future.

(a) No provision would be recognised as the decision has not been communicated.
(b) A provision would be made in the 20X9 financial statements.
(c) A provision for such costs is appropriate.
(d) No present obligation exists and under FRS 12 no provision would be appropriate. This is because the entity could avoid the future expenditure by its future actions, maybe by changing its method of operation.

1.2.2 Probable transfer of economic benefits

For the purpose of the FRS, a transfer of economic benefits is regarded as **'probable'** if the event is **more likely than not** to occur. This appears to indicate a probability of more than 50%. However, the standard makes it clear that where there is a number of similar obligations the probability should be based on considering all the obligations, rather than one single item.

1.2.3 Example: Transfer of economic benefits

If a company has entered into a warranty obligation then the probability of transfer of economic benefits may well be extremely small in respect of one specific item. However, when considering all the warranties, the probability of some transfer of economic benefits is quite likely to be much higher. If there is a **greater than 50% probability** of some transfer of economic benefits then a **provision** should be made for the **expected amount**.

1.2.4 Measurement of provisions

oint to note

The amount recognised as a provision should be the best estimate of the expenditure required to settle the present obligation at the balance sheet date.

The estimates will be determined by the **judgement** of the entity's management supplemented by the experience of similar transactions.

Allowance is made for **uncertainty**.

Where the effect of the **time value of money** is material, the amount of a provision should be the **present value** of the expenditure required to settle the obligation. An appropriate **discount** rate should be used.

1.2.5 Provisions for restructuring

One of the main purposes of FRS 12 was to target abuses of provisions for restructuring. Accordingly, FRS 12 lays down **strict criteria** to determine when such a provision can be made.

ey term

FRS 12 defines a **restructuring** as:

A programme that is planned and is controlled by management and materially changes either:

• The scope of a business undertaken by an entity
• The manner in which that business is conducted.

The FRS gives the following **examples** of events that may fall under the definition of restructuring.

• The **sale or termination** of a line of business
• The **closure of business locations** in a country or region or the **relocation** of business activities from one country region to another
• **Changes in management structure**, for example, the elimination of a layer of management

- **Fundamental reorganisations** that have a material effect on the **nature and focus** of the entity's operations

The question is whether or not an entity has an obligation – legal or constructive – at the balance sheet date.

- An entity must have a **detailed formal plan** for the restructuring.
- It must have **raised a valid expectation** in those affected that it will carry out the restructuring by starting to implement that plan or announcing its main features to those affected by it

Point to note

> **A mere management decision is not normally sufficient.** Management decisions may sometimes trigger off recognition, but only if earlier events such as negotiations with employee representatives and other interested parties have been concluded subject only to management approval.

Where the restructuring involves the **sale of an operation** then FRS 12 states that no obligation arises until the entity has entered into a **binding sale agreement**. This is because until this has occurred the entity will be able to change its mind and withdraw from the sale even if its intentions have been announced publicly.

1.2.6 Costs to be included within a restructuring provision

The FRS states that a restructuring provision should include only the **direct expenditures** arising from the restructuring, which are those that are both:

- **Necessarily entailed** by the restructuring
- Not associated with the **ongoing activities** of the entity.

The following costs should specifically **not** be included within a restructuring provision.

- **Retraining** or relocating continuing staff
- **Marketing**
- **Investment in new systems** and distribution networks

1.2.7 Disclosure

Disclosures for provisions fall into two parts.

- Disclosure of details of the **change in carrying value** of a provision from the beginning to the end of the year
- Disclosure of the **background** to the making of the provision and the uncertainties affecting its outcome

1.3 Contingent liabilities

Now you understand provisions it will be easier to understand contingent assets and liabilities.

Key term

> FRS 12 defines a **contingent liability** as:
>
> - A possible obligation that arises from past events and whose existence will be confirmed only by the occurrence or non-occurrence of one or more uncertain future events not wholly within the entity's control; or
>
> - A present obligation that arises from past events but is not recognised because:
>   - It is not probable that a transfer of economic benefits will be required to settle the obligation
>   - Or the amount of the obligation cannot be measured with sufficient reliability.

As a rule of thumb, probable means more than 50% likely. **If an obligation is probable, it is not a contingent liability** – instead, a **provision is needed**.

1.3.1 Treatment of contingent liabilities

Contingent liabilities **should not be recognised in financial statements** but they **should be disclosed**. The required disclosures are:

- A brief description of the nature of the contingent liability
- An estimate of its financial effect
- An indication of the uncertainties that exist
- The possibility of any reimbursement

1.4 Contingent assets

Key term

FRS 12 defines a **contingent asset** as:

A possible asset that arises from past events and whose existence will be confirmed by the occurrence of one or more uncertain future events not wholly within the entity's control.

A contingent asset must not be recognised. Only when the realisation of the related economic benefits is **virtually certain** should recognition take place. At that point, **the asset is no longer a contingent asset**!

1.5 When to provide

Before trying Question 4, study the flow chart, taken from FRS 12, which is a good summary of the requirements of the standard.

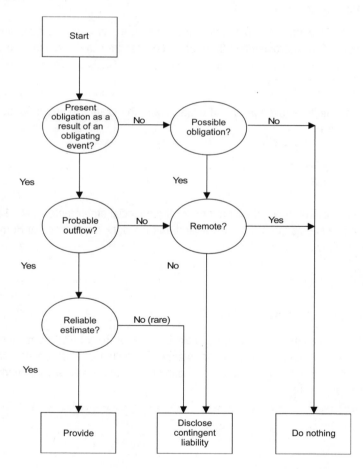

Question

During 20X9 Smack Ltd gives a guarantee of certain borrowings of Pony Ltd, whose financial condition at that time is sound. During 20Y0, the financial condition of Pony Ltd deteriorates and at 30 June 20Y0 Pony Ltd files for protection from its creditors.

What accounting treatment is required:

(a)　At 31 December 20X9?
(b)　At 31 December 20Y0?

Answer

(a)　At 31 December 20X9

There is a present obligation as a result of a past obligating event. The obligating event is the giving of the guarantee, which gives rise to a legal obligation. However, at 31 December 20X9 no transfer of economic benefits is probable in settlement of the obligation.

No provision is recognised. The guarantee is disclosed as a contingent liability unless the probability of any transfer is regarded as remote.

(b)　At 31 December 20Y0

As above, there is a present obligation as a result of a past obligating event, namely the giving of the guarantee.

At 31 December 20Y0 it is probable that a transfer of economic events will be required to settle the obligation. A provision is therefore recognised for the best estimate of the obligation.

Exam focus point

You will certainly be given **practical examples** in the exam. So you must be able to apply the theory to a given situation.

Question

Note to accounts

From the question above, draft the note to the financial statements as at 31 December 20X9. Assume that Pony Ltd is a subsidiary of Smack Ltd and that the bank borrowings of Pony Ltd at 31 December 20X9 were £2 million.

Answer

Note: Contingent liability

The company has given a guarantee to the bankers of Pony Ltd, a subsidiary of the company. This guarantee is in respect of borrowings totalling £2 million as at 31 December 20X9. However, Pony Ltd's financial condition is sound and the company does not foresee any payments becoming due under this guarantee at the current time.

- Financial statements must include **all the information necessary for an understanding of the company's financial position**. Provisions, contingent liabilities and contingent assets are 'uncertainties' that must be accounted for consistently if they are to achieve this understanding.

Quick Quiz

1   A company is being sued for £10,000 by a customer. The company's lawyers reckon that it is likely that the claim will be upheld. Legal fees are currently £5,000.

How should the company account for this?

A   Provision
B   Contingent liability

2   Given the facts in 1 above, how much of a provision should be made if further legal fees of £2,000 are likely to be incurred?

A   £10,000
B   £5,000
C   £15,000
D   £12,000

3   A company has a provision for warranty claims b/f of £50,000. It does a review and decides that the provision needed in future should be £45,000. What is the effect on the financial statements?

	P & L account	Balance sheet
A	Increase expenses by £5,000	Provision £50,000
B	Increases expenses by £5,000	Provision £45,000
C	Decrease expenses by £5,000	Provision £50,000
D	Decrease expenses by £5,000	Provision £45,000

4   A contingent liability is always disclosed on the face of the balance sheet.

Is this statement

A   True
B   False

5   How does a company account for a contingent asset that is not probable?

A   By way of note
B   As an asset in the balance sheet
C   It does nothing

1   A

2   D   The legal fees currently incurred of £5,000 is a current liability and should already be included in the accounts. The provision is for the claim of £10,000 plus the additional legal fees of £2,000.

3   D

PROVISION ACCOUNT

	£		£
P&L account	5,000	Bal b/f	50,000
Bal c/f	45,000		
	50,000		50,000

Note. We are debiting provision account £5,000 and so crediting P&L £5,000. Therefore, we are **decreasing** expenses.

4   B   False. A contingent liability is disclosed by way of notes to the statements.

5   C

Now try the question below from the Exam Question Bank

Number	Level	Marks	Time
Q22	Examination	1	1 min

Preparing a trial balance

Control accounts

Introduction

So far in this text we have assumed that the bookkeeping and double entry (and subsequent preparation of financial accounts) has been carried out by a business without any mistakes. This is not likely to be the case in real life: even the bookkeeper of a very small business with hardly any accounting entries to make will be prone to human error.

If a debit is written as £123 and the corresponding credit as £321, then the books of the business are immediately out of balance by £198.

Once an error has been detected, it has to be corrected.

In this chapter and in the following two chapters, we explain how errors can be detected, what kinds of error might exist, and how to post corrections and adjustments to produce final accounts.

Study guide

		Intellectual level
D1	**Sales and purchases**	
(e)	Account for discounts allowed and discounts received	1
D8	**Debtors and creditors**	
(j)	Account for contras between trade debtors and creditors	1
(k)	Prepare, reconcile and understand the purpose of supplier statements	1
E3	**Control accounts and reconciliations**	
(a)	Understand the purpose of control accounts for debtors and creditors	1
(b)	Understand how control accounts relate to the double entry system	1
(c)	Prepare ledger control accounts from given information	1
(d)	Perform control account reconciliations for debtors and creditors	1
(e)	Identify errors which would be highlighted by performing a control account reconciliation	1
(f)	Identify and correct errors in control accounts and ledger accounts	1

Exam guide

These are important topics. You are likely to find questions on control accounts in the exam. The questions will mainly be computational, although you could be asked to explain the reasons for keeping a control account.

1 Discounts

FAST FORWARD

A discount is a reduction in the price of goods below the amount at which those goods would normally be sold to other customers of the supplier.

1.1 Types of discount

A distinction must be made between:

- **Trade discount**
- **Cash discount** (also known in business as **settlement discount**).

Key term

Trade discount is a reduction in the cost of goods owing to the nature of the trading transaction. It usually results from buying goods in bulk.

1.2 Examples of trade discount

(a) A customer might be quoted a price of £1 per unit for a particular item, but a lower price of, say, 95 pence per unit if the item is bought in quantities of, say, 100 units or more at a time.

(b) An important customer or a regular customer might be offered a discount on all the goods he buys, regardless of the size of each individual order, because the total volume of his purchases over time is so large.

1.3 Accounting for trade discounts

Trade discounts received are deducted from the cost of purchases. **Cash discounts received** are included as 'other income' of the period. **Trade discounts allowed** are deducted from sales and **cash discounts allowed** are shown as expenses of the period.

A trade discount is a reduction in the amount of money demanded from a customer.

(a) If a trade discount is received by a business for goods purchased from a supplier, the amount of money demanded from the business by the supplier will be net of discount (ie it will be the normal sales value less the discount).

(b) Similarly, if a trade discount is given by a business for goods sold to a customer, the amount of money demanded by the business will be after deduction of the discount.

Trade discounts should therefore be accounted for as follows.

(a) **Trade discounts received** should be deducted from the gross cost of purchases. In other words, the cost of purchases in the trading account will be stated at gross cost minus discount (ie it will be stated at the invoiced amount).

(b) **Trade discounts allowed** should be deducted from the gross sales price, so that sales for the period will be reported in the trading account at their invoice value.

1.4 Cash discounts received

Cash discount is a reduction in the amount payable to the supplier, in return for prompt payment.

When a business is given the opportunity to take advantage of a cash discount or a settlement discount for prompt payment, the decision as to whether or not to take the discount is a matter of financing policy, not of trading policy.

1.5 Example: Cash discounts received

Suppose that A buys goods from B, on the understanding that A will be allowed a period of credit before having to pay for the goods. The terms of the transaction might be as follows.

(a) Date of sale: 1 July 20X6
(b) Credit period allowed: 30 days
(c) Invoice price of the goods: £2,000 (the invoice will be issued at this price when the goods are delivered)
(d) Cash discount offered: 4% discount for prompt payment

A has the choice between:

(a) Holding on to his money for 30 days and then paying the full £2,000.
(b) Paying £2,000 less 4% – ie £1,920 now.

This is a financing decision about whether it is worthwhile for A to save £80 by paying its debts sooner, or whether it can employ its cash more usefully for 30 days, and pay the debt at the latest acceptable moment.

If A decides to take the cash discount, he will pay £1,920, instead of the invoiced amount £2,000. The cash discount received (£80) will be accounted for in the books of A as follows.

(a) In the trading account, the cost of purchases will be at the invoiced price (or 'full trade' price) of £2,000. When the invoice for £2,000 is received by A, it will be recorded in his books of account at that price, and the subsequent financing decision about accepting the cash discount is ignored.

(b) In the profit and loss account, the cash discount received is shown as though it were income received. There is no expense in the P & L account from which the cash discount can be deducted, and so there is no alternative other than to show the discount received as income.

In our example, we would have:

	£
Cost of purchase from B by A (trading account)	2,000
Discount received (income in the P & L account)	(80)
Net cost	1,920

Settlement discounts received are accounted for in exactly the same way as cash discounts received.

Double entry

		£	£
DEBIT	Total creditors	2,000	
CREDIT	Discount received		80
CREDIT	Cash account		1,920

In the payments section of the cash book, this will be posted to the columns as follows:

Date	Payee	Payment	Discount received	Purchase ledger
X.X.XX	B	1,920	80	2,000

Question

Soft Supplies Ltd recently purchased from Hard Imports Ltd 10 printers originally priced at £200 each. A 10% trade discount was negotiated together with a 5% cash discount if payment was made within 14 days. Calculate the following.

(a)   The total of the trade discount
(b)   The total of the cash discount

Answer

(a)   £200 (£200 × 10 × 10%)
(b)   £90 (£200 × 10 × 90% × 5%)

1.6 Cash discounts allowed

The same principle is applied in accounting for cash discounts or settlement discounts allowed to customers. Goods are sold at a trade price, and the offer of a discount on that price is a matter of financing policy for the business and not a matter of trading policy.

1.7 Example: Cash discounts allowed

X sells goods to Y at a price of £5,000. Y is allowed 60 days' credit before payment, but is also offered a cash discount of 2% for payment within 10 days of the invoice date.

X will issue an invoice to Y for £5,000 when the goods are sold. X has no idea whether or not Y will take advantage of the discount. In trading terms, and in terms of the amount charged in the invoice to Y, Y is a debtor for £5,000.

If Y subsequently decides to take the discount, he will pay £5,000 less 2% – ie £4,900 – ten days later. The discount allowed (£100) will be accounted for by X as follows:

(a)   in the trading account, sales will be valued at their full invoice price, £5,000;
(b)   in the profit and loss account, the discount allowed will be shown as an expense.

In our example, we would have:

	£
Sales (trading account)	5,000
Discounts allowed (P & L account)	(100)
Net sales	4,900

Double entry

		£	£
DEBIT	Cash account	4,900	
DEBIT	Discount allowed	100	
CREDIT	Total debtors		5,000

In the cash receipts section of the cash book, this will be posted to the columns as follows:

Date	Description	Total	Discount allowed	Sales ledger
X.X.XX	Y	4,900	100	5,000

Question

Discounts

You are required to prepare the trading, profit and loss account of Seesaw Timber Merchants for the year ended 31 March 20X6, given the following information.

	£
Goods in stock, 1 April 20X5	18,000
Purchases at gross cost	120,000
Trade discounts received	4,000
Cash discounts received	1,500
Goods in stock, 31 March 20X6	25,000
Cash sales	34,000
Credit sales at invoice price	150,000
Cash discounts allowed	8,000
Selling expenses	32,000
Administrative expenses	40,000
Drawings by proprietor, Tim Burr	22,000

Answer

SEESAW TIMBER MERCHANTS
TRADING, PROFIT AND LOSS ACCOUNT
FOR THE YEAR ENDED 31 MARCH 20X6

	£	£
Sales (note 1)		184,000
Opening stocks	18,000	
Purchases (note 2)	116,000	
	134,000	
Less closing stocks	25,000	
Cost of goods sold		109,000
Gross profit		75,000
Discounts received		1,500
		76,500
Expenses		
Selling expenses	32,000	
Administrative expenses	40,000	
Discounts allowed	8,000	
		80,000
Net loss transferred to balance sheet		(3,500)

Notes

1   £(34,000 + 150,000)
2   £(120,000 – 4,000)

3   Drawings are not an expense, but an appropriation of profit.

1.8 VAT and discounts

Point to learn!

When a discount is offered, then the VAT is **always** calculated on the discounted price, regardless of whether the discount is actually taken.

Therefore if a sales invoice shows total sales of £20,000 and a cash discount of 5% if paid within 30 days, the VAT is calculated on the discounted price of £19,000. So if VAT is at 15%, the VAT will be £2,850. This applies even if the customer does not pay within 30 days.

Exam focus point

The June 2008 exam included a question on recording discounts allowed. Remember that only cash discounts are recorded in the books, sales and purchases are recorded net of trade discounts. This question included both cash and trade discounts, and the examiner commented the students showed a 'lack of knowledge in the treatment of discounts'.

1.9 Supplier statements

A supplier will usually send a monthly statement showing invoices issued, credit notes, payments received and discounts given. It is **vitally important** that these statements are compared to the supplier's personal account in the purchase ledger. Any discrepancies need to be identified and any errors corrected.

A statement of account is reproduced below.

STATEMENT OF ACCOUNT

**Pickett (Handling Equipment) Limited
Unit 7, Western Industrial Estate
Dunford   DN2 7RJ**

Tel: (01990) 72101   Fax: (01990) 72980   VAT Reg No 982 7213 49

Accounts Department
Finstar Ltd
67 Laker Avenue
Dunford DN4 5PS

RECEIVED
1 JUN X1

Date: 31 May 20X1

A/c No: F023

Date	Details	Debit £ p	Credit £ p	Balance £ p
30/4/X1	Balance brought forward from previous statement			492 22
3/5/X1	Invoice no. 34207	129 40√		621 62
4/5/X1	Invoice no. 34242	22 72√		644 34
5/5/X1	Payment received - thank you		412 17√	232 17
17/5/X1	Invoice no. 34327	394 95√		627 12
18/5/X1	Credit note no. 00192		64 40√	562 72
21/5/X1	Invoice no. 34392	392 78		955 50
28/5/X1	Credit note no. 00199		107 64√	847 86
	Amount now due		£	847 86

Terms: 30 days net, 1% discount for payment in 7 days. E & OE

Registered office: 4 Arkwright Road, London E16 4PQ Registered in England No 2182417

The statement is received on 1 June 20X1 and is passed to Linda Kelly who is the purchase ledger clerk at Finstar Ltd. Linda obtains a printout of the transactions with Pickett (Handling Equipment) Ltd from Finstar's purchase ledger system. (The reason why Linda has made ticks on the statement and on the printout which follows will be explained below.)

FINSTAR LIMITED		PURCHASE LEDGER
ACCOUNT NAME:	PICKETT (HANDLING EQUIPMENT) LIMITED	
ACCOUNT REF:	PO42	
DATE OF REPORT:	1 JUNE 20X1	
Date	*Transaction* £	*(Debit)/Credit*
16.03.X1	Invoice 33004	350.70
20.03.X1	Invoice 33060	61.47
06.04.X1	Invoice 34114	80.05
03.05.X1	Invoice 34207	129.40 ✓
04.05.X1	Payment	(412.17) ✓
06.05.X1	Invoice 34242	22.72 ✓
19.05.X1	Invoice 34327	394.95 ✓
19.05.X1	Credit note 00192	(64.40) ✓
28.05.X1	Payment	(117.77)
30.05.X1	Credit note 00199	(107.64) ✓
	Balance	337.31

The purchase ledger of Finstar shows a balance due to Pickett of £337.31, while Pickett's statement shows a balance due of £847.86.

1.9.1 Supplier statement reconciliations

Linda wants to be sure that her purchase ledger record for Pickett is correct and so she prepares a **supplier statement reconciliation**.

These are the steps to follow.

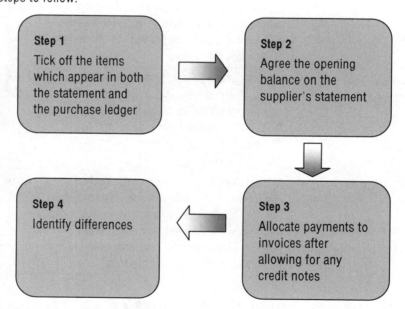

Step 1
Tick off the items which appear in both the statement and the purchase ledger

Step 2
Agree the opening balance on the supplier's statement

Step 3
Allocate payments to invoices after allowing for any credit notes

Step 4
Identify differences

1.9.2 Example: Supplier reconciliation

Linda applies the above steps to Pickett's statement.

Step 1   The common items have been ticked off on the statement and purchase ledger above.

Step 2   The balance brought forward at 30.4.X1 consists of three invoices.

		£
33004		350.70
33060		61.47
34114		80.05
		492.22

Step 3   Invoices 33004 and 33060 were paid on 4 May and 34114 was part of the payment on 28 May.

Step 4   Pickett's statement does not show the payment of £117.77 made on 28 May. However this is reasonable, as the cheque was probably still in the post. The statement also shows an invoice 34392 dated 21 May, which is not in the purchase ledger. This is surprising. Finstar needs to check if the invoice has been received (using the purchase day book), if so has it been posted to the wrong account? If it has not been received, Linda will need to contact Pickett and ask for a duplicate.

SUPPLIER STATEMENT RECONCILIATION
ACCOUNT: PICKETT (HANDLING EQUIPMENT) LTD (PO42)

	£
Balance per supplier's statement	847.86
Less: Payment (28 May) not on statement	(117.77)
Invoice (supplier no 34392) on statement, not on purchase ledger	(392.78)
Balance per purchase ledger	337.31

1.9.3 The reasons for reconciling items

Reconciling items may occur as a result of the following items.

Reconciling item	Effect	Status
Payments in transit	A payment will go in the purchase ledger when the cheque is issued or when a bank transfer instruction is made. There will be delay (postal, processing) before this payment is entered in the records of the supplier. Any statement of account received by post will also be out of date by the length of time taken to deliver it.	Timing difference
Omitted invoices and credit notes	Invoices or credit notes may appear in the ledger of one business but not in that of the other due to error or omission. However, the most common reason will be a timing difference in recording the items in the different ledgers.	Error or omission or timing difference
Other errors	Addition errors can occur, particularly if a statement of account is prepared manually. Invoice, credit note or payment amounts can be misposted. Regular reconciliation of supplier statements will minimise the possibility of missing such errors.	Error

2 What are control accounts?

FAST FORWARD   A control account keeps a total record of a number of individual items. It is an **impersonal** account which is part of the double entry system.

2.1 Definitions

> A **control account** is an account in the nominal ledger in which a record is kept of the total value of a number of similar but individual items. Control accounts are used chiefly for debtors and creditors.
>
> A **debtors control account** (debtors account or total debtors account) is an account in which records are kept of transactions involving all debtors in total. The balance on the debtors control account at any time will be the total amount due to the business at that time from its debtors.
>
> A **creditors control account** (creditors account or total creditors account) is an account in which records are kept of transactions involving all creditors in total, and the balance on this account at any time will be the total amount owed by the business at that time to its creditors.

Although control accounts are used mainly in accounting for debtors and creditors, they can also be kept for other items, such as stocks of goods, wages and salaries. The first important idea to remember, however, is that a control account is an account which keeps a total record for a collective item (eg debtors) which in reality consists of many individual items (eg individual debtors).

A control account is an (impersonal) ledger account which will appear in the nominal ledger. Before we look at the reasons for having control accounts, we will first look at how they are made up.

2.2 Control accounts and personal accounts

The personal accounts of individual debtors are kept in the sales ledger, and the amount owed by each debtor will be a balance on his personal account. The amount owed by all the debtors together will be a balance on the debtors control account.

At any time the balance on the debtors control account should be equal to the sum of the individual balances on the personal accounts in the sales ledger.

For example, if a business has three debtors, A Arnold who owes £80, B Bagshaw who owes £310 and C Cloning who owes £200, the debit balances on the various accounts would be:

Sales ledger (personal accounts)

	£
A Arnold	80
B Bagshaw	310
C Cloning	200
	590

Nominal ledger – debtors control account   590

What has happened here is that the three entries of £80, £310 and £200 were first entered into the sales day book. They were also recorded in the three personal accounts of Arnold, Bagshaw and Cloning in the sales ledger – but remember that this **is not part** of the double entry system (see Chapter 5).

Later, the **total** of £590 is posted from the sales day book into the debtors (control) account. It is fairly obvious that if you add up all the debit figures on the personal accounts, they also total £590, as shown above.

3 The operation of control accounts

The two most important **control accounts** are those for **debtors** and **creditors**. They are part of the double entry system.

3.1 Example: Accounting for debtors

Reference numbers are shown in the accounts to illustrate the cross-referencing that is needed, and in the example Reference numbers beginning:

(a) SDB, refer to a page in the sales day book

(b) SL, refer to a particular account in the sales ledger

(c) NL, refer to a particular account in the nominal ledger

(d) CB, refer to a page in the cash book.

At 1 July 20X2, the Outer Business Company had no debtors at all. During July, the following transactions affecting credit sales and customers occurred.

(a) July 3: invoiced A Arnold for the sale on credit of hardware goods: £100

(b) July 11: invoiced B Bagshaw for the sale on credit of electrical goods: £150

(c) July 15: invoiced C Cloning for the sale on credit of hardware goods: £250

(d) July 10: received payment from A Arnold of £90, in settlement of his debt in full, having taken a permitted discount of £10 for payment within seven days

(e) July 18: received a payment of £72 from B Bagshaw in part settlement of £80 of his debt. A discount of £8 was allowed for payment within seven days of invoice

(f) July 28: received a payment of £120 from C Cloning, who was unable to claim any discount.

Account numbers are as follows:

SL 4	Personal account: A Arnold
SL 9	Personal account: B Bagshaw
SL 13	Personal account: C Cloning
NL 6	Debtors control account
NL 7	Discounts allowed
NL 21	Sales: hardware
NL 22	Sales: electrical
NL 1	Cash control account

The accounting entries, suitably dated, would be as follows.

SALES DAY BOOK   SDB 35

Date 20X2	Name	Reference	Total £	Hardware £	Electrical £
July 3	A Arnold	SL 4 Dr	100.00	100.00	
11	B Bagshaw	SL 9 Dr	150.00		150.00
15	C Cloning	SL13 Dr	250.00	250.00	
			500.00	350.00	150.00
			NL 6 Dr	NL 21 Cr	NL 22 Cr

Note. The personal accounts in the sales ledger are debited on the day the invoices are sent out. The double entry in the ledger accounts might be made at the end of each day, week or month; here it is made at the end of the month, by posting from the sales day book as follows.

			£	£
DEBIT	NL 6	Debtors control account	500	
CREDIT	NL 21	Sales: hardware		350
	NL 22	Sales: electrical		150

CASH BOOK EXTRACT

RECEIPTS CASH BOOK – JULY 20X2

CB 23

Date 20X2	Narrative	Reference	Total £	Discount £	Debtors £
July 10	A Arnold	SL 4 Cr	90.00	10.00	100.00
18	B Bagshaw	SL 9 Cr	72.00	8.00	80.00
28	C Cloning	SL13 Cr	120.00	–	120.00
			282.00	18.00	300.00
			NL 1 Dr	NL 7 Dr	NL 6 Cr

At the end of July, the cash book is posted to the nominal ledger.

		£	£
DEBIT	Cash at bank	282.00	
	Discount allowed	18.00	
CREDIT	Debtors control account		300.00

The personal accounts in the sales ledger are memorandum accounts, because they are not a part of the double entry system.

MEMORANDUM SALES LEDGER
ARNOLD
A/c no: SL 4

Date 20X2	Narrative	Reference	£	Date 20X2	Narrative	Reference	£
July 3	Sales	SDB 35	100.00	July 10	Cash	CB 23	90.00
					Discount	CB 23	10.00
			100.00				100.00

B BAGSHAW
A/c no: SL 9

Date 20X2	Narrative	Reference	£	Date 20X2	Narrative	Reference	£
July 11	Sales	SDB 35	150.00	July 18	Cash	CB 23	72.00
					Discount	CB 23	8.00
				July 31	Balance	c/d	70.00
			150.00				150.00
Aug 1	Balance	b/d	70.00				

C CLONING
A/c no: SL 13

Date 20X2	Narrative	Reference	£	Date 20X2	Narrative	Reference	£
July 15	Sales	SDB 35	250.00	July 28	Cash	CB 23	120.00
				July 31	Balance	c/d	130.00
			250.00				250.00
Aug 1	Balance	b/d	130.00				

In the nominal ledger, the accounting entries can be made from the books of prime entry to the ledger accounts, in this example at the end of the month.

NOMINAL LEDGER (EXTRACT)
TOTAL DEBTORS (SALES LEDGER CONTROL ACCOUNT)
A/c no: NL 6

Date 20X2	Narrative	Reference	£	Date 20X2	Narrative	Reference	£
July 31	Sales	SDB 35	500.00	July 31	Cash and discount	CB 23	300.00
				July 31	Balance	c/d	200.00
			500.00				500.00
Aug 1	Balance	b/d	200.00				

Note. At 31 July the closing balance on the debtors control account (£200) is the same as the total of the individual balances on the personal accounts in the sales ledger (£0 + £70 + £130).

DISCOUNT ALLOWED
A/c no: NL 7

Date 20X2	Narrative	Ref	£	Date	Narrative	Ref	£
July 31	Debtors	CB 23	18.00				

CASH CONTROL ACCOUNT

A/c no: NL 1

Date 20X2	Narrative	Ref	£	Date	Narrative	Ref	£
July 31	Cash received	CB 23	282.00				

SALES – HARDWARE

A/c no: NL 21

Date	Narrative	Ref	£	Date 20X2	Narrative	Ref	£
				July 31	Debtors	SDB 35	350.00

SALES – ELECTRICAL

A/c no: NL 22

Date	Narrative	Ref	£	Date 20X2	Narrative	Ref	£
				July 31	Debtors	SDB 35	150.00

If we took the balance on the accounts shown in this example as at 31 July 20X2 the trial balance (insofar as it is appropriate to call these limited extracts by this name) would be as follows.

TRIAL BALANCE

	Debit £	Credit £
Cash (all receipts)	282	
Debtors	200	
Discount allowed	18	
Sales: hardware		350
Sales: electrical		150
	500	500

The trial balance is shown here to emphasise the point that a trial balance **includes** the balances on control accounts, but **excludes** the balances on the personal accounts in the sales ledger and purchase ledger.

3.2 Accounting for creditors

If you were able to follow the example above dealing with the debtors control account, you should have no difficulty in dealing with similar examples relating to purchases/creditors. If necessary refer back to revise the entries made in the purchase day book and purchase ledger personal accounts.

3.3 Entries in control accounts

Typical entries in the control accounts are listed below. Reference 'Jnl' indicates that the transaction is first lodged in the journal before posting to the control account and other accounts indicated. References SRDB and PRDB are to sales returns and purchase returns day books.

SALES LEDGER (DEBTORS) CONTROL

	Ref	£		Ref	£
Opening debit balances	b/f	7,000	Opening credit balances		
Sales	SDB	52,390	(if any)	b/f	200
Dishonoured bills or	Jnl	1,000	Cash received	CB	52,250
cheques			Discounts allowed	CB	1,250
Cash paid to clear credit			Returns inwards from		
balances	CB	110	debtors	SRDB	800
Interest charged on late paid	Jnl	30	Irrecoverable debts	Jnl	300
accounts					
Closing credit balances	c/f	90	Closing debit balances	c/f	5,820
		60,620			60,620
Debit balances b/f		5,820	Credit balances b/f		90

Note. Opening credit balances are unusual in the debtors control account. They represent debtors to whom the business owes money, probably as a result of the over payment of debts or for advance payments of debts for which no invoices have yet been sent.

PURCHASE LEDGER (CREDITORS) CONTROL

	Ref	£		Ref	£
Opening debit balances			Opening credit balances	b/f	8,300
(if any)	b/f	70	Purchases and other		
Cash paid	CB	29,840	expenses	PDB	31,000
			Interest paid on overdue	CB	35
			accounts		
Discounts received	CB	35	Cash received clearing		
Returns outwards to	PRDB		debit balances	CB	25
suppliers		60	Closing debit balances		
Closing credit balances	c/f	9,400	(if any)	c/f	45
		39,405			39,405
Debit balances	b/f	45	Credit balances	b/f	9,400

Note. Opening debit balances in the creditors control account would represent suppliers who owe the business money, perhaps because debts have been overpaid or because debts have been prepaid before the supplier has sent an invoice.

Posting from the journal to the memorandum sales or bought ledgers and to the nominal ledger may be effected as in the following example, where C Cloning has returned goods with a sales value of £50.

Journal entry	Reference	Dr	Cr
		£	£
Sales	NL 21	50	
To debtors' control	NL 6		50
To C Cloning (memorandum)	SL 13	–	50

Return of electrical goods inwards.

3.4 Contra entries

Sometimes a business may be both a debtor and a creditor. For example, you run a printing business and A Ltd supplies you with ink costing £5,000. You then print some leaflets for A Ltd for £2,500.

In your books, A Ltd is a creditor for £5,000 and a debtor for £2,500. Rather than paying A Ltd £5,000 and waiting for the £2,500 A Ltd owes you, you may agree with A Ltd to 'contra' the lower amount and just pay the balance of £2,500 to A Ltd.

The contra entry is recorded as follows.

		£	£
DEBIT	Creditors control account	2,500	
CREDIT	Debtors control account		2,500

Don't forget to record this in the memorandum sales and purchase ledgers. This clears the balance on the debtors account and reduces the balance on the creditors account to £2,500 (£5,000 – £2,500).

Question

Creditors control account

A creditors control account contains the following entries:

	£
Bank	79,500
Credit purchases	83,200
Discounts received	3,750
Contra with debtors control account	4,000
Balance c/f at 31 December 20X8	12,920

There are no other entries in the account. What was the opening balance brought forward at 1 January 20X8?

Answer

	£	£
Amounts due to creditors at 1 January (balancing figure)		16,970
Purchases in year		83,200
		100,170
Less: cash paid to creditors in year	79,500	
Discounts received	3,750	
Contra with debtors control	4,000	
		87,250
Amounts still unpaid at 31 December		12,920

Question

Sales discrepancy

The total of the balances in a company's sales ledger is £800 more than the debit balance on its debtors control account. Which one of the following errors could by itself account for the discrepancy?

A   The sales day book has been undercast by £800
B   Settlement discounts totalling £800 have been omitted from the nominal ledger
C   One sales ledger account with a credit balance of £800 has been treated as a debit balance
D   The cash receipts book has been undercast by £800

Answer

A   The total of sales invoices in the day book is debited to the control account. If the total is understated by £800, the debits in the control account will also be understated by £800. Options B and D would have the opposite effect: credit entries in the control account would be understated. Option C would lead to a discrepancy of 2 × £800 = £1,600.

3.5 Summary of entries

It may help you to see how the debtors ledger and debtors (control) account are used set out in flowchart form.

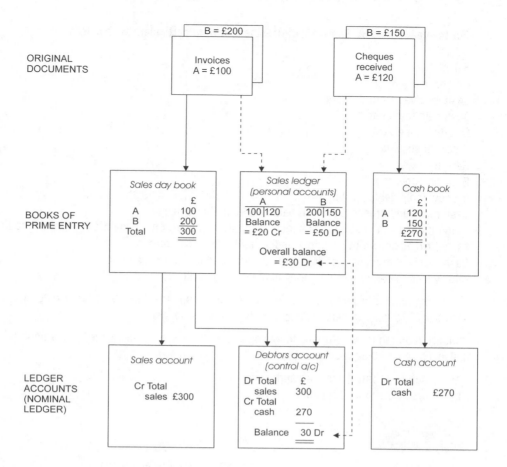

ints to
te

- Cash received is entered in the cash book. The total amount is then debited to the 'cash' or 'cash at bank' account in the nominal ledger and credited to the debtors control account.

- The debtors ledger is not part of the double entry system (it is not used to post the ledger accounts).

- Nevertheless, the total balance on the **debtors ledger** (ie all the personal account balances added up) should equal the balance on the **debtors control account**.

portant!

The diagram shows the personal accounts being written up from the original documents. An alternative way is to transfer the information from the books of prime entry. The system shown has the advantage of helping to reduce errors (as an error made in the books of prime entry will not be transferred to the personal accounts and so will be spotted in the control account reconciliation).

See now whether you can do the following question yourself.

 Question   **Control account transactions**

On examining the books of Exports Ltd, you ascertain that on 1 October 20X8 the debtors' ledger balances were £8,024 debit and £57 credit, and the creditors' ledger balances on the same date £6,235 credit and £105 debit.

For the year ended 30 September 20X9 the following particulars are available.

	£
Sales	63,728
Purchases	39,974
Cash received from debtors	55,212
Cash paid to creditors	37,307
Discount received	1,475
Discount allowed	2,328
Returns inwards	1,002
Returns outwards	535
Irrecoverable debts written off	326
Cash received in respect of debit balances in creditors' ledger	105
Amount due from customer as shown by debtors' ledger, offset against amount due to the same firm as shown by creditors' ledger (settlement by contra)	434
Cash received in respect of debt written off as bad in a previous period	94
Allowances to customers on goods damaged in transit	212

On 30 September 20X9 there were no credit balances in the debtors' ledger except those outstanding on 1 October 20X8, and no debit balances in the creditors' ledger.

You are required to write up the following accounts recording the above transactions bringing down the balances as on 30 September 20X9:

(a)   debtors control account; and
(b)   creditors control account.

Answer

(a)

DEBTORS CONTROL ACCOUNT

20X8		£	20X8		£
Oct 1	Balances b/f	8,024	Oct 1	Balances b/f	57
20X9			20X9		
Sept 30	Sales	63,728	Sept 30	Cash received from debtors	55,212
	Balances c/f	57		Discount allowed	2,328
				Returns	1,002
				Irrecoverable debts written off	326
				Transfer creditors control account	434
				Allowances on goods damaged	212
				Balances c/f	12,238
		71,809			71,809

(b)

CREDITORS CONTROL ACCOUNT

		£			£
20X8			20X8		
Oct 1	Balances b/f	105	Oct 1	Balances b/f	6,235
20X9			• 20X9		
Sept 30	Cash paid to creditors	37,307	Sept 30	Purchases	39,974
	Discount received	1,475		Cash	105
	Returns outwards	535			
	Transfer debtors control account	434			
	Balances c/f	6,458			
		46,314			46,314

Note. The double entry in respect of cash received for the irrecoverable debt written off in a previous period is:

DEBIT	Cash	£94
CREDIT	Irrecoverable debts account	£94

4 The purpose of control accounts

Cash books and day books are totalled periodically and the totals posted to the control accounts. At suitable intervals, the balances on the personal accounts are extracted and totalled. These balance totals should agree to the balance on the control account. In this way, errors can be located and corrected.

4.1 Reasons for having control accounts

The reasons for having control accounts are as follows.

(a) They provide a **check on the accuracy** of entries made in the personal accounts in the sales ledger and purchase ledger. It is very easy to make a mistake in posting entries, because there might be hundreds of entries to make. Figures might get transposed. Some entries might be omitted altogether, so that an invoice or a payment transaction does not appear in a personal account as it should. By comparing:

- The total balance on the debtors control account with the total of individual balances on the personal accounts in the sales ledger
- The total balance on the creditors control account with the total of individual balances on the personal accounts in the purchase ledger

    It is possible to identify the fact that errors have been made.

(b) The control accounts could also assist in the **location of errors**, where postings to the control accounts are made daily or weekly, or even monthly. If a clerk fails to record an invoice or a payment in a personal account, or makes a transposition error, it would be a formidable task to locate the error or errors at the end of a year, say, given the hundreds or thousands of transactions during the year. By using the control account, a comparison with the individual balances in the sales or purchase ledger can be made for every week or day of the month, and the error found much more quickly than if control accounts did not exist.

(c) Where there is a separation of clerical (bookkeeping) duties, the control account provides an **internal check**. The person posting entries to the control accounts will act as a check on a different person whose job it is to post entries to the sales and purchase ledger accounts.

(d) To provide debtors' and creditors' balances more quickly for producing a trial balance or balance sheet. A single balance on a control account is obviously **extracted more simply and quickly** than many individual balances in the sales or purchase ledger. This means also that the number of accounts in the double entry bookkeeping system can be kept down to a manageable size, since the personal accounts are memorandum accounts only and the control accounts instead provide the accounts required for a double entry system.

However, particularly in computerised systems, it may be feasible to use sales and purchase ledgers without the need for operating separate control accounts. In such a system, the sales or purchase ledger printouts produced by the computer constitute the list of individual balances as well as providing a total balance which represents the control account balance.

In the December 2008 exam, there was a question asking which of four errors would be revealed by a debtors control account reconciliation. The examiner commented that only 29% of students chose the correct answer.

4.2 Balancing and agreeing control accounts with sales and purchase (bought) ledgers

The control accounts should be **balanced regularly** (at least monthly), and the balance on the account agreed with the sum of the individual debtors' or creditors' balances extracted from the sales or bought ledgers respectively. It is one of the sad facts of an accountant's life that more often than not the balance on the control account does not agree with the sum of balances extracted, for one or more of the following reasons.

(a)   An **incorrect amount** may be **posted** to the control account because of a miscast of the total in the book of prime entry (ie adding up incorrectly the total value of invoices or payments). The nominal ledger debit and credit postings will then balance, but the control account balance will not agree with the sum of individual balances extracted from the (memorandum) sales ledger or purchase ledger. A journal entry must then be made in the nominal ledger to correct the control account and the corresponding sales or expense account.

(b)   A **transposition** error may occur in posting an individual's balance from the book of prime entry to the memorandum ledger, eg the sale to C Cloning of £250 might be posted to his account as £520. This means that the sum of balances extracted from the memorandum ledger must be corrected. No accounting entry would be required to do this, except to alter the figure in C Cloning's account.

(c)   A transaction may be recorded in the control account and not in the memorandum ledger, or vice versa. This requires an entry in the ledger that has been **missed out** which means a double posting if the control account has to be corrected, and a single posting if it is the individual's balance in the memorandum ledger that is at fault.

(d)   The sum of balances extracted from the memorandum ledger may be **incorrectly extracted** or **miscast**. This would involve simply correcting the total of the balances.

4.3 Example: Agreeing control account balances with the sales and bought ledgers

Reconciling the control account balance with the sum of the balances extracted from the (memorandum) sales ledger or bought ledger should be done in two stages.

(a)   Correct the total of the balances extracted from the memorandum ledger. (The errors must be located first of course.)

	£	£
Sales ledger total		
Original total extracted		15,320
Add difference arising from transposition error (£95 written as £59)		36
		15,356
Less		
Credit balance of £60 extracted as a debit balance (£60 × 2)	120	
Overcast of list of balances	90	
		210
		15,146

(b)   Bring down the balance before adjustments on the control account, and adjust or post the account with correcting entries.

DEBTORS CONTROL

	£		£
Balance before adjustments	15,091	Petty cash – posting omitted	10
		Returns inwards – individual posting omitted from control account	35
Undercast of total invoices issued in sales day book	100	Balance c/f (now in agreement with the corrected total of individual balances in (a))	15,146
	15,191		15,191
Balance b/f	15,146		

Question

April Showers sells goods on credit to most of its customers. In order to control its debtors collection system, the company maintains a debtors control account. In preparing the accounts for the year to 30 October 20X3 the accountant discovers that the total of all the personal accounts in the sales ledger amounts to £12,802, whereas the balance on the debtors control account is £12,550.

Upon investigating the matter, the following errors were discovered.

(a)   Sales for the week ending 27 March 20X3 amounting to £850 had been omitted from the control account.

(b)   A customer's account balance of £300 had not been included in the list of balances.

(c)   Cash received of £750 had been entered in a personal account as £570.

(d)   Discounts allowed totalling £100 had not been entered in the control account.

(e)   A personal account balance had been undercast by £200

(f)   A contra item of £400 with the purchase ledger had not been entered in the control account.

(g)   An irrecoverable debt of £500 had not been entered in the control account.

(h)   Cash received of £250 had been debited to a personal account.

(i)   Discounts received of £50 had been debited to Bell's sales ledger account.

(j)   Returns inwards valued at £200 had not been included in the control account.

(k)   Cash received of £80 had been credited to a personal account as £8.

(l)   A cheque for £300 received from a customer had been dishonoured by the bank, but no adjustment had been made in the control account.

Required

(a)   Prepare a corrected debtors control account, bringing down the amended balance as at 1 November 20X3.

(b)   Prepare a statement showing the adjustments that are necessary to the list of personal account balances so that it reconciles with the amended debtors control account balance.

Answer

(a)

DEBTORS CONTROL ACCOUNT

	£		£
Uncorrected balance b/f	12,550	Discounts omitted (d)	100
Sales omitted (a)	850	Contra entry omitted (f)	400
Bank: cheque dishonoured (l)	300	Irrecoverable debt omitted (g)	500
		Returns inwards omitted (j)	200
		Amended balance c/d	12,500
	13,700		13,700
Balance b/d	12,500		

Note. Items (b), (c), (e), (h), (i) and (k) are matters affecting the personal accounts of customers. They have no effect on the control account.

(b)   STATEMENT OF ADJUSTMENTS TO LIST OF PERSONAL ACCOUNT BALANCES

	£	£
Original total of list of balances		12,802
Add: debit balance omitted (b)	300	
debit balance understated (e)	200	
		500
		13,302
Less: transposition error (c): understatement of cash received	180	
cash debited instead of credited (2 × £250) (h)	500	
discounts received wrongly debited to Bell (i)	50	
understatement of cash received (k)	72	
		802
		12,500

Question   **Creditors control account**

ABC has a creditors control account balance of £12,500 at 31 December 20X6. However the extract of balances from the purchase ledger totals £12,800. Investigation finds the following errors: purchases for week 52 of £1,200 had been omitted form the control account; a supplier account of £900 had been omitted form the list of balances.

What is the correct purchases balance at 31 December 20X6?

A   £12,500
B   £13,400
C   £12,800
D   £13,700

Answer

D

CREDITORS CONTROL

	£		£
		Bal b/f	12,500
Bal c/f	13,700	Purchases – week 52	1,200
	13,700		13,700

Corrected list of balances:

	£
Original	12,800
Omitted account	900
	13,700

Chapter Roundup

- A discount is a reduction in the price of goods below the amount at which those goods would normally be sold to other customers of the supplier.

- **Trade discounts received** are deducted from the cost of purchases. **Cash discounts received** are included as 'other income' of the period. **Trade discounts allowed** are deducted from sales and **cash discounts allowed** are shown as expenses of the period.

- A control account keeps a total record of a number of individual items. It is an **impersonal** account which is part of the double entry system.

- The two most important **control accounts** are those for **debtors** and **creditors**. They are part of the double entry system.

- Cash books and day books are totalled periodically and the totals posted to the control accounts. At suitable intervals, the balances on the personal accounts are extracted and totalled. These balance totals should agree to the balance on the control account. In this way, errors can be located and corrected.

Quick Quiz

1   Which of the following accounting items may have control accounts in the nominal ledger?

    (i)   Debtors and creditors
    (ii)   Stock
    (iii)   Cash
    (iv)   Salaries and wages

    A   (i) and (ii)
    B   (i), (ii) and (iv)
    C   (i), (ii) and (iii)
    D   (i), (ii), (iii) and (iv)

2   Sales of £4,000 have been omitted from the debtors control account. What is the entry to correct this?

    A   Debit DCA   £4,000
    B   Credit DCA   £4,000

3   During a period, A Ltd has the following transactions on debtors control account. Sales £125,000, cash received £50,000, discounts allowed £2,000. The balance carried forward is £95,000. What was the opening balance at the beginning of the period?

    A   £22,000 debit
    B   £22,000 credit
    C   £18,000 debit
    D   £20,000 debit

4   An invoice amount has been incorrectly posted to the sales day book. The memorandum accounts are posted direct from the invoices. A debtors control account reconciliation will reveal this error. True or false?

5   A transaction for £10,000 of sales offers 2% trade discount and 5% cash discount. If both discounts are taken, how much is posted to discounts allowed?

    A   £490
    B   £690

1   D

2   A

3   A

DEBTORS CONTROL

	£		£
Bal b/f (bal figure)	22,000	Cash	50,000
Sales	125,000	Discounts allowed	2,000
		Bal c/f	95,000
	147,000		147,000

If you had answer B, you reversed the double entry and so produced a creditors control account. In answer D, you omitted the discounts allowed figure; while in answer C you put discounts allowed on the debit instead of the credit side of the control account.

4   True. However, if the memorandum accounts were posted from the sales day book, then the answer would be false.

5   A   The sales is recorded as £9,800 (£10,000 – £200 trade discount).
Discount allowed is then 5% × £9,800 = £490

Now try the questions below from the Exam Question Bank

Number	Level	Marks	Time
Q23	Examination	2	2 mins
Q24	Examination	2	2 mins
Q25	Examination	2	2 mins
Q26	Examination	2	2 mins

15

Bank reconciliations

Topic list	Syllabus reference
1 Bank statement and cash book	E4(b)
2 The bank reconciliation	E4(a), (c)-(f)
3 Worked examples	E4(c)-(f)

Introduction

It is very likely that you will have had to do a bank reconciliation at work. If not, you will probably have done one on your own bank account without even being aware of it.

The first two sections of this chapter explain why we need a bank reconciliation, and the sort of differences that need to be reconciled. The third section takes you through some examples of increasing complexity.

Study guide

		Intellectual level
E4	**Bank reconciliations**	
(a)	Understand the purpose of bank reconciliations	1
(b)	Identify the main reasons for differences between the cash book and the bank statement	1
(c)	Correct cash book errors and/or omissions	1
(d)	Prepare bank reconciliation statements	1
(e)	Derive bank statement and cash book balances from given information	1
(f)	Identify the bank balance to be reported in the final accounts	1

Exam guide

Bank reconciliations test your understanding of double entry. You are extremely likely to have a bank reconciliation question in the exam.

1 Bank statement and cash book

FAST FORWARD

In theory, the entries appearing on a business's **bank statement** should be exactly the same as those in the business cash book. The balance shown by the bank statement should be the same as the **cash book** balance on the same date.

The cash book of a business is the record of **how much cash the business believes** that it **has in the bank**. In the same way, you yourself might keep a private record of how much money you think you have in your own personal account at your bank, perhaps by making a note in your cheque book of income received and the cheques you write. If you do keep such a record you will probably agree that when your bank sends you a bank statement from time to time the amount it shows as being the balance in your account is rarely exactly the amount that you have calculated for yourself as being your current balance.

Why might your own estimate of your bank balance be different from the amount shown on your bank statement? There are three common explanations.

(a) **Error**. Errors in calculation, or recording income and payments, are more likely to have been made by you than by the bank, but it is conceivable that the bank has made a mistake too.

(b) **Bank charges or bank interest**. The bank might deduct charges for interest on an overdraft or for its services, which you are not informed about until you receive the bank statement.

(c) **Time differences**

(i) There might be some cheques that you have received and paid into the bank, but which have not yet been **'cleared'** and added to your account. So although your own records show that some cash has been added to your account, it has not yet been acknowledged by the bank - although it will be in a very short time when the cheque is eventually cleared.

(ii) Similarly, you might have made some payments by cheque, and reduced the balance in your account accordingly in the record that you keep, but the person who receives the cheque might not bank it for a while. Even when it is banked, it takes a day or two for the banks to process it and for the money to be deducted from your account.

If you do keep a personal record of your cash position at the bank, and if you do check your periodic bank statements against what you think you should have in your account, you are doing exactly the same thing that the bookkeepers of a business do when they make a bank reconciliation.

A **bank reconciliation** is a comparison of a bank statement (sent monthly, weekly or even daily by the bank) with the cash book. Differences between the balance on the bank statement and the balance in the cash book will be errors or timing differences, and they should be identified and satisfactorily explained.

2 The bank reconciliation

FAST FORWARD

Differences between the cash book and the bank statement arise for three reasons:

- Errors – usually in the cash book
- Omissions – such as bank charges not posted in the cash book
- Timing differences – such as unpresented cheques

2.1 The bank statement

It is a common practice for a business to issue a monthly statement to each credit customer, itemising:

(a)   The **balance** he owed on his account at the **beginning** of the month
(b)   **New debts** incurred by the customer during the month
(c)   **Payments** made by him during the month
(d)   The **balance** he owes on his account at the **end** of the month.

In the same way, a bank statement is sent by a bank to its short-term debtors and creditors - ie customers with bank overdrafts and customers with money in their account - itemising the balance on the account at the beginning of the period, receipts into the account and payments from the account during the period, and the balance at the end of the period.

However, remember that if a customer has money in his account, the bank owes him that money, and the customer is therefore a **creditor** of the bank (hence the phrase 'to be in credit' means to have money in your account). If a business has £8,000 cash in the bank, it will have a debit balance in its own cash book, but the bank statement will show a credit balance of £8,000. (**Think of sales and purchases: in the customer's books, the supplier is a creditor; in the supplier's books, the customer is a debtor.**)

2.2 Why is a bank reconciliation necessary?

A bank reconciliation is needed to identify and account for the differences between the cash book and the bank statement.

Question   Differences

These differences fall into three categories. What are they?

Answer

Error, bank charges or interest, time differences

2.3 What to look for when doing a bank reconciliation

The cash book and bank statement will rarely agree at a given date. If you are doing a bank reconciliation, you may have to look for the following items.

(a)   **Corrections and adjustments to the cash book:**

   (i)   Payments made into the account or from the account by way of standing order, which have not yet been entered in the cash book.

(ii)   Dividends received (on investments held by the business), paid direct into the bank account but not yet entered in the cash book.

(iii)   Bank interest and bank charges, not yet entered in the cash book.

(b)   **Items reconciling the correct cash book balance to the bank statement:**

(i)   Cheques drawn (ie paid) by the business and credited in the cash book, which have not yet been presented to the bank, or 'cleared' and so do not yet appear on the bank statement.

(ii)   Cheques received by the business, paid into the bank and debited in the cash book, but which have not yet been cleared and entered in the account by the bank, and so do not yet appear on the bank statement.

Exam focus point

> You are likely to have a bank reconciliation question. You may have to adjust the cash book, the bank balance or both.

3 Worked examples

FAST FORWARD

> When the differences between the bank statement and the cash book are identified, the cash book must be corrected for any errors or omissions. Any remaining difference can then be shown to be due to timing differences.

3.1 Example: Bank reconciliation

At 30 September 20X6, the balance in the cash book of Wordsworth Ltd was £805.15 debit. A bank statement on 30 September 20X6 showed Wordsworth Ltd to be in credit by £1,112.30.

On investigation of the difference between the two sums, it was established that:

(a)   The cash book had been undercast by £90.00 on the debit side*.

(b)   Cheques paid in not yet credited by the bank amounted to £208.20.

(c)   Cheques drawn not yet presented to the bank amounted to £425.35.

* *Note.* 'Casting' is an accountant's term for adding up.

Required

(a)   Show the correction to the cash book.

(b)   Prepare a statement reconciling the balance per bank statement to the balance per cash book.

Solution

		£
(a)		
	Cash book balance brought forward	805.15
	Add	
	Correction of undercast	90.00
	Corrected balance	895.15

		£	£
(b)			
	Balance per bank statement		1,112.30
	Add		
	Cheques paid in, recorded in the cash book, but not yet credited to the account by the bank	208.20	
	Less		
	Cheques paid by the company but not yet presented to the company's bank for settlement	425.35	
			(217.15)
	Balance per cash book		895.15

Question

On 31 January 20X8 a company's cash book showed a credit balance of £150 on its current account which did not agree with the bank statement balance. In performing the reconciliation the following points come to light.

	£
Not recorded in the cash book	
Bank charges	36
Transfer from deposit account to current account	500
Not recorded on the bank statement	
Unpresented cheques	116
Outstanding lodgements	630

It was also discovered that the bank had debited the company's account with a cheque for £400 in error. What was the original balance on the bank statement?

Answer

CASH ACCOUNT

	£		£
		Balance b/f	150
Transfer from deposit a/c	500	Charges	36
		Balance c/f	314
	500		500

	£
Balance per cash book	314
Add unpresented cheques	116
Less uncleared lodgements	(630)
Less error by bank	(400)
Balance per bank statement	(600)

Note that on the bank statement Dr is overdrawn, so the bank statement will show a balance of £600 debit.

You may well be asked to reconstruct opening figures in the exam. If so then you may need to reverse the usual workings, as illustrated in the example above.

Question

A company's bank statement shows £715 direct debits and £353 investment income not recorded in the cash book. The bank statement does not show a customer's cheque for £875 entered in the cash book on the last day of the accounting period. If the cash book shows a credit balance of £610 what balance appears on the bank statement?

A   £1,847 debit
B   £1,847 credit
C   £972 credit
D   £972 debit

A

	£	£
Balance per cash book		(610)
Items on statement, not in cash book		
Direct debits	(715)	
Investment income	353	
		(362)
Corrected balance per cash book		(972)
Item in cash book not on statement:		
Customer's cheque		(875)
Balance per bank statement		(1,847)

As the balance is overdrawn, this is a debit on the bank statement.

Question

Bank balance

Given the facts in the question above, what is the figure for the bank balance to be reported in the final accounts?

A   £1,847 credit
B   £972 credit
C   £972 debit
D   £1,847 debit

Answer

B   The figure to go in the balance sheet is the corrected cash book figure. This is £972 credit (or overdrawn). So the bank figure will appear in liabilities.

3.2 Example: More complicated bank reconciliation

On 30 June 20X0, Cook's cash book showed that he had an overdraft of £300 on his current account at the bank. A bank statement as at the end of June 20X0 showed that Cook was in credit with the bank by £65.

On checking the cash book with the bank statement you find the following.

(a)   Cheques drawn, amounting to £500, had been entered in the cash book but had not been presented.

(b)   Cheques received, amounting to £400, had been entered in the cash book, but had not been credited by the bank.

(c)   On instructions from Cook the bank had transferred interest received on his deposit account amounting to £60 to his current account, recording the transfer on 5 July 20X0. This amount had, however, been credited in the cash book as on 30 June 20X0.

(d)   Bank charges of £35 shown in the bank statement had not been entered in the cash book.

(e)   The payments side of the cash book had been undercast by £10.

(f)   Dividends received amounting to £200 had been paid direct to the bank and not entered in the cash book.

(g)   A cheque for £50 drawn on deposit account had been shown in the cash book as drawn on current account.

(h)   A cheque issued to Jones for £25 was replaced when out of date. It was entered again in the cash book, no other entry being made. Both cheques were included in the total of unpresented cheques shown above.

Required

(a) Indicate the appropriate adjustments in the cash book.

(b) Prepare a statement reconciling the amended balance with that shown in the bank statement.

Solution

(a) The errors to correct are given in notes (c) (e) (f) (g) and (h) of the problem. Bank charges (note (d)) also call for an adjustment.

CASH BOOK

		£			£
20X0			20X0		
Jun 30	Bank interest - reversal of incorrect entry (c)	60	Jun 30	Balance brought down	300
	Bank interest account (c)(Note 1)	60		Bank charges (d)	35
	Dividends paid direct to bank (f)	200		Correction of undercast (e)	10
	Cheque drawn on deposit account written back (g)	50		Balance carried down	50
	Cheque issued to Jones Cancelled (h) (Note 2)	25			
		395			395

Notes

1. Item (c) is rather complicated. The transfer of interest from the deposit to the current account was presumably given as an instruction to the bank on or before 30 June 20X0. Since the correct entry is to debit the current account (and credit the deposit account) the correction in the cash book should be to debit the current account with $2 \times £60 = £120$ - ie to cancel out the incorrect credit entry in the cash book and then to make the correct debit entry. However, the bank does not record the transfer until 5 July, and so it will not appear in the bank statement.

2. Item (h). Two cheques have been paid to Jones, but one is now cancelled. Since the cash book is credited whenever a cheque is paid, it should be debited whenever a cheque is cancelled. The amount of cheques paid but not yet presented should be reduced by the amount of the cancelled cheque.

(b) BANK RECONCILIATION STATEMENT AT 30 JUNE 20X0

	£	£
Balance per bank statement		65
Add: outstanding lodgements		
(ie cheques paid in but not yet credited) (b)	400	
deposit interest not yet credited (c)	60	
		460
		525
Less: unpresented cheques (a)	500	
less cheque to Jones cancelled (h)	(25)	
		475
Balance per corrected cash book		50

> **Exam focus point**
>
> Notice that in preparing a bank reconciliation it is good practice to begin with the balance shown by the bank statement and end with the balance shown by the cash book. It is this corrected cash book balance which will appear in the balance sheet as 'cash at bank'. But examination questions sometimes ask for the reverse order: as always, read the question carefully.

 Question

Bank reconciliation

From the information given below relating to PWW Ltd you are required:

(a) To make such additional entries in the cash at bank account of PWW Ltd as you consider necessary to show the correct balance at 31 October 20X2.

(b) To prepare a statement reconciling the correct balance in the cash at bank account as shown in (a) above with the balance at 31 October 20X2 that is shown on the bank statement from Z Bank plc.

CASH AT BANK ACCOUNT IN THE LEDGER OF PWW LIMITED

20X2 October		£	20X2 October		£
1	Balance b/f	274	1	Wages	3,146
8	Q Manufacturing	3,443	1	Petty Cash	55
8	R Cement	1,146	8	Wages	3,106
11	S Limited	638	8	Petty Cash	39
11	T & Sons	512	15	Wages	3,029
11	U & Co	4,174	15	Petty Cash	78
15	V plc	1,426	22	A & Sons	929
15	W Electrical	887	22	B Limited	134
22	X and Associates	1,202	22	C & Company	77
26	Y Limited	2,875	22	D & E	263
26	Z Limited	982	22	F Limited	1,782
29	ABC plc	1,003	22	G Associates	230
29	DEE Corporation	722	22	Wages	3,217
29	GHI Limited	2,461	22	Petty Cash	91
31	Balance c/f	14	25	H & Partners	26
			26	J Sons & Co Ltd	868
			26	K & Co	107
			26	L, M & N	666
			28	O Limited	112
			29	Wages	3,191
			29	Petty Cash	52
			29	P & Sons	561
		21,759			21,759

Z BANK PLC - STATEMENT OF ACCOUNT WITH PWW LIMITED

20X2 October		Payments £	Receipts £		Balance £
1					1,135
1	cheque	55			
1	cheque	3,146			
1	cheque	421		O/D	2,487
2	cheque	73			
2	cheque	155		O/D	2,715
6	cheque	212		O/D	2,927
8	sundry credit		4,589		
8	cheque	3,106			
8	cheque	39		O/D	1,483
11	sundry credit		5,324		3,841
15	sundry credit		2,313		
15	cheque	78			
15	cheque	3,029			3,047
22	sundry credit		1,202		
22	cheque	3,217			
22	cheque	91			941
25	cheque	1,782			
25	cheque	134		O/D	975
26	cheque	929			
26	sundry credit		3,857		
26	cheque	230			1,723
27	cheque	263			
27	cheque	77			1,383

20X2		Payments	Receipts	Balance
29	sundry credit		4,186	
29	cheque	52		
29	cheque	3,191		
29	cheque	26		
29	dividends on investments		2,728	
29	cheque	666		4,362
31	bank charges	936		3,426

Answer

(a)

CASH BOOK

		£			£
31 Oct	Dividends received	2,728	31 Oct	Unadjusted balance b/f (overdraft)	14
			31 Oct	Bank charges	936
			31 Oct	Adjusted balance c/f	1,778
		2,728			2,728

(b) BANK RECONCILIATION STATEMENT
AT 31 OCTOBER 20X2

	£	£
Corrected balance as per cash book		1,778
Cheques paid out but not yet presented	1,648	
Cheques paid in but not yet cleared by bank	0	
		1,648
Balance as per bank statement		3,426

Workings

1	Payments shown on bank statement but not in cash book* £(421 + 73 + 155 + 212) * Presumably recorded in cash book before 1 October 20X2 but not yet presented for payment as at 30 September 20X2	£861
2	Payments in the cash book and on the bank statement £(3,146 + 55 + 3,106 + 39 + 78 + 3,029 + 3,217 + 91 + 1,782 + 134 + 929 + 230 + 263 + 77 + 52 + 3,191 + 26 + 666)	£20,111
3	Payments in the cash book but not on the bank statement = Total payments in cash book £21,759 minus £20,111 =	£1,648

(Alternatively		£
	J & Sons	868
	K & Co	107
	O Ltd	112
	P & Sons	561
		1,648

4	Bank charges, not in the cash book	£936
5	Receipts recorded by bank statement but not in cash book: dividends on investments	£2,728
6	Receipts in the cash book and also bank statement (8 Oct £4,589; 11 Oct £5,324; 15 Oct £2,313; 22 Oct £1,202; 26 Oct £3,857; 29 Oct £4,186)	£21,471
7	Receipts recorded in cash book but not bank statement	None

Chapter Roundup

- In theory, the entries appearing on a business's **bank statement** should be exactly the same as those in the business cash book. The balance shown by the bank statement should be the same as the **cash book** balance on the same date.

- Differences between the cash book and the bank statement arise for three reasons:

    - Errors – usually in the cash book
    - Omissions – such as bank charges not posted in the cash book
    - Timing differences – such as unpresented cheques

- When the differences between the bank statement and the cash book are identified, the cash book must be corrected for any errors or omissions. Any remaining difference can then be shown to be due to timing differences.

Quick Quiz

1   Which of the following are common reasons for differences between the cash book and the bank statements?

    (i)   Timing differences
    (ii)   Errors
    (iii) Omissions
    (iv) Contra entries

    A   (i) and (ii)
    B   (i) and (iv)
    C   (ii), (iii) and (iv)
    D   (i), (ii) and (iii)

2   A cash book and a bank statement will never agree.

    Is this statement?

    A   True
    B   False

3   A bank statement shows a balance of £1,200 in credit. An examination of the statement shows a £500 cheque paid in per the cash book but not yet on the bank statement and a £1,250 cheque paid out but not yet on the statement. In addition the cash book shows deposit interest received of £50 but this is not yet on the statement. What is the balance per the cash book?

    A   £1,900 overdrawn
    B   £500 overdrawn
    C   £1,900 in hand
    D   £500 in hand

4   Comparing the cash book with the bank statements is called a ....
    (complete the blanks)

5   Why is it necessary to compare the cash book and bank statement?

Answers to Quick Quiz

1   D   Contra entries only occur between the debtors and creditors control accounts.

2   B   False. In very small businesses, with few transactions, the cash book and bank statement could well agree.

3   D

	£	£
Balance per bank statement		1,200
Add: outstanding lodgements	500	
deposit interest not yet credited	50	550
	1,750	
Less: unpresented cheques		(1,250)
Balance per cash book		500

4   Bank reconciliation

5   It highlights errors and omissions in the cash book and helps to prevent fraud. It also checks the bank figure and helps to spot any bank errors.

Now try the questions below from the Exam Question Bank

Number	Level	Marks	Time
Q27	Examination	2	2 mins
Q28	Examination	2	2 mins

Correction of errors

Topic list	Syllabus reference
1 Types of error in accounting	E2(a), (b)
2 The correction of errors	E2(d)-(e), E5(a)-(d)
3 Material errors	E2(c)

Introduction

This chapter continues the subject of errors in accounts. You have already learned about errors which arise in the context of the cash book or the sales and purchase ledgers and debtors and creditors control accounts.

Here we deal with errors that may be corrected by means of the journal or a suspense account. In addition we look at the correction of material errors from a **prior period**.

By the end of this chapter you should be able to prepare a set of final accounts for a sole trader from a trial balance after incorporating adjustments to profit for errors.

Study guide

		Intellectual level
E2	**Correction of errors**	
(a)	Identify the types of error which may occur in bookkeeping systems	1
(b)	Identify errors which would be highlighted by the extraction of a trial balance	1
(c)	Understand the provision of FRSs governing financial statements regarding material errors which result in prior period adjustments	1
(d)	Prepare journal entries to correct errors	1
(e)	Calculate and understand the impact of errors on the profit and loss account and balance sheet	1
E5	**Suspense account**	
(a)	Understand the purpose of a suspense account	1
(b)	Identify errors leading to the creation of a suspense account	1
(c)	Record entries in a suspense account	1
(d)	Make journal entries to clear a suspense account	1

Exam guide

Be prepared for theoretical questions on errors as well as questions asking you to correct errors.

Exam focus point

At the 2009 ACCA Teachers' Conference, the examiner highlighted suspense accounts and errors as areas that are consistently answered badly in the exam.

1 Types of error in accounting

FAST FORWARD

There are five main types of error. Some can be corrected by journal entry, some require the use of a suspense account.

1.1 Introduction

It is not really possible to draw up a complete list of all the errors which might be made by bookkeepers and accountants. Even if you tried, it is more than likely that as soon as you finished, someone would commit a completely new error that you had never even dreamed of! However, it is possible to describe five **types of error** which cover most of the errors which might occur. They are as follows.

- Errors of **transposition**
- Errors of **omission**
- Errors of **principle**
- Errors of **commission**
- **Compensating** errors

Some of these we have already looked at in the context of the cash book, sales and purchase ledgers and debtors and creditors control accounts.

Once an error has been detected, it needs to be put right.

(a) If the correction **involves a double entry** in the ledger accounts, then it is done by using a **journal entry** in the journal.

(b)   When the error **breaks the rule of double entry**, then it is corrected by the use of a **suspense account** as well as a journal entry.

In this chapter we will:

(a)   Look at the five common types of error
(b)   Review journal entries (which we briefly looked at earlier in this text)
(c)   Define a **suspense account**, and describe how it is used.

1.2 Errors of transposition

> An **error of transposition** is when two digits in an amount are accidentally recorded the wrong way round.

For example, suppose that a sale is recorded in the sales account as £6,843, but it has been incorrectly recorded in the total debtors account as £6,483. The error is the transposition of the 4 and the 8. The consequence is that total debits will not be equal to total credits. *Note: Differences arising from transposition errors are always divisible by 9. If you have a difference that is a multiple of 9, this might be an indication that you should be looking for a transposition error. For example, £6,843 – £6,483 = £360; £360 ÷ 9 = 40.*

1.3 Errors of omission

> An **error of omission** means failing to record a transaction at all, or making a debit or credit entry, but not the corresponding double entry.

Here are two examples.

(a)   If a business receives an invoice from a supplier for £250, the transaction might be omitted from the books entirely. As a result, both the total debits and the total credits of the business will be out by £250.

(b)   If a business receives an invoice from a supplier for £300, the purchase ledger control account might be credited, but the debit entry in the purchases account might be omitted. In this case, the total credits would not equal total debits (because total debits are £300 less than they ought to be).

1.4 Errors of principle

> An **error of principle** involves making a double entry in the belief that the transaction is being entered in the correct accounts, but subsequently finding out that the accounting entry breaks the 'rules' of an accounting principle or concept.

A typical example of such an error is to treat certain revenue expenditure incorrectly as capital expenditure.

(a)   For example, repairs to a machine costing £150 should be treated as revenue expenditure, and debited to a repairs account. If, instead, the repair costs are added to the cost of the fixed asset (capital expenditure) an error of principle would have occurred. As a result, although total debits still equal total credits, the repairs account is £150 less than it should be and the cost of the fixed asset is £150 greater than it should be.

(b)   Similarly, suppose that the proprietor of the business sometimes takes cash out of the till for his personal use and during a certain year these drawings amount to £280. The book-keeper states that he has reduced cash sales by £280 so that the cash book could be made to balance. This would be an error of principle, and the result of it would be that the drawings account is understated by £280, and so is the total value of sales in the sales account.

1.5 Errors of commission

Key term

Errors of commission are where the bookkeeper makes a mistake in carrying out his or her task of recording transactions in the accounts.

Here are two common errors of commission.

(a) **Putting a debit entry or a credit entry in the wrong account**. For example, if telephone expenses of £540 are debited to the electricity expenses account, an error of commission would have occurred. The result is that although total debits and total credits balance, telephone expenses are understated by £540 and electricity expenses are overstated by the same amount.

(b) **Errors of casting (adding up).** Suppose for example that the total daily credit sales in the sales day book of a business should add up to £28,425, but are incorrectly added up as £28,825. The total sales in the sales day book are then used to credit total sales and debit total debtors in the ledger accounts, so that total debits and total credits are still equal, although incorrect.

1.6 Compensating errors

Key term

Compensating errors are errors which are, coincidentally, equal and opposite to one another.

For example, two transposition errors of £540 might occur in extracting ledger balances, one on each side of the double entry. In the administration expenses account, £2,282 might be written instead of £2,822, while in the sundry income account, £8,391 might be written instead of £8,931. Both the debits and the credits would be £540 too low, and the mistake would not be apparent when the trial balance is cast. Consequently, compensating errors hide the fact that there are errors in the trial balance.

1.7 Summary: errors that can be detected by a trial balance

- Errors of transposition
- Errors of omission (if one-sided)
- Errors of commission (if one-sided, or two debit entries are made for example)

Other errors will not be detected by extracting a trial balance but may be spotted by other controls (such as bank or control account reconciliations).

2 The correction of errors

FAST FORWARD

Errors which leave total debits and credits in the ledger accounts in balance can be corrected by using **journal entries**. Otherwise a suspense account has to be opened first, and later cleared by a journal entry.

2.1 Journal entries

Some errors can be corrected by **journal entries**. To remind you, the format of a journal entry is:

Date	Reference	Debit £	Credit £
Account to be debited		X	
Account to be credited			X
(Narrative to explain the transaction)			

Exam focus point

As already indicated, in the exam you are often required to present answers in the form of journal entries.

The journal requires a debit and an equal credit entry for each 'transaction' – ie for each correction. This means that if total debits equal total credits before a journal entry is made then they will still be equal after the journal entry is made. This would be the case if, for example, the original error was a debit wrongly posted as a credit or vice versa.

Similarly, if total debits and total credits are unequal before a journal entry is made, then they will still be unequal (by the same amount) after it is made.

For example, a bookkeeper accidentally posts a bill for £40 to the rates account instead of to the electricity account. A trial balance is drawn up, and total debits are £40,000 and total credits are £40,000. A journal entry is made to correct the misposting error as follows.

1.7.20X7

| DEBIT | Electricity account | £40 | |
| CREDIT | Rates account | | £40 |

To correct a misposting of £40 from the rates account to electricity account.

After the journal has been posted, total debits will still be £40,000 and total credits will be £40,000. Total debits and totals credits are still equal.

Now suppose that, because of some error which has not yet been detected, total debits were originally £40,000 but total credits were £39,900. If the same journal correcting the £40 is put through, total debits will remain £40,000 and total credits will remain £39,900. Total debits were different by £100 *before* the journal, and they are still different by £100 *after* the journal.

This means that journals can only be used to correct errors which require both a credit and (an equal) debit adjustment.

2.2 Example: journal entries

Listed below are five errors which were used as examples earlier in this chapter. Write out the journal entries which would correct these errors.

(a)   A business receives an invoice for £250 from a supplier which was omitted from the books entirely.
(b)   Repairs worth £150 were incorrectly debited to the fixed asset (machinery) account instead of the repairs account.
(c)   The bookkeeper of a business reduces cash sales by £280 because he was not sure what the £280 represented. In fact, it was drawings.
(d)   Telephone expenses of £540 are incorrectly debited to the electricity account.
(e)   A page in the sales day book has been added up to £28,425 instead of £28,825.
(f)   The error of casting in Section 1.5 (b) above.

Solution

(a)
| DEBIT | Purchases | £250 | |
| CREDIT | Creditors | | £250 |

A transaction previously omitted.

(b)
| DEBIT | Repairs account | £150 | |
| CREDIT | Fixed asset (machinery) a/c | | £150 |

The correction of an error of principle. Repairs costs incorrectly added to fixed asset costs.

(c)
| DEBIT | Drawings account | £280 | |
| CREDIT | Sales | | £280 |

An error of principle, in which sales were reduced to compensate for cash drawings not accounted for.

(d)
| DEBIT | Telephone expenses | £540 | |
| CREDIT | Electricity expenses | | £540 |

Correction of an error of commission. Telephone expenses wrongly charged to the electricity account.

			£400	
(e)	DEBIT	Debtors		
	CREDIT	Sales		£400

The correction of a casting error in the sales day book.
(£28,825 − £28,425 = £400)

			£400	
(f)	DEBIT	Sales		
	CREDIT	Debtors		£400

Correction of error of commission.

2.3 Use of journal entries in examinations

Occasionally an examination question might ask you to 'journalise' a transaction (ie write it out in the form of a journal entry), even though the transaction is perfectly normal and nothing to do with an error. This is just the examiner's way of finding out whether you know your debits and credits. For example:

Question: A business sells £500 of goods on credit. Journalise the transaction.

Answer.

		£500	
DEBIT	Debtors		
CREDIT	Sales		£500

Goods to the value of £500 sold on credit.

No error has occurred here, just a normal credit sale of £500. By asking you to put it in the form of a journal, the examiner can see that you understand the double-entry bookkeeping.

2.4 Suspense accounts

Suspense accounts, as well as being used to correct some errors, are also opened when it is not known immediately where to post an amount. When the mystery is solved, the suspense account is closed and the amount correctly posted using a journal entry.

Key term

A **suspense account** is an account showing a balance equal to the difference in a trial balance.

A suspense account is a **temporary** account which can be opened for a number of reasons. The most common reasons are as follows.

(a)   A trial balance is drawn up which does not balance (ie total debits do not equal total credits).

(b)   The bookkeeper of a business knows where to post the credit side of a transaction, but does not know where to post the debit (or vice versa). For example, a cash payment might be made and must obviously be credited to cash. But the bookkeeper may not know what the payment is for, and so will not know which account to debit.

In both these cases, a temporary suspense account is opened up until the problem is sorted out. The next few paragraphs explain exactly how this works.

2.5 Use of suspense account: when the trial balance does not balance

When an error has occurred which results in an imbalance between total debits and total credits in the ledger accounts, the first step is to open a suspense account. For example, suppose an accountant draws up a trial balance and finds that, for some reason he cannot immediately discover, total debits exceed total credits by £162.

He knows that there is an error somewhere, but for the time being he opens a suspense account and enters a credit of £162 in it. This serves two purposes.

(a)   Because the suspense account now exists, the accountant will not forget that there is an error (of £162) to be sorted out.

(b)   Now that there is a credit of £162 in the suspense account, the trial balance balances.

When the cause of the £162 discrepancy is tracked down, it is corrected by means of a journal entry. For example, suppose it turned out that the accountant had accidentally failed to make a credit of £162 to purchases. The journal entry would be:

DEBIT	Suspense a/c	£162	
CREDIT	Purchases		£162

To close off suspense a/c and correct error.

Whenever an error occurs which results in total debits not being equal to total credits, the first step an accountant makes is to open up a suspense account. Three more examples are given below.

2.6 Example: Transposition error

The bookkeeper of Mixem Gladly Ltd made a transposition error when entering an amount for sales in the sales account. Instead of entering the correct amount of £37,453.60 he entered £37,543.60, transposing the 4 and 5. The debtors were posted correctly, and so when total debits and credits on the ledger accounts were compared, it was found that credits exceeded debits by £(37,543.60 – 37,453.60) = £90.

The initial step is to equalise the total debits and credits by posting a debit of £90 to a suspense account.

When the cause of the error is discovered, the double entry to correct it should be logged in the journal as:

DEBIT	Sales	£90	
CREDIT	Suspense a/c		£90

To close off suspense a/c and correct transposition error.

2.7 Example: Error of omission

When Guttersnipe Builders paid the monthly salary cheques to its office staff, the payment of £5,250 was correctly entered in the cash account, but the bookkeeper omitted to debit the office salaries account. As a consequence, the total debit and credit balances on the ledger accounts were not equal, and credits exceeded debits by £5,250.

The initial step in correcting the situation is to debit £5,250 to a suspense account, to equalise the total debits and total credits.

When the cause of the error is discovered, the double entry to correct it should be logged in the journal as:

DEBIT	Office salaries account	£5,250	
CREDIT	Suspense account		£5,250

To close off suspense account and correct error of omission.

2.8 Example: Error of commission

A bookkeeper might make a mistake by entering what should be a debit entry as a credit, or vice versa. For example, suppose that a credit customer pays £460 of the £660 he owes to Ashdown Tree Felling Contractors, but Ashdown's bookkeeper has debited £460 on the debtors account in the nominal ledger by mistake instead of crediting the payment received.

The total debit balances in Ashdown's ledger accounts would now exceed the total credits by 2 × £460 = £920. The initial step in correcting the error would be to make a credit entry of £920 in a suspense account. When the cause of the error is discovered, it should be corrected as follows.

DEBIT	Suspense account	£920	
CREDIT	Debtors		£920

To close off suspense account and correct error of commission.

In the debtors account in the nominal ledger, the correction would appear therefore as follows.

DEBTORS ACCOUNT

	£		£
Balance b/f	660	Suspense account: error corrected	920
Payment incorrectly debited	460	Balance c/f	200
	1,120		1,120

2.9 Use of suspense account: not knowing where to post a transaction

Another use of suspense accounts occurs when a bookkeeper does not know in which account to post one side of a transaction. Until the mystery is sorted out, the credit entry can be recorded in a suspense account. A typical example is when the business receives cash through the post from a source which cannot be determined. The double entry in the accounts would be a debit in the cash book, and a credit to a suspense account.

2.10 Example: not knowing where to post a transaction

Windfall Garments received a cheque in the post for £620. The name on the cheque is R J Beasley Esq, but Windfall Garments have no idea who this person is, nor why he should be sending £620. The bookkeeper decides to open a suspense account, so that the double entry for the transaction is:

		£620	
DEBIT	Cash		
CREDIT	Suspense account		£620

Eventually, it transpires that the cheque was in payment for a debt owed by the Haute Couture Corner Shop and paid out of the proprietor's personal bank account. The suspense account can now be cleared, as follows.

		£620	
DEBIT	Suspense account		
CREDIT	Debtors		£620

 Question Journal and suspense

You are assisting the accountant, of Beavis Ltd in preparing the accounts for the year ended 31 December 20X7. You draw up a trial balance and you notice that the credit side is greater than the debit side by £11,482.29. You enter this difference in a suspense account.

On investigation, the following errors and omissions are found to have occurred.

(a) An invoice for £3,217.20 for general insurance has been posted to cash but not to the ledger account.

(b) A customer went into liquidation just before the year end, owing Beavis Ltd £1,425.53. The amount was taken off debtors but the corresponding entry to expense the irrecoverable debt has not been made.

(c) A cheque paid for purchases has been posted to the purchases account as £4,196.29, when the cheque was made out for £4,916.29.

(d) A van was purchased during the year for £3,059.78, but this amount was credited to the motor vehicles account.

Required

(a) Show the journal required to clear the suspense account.

(b) Show the suspense account in ledger account form.

(a)   Journal

			£	£
DEBIT	Insurance		3,217.20	
	Irrecoverable debt expense		1,425.53	
	Purchases (£4,916.29 – £4,196.29)		720.00	
	Motor vehicles (£3,059.78 × 2)		6,119.56	
CREDIT	Suspense account			11,482.29

(b)   *In ledger account form*

SUSPENSE ACCOUNT

	£		£
Balance b/f	11,482.29	Insurance	3,217.20
		Irrecoverable debt expense	1,425.53
		Purchases	720.00
		Motor vehicles	6,119.56
	11,482.29		11,482.29

2.11 Suspense accounts might contain several items

If more than one error or unidentifiable posting to a ledger account arises during an accounting period, they will all be merged together in the same suspense account. Indeed, until the causes of the errors are discovered, the bookkeepers are unlikely to know exactly how many errors there are. An examination question might give you a balance on a suspense account, together with enough information to make the necessary corrections, leaving a nil balance on the suspense account and correct balances on various other accounts. In practice, of course, finding these errors is far from easy!

2.12 Suspense accounts are temporary

FAST FORWARD **Suspense accounts are only temporary**. None should exist when it comes to drawing up the financial statements at the end of the accounting period.

It must be stressed that a suspense account can only be temporary. Postings to a suspense account are only made when the bookkeeper doesn't know yet what to do, or when an error has occurred. Mysteries must be solved, and errors must be corrected. Under no circumstances should there still be a suspense account when it comes to preparing the balance sheet of a business. The suspense account must be cleared and all the correcting entries made before the final accounts are drawn up.

Question   Suspense account

At the year end of T Down & Co, an imbalance in the trial balance was revealed which resulted in the creation of a suspense account with a credit balance of £1,040.

Investigations revealed the following errors.

(i)   A sale of goods on credit for £1,000 had been omitted from the sales account.

(ii)   Delivery and installation costs of £240 on a new item of plant had been recorded as a revenue expense.

(iii)   Cash discount of £150 on paying a creditor, JW, had been taken, even though the payment was made outside the time limit.

(iv)   Stock of stationery at the end of the period of £240 had been ignored.

(v) A purchase of raw materials of £350 had been recorded in the purchases account as £850.

(vi) The purchase returns day book included a sales credit note for £230 which had been entered correctly in the account of the debtor concerned, but included with purchase returns in the nominal ledger.

Required

(a) Prepare journal entries to correct *each* of the above errors. Narratives are *not* required.

(b) Open a suspense account and show the corrections to be made.

(c) Prior to the discovery of the errors, T Down & Co's gross profit for the year was calculated at £35,750 and the net profit for the year at £18,500. Calculate the revised gross and net profit figures after the correction of the errors.

Answer

(a)

			Dr £	Cr £
(i)	DEBIT	Suspense a/c	1,000	
	CREDIT	Sales		1,000
(ii)	DEBIT	Plant	240	
	CREDIT	Delivery cost		240
(iii)	DEBIT	Cash discount received	150	
	CREDIT	JW a/c		150
(iv)	DEBIT	Stock of stationery	240	
	CREDIT	Stationery expense		240
(v)	DEBIT	Suspense a/c	500	
	CREDIT	Purchases		500
(vi)	DEBIT	Purchase returns	230	
	DEBIT	Sales returns	230	
	CREDIT	Suspense a/c		460

(b)

SUSPENSE A/C

		£			£
(i)	Sales	1,000		End of year balance	1,040
(v)	Purchases	500	(vi)	Purchase returns/sales returns	460
		1,500			1,500

(c)

	£
Gross profit originally reported	35,750
Sales omitted	1,000
Plant costs wrongly allocated	240
Incorrect recording of purchases	500
Sales credit note wrongly allocated	(460)
Adjusted gross profit	37,030

	£
Net profit originally reported	18,500
Adjustments to gross profit £(37,030 – 35,750)	1,280
Cash discount incorrectly taken	(150)
Stationery stock	240
Adjusted net profit	19,870

Note. It has been assumed that the delivery and installation costs on plant have been included in purchases.

There was a question in the December 2007 exam on suspense accounts that the examiner highlighted as being badly answered. You were asked to calculate the balance remaining on the suspense account after certain errors had been adjusted. The key to the question was recognising which errors affected the suspense account, then putting the adjustments through correctly as in the above example.

3 Material errors

Errors discovered during a current period which **relate to a prior period** may arise through:

(a) Mathematical mistakes
(b) Mistakes in the application of accounting policies
(c) Misinterpretation of facts
(d) Oversights
(e) Fraud

Most of the time these errors can be **corrected through net profit or loss for the current period**. Where they fulfil the definition of material errors (given above), however, this is not appropriate.

The amount of the correction of a material error that relates to prior periods should be reported by **adjusting the opening balance of retained earnings**. Comparative information should be restated (unless this is impracticable).

This treatment means that the financial statements appear as if the material error had been **corrected in the period it was made**. Financial statements include comparatives for the previous period, so any amount relating to the previous period immediately prior to the current one will be included in the net profit or loss for that period. Amounts relating to periods before that will be used to adjust the opening reserves figure of the previous period shown.

Various **disclosures** are required:

(a) **Nature** of the material error
(b) **Amount of the correction** for the current period and for each prior period presented
(c) Amount of the correction relating to periods prior to those included in the **comparative** information
(d) The fact that comparative information has been **restated** or that it is impracticable to do so

Question	Prior period error

During 20X7 Lubi Co discovered that certain items had been included in stock at 31 December 20X6, valued at £4.2m, which had in fact been sold before the year end. The following figures for 20X6 (as reported) and 20X7 (draft) are available.

	20X6	20X7 (draft)
	£'000	£'000
Sales	47,400	67,200
Cost of goods sold	(34,570)	(55,800)
Profit before taxation	12,830	11,400
Tax	(3,880)	(3,400)
Net profit	8,950	8,000

Reserves at 1 January 20X6 were £13m. The cost of goods sold for 20X7 includes the £4.2m error in opening stock. The tax rate was 30% for 20X6 and 20X7.

Required

Show the profit and loss account for 20X7, with the 20X6 comparative, and the adjusted retained earnings.

PROFIT AND LOSS ACCOUNT

	20X6	20X7
	£'000	£'000
Sales	47,400	67,200
Cost of goods sold (W1)	(38,770)	(51,600)
Profit before tax	8,630	15,600
Tax (W2)	(2,620)	(4,660)
Net profit	6,010	10,940

RETAINED EARNINGS

Opening retained earnings		
As previously reported	13,000	21,950
Correction of prior period		
error (4,200 – 1,260)	–	(2,940)
As restated	13,000	19,010
Net profit for year	6,010	10,940
Closing retained earnings	19,010	29,950

Working

1   *Cost of goods sold*

	20X6	20X7
	£'000	£'000
As stated in question	34,570	55,800
Stock adjustment	4,200	(4,200)
	38,770	51,600

2   *Tax*

	20X6	20X7
	£'000	£'000
As stated in question	3,880	3,400
Stock adjustment (4,200 × 30%)	1,260	1,260
	2,620	4,660

Chapter Roundup

- There are five main types of error. Some can be corrected by journal entry, some require the use of a suspense account.

- Errors which leave total debits and credits in the ledger accounts in balance can be corrected by using **journal entries**. Otherwise a suspense account has to be opened first, and later cleared by a journal entry.

- **Suspense accounts**, as well as being used to correct some errors, are also opened when it is not known immediately where to post an amount. When the mystery is solved, the suspense account is closed and the amount correctly posted using a journal entry.

- **Suspense accounts are only temporary**. None should exist when it comes to drawing up the financial statements at the end of the accounting period.

Quick Quiz

1   List five types of error made in accounting.

2   What is a journal used for?

    A   To correct errors
    B   To correct errors and post unusual transactions
    C   To correct errors and clear suspense account
    D   To make adjustments to the double entry

3   A suspense account is a temporary account to make the trial balance balance.

    Is this statement

    A   True
    B   False

4   What must be done with a suspense account before preparing a balance sheet?

    A   Include in assets
    B   Clear it to nil
    C   Include in liabilities
    D   Write it off to capital

5   Sales returns of £460 have inadvertently been posted to the purchase returns, although the correct entry has been made to the debtors control. A suspense account needs to be set up for how much?

    A   £460 debit
    B   £460 credit
    C   £920 debit
    D   £920 credit

1 Transposition, omission, principle, commission and compensating errors.

2 D Although A, B and C are correct as far as they go, they don't cover everything. Selection D is the most comprehensive answer.

3 A

4 B All errors must be identified and the suspense account cleared to nil.

5 C The sales returns of £460 have been credited to debtors and also £460 has been credited to purchase returns. Therefore the trial balance needs a debit of 2 × £460 = £920 to balance.

Now try the questions below from the Exam Question Bank

Number	Level	Marks	Time
Q29	Examination	2	2 mins
Q30	Examination	2	2 mins
Q31	Examination	2	2 mins
Q32	Examination	2	2 mins

17

Preparation of financial statements for sole traders

Topic list	Syllabus reference
1 Preparation of final accounts	F1(d), F2(a)

Introduction

We have now reached our goal of preparing of the final accounts of a sole trader!

We will deal with the case of a trial balance and then making adjustments to produce final accounts.

This chapter also acts as a review of what we have covered to date. Use this period to review all the work covered to date. If you have any problems with the examples and questions, thoroughly revise the appropriate chapter before proceeding to the next part.

Study guide

Exam guide

This chapter covers a lot of ground, all of which is examinable. Use it as useful revision of what you have learned to date.

Exam focus point

At the 2009 ACCA Teachers' Conference, the examiner emphasised the need to practise full questions particularly in certain key areas. One of these key areas was accounts preparation. Therefore do not neglect this chapter. It will also serve as a good foundation for your later studies at F7.

1 Preparation of final accounts

FAST FORWARD

You should now be able to prepare a set of final accounts for a sole trader from a trial balance after incorporating period end adjustments for depreciation, stock, prepayments, accruals, irrecoverable debts, and allowances for debtors.

1.1 Adjustments to accounts

You should now use what you have learned to produce a solution to the following exercise, which involves preparing a profit and loss account and balance sheet. We have met Newbegin Tools before, but now we add a lot more information.

Question   **Adjustment to accounts**

The financial affairs of Newbegin Tools prior to the commencement of trading were as follows.

NEWBEGIN TOOLS
BALANCE SHEET AS AT 1 AUGUST 20X5

	£	£
Fixed assets		
Motor vehicle		2,000
Shop fittings		3,000
		5,000
Current assets		
Stock	12,000	
Cash	1,000	
	13,000	
Current liabilities		
Bank overdraft	2,000	
Trade creditors	4,000	
	6,000	
Net current assets		7,000
		12,000
Capital		12,000

At the end of six months the business had made the following transactions.

(a) Goods were purchased on credit at a list price of £10,000.

(b) Trade discount received was 2% on list price and there was a settlement discount received of 5% on settling debts to suppliers of £8,000. These were the only payments to suppliers in the period.

(c) Closing stocks of goods were valued at £5,450.

(d) All sales were on credit and amounted to £27,250.

(e) Outstanding debtors balances at 31 January 20X6 amounted to £3,250 of which £250 were to be written off. An allowance for debtors is to be made amounting to 2% of the remaining outstanding debtors.

(f) Cash payments were made in respect of the following expenses.

		£
(i)	Stationery, postage and wrapping	500
(ii)	Telephone charges	200
(iii)	Electricity	600
(iv)	Cleaning and refreshments	150

(g) Cash drawings by the proprietor, Alf Newbegin, amounted to £6,000.

(h) The outstanding overdraft balance as at 1 August 20X5 was paid off. Interest charges and bank charges on the overdraft amounted to £40.

Prepare the profit and loss account of Newbegin Tools for the six months to 31 January 20X6 and a balance sheet as at that date. Ignore depreciation.

Answer

PROFIT AND LOSS ACCOUNT
FOR THE SIX MONTHS ENDED 31 JANUARY 20X6

	£	£
Sales		27,250
Cost of sales: Opening stock	12,000	
Purchases (note (a))	9,800	
	21,800	
Less closing stock	5,450	
Cost of goods sold		16,350
Gross profit		10,900
Discounts received (note (b))		400
		11,300
Electricity (note (c))	600	
Stationery, postage and wrapping	500	
Irrecoverable debts written off	250	
Allowance for debtors (note (d))	60	
Telephone charges	200	
Cleaning and refreshments	150	
Interest and bank charges	40	
		1,800
Net profit		9,500

Notes

(a) Purchases at cost £10,000 less 2% trade discount.

(b) 5% of £8,000 = £400.

(c) Expenses are grouped into sales and distribution expenses (here assumed to be electricity, stationery and postage, irrecoverable debts and allowance for debtors) administration expenses (here assumed to be telephone charges and cleaning) and finance charges.

(d) 2% of £3,000 = £60.

The preparation of a balance sheet is not so easy, because we must calculate the value of creditors and cash in hand.

(a)   *Creditors as at 31 January 20X6*

The amount owing to creditors is the sum of the amount owing at the beginning of the period, plus the cost of purchases during the period (net of all discounts), less the payments already made for purchases.

	£
Creditors as at 1 August 20X5	4,000
Add purchases during the period, net of trade discount	9,800
	13,800
Less settlement discounts received	(400)
	13,400
Less payments to creditors during the period*	(7,600)
	5,800

* £8,000 less cash discount of £400.

(b)   *Cash at bank and in hand at 31 January 20X6*

You need to identify cash payments received and cash payments made.

		£
(i)	*Cash received from sales*	
	Total sales in the period	27,250
	Add debtors as at 1 August 20X5	0
		27,250
	Less unpaid debts as at 31 January 20X6	3,250
	Cash received	24,000
(ii)	*Cash paid*	
	Trade creditors (see (a))	7,600
	Stationery, postage and wrapping	500
	Telephone charges	200
	Electricity	600
	Cleaning and refreshments	150
	Bank charges and interest	40
	Bank overdraft repaid	2,000
	Drawings by proprietor	6,000
		17,090

Note. It is easy to forget some of these payments, especially drawings.

		£
(iii)	Cash in hand at 1 August 20X5	1,000
	Cash received in the period	24,000
		25,000
	Cash paid in the period	(17,090)
	Cash at bank and in hand as at 31 January 20X6	7,910

(c)   When irrecoverable debts are written off, the value of outstanding debtors must be reduced by the amount written off. Debtors in the balance sheet will be valued at £3,250 less irrecoverable debts £250 and the allowance for debtors of £60 – ie at £2,940.

(d) Fixed assets should be depreciated. However, in this exercise depreciation has been ignored.

NEWBEGIN TOOLS
BALANCE SHEET AS AT 31 JANUARY 20X6

	£	£
Fixed assets		
Motor vehicles		2,000
Shop fittings		3,000
		5,000
Current assets		
Stock	5,450	
Debtors, less allowance for debtors	2,940	
Cash	7,910	
	16,300	
Current liabilities		
Trade creditors	(5,800)	
Net current assets		10,500
		15,500
Capital		
Capital at 1 August 20X5		12,000
Net profit for the period		9,500
		21,500
Less drawings		6,000
Capital at 31 January 20X6		15,500

The bank overdraft has now been repaid and is therefore not shown.

Exam focus point

> Although your exam is all MCQs, you might be given a lot of information and asked to calculate a figure to go in the profit and loss account and/or balance sheet. Therefore calculating account balances and preparing financial statements must become second nature to you.

1.2 Example: accounts preparation from a trial balance

The following trial balance was extracted from the ledger of Stephen Chee, a sole trader, as at 31 May 20X1 – the end of his financial year.

STEPHEN CHEE
TRIAL BALANCE AS AT 31 MAY 20X1

	Dr £	Cr £
Property, at cost	120,000	
Equipment, at cost	80,000	
Provisions for depreciation (as at 1 June 20X0)		
– on property		20,000
– on equipment		38,000
Purchases	250,000	
Sales		402,200
Stock, as at 1 June 20X0	50,000	
Discounts allowed	18,000	
Discounts received		4,800
Returns out		15,000
Wages and salaries	58,800	
Irrecoverable debts	4,600	
Loan interest	5,100	
Other operating expenses	17,700	
Trade creditors		36,000
Trade debtors	38,000	
Cash in hand	300	
Bank	1,300	
Drawings	24,000	
Allowance for debtors		500
17% long term loan		30,000
Capital, as at 1 June 20X0		121,300
	667,800	667,800

The following additional information as at 31 May 20X1 is available.

(a) Stock as at the close of business has been valued at cost at £42,000.

(b) Wages and salaries need to be accrued by £800.

(c) Other operating expenses are prepaid by £300.

(d) The allowance for debtors is to be adjusted so that it is 2% of trade debtors.

(e) Depreciation for the year ended 31 May 20X1 has still to be provided for as follows.

Property: 1.5% per annum using the straight line method; and
Equipment: 25% per annum using the reducing balance method.

Required

Prepare Stephen Chee's profit and loss account for the year ended 31 May 20X1 and his balance sheet as at that date.

Tutorial note. Again you have met a simplified form of Stephen Chee before. However this version contains a lot more information for you to deal with before you can prepare accounts.

Solution

STEPHEN CHEE
PROFIT AND LOSS ACCOUNT
FOR THE YEAR ENDED 31 MAY 20X1

	£	£
Sales		402,200
Cost of sales:		
Opening stock	50,000	
Purchases	250,000	
Purchases returns	(15,000)	
	285,000	
Closing stock	42,000	
		243,000
Gross profit		159,200
Other income – discounts received		4,800
		164,000
Expenses:		
Operating expenses		
Wages and salaries (£58,800 + £800)	59,600	
Discounts allowed	18,000	
Irrecoverable debts (W1)	4,860	
Loan interest	5,100	
Depreciation (W2)	12,300	
Other operating expenses (£17,700 – £300)	17,400	
		117,260
Net profit for the year		46,740

STEPHEN CHEE
BALANCE SHEET AS AT 31 MAY 20X0

	Cost	Accumulated depn.	Net book value
Fixed assets	£	£	£
Property	120,000	21,800	98,200
Equipment	80,000	48,500	31,500
	200,000	70,300	129,700
Current assets			
Stock		42,000	
Trade debtors net of allowance for debtors (£38,000 – 760 (W1))		37,240	
Prepayments		300	
Bank		1,300	
Cash in hand		300	
		81,140	
Current liabilities			
Trade creditors		36,000	
Accruals		800	
		36,800	
Net current assets			44,340
Net assets			174,040
Long term liabilities			
17% loan			(30,000)
			144,040
Capital			
Balance at 1 June 20X0			121,300
Net profit for the year			46,740
			168,040
Drawings			24,000
			144,040

Workings

1	Irrecoverable debts	£
	Previous allowance	500
	New allowance (2% × 38,000)	760
	Increase	260
	Per trial balance	4,600
	P&L	4,860

2	Depreciation	
	Property	
	Opening provision	20,000
	Provision for the year (1.5% × 120,000)	1,800
	Closing provision	21,800
	Equipment	
	Opening provision	38,000
	Provision for the year (25% × 42,000)	10,500
	Closing provision	48,500
	Total charge in P&L	12,300

Question

Final accounts

Donald Brown, a sole trader, extracted the following trial balance on 31 December 20X0.

TRIAL BALANCE AS AT 31 DECEMBER 20X0

	Debit £	Credit £
Capital at 1 January 20X0		26,094
Debtors	42,737	
Cash in hand	1,411	
Creditors		35,404
Fixtures and fittings at cost	42,200	
Discounts allowed	1,304	
Discounts received		1,175
Stock at 1 January 20X0	18,460	
Sales		491,620
Purchases	387,936	
Motor vehicles at cost	45,730	
Lighting and heating	6,184	
Motor expenses	2,862	
Rent	8,841	
General expenses	7,413	
Bank overdraft		19,861
Provision for depreciation		
Fixtures and fittings		2,200
Motor vehicles		15,292
Drawings	26,568	
	591,646	591,646

The following information as at 31 December is also available.

(a)   £218 is owing for motor expenses.

(b)   £680 has been prepaid for rent.

(c)   Depreciation is to be provided of the year as follows.

Motor vehicles: 20% on cost
Fixtures and fittings: 10% reducing balance method

(d)   Stock at the close of business was valued at £19,926.

Required

Prepare Donald Brown's profit and loss account for the year ended 31 December 20X0 and his balance sheet at that date.

Answer

Tutorial note. You should note these points.

(a)   Discounts allowed are an expense of the business and should be shown as a deduction from gross profit. Similarly, discounts received is a revenue item and should be added to gross profit.

(b)   The figure for depreciation in the trial balance represents accumulated depreciation up to and including 20W9. You have to calculate the charge for the year 20X0 for the profit and loss account and add this to the trial balance figure to arrive at the accumulated depreciation figure to be included in the balance sheet.

DONALD BROWN
PROFIT AND LOSS ACCOUNT
FOR THE YEAR ENDED 31 DECEMBER 20X0

	£	£
Sales		491,620
Less cost of sales		
Opening stock	18,460	
Purchases	387,936	
	406,396	
Closing stock	19,926	
		386,470
Gross profit		105,150
Discounts received		1,175
		106,325
Less expenses:		
discounts allowed	1,304	
lighting and heating	6,184	
motor expenses (2,862 + 218)	3,080	
rent (8,841 − 680)	8,161	
general expenses	7,413	
depreciation (W)	13,146	
		39,288
Net profit		67,037

Working: depreciation charge

Motor vehicles: £45,730 × 20% = £9,146

Fixtures and fittings: 10% × £(42,200 − 2,200) = £4,000

Total: £4,000 + £9,146 = £13,146.

DONALD BROWN
BALANCE SHEET AS AT 31 DECEMBER 20X0

	Cost £	Depreciation £	Net £
Fixed assets			
Fixtures and fittings	42,200	6,200	36,000
Motor vehicles	45,730	24,438	21,292
	87,930	30,638	57,292
Current assets			
Stock		19,926	
Debtors		42,737	
Prepayments		680	
Cash in hand		1,411	
		64,754	
Current liabilities			
Creditors		35,404	
Accruals		218	
Bank overdraft		19,861	
		55,483	
Net current assets			9,271
			66,563
Capital			
Balance b/f			26,094
Net profit for year			67,037
			93,131
Less drawings			26,568
			66,563

Exam focus point

In the June 2008 exam, there was a question giving a number of adjustments and asking for the effect on profit. The examiner commented that only 30% of students got this right. You need to follow the procedure shown the question below.

 Question

Effect on profit

Given the facts in Final accounts (Donald Brown) above, what is the net effect on profit of the adjustments in (a) to (c)?

Answer

(a) Motor expenses accrual – £218 additional expense, so reduction in profit

(b) Rent prepayment – £680 reduction in expense, so increase in profit.

(c) Depreciation – total charge £13,146 – additional expanse, so reduction in profit

Total effect on net profit = + 680 – 218 – 13,146
= 12,684 reduction

Chapter Roundup

- You should now be able to prepare a set of final accounts for a sole trader from a trial balance after incorporating period end adjustments for depreciation, stock, prepayments, accruals, irrecoverable debts, and allowances for debtors.

Quick Quiz

1   Which of the following is the correct formula for cost of sales?

   A   Opening stock – purchases + closing stock.
   B   Purchases – closing stock + sales.
   C   Opening stock – closing stock + purchases.
   D   Opening stock + closing stock – purchases.

2   If an owner takes goods out of stock for his own use, how is this dealt with?

   A   Credited to drawings at cost
   B   Credited to drawings at selling price
   C   Debited to drawings at cost
   D   Debited to drawings at selling price

3   A business starts trading on 1 September 20X0. During the year, it has sales of £500,000, purchases of £250,000 and closing stock of £75,000. What is the gross profit for the year?

   A   £175,000
   B   £675,000
   C   £325,000
   D   £250,000

4   Mario's trial balance includes the following items: fixed assets £50,000, stock £15,000, creditors £10,000, debtors £5,000, bank £110,000, allowance for debtors £1,000.

   What is the figure for current assets?

   A   £180,000
   B   £170,000
   C   £129,000
   D   £134,000

5   Using the information in Question 4 above, what is the figure for total assets?

   A   £184,000
   B   £179,000

Answers to Quick Quiz

1	C	Correct, this is a version of the more normal formula: opening stock + purchases – closing stock.
	A	Incorrect.
	B	Incorrect. Sales should never form part of cost of sales.
	C	Incorrect.
2	C	Although we have not specifically covered this point, you should have realised that goods for own use must be treated as drawings (and so debited to drawings). Thinking about prudence, if the goods were transferred at selling price, the business would show a profit on the sale of the goods that it has not made. So the transaction must be shown at cost. (Now think about where the credit entry goes before trying the question from the EQB.)

3   C

	£
Sales	500,000
Purchases	250,000
Closing stock	(75,000)
Cost of sales	175,000
Gross profit	325,000

4   C

	£
Current assets	
Stock	15,000
Debtors (5,000 – 1,000)	4,000
Bank	110,000
	129,000

5   B   Total assets = fixed assets + current assets
            = 50,000 + 129,000
            = 179,000

Now try the question below from the Exam Question Bank

Number	Level	Marks	Time
Q33	Examination	1	1 min

Preparing basic financial statements

Incomplete records

Topic list	Syllabus reference
1 Incomplete records questions	F6(a)
2 The opening balance sheet	F6(a)
3 Credit sales and debtors	F6(a)
4 Purchases and trade creditors	F6(a)
5 Establishing cost of sales	F6(a)
6 Stolen goods or goods destroyed	F6(a)
7 The cash book	F6(a)
8 Accruals and prepayments	F6(a)
9 Drawings	F6(a)
10 The business equation	F6(a)
11 Comprehensive worked examples	F6(a)

Introduction

So far in your work on preparing the final accounts for a sole trader we have
assumed that a full set of records are kept. In practice many sole traders do not
keep a full set of records and you must apply certain techniques to arrive at the
necessary figures.

**Incomplete records questions are a very good test of your understanding of
the way in which a set of accounts is built up.**

Limited companies are obliged by law to keep proper accounting records. They
will be considered in Chapters 20 and 21.

Study guide

		Intellectual level
F6	**Incomplete records**	
(a)	Understand and apply techniques used in incomplete record situations	1
	(i) Use of accounting equation	
	(ii) Use of ledger accounts to calculate missing figures	
	(iii) Use of cash and/or bank summaries	
	(iv) Use of profit percentages to calculate missing figures	

Exam guide

Incomplete record questions are likely to appear regularly. Learn the tricks presented in this chapter and you should be able to tackle anything the examiner throws at you. Make sure you understand the difference between **margin** and **mark-up**.

1 Incomplete records questions

FAST FORWARD

Incomplete records problems occur when a business does not have a full set of accounting records, either because:

- The proprietor of the business does not keep a full set of accounts, or
- Some of the business accounts are accidentally lost or destroyed.

The problem for the accountant is to prepare a set of year-end accounts for the business; ie a trading, profit and loss account, and a balance sheet. Since the business does not have a full set of records, preparing the final accounts is not a simple matter of closing off accounts and transferring balances. The task of preparing the final accounts involves:

- (a) Establishing the **cost of purchases** and **other expenses**
- (b) Establishing the **total amount of sales**
- (c) Establishing the amount of **creditors, accruals, debtors** and **prepayments** at the end of the year

Examination questions often take incomplete records problems a stage further, by introducing an 'incident' – such as fire or burglary– which leaves the owner of the business uncertain about how much stock has been destroyed or stolen.

The great merit of incomplete records problems is that they focus attention on the relationship between cash received and paid, sales and debtors, purchases and creditors, and stocks, as well as calling for the preparation of final accounts from basic principles.

To understand what incomplete records are about, it will obviously be useful now to look at what exactly might be incomplete. The items we shall consider in turn are:

- (a) The opening balance sheet
- (b) Credit sales and debtors
- (c) Purchases and trade creditors
- (d) Purchases, stocks and the cost of sales
- (e) Stolen goods or goods destroyed
- (f) The cash book
- (g) Accruals and prepayments
- (h) Drawings

2 The opening balance sheet

In practice there should not be any missing item in the opening balance sheet of the business, because it should be available from the preparation of the previous year's final accounts.

However, an examination problem might provide information about the assets and liabilities of the business at the beginning of the period under review, but then leave the balancing figure – ie the proprietor's business capital – unspecified. If you remember the accounting equation (A = C + L), the problem is quite straightforward.

2.1 Example: Opening balance sheet

Suppose a business has the following assets and liabilities as at 1 January 20X3.

	£
Fixtures and fittings at cost	7,000
Provision for depreciation, fixtures and fittings	4,000
Motor vehicles at cost	12,000
Provision for depreciation, motor vehicles	6,800
Stock in trade	4,500
Trade debtors	5,200
Cash at bank and in hand	1,230
Trade creditors	3,700
Prepayment	450
Accrued rent	2,000

You are required to prepare a balance sheet for the business, inserting a balancing figure for proprietor's capital.

Solution

Balance sheet as at 1 January 20X3

	£	£
Fixed assets		
Fixtures and fittings at cost	7,000	
Less accumulated depreciation	4,000	
		3,000
Motor vehicles at cost	12,000	
Less accumulated depreciation	6,800	
		5,200
		8,200
Current assets		
Stock in trade	4,500	
Trade debtors	5,200	
Prepayment	450	
Cash	1,230	
	11,380	
Current liabilities		
Trade creditors	3,700	
Accrual	2,000	
	5,700	
Net current assets		5,680
		13,880
Proprietor's capital as at 1 January 20X3 (balancing figure)		13,880

3 Credit sales and debtors

FAST FORWARD

If a business does not keep a record of its sales on credit, the value of these sales can be derived from the opening balance of trade debtors, the closing balance of trade debtors, and the payments received from trade debtors during the period.

Formula to learn

Credit sales are:	£
Payments received from trade debtors	X
Plus closing balance of trade debtors (since these represent sales in the current period for which cash payment has not yet been received)	X
Less opening balance of trade debtors (unless these become irrecoverable debts, they will pay what they owe in the current period for sales in a previous period)	(X)
	X

For example, suppose that a business had trade debtors of £1,750 on 1 April 20X4 and trade debtors of £3,140 on 31 March 20X5. If payments received from trade debtors during the year to 31 March 20X5 were £28,490, and if there are no irrecoverable debts, then credit sales for the period would be:

	£
Cash received from debtors	28,490
Plus closing debtors	3,140
Less opening debtors	(1,750)
Credit sales	29,880

If there are irrecoverable debts during the period, the value of sales will be increased by the amount of irrecoverable debts written off, no matter whether they relate to opening debtors or credit sales during the current period.

The same calculation could be made in a T account, with credit sales being the balancing figure to complete the account.

DEBTORS

	£		£
Opening balance b/f	1,750	Cash received	28,490
Credit sales (balancing fig)	29,880	Closing balance c/f	3,140
	31,630		31,630

You should recognise that this is, in fact, the **debtors control account**.

The same interrelationship between credit sales, cash from debtors, and opening and closing debtors balances can be used to derive a missing figure for cash from debtors, or opening or closing debtors, given the values for the three other items. For example, if we know that opening debtors are £6,700, closing debtors are £3,200 and credit sales for the period are £69,400, then cash received from debtors during the period would be as follows.

DEBTORS

	£		£
Opening balance	6,700	Cash received (balancing figure)	72,900
Sales (on credit)	69,400	Closing balance c/f	3,200
	76,100		76,100

An alternative way of presenting the same calculation would be:

	£
Opening balance of debtors	6,700
Credit sales during the period	69,400
Total money owed to the business	76,100
Less closing balance of debtors	(3,200)
Equals cash received during the period	72,900

4 Purchases and trade creditors

FAST FORWARD

A similar relationship exists between purchases of stock during a period, the opening and closing balances for trade creditors, and amounts paid to trade creditors during the period.

Formula to learn

If we wish to calculate an unknown amount for purchases, the amount would be derived as follows:

	£
Payments to trade creditors during the period	X
Plus closing balance of trade creditors (since these represent purchases in the current period for which payment has not yet been made)	X
Less opening balance of trade creditors (these relate to purchases in a previous period)	(X)
Purchases during the period	X

For example, suppose that a business had trade creditors of £3,728 on 1 October 20X5 and trade creditors of £2,645 on 30 September 20X6. If payments to trade creditors during the year to 30 September 20X6 were £31,479, then purchases during the year would be:

	£
Payments to trade creditors	31,479
Plus closing balance of trade creditors	2,645
Less opening balance of trade creditors	(3,728)
Purchases	30,396

The same calculation could be made in a T account, with purchases being the balancing figure to complete the account.

CREDITORS

	£		£
Cash payments	31,479	Opening balance b/f	3,728
Closing balance c/f	2,645	Purchases (balancing figure)	30,396
	34,124		34,124

Once again, you should recognise that this is the **creditors control account**.

Question   Purchases

Mr Harmon does not keep full accounting records, but the following information is available in respect of his accounting year ended 31 December 20X9.

	£
Cash purchases in year	3,900
Cash paid for goods supplied on credit	27,850
Creditors at 1 January 20X9	970
Creditors at 31 December 20X9	720

In his trading account for 20X9, what will be Harmon's figure for purchases?

Answer

CREDITORS

	£		£
Cash payments	31,750	Opening balance b/f	970
Closing balance c/f	720	Purchases (balancing figure)	31,500
	32,470		32,470

Alternatively, you could prepare the creditors control account to just include credit purchases and then add on the cash purchases, as a separate calculation.

5 Establishing cost of sales

FAST FORWARD

When the value of purchases is not known, a different approach might be required to find out what they were, depending on the nature of the information given to you.

One approach would be to use information about the cost of sales, and opening and closing stocks, in other words, to use the trading account rather than the trade creditors account to find the cost of purchases.

Formula to learn

		£
Since	Opening stocks	X
	Plus purchases	X
	Less closing stocks	(X)
	Equals the cost of goods sold	X
Then	The cost of goods sold	X
	Plus closing stocks	X
	Less opening stocks	(X)
	Equals purchases	X

The stock in trade of a business on 1 July 20X6 has a balance sheet value of £8,400, and a stock taking exercise at 30 June 20X7 showed stock to be valued at £9,350. Sales for the year to 30 June 20X7 are £80,000, and the business makes a gross profit of $33^1/3$% on cost for all the items that it sells. What were the purchases during the year?

You should remember that sales – cost of sales = gross profit. In the example we are told that gross profit is $33^1/3$% **on cost.** So cost of sales is 100% and sales must be $133^1/3$% ($133^1/3$% – 100% = $33^1/3$%)

	£
Sales ($133^1/3$%)	80,000
Cost of sales (100%)	60,000
Gross profit ($33^1/3$%)	20,000

	£
Cost of goods sold	60,000
Plus closing stock	9,350
Less opening stocks	(8,400)
Purchases	60,950

The above example illustrates **markup**. We are told that the business makes a gross profit of $33^1/3$% on **cost**. From this we were able to deduce that cost of sales were 100% and sales $133^1/3$%. In other words, the business has a markup of $33^1/3$% on cost.

Another way of calculating cost of sales uses gross profit **margin**. Suppose that we were told that the sales were £80,000 and the business had a gross profit margin of $33^1/3$%. This means that sales are 100% and so cost of sales are $66^2/3$%.

	£
Sales (100%)	80,000
Cost of sales ($66^2/3$%)	53,333
Gross profit ($33^1/3$%)	26,667

Attention!

Markup means that cost of sales is the 100% figure.

Margin means that sales is the 100% figure.

BPP LEARNING MEDIA

Question

Harry has budgeted that his sales for the coming year will be £175,000. He achieves a constant gross mark-up of 40% on cost. He plans to reduce his stock level by £13,000 over the year.

What will Harry's purchases be for the year?

Answer

First we will need to calculate cost of sales. Markup means that cost of sales is the 100% figure.

Cost of sales   = 100/140 × £175,000
        = £125,000

We do not know the figure for opening stock, so let's call it £x. Closing stock will be (£x – £13,000).

Opening stock + purchases – closing stock   = cost of sales

£x + purchases – (£x – £13,000)   = £125,000
£x + purchases – £x + £13,000   = £125,000
∴ Purchases   = £125,000 – £13,000
                = £112,000

Question

Using the same facts as in the question above, calculate Harry's purchases for the year if he achieves a constant **margin** of 40% on sales.

Answer

Gross profit = 40% of sales, so cost of sales = 60% of sales.

Cost of sales $= \dfrac{60}{100} \times £175,000$

      = £105,000

Since the stock level is being allowed to fall, it means purchases will be £13,000 less than £105,000 = £92,000.

6 Stolen goods or goods destroyed

AST FORWARD

A similar type of calculation might be required to derive the value of goods stolen or destroyed.

When an unknown quantity of goods is lost, whether they are stolen, destroyed in a fire, or lost in any other way such that the quantity lost cannot be counted, then the cost of the goods lost is the difference between:

(a) The **cost of goods sold**
(b) **Opening stock of the goods** (at cost) plus **purchases** less **closing stock of the goods** (at cost)

In theory (a) and (b) should be the same. However, if (b) is a larger amount than (a), it follows that the difference must be the cost of the goods purchased and neither sold nor remaining in stock – ie the cost of the goods lost.

6.1 Example: Cost of goods destroyed

Orlean Flames is a shop which sells fashion clothes. On 1 January 20X5, it had stock in trade which cost £7,345. During the 9 months to 30 September 20X5, the business purchased goods from suppliers costing £106,420. Sales during the same period were £154,000. The shop makes a gross profit markup of 40% on cost for everything it sells. On 30 September 20X5, there was a fire in the shop which destroyed most of the stock in it. Only a small amount of stock, known to have cost £350, was undamaged and still fit for sale.

How much stock was lost in the fire?

Solution

	£
(a)	
Sales (140%)	154,000
Gross profit (40%)	44,000
Cost of goods sold (100%)	110,000

	£
(b)	
Opening stock, at cost	7,345
Plus purchases	106,420
	113,765
Less closing stock, at cost	350
Equals cost of goods sold and goods lost	113,415

	£
(c)	
Cost of goods sold and lost	113,415
Cost of goods sold	110,000
Cost of goods lost	3,415

6.2 Example: Cost of goods stolen

Beau Gullard runs a jewellery shop in the High Street. On 1 January 20X9, his stock in trade, at cost, amounted to £4,700 and his trade creditors were £3,950.

During the six months to 30 June 20X9, sales were £42,000. Beau Gullard makes a gross profit margin of $33^{1}/_{3}\%$ on the sales value of everything he sells.

On 30 June, there was a burglary at the shop, and all the stock was stolen.

In trying to establish how much stock had been taken, Beau Gullard was only able to say that:

(a) He knew from his bank statements that he had paid £28,400 to creditors in the 6 month period to 30 June 20X9.

(b) He currently owed creditors £5,550.

Required

(a) Calculate the amount of stock stolen.
(b) Prepare a trading account for the 6 months to 30 June 20X9.

Solution

Step 1. The first 'unknown' is the amount of purchases during the period. This is established by the method previously described in Section 4.

CREDITORS

	£		£
Payments to creditors	28,400	Opening balance b/f	3,950
Closing balance c/f	5,550	Purchases (balancing figure)	30,000
	33,950		33,950

Step 2. The cost of goods sold is also unknown, but this can be established from the gross profit margin and the sales for the period.

		£
Sales	(100%)	42,000
Gross profit	(33⅓%)	14,000
Cost of goods sold	(66⅔%)	28,000

Step 3. The cost of the goods stolen is:

	£
Opening stock at cost	4,700
Purchases	30,000
	34,700
Less closing stock (after burglary)	0
Cost of goods sold and goods stolen	34,700
Cost of goods sold (see Step 2 above)	28,000
Cost of goods stolen	6,700

Step 4. The cost of the goods stolen will not be a charge in the trading account, and so the trading account for the period is as follows:

BEAU GULLARD
TRADING ACCOUNT FOR THE SIX MONTHS TO 30 JUNE 20X9

	£	£
Sales		42,000
Less cost of goods sold		
Opening stock	4,700	
Purchases	30,000	
	34,700	
Less stock stolen	6,700	
		28,000
Gross profit		14,000

6.3 Accounting for stock destroyed, stolen or otherwise lost

When stock is stolen, destroyed or otherwise lost, the loss must be accounted for somehow. The procedure was described briefly in the earlier chapter on accounting for stocks. Since the loss is not a trading loss, the cost of the goods lost is not included in the trading account, as the previous example showed.

The account that is to be debited is one of two possibilities, depending on whether or not the lost goods were insured against the loss.

(a) If the lost goods were not insured, the business must bear the loss, and the loss is shown in the P & L account: ie

DEBIT   Profit and loss
CREDIT   Trading account

(b) If the lost goods were insured, the business will not suffer a loss, because the insurance will pay back the cost of the lost goods. This means that there is no charge at all in the P&L account, and the appropriate double entry is:

DEBIT   Insurance claim account (debtor account)
CREDIT   Trading account

with the cost of the loss. The insurance claim will then be a current asset, and shown in the balance sheet of the business as such. When the claim is paid, the account is then closed by

DEBIT   Cash
CREDIT   Insurance claim account

7 The cash book

FAST FORWARD

> The construction of a cash book, largely from bank statements showing receipts and payments of a business during a given period, is often an important feature of incomplete records problems.

Exam focus point

> In an examination, the purpose of an incomplete records question is largely to test the understanding of candidates about how various items of receipts or payments relate to the preparation of a final set of accounts for a business.

We have already seen in this chapter that information about cash receipts or payments might be needed to establish:

(a)   The amount of purchases during a period
(b)   The amount of credit sales during a period

Other items of receipts or payments might be relevant to establishing:

(a)   The amount of cash sales
(b)   The amount of certain expenses in the P & L account
(c)   The amount of drawings by the business proprietor

It might therefore be helpful, if a business does not keep a cash book day-to-day, to construct a cash book at the end of an accounting period. A business which typically might not keep a day-to-day cash book is a shop, where:

(a)   Many sales, if not all sales, are cash sales (ie with payment by notes and coins, cheques, or credit cards at the time of sale).

(b)   Some payments are made in notes and coins out of the till rather than by payment out of the business bank account by cheque.

Where there appears to be a sizeable volume of receipts and payments in cash (ie notes and coins), then it is also helpful to construct a two column cash book.

Key term

> A **two column cash book** is a cash book with one column for cash, and one column for the business bank account.

An example will illustrate the technique and the purpose of a two column cash book.

7.1 Example: Two column cash book

Jonathan Slugg owns and runs a shop selling fishing tackle, making a gross profit of 25% on the cost of everything he sells. He does not keep a cash book.

On 1 January 20X7 the balance sheet of his business was as follows.

	£	£
Net fixed assets		20,000
Stock	10,000	
Cash in the bank	3,000	
Cash in the till	200	
	13,200	
Trade creditors	1,200	
		12,000
		32,000
Proprietor's capital		32,000

In the year to 31 December 20X7:

(a)   There were no sales on credit

(b)   £41,750 in receipts were banked

(c)   The bank statements of the period show the payments:

		£
(i)	To trade creditors	36,000
(ii)	Sundry expenses	5,600
(iii)	In drawings	4,400

(d)   Payments were also made in cash out of the till:

		£
(i)	To trade creditors	800
(ii)	Sundry expenses	1,500
(iii)	In drawings	3,700

At 31 December 20X7, the business had cash in the till of £450 and trade creditors of £1,400. The cash balance in the bank was not known and the value of closing stock has not yet been calculated. There were no accruals or prepayments. No further fixed assets were purchased during the year. The depreciation charge for the year is £900.

Required

(a)   Prepare a two column cash book for the period.

(b)   Prepare the trading, profit and loss account for the year to 31 December 20X7 and the balance sheet as at 31 December 20X7.

7.2 Discussion and solution

A two column cash book is completed as follows.

Step 1.   Enter the opening cash balances.

Step 2.   Enter the information given about cash payments (and any cash receipts, if there had been any such items given in the problem).

Step 3.   The cash receipts banked are a 'contra' entry, being both a debit (bank column) and a credit (cash in hand column) in the same account.

Step 4.   Enter the closing cash in hand (cash in the bank at the end of the period is not known).

CASH BOOK

	Cash in hand £	Bank £		Cash in hand £	Bank £
Balance b/f	200	3,000	Trade creditors	800	36,000
Cash receipts banked		41,750	Sundry expenses	1,500	5,600
			Drawings	3,700	4,400
Sales*	48,000		Cash receipts banked	41,750	
			Balance c/f	450	
Balance c/f		*1,250			
	48,200	46,000		48,200	46,000

* Balancing figure

Step 5.   The closing balance of money in the bank is a balancing figure. Notice that this is a credit balance ie an overdraft.

Step 6.   Since all sales are for cash, a balancing figure that can be entered in the cash book is sales, in the cash in hand (debit) column.

It is important to notice that since not all receipts from cash sales are banked, the value of cash sales during the period is:

	£
Receipts banked	41,750
Plus expenses and drawings paid out of the till in cash	
£(800 + 1,500 + 3,700)	6,000
Plus any cash stolen (here there is none)	0
Plus the closing balance of cash in hand	450
	48,200
Less the opening balance of cash in hand	(200)
Equals cash sales	48,000

The cash book constructed in this way has enabled us to establish both the closing balance for cash in the bank and also the volume of cash sales. The trading, profit and loss account and the balance sheet can also be prepared, once a value for purchases has been calculated.

CREDITORS

	£		£
Cash book:		Balance b/f	1,200
Payments from bank	36,000	Purchases (balancing figure)	37,000
Cash book:			
Payments in cash	800		
Balance c/f	1,400		
	38,200		38,200

The gross profit markup of 25% on cost indicates that the cost of the goods sold is £38,400, ie:

	£
Sales (125%)	48,000
Gross profit (25%)	9,600
Cost of goods sold (100%) ($^{100}/_{125} \times$ £48,000)	38,400

The closing stock amount is now a balancing figure in the trading account.

JONATHAN SLUGG
TRADING, PROFIT AND LOSS ACCOUNT
FOR THE YEAR ENDED 31 DECEMBER 20X7

	£	£
Sales		48,000
Less cost of goods sold		
Opening stock	10,000	
Purchases	37,000	
	47,000	
Less closing stock (balancing figure)	8,600	
		38,400
Gross profit (25/125 × £48,000)		9,600
Expenses		
Sundry £(1,500 + 5,600)	7,100	
Depreciation	900	
		8,000
Net profit		1,600

JONATHAN SLUGG
BALANCE SHEET AS AT 31 DECEMBER 20X7

	£	£
Net fixed assets £(20,000 – 900)		19,100
Stock	8,600	
Cash in the till	450	
	9,050	
Bank overdraft	1,250	
Trade creditors	1,400	
	2,650	
Net current assets		6,400
		25,500
Proprietor's capital		
Balance b/f		32,000
Net profit for the year		1,600
		33,600
Drawings £(3,700 + 4,400)		(8,100)
Balance c/f		25,500

7.3 Theft of cash from the till

When cash is stolen from the till, the amount stolen will be a credit entry in the cash book, and a debit in either the P&L account or insurance claim account, depending on whether the business is insured. The missing figure for cash sales, if this has to be calculated, must not ignore cash received but later stolen – see Step 6 above.

8 Accruals and prepayments

Where there is an accrued expense or a prepayment, the charge to be made in the P&L account for the item concerned should be found from the opening balance b/f, the closing balance c/f, and cash payments for the item during the period. The charge in the P&L account is perhaps most easily found as the balancing figure in a T account.

For example, on 1 April 20X6 a business had prepaid rent of £700 which relates to the next accounting period. During the year to 31 March 20X7 it pays £9,300 in rent, and at 31 March 20X7 the prepayment of rent is £1,000. The cost of rent in the P&L account for the year to 31 March 20X7 would be the balancing figure in the following T account. (Remember that a prepayment is a current asset, and so is a debit balance b/f.)

RENT

	£		£
Prepayment: balance b/f	700	P & L account (balancing figure)	9,000
Cash	9,300	Prepayment: balance c/f	1,000
	10,000		10,000
Balance b/f	1,000		

Similarly, if a business has accrued telephone expenses as at 1 July 20X6 of £850, pays £6,720 in telephone bills during the year to 30 June 20X7, and has accrued telephone expenses of £1,140 as at 30 June 20X7, then the telephone expense to be shown in the P&L account for the year to 30 June 20X7 is the balancing figure in the following T account. (Remember that an accrual is a current liability, and so is a credit balance b/f.)

TELEPHONE EXPENSES

	£		£
Cash	6,720	Balance b/f (accrual)	850
Balance c/f (accrual)	1,140	P&L a/c (balancing figure)	7,010
	7,860		7,860
		Balance b/f	1,140

9 Drawings

FAST FORWARD

Drawings often feature as the missing item in an incomplete records problem. The trader has been drawing money but does not know how much.

Drawings would normally represent no particular problem at all in preparing a set of final accounts from incomplete records, but it is not unusual for examination questions to introduce a situation in which:

(a) The business owner pays income into his bank account which has nothing whatever to do with the business operations. For example, the owner might pay dividend income, or other income from personal investments into the bank. (In other words, there are no investments in the business balance sheet, and so income from investments cannot possibly be income of the business).

(b) The business owner pays money out of the business bank account for items which are not business expenses, such as life insurance premiums or a payment for his family's holidays etc.

Where such **personal items of receipts or payments** are made:

(a) Receipts should be set off against drawings. For example, if a business owner receives £600 in dividend income and pays it into his business bank account, although the dividends are from investments not owned by the business, then the accounting entry is:

DEBIT   Cash
CREDIT   Drawings

(b) Payments should be charged to drawings; ie

DEBIT   Drawings
CREDIT   Cash

9.1 Drawings: Beware of the wording in an examination question

You should note that:

(a) If a question states that a proprietor's drawings during a given year are 'approximately £40 per week' then you should assume that drawings for the year are £40 × 52 weeks = £2,080.

(b) However, if a question states that drawings in the year are 'between £35 and £45 per week', do not assume that the drawings average £40 per week and so amount to £2,080 for the year. You could not be certain that the actual drawings did average £40, and so you should treat the drawings figure as a missing item that needs to be calculated.

10 The business equation

FAST FORWARD

Where no trading records have been kept, profit can be derived from opening and closing net assets by use of the **business equation.**

The most obvious incomplete records situation is that of a sole trader who has kept no trading records. It may not be possible to reconstruct his whole profit and loss account, but it will be possible to compute his profit for the year using the **business equation**.

Here is the basic balance sheet format:

Assets	X	
Liabilities	(X)	XX
Capital		XX

So this gives us a figure for capital – assets less liabilities, or **net assets**.

What will increase or decrease capital?

Capital is changed by:

(a)   Money paid in by the trader
(b)   Drawings by the trader
(c)   Profits or losses

So, if we are able to establish the traders net assets at the beginnings and end of the period, we can compute profits as follows:

Profit (loss) = movement in net assets − capital introduced + drawings

This can also be written as:

$$P = I - C_i + D$$

We want to eliminate any movement caused by money paid in or taken out for personal use by the trader. So we take out capital introduced and add back in drawings.

10.1 Example: Business equation

Joe starts up his camera shop on 1 January 20X1, from rented premises, with £5,000 stock and £3,000 in the bank. All of his sales are for cash. He keeps no record of his takings.

At the end of the year he has stock worth £6,600 and £15,000 in the bank. He owes £3,000 to suppliers. He had paid in £5,000 he won on the lottery and drawn out £2,000 to buy himself a motorbike. The motorbike is not used in the business. He has been taking drawings of £100 per week. What is his profit at 31 December 20X1?

Solution

Opening net assets	£
Stock	5,000
Cash	3,000
	8,000

Closing net assets	
Stock	6,600
Cash	15,000
Creditors	(3,000)
	18,600

Movement in net assets (18,600 − 8,000)	10,600
Less capital paid in	(5,000)
Plus drawings ((100 × 52) + 2000)	7,200
Profit	12,800

11 Comprehensive worked examples

A suggested approach to dealing with incomplete records problems brings together the various points described so far in this chapter.

The nature of the 'incompleteness' in the records will vary from problem to problem, but the approach, suitably applied, should be successful in arriving at the final accounts whatever the particular characteristics of the problem might be.

The approach is as follows.

Step 1.   If possible, and if it is not already known, establish the opening balance sheet and the proprietor's interest.

Step 2.   Open up four accounts.

   •   **Trading account** (if you wish, leave space underneath for entering the P&L account later)

- A **cash book**, with two columns if cash sales are significant and there are payments in cash out of the till
- A **debtors account**
- A **creditors account**

Step 3. Enter the opening balances in these accounts.

Step 4. Work through the information you are given line by line; and each item should be entered into the appropriate account if it is relevant to one or more of these four accounts.

You should also try to recognise each item as a 'P&L account income or expense item' or a 'closing balance sheet item'.

It may be necessary to calculate an amount for drawings and an amount for fixed asset depreciation.

Step 5. Look for the balancing figures in your accounts. In particular you might be looking for a value for credit sales, cash sales, purchases, the cost of goods sold, the cost of goods stolen or destroyed, or the closing bank balance. Calculate these missing figures, and make any necessary double entry (eg to the trading account from the creditors account for purchases, to the trading account from the cash book for cash sales, and to the trading account from the debtors account for credit sales).

Step 6. Now complete the P&L account and balance sheet. Working T accounts might be needed where there are accruals or prepayments.

Exam focus point

> Although the following example deals with a long computational question, remember that any of the individual techniques can be examined in a MCQ. In particular a MCQ may ask for the computation of profit given opening and closing net assets. In this case use the business equation: $P = I + D - Ci$ (see above).

An example will illustrate this approach.

11.1 Example: An incomplete records problem

John Snow is the sole distribution agent in the Branton area for Diamond floor tiles. Under an agreement with the manufacturers, John Snow purchases the Diamond floor tiles at a trade discount of 20% off list price and annually in May receives an agency commission of 1% of his purchases for the year ended on the previous 31 March.

For several years, John Snow has obtained a gross profit of 40% on all sales. In a burglary in January 20X1 John Snow lost stock costing £4,000 as well as many of his accounting records. However, after careful investigations, the following information has been obtained covering the year ended 31 March 20X1.

(a) Assets and liabilities at 31 March 20X0 were as follows:

		£
Buildings:	at cost	10,000
	provision for depreciation	6,000
Motor vehicles:	at cost	5,000
	provision for depreciation	2,000
Stock: at cost		3,200
Trade debtors (for sales)		6,300
Agency commission due		300
Prepayments (trade expenses)		120
Balance at bank		4,310
Trade creditors		4,200
Accrued vehicle expenses		230

(b) John Snow has been notified that he will receive an agency commission of £440 on 1 May 20X1.

(c) Stock, at cost, at 31 March 20X1 was valued at an amount £3,000 more than a year previously.

(d) In October 20X0 stock costing £1,000 was damaged by dampness and had to be scrapped as worthless.

(e) Trade creditors at 31 March 20X1 related entirely to goods received whose list prices totalled £9,500.

(f) Discounts allowed amounted to £1,620 whilst discounts received were £1,200.

(g) Trade expenses prepaid at 31 March 20X1 totalled £80.

(h) Vehicle expenses for the year ended 31 March 20X1 amounted to £7,020.

(i) Trade debtors (for sales) at 31 March 20X1 were £6,700.

(j) All receipts are passed through the bank account.

(k) Depreciation is provided annually at the following rates.

Buildings 5% on cost
Motor vehicles 20% on cost.

(l) Commissions received are paid directly to the bank account.

(m) In addition to the payments for purchases, the bank payments were:

	£
Vehicle expenses	6,720
Drawings	4,300
Trade expenses	7,360

(n) John Snow is not insured against loss of stock owing to burglary or damage to stock caused by damp.

Required

Prepare John Snow's trading and profit and loss account for the year ended 31 March 20X1 and a balance sheet on that date.

11.2 Discussion and solution

This is an incomplete records problem because we are told that John Snow has lost many of his accounting records. In particular we do not know sales for the year, purchases during the year, or all the cash receipts and payments.

The first step is to find the opening balance sheet, if possible. In this case, it is. The proprietor's capital is the balancing figure.

JOHN SNOW
BALANCE SHEET AS AT 31 MARCH 20X0

	Cost £	Dep'n £	NBV £
Fixed assets			
Buildings	10,000	6,000	4,000
Motor vehicles	5,000	2,000	3,000
	15,000	8,000	7,000
Current assets			
Stock		3,200	
Trade debtors		6,300	
Commission due		300	
Prepayments		120	
Balance at bank		4,310	
		14,230	
Current liabilities			
Trade creditors		4,200	
Accrued expenses		230	
		4,430	
			9,800
			16,800
Proprietor's capital as at 31 March 20X0			16,800

The next step is to open up a trading account, cash book, debtors account and creditors account and to insert the opening balances, if known. Cash sales and payments in cash are not a feature of the problem, and so a single column cash book is sufficient.

The problem should then be read line by line, identifying any transactions affecting those accounts.

TRADING ACCOUNT

	£	£
Sales (note (f))		60,000
Opening stock	3,200	
Purchases (note (a))	44,000	
	47,200	
Less: damaged stock written off (note (c))	(1,000)	
stock stolen (note (e))	(4,000)	
	42,200	
Less closing stock (note (b))	6,200	
Cost of goods sold		36,000
Gross profit (note (f))		24,000

CASH BOOK

	£		£
Opening balance	4,310	Trade creditors	
Trade debtors (see below)	57,980	(see creditors a/c)	39,400
Agency commission (note (g))	300	Trade expenses	7,360
		Vehicle expenses	6,720
		Drawings	4,300
		Balance c/f	4,810
	62,590		62,590

TRADE DEBTORS

	£		£
Opening balance b/f	6,300	Discounts allowed (note (d))	1,620
Sales (note (f))	60,000	Cash received (balancing figure)	57,980
		Closing balance c/f	6,700
	66,300		66,300

TRADE CREDITORS

	£		£
Discounts received (note (d))	1,200	Opening balance b/f	4,200
Cash paid (balancing figure)	39,400	Purchases (note (a))	44,000
Closing balance c/f (note (i))	7,600		
	48,200		48,200

VEHICLE EXPENSES

	£		£
Cash	6,720	Accrual b/f	230
Accrual c/f (balancing figure)	530	P & L account	7,020
	7,250		7,250

The trading account is complete already, but now the P&L account and balance sheet can be prepared. Remember not to forget items such as the stock losses, commission earned on purchases, discounts allowed and discounts received.

JOHN SNOW – TRADING, PROFIT AND LOSS ACCOUNT
FOR THE YEAR ENDED 31 MARCH 20X1

	£	£
Sales (note (f))		60,000
Opening stock	3,200	
Purchases (note (a))	44,000	
	47,200	
Less: damaged stock written off (note (c))	(1,000)	
stock stolen	(4,000)	
	42,200	
Less closing stock (note (b))	6,200	
Cost of goods sold		36,000
Gross profit (note (f))		24,000
Add: commission on purchases		440
discounts received (note (d))		1,200
		25,640
Expenses		
Trade expenses (note (h))	7,400	
Stock damaged	1,000	
Stock stolen	4,000	
Vehicle expenses	7,020	
Discounts allowed	1,620	
Depreciation		
Buildings	500	
Motor vehicles	1,000	
		22,540
Net profit (to capital account)		3,100

JOHN SNOW
BALANCE SHEET AS AT 31 MARCH 20X1

	Cost £	Dep'n £	NBV £
Fixed assets			
Buildings	10,000	6,500	3,500
Motor vehicles	5,000	3,000	2,000
	15,000	9,500	5,500
Current assets			
Stock		6,200	
Trade debtors		6,700	
Commission due		440	
Prepayments (trade expenses)		80	
Balance at bank		4,810	
		18,230	
Current liabilities			
Trade creditors		7,600	
Accrued expenses		530	
		8,130	
			10,100
			15,600
Proprietor's capital			
As at 31 March 20X0			16,800
Net profit for year to 31 March 20X1		3,100	
Less drawings		(4,300)	
Retained deficit			(1,200)
As at 31 March 20X1			15,600

Notes

(a) The agency commission due on 1 May 20X1 indicates that purchases for the year to 31 March 20X1 were

100%/1% × £440 = £44,000

(b) Closing stock at cost on 31 March 20X1 was £(3,200 + 3,000) = £6,200.

(c) Stock scrapped (£1,000) is accounted for by:

CREDIT   Trading account
DEBIT   P&L account

(d) Discounts allowed are accounted for by:

DEBIT   Discounts allowed account
CREDIT   Debtors

Similarly, discounts received are:

DEBIT   Creditors
CREDIT   Discounts received

Note. Discounts received represents settlement discounts, not *trade* discounts, which are not usually accounted for as they are given automatically at source.

(e) Stocks lost in the burglary are accounted for by:

CREDIT   Trading account
DEBIT   P&L account

(f) The trade discount of 20% has already been deducted in arriving at the value of the purchases. The gross profit is 40% on sales, so with cost of sales = £36,000

		£
Cost	(60%)	36,000
Profit	(40%)	24,000
Sales	(100%)	60,000

(It is assumed that trade expenses are not included in the trading account, and so should be ignored in this calculation.)

(g) The agency commission of £300 due on 1 May 20X0 would have been paid to John Snow at that date.

(h) The P&L account expenditure for trade expenses and closing balance on vehicle expenses account are as follows:

TRADE EXPENSES

	£		£
Prepayment b/f	120	P&L account (balancing figure)	7,400
Cash	7,360	Prepayment c/f	80
	7,480		7,480

(i) Trade creditors at the year end are £9,500 less 20% trade discount, ie £7,600 (80% × £9,500).

Exam focus point

Incomplete records questions in the exam will only be for sole traders (not partnerships). Also, as the average MCQ is worth around 2 marks, you will only have to calculate **some** of these missing figures.

However, you need to practise doing questions with different missing figures, as you do not know which missing figures will be examined eg it could be sales and purchases, or cash sales and stolen stock. Therefore you need to get as much practise as possible on all types of incomplete records questions. Make sure that you make a good attempt at the questions in the exam question bank.

11.3 Using a debtors account to calculate both cash sales and credit sales

A final point which needs to be considered is how a missing value can be found for cash sales and credit sales, when a business has both, but takings banked by the business are not divided between takings from cash sales and takings from credit sales.

11.4 Example: Using a debtors account

A business had, on 1 January 20X8, trade debtors of £2,000, cash in the bank of £3,000, and cash in hand of £300.

During the year to 31 December 20X8 the business banked £95,000 in takings.

It also paid out the following expenses in cash from the till:

Drawings	£1,200
Sundry expenses	£800

On 29 August 20X8 a thief broke into the shop and stole £400 from the till.

At 31 December 20X8 trade debtors amounted to £3,500, cash in the bank £2,500 and cash in the till £150.

What was the value of sales during the year?

Solution

If we tried to prepare a debtors account and a two column cash book, we would have insufficient information, in particular about whether the takings which were banked related to cash sales or credit sales.

DEBTORS

	£		£
Balance b/f	2,000	Payments from debtors (credit sales)	Unknown
Credit sales	Unknown		
		Balance c/f	3,500

CASH BOOK

	Cash £	Bank £		Cash £	Bank £
Balance b/f	300	3,000	Drawings	1,200	
			Sundry expenses	800	
Debtors-payments		Unknown	Cash stolen	400	
Cash sales	Unknown		Balance c/f	150	2,500

All we do know is that the combined sums from debtors and cash takings banked is £95,000.

The value of sales can be found instead by using the debtors account, which should be used to record cash takings banked as well as payments by debtors. The balancing figure in the debtors account will then be a combination of credit sales and some cash sales. The cash book only needs to be a single column.

DEBTORS

	£		£
Balance b/f	2,000	Cash banked	95,000
Sales-to trading account	96,500	Balance c/f	3,500
	98,500		98,500

	£		£
Balance in hand b/f	300	Payments in cash:	
Balance in bank b/f	3,000	Drawings	1,200
Debtors a/c	95,000	Expenses	800
		Other payments	?
		Cash stolen	400
		Balance in hand c/f	150
		Balance in bank c/f	2,500

The remaining 'undiscovered' amount of cash sales is now found as follows.

	£	£
Payments in cash out of the till		
Drawings	1,200	
Expenses	800	
		2,000
Cash stolen		400
Closing balance of cash in hand		150
		2,550
Less opening balance of cash in hand		(300)
Further cash sales		2,250

(This calculation is similar to the one described above for calculating cash sales.)

Total sales for the year are:

	£
From debtors account	96,500
From cash book	2,250
Total sales	98,750

Question

Incomplete records

Mary Grimes, retail fruit and vegetable merchant, does not keep a full set of accounting records. However, the following information has been produced from the business's records.

(a)   Summary of the bank account for the year ended 31 August 20X8

	£		£
1 Sept 20X7 balance brought forward	1,970	Payment to suppliers	72,000
		Purchase of motor van (E471 KBR)	13,000
Receipts from trade debtors	96,000	Rent and rates	2,600
Sale of private yacht	20,000	Wages	15,100
Sale of motor van (A123 BWA)	2,100	Motor vehicle expenses	3,350
		Postages and stationery	1,360
		Drawings	9,200
		Repairs and renewals	650
		Insurances	800
		31 August 20X8 balance c/fwd	2,010
	120,070		120,070
1 Sept 20X8 balance b/fwd	2,010		

(b)   Assets and liabilities, other than balance at bank as at:

		1 Sept 20X7 £	31 Aug 20X8 £
Trade creditors		4,700	2,590
Trade debtors		7,320	9,500
Rent and rates accruals		200	260
Motor vans:			
A123 BWA:	At cost	10,000	–
	Provision for depreciation	8,000	–
E471 KBR:	At cost	–	13,000
	Provision for depreciation	–	To be determined
Stock in trade		4,900	5,900
Insurance prepaid		160	200

(c)   All receipts are banked and all payments are made from the business bank account.

(d)   A trade debt of £300 owing by John Blunt and included in the trade debtors at 31 August 20X8 (see (b) above), is to be written off as a irrecoverable debt.

(e)   It is Mary Grimes' policy to provide depreciation at the rate of 20% on the cost of motor vans held at the end of each financial year; no depreciation is provided in the year of sale or disposal of a motor van.

(f)   Discounts received during the year ended 31 August 20X8 from trade creditors amounted to £1,100.

Required

(a)   Prepare Mary Grimes' trading and profit and loss account for the year ended 31 August 20X8.
(b)   Prepare Mary Grimes' balance sheet as at 31 August 20X8.

Answer

(a)   TRADING AND PROFIT AND LOSS ACCOUNT
         FOR THE YEAR ENDED 31 AUGUST 20X8

	£	£
Sales (W1)		98,180
Opening stock	4,900	
Purchases (W2)	70,990	
	75,890	
Less closing stock	5,900	
		69,990
Gross profit		28,190
Discounts received		1,100
Profit on sale of motor vehicle £2,100 – £(10,000 – 8,000)		100
		29,390
Rent and rates (W3)	2,660	
Wages	15,100	
Motor vehicle expenses	3,350	
Postages and stationery	1,360	
Repairs and renewals	650	
Insurances (W4)	760	
Irrecoverable debt	300	
Depreciation of van (20% × £13,000)	2,600	
		26,780
		2,610

(b)   BALANCE SHEET AS AT 31 AUGUST 20X8

	£	£
Fixed assets		
Motor van: cost	13,000	
depreciation	2,600	
		10,400
Current assets		
Stock	5,900	
Debtors (£9,500 – £300 bad debt)	9,200	
Prepayment	200	
Cash at bank	2,010	
	17,310	
Current liabilities		
Creditors	2,590	
Accrual	260	
	2,850	
Net current assets		14,460
		24,860
Capital account		
Balance at 1 September 20X7 (W5)		11,450
Additional capital: proceeds on sale of yacht		20,000
Net profit for the year	2,610	
Less drawings	9,200	
Retained loss for the year		(6,590)
Balance at 31 August 20X8		24,860

Workings

1   Sales

	£
Cash received from customers	96,000
Add debtors balances at 31 August 20X8	9,500
	105,500
Less debtors balances at 1 September 20X7	7,320
Sales in year	98,180

2   Purchases

	£	£
Payments to suppliers		72,000
Add: creditors balances at 31 August 20X8	2,590	
discounts granted by creditors	1,100	
		3,690
		75,690
Less creditors balances at 1 September 20X7		4,700
		70,990

3   Rent and rates

	£
Cash paid in year	2,600
Add accrual at 31 August 20X8	260
	2,860
Less accrual at 1 September 20X7	200
Charge for the year	2,660

	£
Cash paid in year	800
Add prepayment at 1 September 20X7	160
	960
Less prepayment at 31 August 20X8	200
	760

Workings 1-4 could also be presented in ledger account format as follows.

TOTAL DEBTORS

	£		£
Balance b/f	7,320	Bank	96,000
∴ Sales	98,180	Balance c/f	9,500
	105,500		105,500

TOTAL CREDITORS

	£		£
Bank	72,000	Balance b/f	4,700
Discounts received	1,100	∴ Purchases	70,990
Balance c/f	2,590		
	75,690		75,690

RENT AND RATES

	£		£
Bank	2,600	Balance b/f	200
Balance c/f	260	∴ P & L charge	2,660
	2,860		2,860

INSURANCES

	£		£
Balance b/f	160	∴ P & L charge	760
Bank	800	Balance c/f	200
	960		960

5   *Capital at 1 September 20X7*

	£	£
Assets		
Bank balance		1,970
Debtors		7,320
Motor van £(10,000 – 8,000)		2,000
Stock		4,900
Prepayment		160
		16,350
Liabilities		
Trade creditors	4,700	
Accrual	200	
		4,900
		11,450

Chapter Roundup

- Incomplete records problems occur when a business does not have a full set of accounting records, either because:
  - The proprietor of the business does not keep a full set of accounts, or
  - Some of the business accounts are accidentally lost or destroyed.

- In practice there should not be any missing item in the opening balance sheet of the business, because it should be available from the preparation of the previous year's final accounts.

- If a business does not keep a record of its sales on credit, the value of these sales can be derived from the opening balance of trade debtors, the closing balance of trade debtors, and the payments received from trade debtors during the period.

- A similar relationship exists between purchases of stock during a period, the opening and closing balances for trade creditors, and amounts paid to trade creditors during the period.

- When the value of purchases is not known, a different approach might be required to find out what they were, depending on the nature of the information given to you.

- A similar type of calculation might be required to derive the value of goods stolen or destroyed.

- The construction of a cash book, largely from bank statements showing receipts and payments of a business during a given period, is often an important feature of incomplete records problems.

- **Drawings** often feature as the missing item in an incomplete records problem. The trader has been drawing money but does not know how much.

- Where no trading records have been kept, profit can be derived from opening and closing net assets by use of the **business equation.**

Quick Quiz

1   In the absence of a sales account or sales day book, how can a figure of sales for the year be computed?

2   A business has opening creditors of £75,000 and closing creditors of £65,000. Cash paid to suppliers was £65,000 and discounts received £3,000. What is the figure for purchases?

    A   £58,000
    B   £78,000
    C   £52,000
    D   £55,000

3   What is the difference between 'mark-up' and 'gross profit percentage'?

4   What is the accounting double entry to record the loss of stock by fire or burglary?

    A   DR P&L, CR Cost of sales
    B   DR Cost of sales, CR P&L

5   In what circumstances is a two-column cash book useful?

6   If a business proprietor pays his personal income into the business bank account, what is the accounting double entry to record the transaction?

    A   DR drawings, CR cash
    B   DR cash, CR drawings

7   A business has net assets of £70,000 at the beginning of the year and £80,000 at the end of the year. Drawings were £25,000 and a lottery win of £5,000 was paid into the business during the year. What was the profit for the year?

    A   £10,000 loss
    B   £30,000 profit
    C   £10,000 profit
    D   £30,000 loss

8   A business usually has a mark-up of 20% on cost of sales. During a year, its sales were £90,000. What was cost of sales?

    A   £15,000
    B   £72,000
    C   £18,000
    D   £75,000

Answers to Quick Quiz

1. By using the trade debtors control account to calculate sales as a balancing figure.

2. A

CREDITORS CONTROL

	£		£
Bank	65,000	Opening creditors	75,000
Discounts received	3,000	Purchases (bal fig)	58,000
Closing creditors	65,000		
	133,000		133,000

3. • Mark-up is the profit as a percentage of cost.
   • Gross profit percentage is the profit as a percentage of sales.

4. A   DEBIT   P&L a/c
        CREDIT   Cost of sales

   Assuming that the goods were not insured.

5. Where a large amount of receipts and payments are made in cash.

6. B   DEBIT   Cash
        CREDIT   Drawings

7. B   Profit = movement in net assets − capital introduced + drawings
        = (80,000 − 70,000) − 5,000 + 25,000
        = 30,000

8. D

	£
Sales	90,000
Cost of sales (bal fig)	75,000
Profit $\dfrac{20}{120} \times 90,000$	15,000

Now try the questions below from the Exam Question Bank

Number	Level	Marks	Time
Q34	Examination	2	2 mins
Q35	Examination	2	2 mins
Q36	Examination	2	2 mins
Q37	Examination	2	2 mins

Partnerships

Topic list	Syllabus reference
1 The characteristics of partnerships	F4(a), (c), (d)
2 Preparing partnership accounts	F4(b)-(n)

Introduction

So far we have considered businesses owned by one person: sole traders. Now we will consider how we can account for businesses owned by more than one person. This chapter will examine how we can account for partnerships and the following two chapters will examine how we can account for companies.

Study guide

		Intellectual level
F4	**Accounting for partnerships**	
(a)	Understand and identify the typical content of a partnership agreement, including profit-sharing terms	1
(b)	Understand the nature of:	1
(i)	Capital accounts	
(ii)	Current accounts	
(iii)	Division of profits	
(c)	Calculate and record the partners' shares of profit/losses	1
(d)	Account for guaranteed minimum profit shares	1
(e)	Calculate and record partners' drawings	1
(f)	Calculate and record interest on drawings	1
(g)	Calculate and record interest on capital	1
(h)	Calculate and record partners' salaries	1
(i)	Prepare an extract of a current account	1
(j)	Prepare an extract of a capital account	1
(k)	Prepare extracts of the profit and loss account, including division of profit, and balance sheet of a partnership	1
(l)	Define goodwill, in relation to partnership accounts	1
(m)	Identify the factors leading to the creation of goodwill in relation to partnership accounts	1
(n)	Calculate the value of goodwill from given information	1

Note. Questions on partnerships may include the effect of admission of new partners.

Exam guide

This is an important topic and it is almost certain to appear in the exam. Learn how to prepare partnership accounts and also the advantages and disadvantages of trading as a partnership.

Exam focus point

At the 2009 ACCA Teachers' Conference the examiner highlighted partnership accounts as an area consistently answered badly in the exam. She also emphasised the need to practise full questions on this topic as a good foundation for future studies.

1 The characteristics of partnerships

Try this question to get you thinking.

Question   Partnership

Try to think of reasons why a business should be conducted as a partnership, rather than:

(a)   As a sole trader
(b)   As a company

(a)   The main problems with trading as a sole trader is the limitation on resources it implies. As the business grows, there will be a need for:

(i)   Additional capital. Although some capital may be provided by a bank, it would not be desirable to have the business entirely dependent on borrowing.

(ii) Additional expertise. A sole trader technically competent in his own field may not have, for example, the financial skills that would be needed in a larger business.

(iii) Additional management time. Once a business grows to a certain point, it becomes impossible for one person to look after all aspects of it without help.

(b)   The main disadvantage of incorporating is the regulatory burden faced by limited companies. In addition, there are certain 'businesses' which are not allowed to enjoy limited liability; you may have read about the Lloyd's 'names' who face personal bankruptcy because the option of limited liability was not available to them.

There are also tax factors to consider, but these are beyond the scope of this book.

Key term

> **Partnership** is defined by the Partnership Act 1890 as the relationship which exists between persons carrying on a business in common with a view of profit.

In other words, a partnership is an arrangement between two or more individuals in which they undertake to share the risks and rewards of a joint business operation.

It is usual for a partnership to be established formally by means of a **partnership agreement**. However, if individuals act as though they are in partnership even if no written agreement exists, then it will be presumed in law that a partnership does exist and that its terms of agreement are the same as those laid down in the Partnership Act 1890.

1.1 The partnership agreement

The partnership agreement is a written agreement in which the terms of the partnership are set out, and in particular the financial arrangements as between partners. The items it should cover include the following.

(a)   **Capital**. Each partner puts in a share of the business capital. If there is to be an agreement on how much each partner should put in and keep in the business, as a minimum fixed amount, this should be stated.

(b)   **Profit-sharing ratio**. Partners can agree to share profits in any way they choose. For example, if there are three partners in a business, they might agree to share profits equally but on the other hand, if one partner does a greater share of the work, or has more experience and ability, or puts in more capital, the ratio of profit sharing might be different.

(c)   **Interest on capital**. Partners might agree to pay themselves interest on the capital they put into the business. If they do so, the agreement will state what rate of interest is to be applied.

(d)   **Partners' salaries**. Partners might also agree to pay themselves salaries. These are not salaries in the same way that an employee of the business will be paid a wage or salary, because partners' salaries are an appropriation of profit, and not an expense in the profit and loss account of the business. The purpose of paying salaries is to give each partner a satisfactory basic income before the residual profits are shared out.

(e)   **Drawings**. Partners may draw out their share of profits from the business. However, they might agree to put a limit on how much they should draw out in any period. If so, this limit should be specified in the partnership agreement. To encourage partners to delay taking drawings out of the business until the financial year has ended, the agreement might also be that partners should be charged interest on their drawings during the year.

(f)   **Guaranteed minimum profit shares**. Some partnership agreements may guarantee a minimum share of profits for one or more partners. This would mean that a partner was entitled to a stipulated amount from the profits. If the amount allocated by the **profit-sharing ratio** is lower than this, then the partner would receive the guaranteed minimum profit share and the remainder of the profits would be a shared between the other partners according to the partnership agreement. Occasionally, one partner will guarantee another partner's minimum profit share. In this case that partner will make up the difference between the profit-sharing ratio and the minimum guaranteed amount.

Even in loss making situations, the partner is entitled to the guaranteed minimum profit share.

In the absence of a formal agreement between the partners, certain rules laid down by the **Partnership Act 1890** are presumed to apply instead.

(a) Residual profits are shared equally between the partners

(b) There are no partners' salaries

(c) Partners receive no interest on the capital they invest in the business

(d) Partners are entitled to interest of 5% per annum on any loans they advance to the business in excess of their agreed capital.

1.2 Example: Partners' salaries and profit-sharing

Suppose Bill and Ben are partners sharing profit in the ratio 2:1 and that they agree to pay themselves a salary of £10,000 each. If profits before deducting salaries are £26,000, how much income would each partner receive?

Solution

First, the two salaries are deducted from profit, leaving £6,000 (£26,000 – £20,000).

This £6,000 has to be distributed between Bill and Ben in the ratio 2:1. In other words, Bill will receive twice as much as Ben. You can probably work this out in your head and see that Bill will get £4,000 and Ben £2,000, but we had better see how this is calculated properly.

Add the 'parts' of the ratio together. For our example, 2 + 1 = 3. Divide this total into whatever it is that has to be shared out. In our example, £6,000 ÷ 3 = £2,000. Each 'part' is worth £2,000, so Bill receives 2 × £2,000 = £4,000 and Ben will receive 1 × £2,000 = £2,000.

So the final answer to the question is that Bill receives his salary plus £4,000 and Ben his salary plus £2,000. This could be laid out as follows:

	Bill	Ben	Total
	£	£	£
Salary	10,000	10,000	20,000
Share of residual profits (ratio 2:1)	4,000	2,000	6,000
	14,000	12,000	26,000

Question   Profit share

Suppose Tom, Dick and Harry want to share out £150 in the ratio 7:3:5. How much would each get?

Answer

The sum of the ratio 'parts' is 7 + 3 + 5 = 15. Each part is therefore worth £150 ÷ 15 = £10. So the £150 would be shared as follows:

			£
(a)	Tom:	7 × £10 =	70
(b)	Dick:	3 × £10 =	30

(c)   Harry: 5 × £10 =   <u>50</u>
                                     <u>150</u>

1.3 Guaranteed Minimum Profit Share

Sita, Nisha and Zelda share profits in the ratio of 2:2:1 but Zelda has a guaranteed minimum profit of £18,000. The profits for the year are £75,000.

The sum of the ratio 'parts' is 2+2+1=5. Each part is worth £15,000 so according to the PSR the profits will be allocated

Sita	Nisha	Zelda
30,000	30,000	15,000

However, this leaves Zelda with less than her guaranteed minimum so a further reallocation of profits is made from the other two partners to give her the minimum amount.

Sita	Nisha	Zelda
30,000	30,000	15,000
(1,500)	(1,500)	3,000
28,500	28,500	18,000

1.4 Advantages and disadvantages of trading as a partnership

Operating as a partnership entails certain advantages and disadvantages when compared with both sole traders and limited companies.

1.4.1 Partnership v sole trader

The advantages of operating as a partnership rather than as a sole trader are practical rather than legal. They include the following.

(a)   Risks are spread across a larger number of people.
(b)   The trader will have access to a wider network of contacts through the other partners.
(c)   Partners should bring to the business not only capital but skills and experience.
(d)   It may well be easier to raise finance from external sources such as banks.

Possible disadvantages include the following.

(a)   While the risk is spread over a larger number of people, so are the profits!
(b)   By bringing in more people the former sole trader dilutes control over his business.
(c)   There may be disputes between the partners.

1.4.2 Partnership v limited company

Limited companies (covered in detail in the next chapter) offer limited liability to their owners. This means that the maximum amount that an owner stands to lose in the event that the company becomes insolvent and must pay off its debts is the capital in the business. In the case of partnerships (and sole traders), liability for the debts of the business is unlimited, which means that if the business runs up debts and is unable to pay, the proprietors will become personally liable for the unpaid debts and would be required, if necessary, to sell their private possessions in order to pay for them.

Limited liability is clearly a significant incentive for a partnership to incorporate (become a company). Other advantages of incorporation are that it is easier to raise capital and that the retirement or death of one of its members does not necessitate dissolution and re-formation of the firm.

In practice, however, particularly for small firms, these advantages are more apparent than real. Banks will normally seek personal guarantees from shareholders before making loans or granting an overdraft facility and so the advantage of limited liability is lost to a small owner managed business.

LEARNING MEDIA

In addition, a company faces a greater administrative and financial burden arising from:

(a) Compliance with the Companies Act, notably in having to prepare annual accounts and have them audited, file annual returns and keep statutory books.

(b) Compliance with SSAPs and FRSs.

(c) Formation and annual registration costs.

2 Preparing partnership accounts

FAST FORWARD

Partnership accounts are the same as sole traders except for the allocation of profit and treatment of capital.

2.1 How does accounting for partnerships differ from accounting for sole traders?

Partnership accounts are identical in many respects to the accounts of sole traders.

(a) The assets of a partnership are like the assets of any other business, and are accounted for in the same way. The assets side of a partnership balance sheet is no different from what has been shown in earlier chapters of this Study Text.

(b) The net profit of a partnership is calculated in the same way as the net profit of a sole trader. The only minor difference is that if a partner makes a loan to the business (as distinct from capital contribution) then interest on the loan will be an expense in the profit and loss account, in the same way as interest on any other loan from a person or organisation who is not a partner. We will return to partner loans later in the chapter.

There are two respects in which partnership accounts are different, however.

(a) The funds put into the business by each partner are shown differently.

(b) The net profit must be **appropriated** by the partners. This appropriation of profits must be shown in the partnership accounts.

Exam focus point

Appropriation of profit means sharing out profits in accordance with the partnership agreement.

2.2 Funds employed

When a partnership is formed, each partner puts in some capital to the business. These initial capital contributions are recorded in a series of **capital accounts**, one for each partner. (Since each partner is ultimately entitled to repayment of his capital it is clearly vital to keep a record of how much is owed to whom.) Partners do not have to put in the same amount.

Attention!

The balance for the capital account will always be a brought forward credit entry in the partnership accounts, because the capital contributed by proprietors is a liability of the business.

In addition to a capital account, each partner normally has:

(a) A **current account**.

(b) A **drawings account**.

Key term

A **current account** is used to record the **profits retained in the business** by the partner.

It is therefore a sort of capital account, which increases in value when the partnership makes profits, and falls in value when the partner whose current account it is makes drawings out of the business.

The main differences between the capital and current account in accounting for partnerships are as follows.

(a)   (i)   The balance on the capital account remains static from year to year (with one or two exceptions).

          (ii)   The current account is continually fluctuating up and down, as the partnership makes profits which are shared out between the partners, and as each partner takes out drawings.

(b)   A further difference is that when the partnership agreement provides for interest on capital, partners receive interest on the balance in their capital account, but **not on the balance in their current account.**

The drawings accounts serve exactly the same purpose as the drawings account for a sole trader. Each partner's drawings are recorded in a separate account. At the end of an accounting period, each partner's drawings are cleared to his current account; ie

DEBIT   Current account of partner
CREDIT   Drawings account of partner

(If the amount of the drawings exceeds the balance on a partner's current account, the current account will show a debit balance. However, in normal circumstances, we should expect to find a credit balance on the current accounts.)

The partnership balance sheet will therefore consist of:

(a)   The capital accounts of each partner.
(b)   The current accounts of each partner, net of drawings.

This will be illustrated in an example later.

2.3 Loans by partners

In addition, it is sometimes the case that an existing or previous partner will make a loan to the partnership in which case he becomes a creditor of the partnership. On the balance sheet, such a loan is not included as partners' funds, but is shown separately as a long-term liability (unless repayable within twelve months in which case it is a current liability). This is the case whether or not the loan creditor is also an existing partner.

However, **interest on such loans will be credited to the partner's current account** (if he is an existing partner). This is administratively more convenient, especially when the partner does not particularly want to be paid the loan interest in cash immediately it becomes due. Remember:

(a)   Interest on loans from a partner is accounted for as an expense in the P & L account, and not as an appropriation of profit, even though the interest is added to the current account of the partners.

(b)   If there is no interest rate specified, the Partnership Act 1890 (section 24) provides for interest to be paid at 5% pa on loans by partners.

2.4 Appropriation of net profits

The net profit of a partnership is shared out between them according to the terms of their agreement. This sharing out is shown in a **profit and loss appropriation account**, which follows on from the profit and loss account itself.

The accounting entries are:

(a)   DEBIT   Profit and loss account with net profit c/d
           CREDIT   Profit and loss appropriation account with net profit b/d

(b)   DEBIT   Profit and loss appropriation account
           CREDIT   The current accounts of each partner

With an individual share of profits for each partner.

The way in which profit is shared out depends on the terms of the partnership agreement. The steps to take are as follows.

Step 1. Establish how much the net profit is.

Step 2. Appropriate interest on capital and salaries first. Both of these items are an appropriation of profit and are not expenses in the P & L account.

Step 3. If partners agree to pay interest on their drawings during the year

DEBIT   Current accounts
CREDIT   Appropriation of profit account

Step 4. **Residual profits**: the difference between net profits (plus any interest charged on drawings) and appropriations for interest on capital and salaries is the residual profit. This is shared out between partners in the profit-sharing ratio.

Step 5. Each partner's share of profits is credited to his current account.

Step 6. The balance on each partner's drawings account is debited to his current account.

In practice each partner's capital account will occupy a separate ledger account, as will his current account etc. The examples which follow in this text use the columnar form; they might also ignore the breakdown of net assets employed (fixed, current assets etc) to help to clarify and simplify the illustrations.

Exam focus point

For examination purposes, it is customary to represent the details of these accounts side by side, in columnar form, to save time.

2.5 Example: Partnership accounts

Locke, Niece and Munster are in partnership with an agreement to share profits in the ratio 3:2:1. They also agree that:

(a)   All three should receive interest at 12% on capital.

(b)   Munster should receive a salary of £6,000 per annum.

(c)   Interest will be charged on drawings at the rate of 5% (charged on the end of year drawings balances).

(d)   The interest rate on the loan by Locke is 5%.

The balance sheet of the partnership as at 31 December 20X5 revealed the following:

	£	£
Capital accounts		
Locke	20,000	
Niece	8,000	
Munster	6,000	
		34,000
Current accounts		
Locke	3,500	
Niece	(700)	
Munster	1,800	
		4,600
Loan account (Locke)		6,000
Capital employed to finance net fixed assets and working capital		44,600

Drawings made during the year to 31 December 20X6 were:

	£
Locke	6,000
Niece	4,000
Munster	7,000

The net profit for the year to 31 December 20X6 was £24,530 before deducting loan interest.

Required

Prepare the profit and loss appropriation account for the year to 31 December 20X6, and the partners' capital accounts, and current accounts.

Solution

The interest payable by each partner on their drawings during the year is:

		£
Locke	5% of £6,000	300
Niece	5% of £4,000	200
Munster	5% of £7,000	350
		850

These payments are debited to the current accounts and credited to the profit and loss **appropriation** account.

The interest payable to Locke on his loan is:

5% of £6,000 = £300

We can now begin to work out the appropriation of profits.

		£	£
Net profit, less loan interest (£24,530 – £300)			24,230
Add interest on drawings			850
			25,080
Less Munster salary			6,000
			19,080
Less Interest on capital			
Locke	(12% of £20,000)	2,400	
Niece	(12% of £ 8,000)	960	
Munster	(12% of £ 6,000)	720	
			4,080
			15,000
Residual profits:			
Locke	(3)	7,500	
Niece	(2)	5,000	
Munster	(1)	2,500	
			15,000

Make sure you remember what the various interest figures represent and that you understand exactly what has been calculated here.

(a) The partners can take some drawings out of the business, but if they do they will be charged interest on it.

(b) The partners have capital tied up in the business (of course, otherwise there would be no business) and they have agreed to pay themselves interest on whatever capital each has put in.

(c) Once all the necessary adjustments have been made to net profit, £15,000 remains and is divided up between the partners in the ratio 3:2:1.

Now the accounts for the partnership can be prepared.

LOCKE NIECE MUNSTER
PROFIT AND LOSS APPROPRIATION ACCOUNT
FOR THE YEAR ENDED 31 DECEMBER 20X6

	£	£		£	£
			Net profit b/f		24,230
Salaries – Munster		6,000	Interest on drawings:		
Interest on capital			Current account of		
Locke	2,400		Locke	300	
Niece	960		Niece	200	
Munster	720		Munster	350	
		4,080			850
Residual profits					
Locke	7,500				
Niece	5,000				
Munster	2,500				
		15,000			
		25,080			25,080

PARTNERS' CURRENT ACCOUNTS

	Locke £	Niece £	Munster £		Locke £	Niece £	Munster £
Balance b/f		700		Balance b/f	3,500		1,800
Interest on drawings	300	200	350	Loan interest	300		
Drawings	6,000	4,000	7,000	Interest on capital	2,400	960	720
Balance c/f	7,400	1,060	3,670	Salary			6,000
				Residual profits	7,500	5,000	2,500
	13,700	5,960	11,020		13,700	5,960	11,020
				Balance b/f	7,400	1,060	3,670

PARTNERS' CAPITAL ACCOUNTS

	Locke £	Niece £	Munster £
Balance b/f	20,000	8,000	6,000

The balance sheet as at 31 December 20X6 would be:

	£	£
Capital accounts		
Locke	20,000	
Niece	8,000	
Munster	6,000	
		34,000
Current accounts		
Locke	7,400	
Niece	1,060	
Munster	3,670	
		12,130
		46,130

	£
Net assets	
As at 31 December 20X5	44,600
Added during the year (applying the business equation, this is the difference between net profits and drawings = £24,230 – £17,000)	7,230
Add accrual for loan interest	300
As at 31 December 20X6	52,130
Less long term creditors	
Loan: Locke	(6,000)
	46,130

Again, make sure you understand what has happened here.

(a)   The partners' *capital* accounts have not changed. They were brought forward at £20,000, £8,000 and £6,000, and they are just the same in the new balance sheet.

(b)   The partners' *current* accounts have changed. The balances brought forward from last year's balance sheet of £3,500, (£700) and £1,800 have become £7,400, £1,060 and £3,670 in the new balance sheet. How this came about is shown in the partners' current (ledger) accounts.

(c)   The events recorded in the current accounts are a reflection of how the partnership has distributed its profit, and this was shown in the profit and loss appropriation account.

2.6 Changes in the partnership

Another aspect to consider is how changes in the partnership will affect the profit sharing arrangements. When a partner retires or a new partner is taken on during the year, the profit for that year will have to be apportioned into the periods before and after the change and the two or more sets of profit sharing arrangements applied. Unless told otherwise, assume that profits were earned evenly throughout the year.

2.7 Example: Profit share

Hook and Line have been in partnership for many years, sharing profits equally. On 1 October 20X8, Floater is admitted to the partnership and it is decided that Hook, Line and Floater will now share profits 4:4:2. The net profit for the year to 31 December 20X8 is £150,000. Show how this will be split between the partners.

Solution

There are two distinct periods here – 9 months of Hook and Line and 3 months of Hook, Line and Floater. Profits average £12,500 per month. So we apportion as follows:

	Hook	Line	Floater	Total
Jan-Sept 20X8				
112,500/5:5	56,250	56,250	–	112,500
Oct-Dec 20X8				
37,500/4:4:2	15,000	15,000	7,500	37,500
	71,250	71,250	7,500	150,000

2.8 Goodwill

When a partner retires or a new partner is admitted, it is usual to calculate the 'goodwill' in the business.

Goodwill arises because an existing, thriving business is usually worth more than the value of the net assets in the balance sheet. Customer 'goodwill' means that customers will return because of the good service given. Supplier 'goodwill' can also arise if there are good relationships with suppliers, so that suppliers trust the business. Goodwill is an example of an intangible asset.

Goodwill is allocated to the partners before the change in the old PSR. After the change, goodwill is then written back to all the new partners in the new PSR.

> Goodwill should not be left in the balance sheet.

2.9 Example: goodwill

In the case of Hook, Line and Floater in 2.7 above, assume that the business had goodwill of £300,000 at 1 October 20X8.

The partners request that goodwill is created and then reversed on each change.

Solution

CURRENT ACCOUNTS

	Hook £	Line £	Floater £		Hook £	Line £	Floater £
1/10/X8				1/10/X8			
Goodwill reversed	120,000	120,000	60,000	Goodwill created	150,000	150,000	–

GOODWILL

		£			£
1/10/X8	Current accounts	300,000	1/10/X8	Current accounts	300,000

Notice the effect that this has on the partners' current accounts. Although goodwill does not remain in the books, when Floater is admitted, he effectively pays for his share of the goodwill because Hook and Line's shares have been diminished on his admission.

2.10 Calculation of goodwill

You may have wondered how the goodwill in Section 2.9 was calculated. In real life, the calculation of goodwill can be extremely complex and this is outside the scope of your syllabus.

In the exam, you are only likely to be asked to calculate goodwill using the following formula.

> Goodwill = value of business − net asset value

Question   Calculation of goodwill

Hook, Line and Floater have continued trading for a further year and they are considering admitting Sinker on 31 December 20X9. For the purpose of calculating goodwill, the partners obtain a valuation of the business as if it were to be sold on 31 December 20X9. This valuation is £750,000. The balance sheet at 31 December 20X9 shows net assets of £375,000. Calculate goodwill.

Answer

Goodwill = value of business − net assets value
$$= 750,000 - 375,000$$
$$= £375,000$$

2.11 Summary

If a change in the constitution of a partnership takes place during the financial year the profit and loss appropriation account will have to be prepared in **two stages** in columnar form. Generally it is assumed that profit is earned evenly over a period (unless otherwise stated), but some points to watch out for are as follows.

(a)   If an employee is admitted to partnership in mid-year, his salary whilst an employee is an expense chargeable wholly against profits of the first part of the year and subsequent drawings are debited to his current account.

(b)   If a partner leaves in mid-year and a loan account is created, interest on the loan account is chargeable as an expense against profits of the last part of the year only.

Now try these questions – they are good practice for your exam.

Question

Alice, Bonny & Clyde

You have been approached by a partnership, Alice, Bonny and Clyde, to prepare their accounts for the year ending 31 October 20X4. You have established that profit available for appropriation is £78,000 for the year and have been given the following information.

(a)   Originally only Alice and Bonny were in partnership, sharing profits in a ratio of 2:1. On 1 November 20X3 they admitted the third partner, Clyde. Clyde contributed capital of £10,000 on 1 November 20X3. The new profit sharing ratio is 3:2:1 to Alice, Bonny and Clyde respectively.

(b)   Interest on capital is paid at a rate of 10% based on the year-end capital amount. No interest is allowed on the balance of current accounts.

(c)   Drawings made for the year ending 31 October 20X4 were:

	£
Alice	38,000
Bonny	19,500
Clyde	15,000

(d)   Alice is entitled to a salary of £10,000 per annum, and Clyde is entitled to £5,000 per annum.

(e)   You have been supplied with the balance sheet of the partnership as at 31 October 20X3.

Part F Preparing basic financial statements | **19: Partnerships**   341

BALANCE SHEET OF ALICE AND BONNY AS AT 31 OCTOBER 20X3

	£	£
Fixed assets		
Motor cars	20,000	
Fixtures and fittings	4,000	
		24,000
Current assets		
Stock	8,000	
Debtors	3,500	
	11,500	
Current liabilities		
Creditors	2,000	
Bank overdraft	3,000	
	5,000	
Net current assets		6,500
Total assets less current liabilities		30,500
Represented by:		
Capital accounts		
Alice	14,000	
Bonny	10,000	
		24,000
Current accounts		
Alice	4,000	
Bonny	2,500	
		6,500
		30,500

Tasks

(a)   Based on the above information, draw up an appropriation account for the partnership of Alice, Bonny and Clyde for the year ended 31 October 20X4.

(b)   Prepare the partners' current and capital accounts for the year ended 31 October 20X4 showing clearly the effect of admitting Clyde to the partnership.

Answer

Tutorial note. Because interest is calculated on the year-end balance of capital, it is necessary to prepare the capital accounts in Part (b) before you can complete the appropriation account in Part (a).

(a)   ALICE, BONNY AND CLYDE
APPROPRIATION ACCOUNT FOR THE YEAR ENDED 31 OCTOBER 20X4

	£	£
Profit available for appropriation		78,000
Less salaries: Alice	10,000	
Clyde	5,000	
		(15,000)
Less interest on capital		
Alice: 14,000 × 10%	1,400	
Bonny: 10,000 × 10%	1,000	
Clyde: 10,000 × 10%	1,000	
		(3,400)
Balance of net profit		59,600
Alice 3/6	29,800	
Bonny 2/6	19,867	
Clyde 1/6	9,933	
		59,600

(b)

CAPITAL ACCOUNTS

	Alice £	Bonny £	Clyde £		Alice £	Bonny £	Clyde £
Balance c/f	14,000	10,000	10,000	Balance b/f	14,000	10,000	–
				Bank	–	–	10,000
	14,000	10,000	10,000		14,000	10,000	10,000

CURRENT ACCOUNTS

	Alice £	Bonny £	Clyde £		Alice £	Bonny £	Clyde £
Drawings	38,000	19,500	15,000	Balance b/f	4,000	2,500	–
Balance c/f	7,200	3,867	933	Salary	10,000	–	5,000
				Interest on capital	1,400	1,000	1,000
				Profit	29,800	19,867	9,933
	45,200	23,367	15,933		45,200	23,367	15,933

Question

Blake, Turner & Reynolds

Amanda Blake, John Turner and Fred Reynolds are in partnership together as wholesale distributors of prints of popular paintings. Amanda has produced a draft profit and loss account for the partnership for the year ended 31 December 20X7 and has asked you to finalise the partnership accounts. She has given you the following information that is relevant to the year in question.

(a) Interest on capital is to be paid at a rate of 10% on the balance at the year end on the capital accounts. No interest is paid on the current accounts.

(b) Cash drawings in the year amounted to:

Amanda	£51,000
John	£38,000
Fred	£24,000

(c) The partners are entitled to the following salaries per annum:

Amanda	£14,000
John	£11,000
Fred	£8,000

(d) On 1 January 20X7, the partners admitted Fred Reynolds into the partnership. He paid £45,000 cash into the partnership on that date. The profit-sharing ratios in the old partnership were:

Amanda	6/10
John	4/10

The new profit-sharing ratios are now:

Amanda	6/12
John	4/12
Fred	2/12

(e) The balances on the current and capital accounts at the beginning of the year, before any adjustments have been made for the admission of Fred into the partnership, were as follows.

Capital accounts:

Amanda	£36,600
John	£31,200

Current accounts:

Amanda	£4,200
John	£3,600

(f) The net profit per the accounts given to you by Amanda amounted to £152,280.

Tasks

(a) Prepare the partners' capital accounts for the year ended 31 December 20X7 from the information provided above.

(b) Prepare an appropriation account for the partnership for the year ended 31 December 20X7.

(c) Prepare the partners' current accounts for the year ended 31 December 20X7.

(a)

CAPITAL ACCOUNTS

	Amanda £	John £	Fred £	Amanda £	John £	Fred £
Bal b/d 1.1.X7				36,600	31,200	–
Cash						45,000
Bal c/d 31.12.X7	36,600	31,200	45,000			
	36,600	31,200	45,000	36,600	31,200	45,000

(b) APPROPRIATION ACCOUNTS FOR THE YEAR ENDED
31 DECEMBER 20X7

			£	£
Net profit per accounts				152,280
Less partners' salaries	Amanda		14,000	
	John		11,000	
	Fred		8,000	
				(33,000)
Less interest on capital				
Amanda (10% × 36,600)			3,660	
John (10% × 31,200)			3,120	
Fred (10% × 45,000)			4,500	
				(11,280)
				108,000
Profit available for appropriation				
Profit share	Amanda	6/12	54,000	
	John	4/12	36,000	
	Fred	2/12	18,000	
				108,000

(c)

CURRENT ACCOUNTS

	Amanda £	John £	Fred £	Amanda £	John £	Fred £
Bal b/d 1.1.X7				4,200	3,600	
Interest on capital				3,660	3,120	4,500
Salaries				14,000	11,000	8,000
Drawings	51,000	38,000	24,000			
Profit				54,000	36,000	18,000
Bal c/d 31.12.X7	24,860	15,720	6,500			
	75,860	53,720	30,500	75,860	53,720	30,500

Exam focus point

In the December 2007 exam, there was a question asking for the net increase in a partner's current account during the year. The examiner commented that most students chose the option giving the closing balance. Remember to read the requirement carefully and to answer the question actually asked.

In the question above, Amanda's closing balance is £24,860 but the net increase in her account is £20,660 (3,660 + 14,000 + 54,000 − 51,000).

One of the competences you require to fulfil performance objective 5 of the PER is the ability to communicate effectively. Your examination is a means of demonstrating this competence by answering the question set.

Chapter Roundup

- Partnership accounts are the same as sole traders except for the allocation of profit and treatment of capital.

Quick Quiz

1 What is a partnership?

2 A partner's salary is an expense of the partnership. Is this statement:

    A   True
    B   False

3 Why might a sole trader take on a partner?

4 What is the difference between a partner's capital account and a partner's current account?

5 How is profit shared between partners?

6 A, B and C are in partnership with a profit sharing ratio of 3:2:1. For the year ended 31.12.X9, the partnership profits are £18,000. What is B's share of the profits?

    A   £3,000
    B   £6,000
    C   £9,000
    D   £18,000

7 X, Y and Z are in partnership. X receives a salary of £14,000. If the profits for the year are £80,000 and the partners share profits equally, what is Y's share of the profits?

    A   £14,000
    B   £22,000
    C   £26,000
    D   £26,667

8 Profits for the year are £75,000. A, B and C share profits in the ratio 4:3:3. Opening balances on their current accounts were £10,000, £12,000 and £15,000 respectively. If each partner had drawings of £20,000, what is the closing balance on B's account?

    A   £17,500
    B   £20,000
    C   £14,500
    D   £22,500

9 Goodwill is brought into the partnership accounts in the old PSR and written off in the new PSR. Is this statement:

    A   True
    B   False

1   An arrangement between two or more individuals to carry on the risks and rewards of a business together.

2   B   False. It is an appropriation of profit.

3   See 1.3.

4   The capital account reflects the amount of money invested in the business by each partner. The current account reflects each partner's share of the profits less drawings.

5   According to the terms of the partnership agreements. This may allow interest on capital accounts, charge interest on drawings, allow salaries and then divide the residual profits according to the profit sharing ratio.

6   B   Each 'share' is worth $\dfrac{£18,000}{6}$ (£3,000). B's share is, therefore, £6,000.

7   B

		£
Appropriation account		
Profits		80,000
X's salary		(14,000)
		66,000

Shared equally:		
X	22,000	
Y	22,000	
Z	22,000	66,000

So Y's share of the profits is £22,000.

8   C

CURRENT ACCOUNTS

	A	B	C		A	B	C
	£	£	£		£	£	£
Drawings	20,000	20,000	20,000	Opening balance	10,000	12,000	15,000
Closing balance	20,000	14,500	17,500	Profits (4:3:3)	30,000	22,500	22,500
	40,000	24,500	37,500		40,000	34,500	37,500

9   A   True.

Now try the questions below from the Exam Question Bank

Number	Level	Marks	Time
Q38	Examination	2	2 mins
Q39	Examination	1	1 min
Q40	Examination	2	2 mins

Introduction to company accounting

20

Topic list	Syllabus reference
1 Limited liability and accounting records	D10(a)
2 Share capital	D10(a)
3 Reserves	D10(b), (c), (j), F1(b), F1(c)
4 Bonus and rights issues	D10(d)-(g)
5 Ledger accounts and limited companies	D10(h)-(i)

Introduction

We begin this chapter by considering the **status of limited** companies and the type of accounting records they maintain in order to prepare financial statements.

Then we will look at those accounting entries unique to limited companies: share capital, reserves, and bonus and rights issues.

This chapter provides the grounding for Chapter 21, where you will learn to prepare company financial statements.

Study guide

		Intellectual level
D10	**Capital structure and finance costs**	
(a)	Understand the capital structure of a limited liability company including:	1
(i)	Ordinary shares	
(ii)	Preference shares (redeemable and irredeemable)	
(iii)	Loan notes	
(b)	Record movements in the share capital and share premium accounts	1
(c)	Identify and record the other reserves which may appear in the company balance sheet	1
(d)	Define a bonus (capitalisation) issue and its advantages and disadvantages	1
(e)	Define a rights issue and its advantages and disadvantages	1
(f)	Record and show the effects of a bonus (capitalisation) issue in the balance sheet	1
(g)	Record and show the effect of a rights issue in the balance sheet	1
(h)	Record dividends in ledger accounts and the financial statements	1
(i)	Calculate and record interest in ledger accounts and the financial statements	1
(j)	Identify the components of the statement of movements in reserves	1
F1	**Balance sheets**	
(b)	Understand the nature of reserves	1
(c)	Identify and report reserves in a company balance sheet	1

Exam guide

Your later financial accounting studies will be concerned almost entirely with company accounts so it is vital that you acquire a sound understanding of the basic concepts now. This is a key exam area.

1 Limited liability and accounting records

FAST FORWARD

As we should expect, the accounting rules and conventions for recording the business transactions of limited companies and then preparing their final accounts are much the same as for sole traders. However there are some important differences as well.

So far, this Study Text has dealt mainly with the accounts of businesses in general. In this chapter we shall turn our attention to the accounts of limited companies. As we should expect, the accounting rules and conventions for recording the business transactions of limited companies and then preparing their final accounts are much the same as for sole traders.

For example, companies will have a cash book, sales day book, purchase day book, journal, sales ledger, purchase ledger and nominal ledger. They will also prepare a profit and loss account annually and a balance sheet at the end of the accounting year.

There are, however, some **differences** in the accounts of limited companies, of which the following are perhaps the most significant.

(a)   The **legislation** governing the activities of limited companies is very extensive. Amongst other things, the Companies Acts define certain minimum accounting records which must be maintained by companies.

(i) They specify that the **annual accounts** of a company must be filed with the Registrar of Companies and so available for public inspection

(ii) They contain detailed requirements on the **minimum information** which must be disclosed in a company's accounts. Businesses which are not limited companies (non-incorporated businesses) enjoy comparative freedom from statutory regulation.

(b) The owners of a company (its **members** or **shareholders**) may be very numerous. Their capital is shown differently from that of a sole trader; and similarly the 'appropriation account' of a company is different.

1.1 Limited liability

> **Unlimited liability** means that if the business runs up debts that it is unable to pay, the proprietors will become personally liable for the unpaid debts, and would be required, if necessary, to sell their private possessions in order to repay them.

It is worth recapping the relative **advantages and disadvantages** of limited liability (which we have mentioned in earlier parts of the text). Sole traders and partnerships are, with some significant exceptions, generally fairly small concerns. The amount of capital involved may be modest, and the proprietors of the business usually participate in managing it. Their liability for the debts of the business is unlimited, which means that if the business runs up debts that it is unable to pay, the proprietors will become personally liable for the unpaid debts, and would be required, if necessary, to sell their private possessions in order to repay them. For example, if a sole trader has some capital in his business, but the business now owes £40,000 which it cannot repay, the trader might have to sell his house to raise the money to pay off his business debts.

Limited companies offer limited liability to their owners.

> **Limited liability** means that the maximum amount that an owner stands to lose in the event that the company becomes insolvent and cannot pay off its debts, is his share of the capital in the business.

Thus limited liability is a major advantage of turning a business into a limited company. However, in practice, banks will normally seek personal guarantees from shareholders of a small owner managed company before making loans or granting an overdraft facility, and so the advantage of limited liability is lost.

There are other disadvantages too. In comparison with sole trader businesses, there is a significantly increased administrative and financial burden. This arises from:

(a) Compliance with the Companies Act 2006, notably in having to prepare annual accounts and have them audited, in keeping statutory registers and having to publish accounts

(b) Having to comply with all SSAPs and FRSs

(c) Formation and annual registration costs

As a business grows, it needs more capital to finance its operations, and significantly more than the people currently managing the business can provide themselves. One way of obtaining more capital is to invite **investors from outside** the business to invest in the ownership or equity of the business. These new co-owners would not usually be expected to help with managing the business. To such investors, **limited liability is very attractive**.

Investments are always risky undertakings, but with limited liability the investor knows the maximum amount that he stands to lose when he puts some capital into a company.

1.2 Public and private companies

There are two classes of limited company.

(a) **Private companies**. These have the word 'limited' at the end of their name. Being private, they cannot invite members of the public to invest in their equity (ownership).

(b) **Public companies**. These are much fewer in number than private companies, but are generally much larger in size. They have the words 'public limited company' – shortened to PLC or plc (or the Welsh language equivalent) at the end of their name. Public limited companies can invite members of the general public to invest in their equity, and the 'shares' of these companies may be traded on The Stock Exchange.

Question
Limited liability

Limited liability means that the directors do not have to account for their mistakes. True or false?

Answer

False. But what *does* it mean? Look back to Section 1.1.

1.3 The accounting records of limited companies

FAST FORWARD

> There is a legal requirement for companies in the UK to keep **accounting records** which are sufficient to show and explain the company's transactions.

The records should:

(a) Disclose the company's current financial position at any time.

(b) Contain:
  (i)   Day-to-day entries of money received and spent.
  (ii) A record of the company's assets and liabilities.
  (iii) Where the company deals in goods:
     • A statement of stocks held at the year end, and supporting stocktaking sheets.
     • With the exception of retail sales, statements of goods bought and sold which identify the sellers and buyers of those goods.

(c) Enable the directors of the company to ensure that the final accounts of the company give a true and fair view of the company's profit or loss and balance sheet position.

1.3.1 Registers: the statutory books

A company must also keep a number of non-accounting registers. These include:

• Register of members
• Register of shareholders' 3 per cent interests
• Register of charges and a register of debenture holders
• Register of directors and company secretaries
• Register of directors' interests (in shares or debentures of the company)

These registers are known collectively as the **statutory books** of the company.

2 Share capital

FAST FORWARD

> In preparing a balance sheet you must be able to deal with:
>
> • ordinary and preference share capital
> • reserves
> • loan stock
>
> The proprietors' capital in a limited company consists of **share capital**.

2.1 The capital of limited companies

When a company is set up for the first time, it issues shares. These are paid for by investors, who then become shareholders of the company. Shares are denominated in units of 25 pence, 50 pence, £1 or whatever seems appropriate. This 'face value' of the shares is called their **nominal value**.

For example, when a company is set up with a share capital of, say, £100,000, it may be decided to issue:

(a)   100,000 shares of £1 each nominal value
(b)   200,000 shares of 50p each
(c)   400,000 shares of 25p each
(d)   250,000 shares of 40p each etc

The amount at which the shares are issued may exceed their nominal value. For example, a company might issue 100,000 £1 shares at a price of £1.20 each. Subscribers will then pay a total of £120,000. The issued share capital of the company would be shown in its accounts at nominal value, £100,000; the excess of £20,000 is described not as share capital, but **as share premium** (see Section 3.2).

2.2 Authorised, issued, called-up and paid-up share capital

A distinction must be made between authorised, issued, called-up and paid-up share capital.

(a)   **Authorised (or nominal) capital** is the maximum amount of share capital that a company is empowered to issue. The amount of authorised share capital varies from company to company, and can change by agreement.

For example, a company's authorised share capital might be 5,000,000 ordinary shares of £1 each. This would then be the maximum number of shares it could issue, unless the maximum were to be changed by agreement.

(b)   **Issued capital** is the nominal amount of share capital that has been issued to shareholders. The amount of issued capital cannot exceed the amount of authorised capital.

Continuing the example above, the company with authorised share capital of 5,000,000 ordinary shares of £1 might have issued 4,000,000 shares. This would leave it the option to issue 1,000,000 more shares at some time in the future.

When share capital is issued, shares are allotted to shareholders. The term 'allotted' share capital means the same thing as issued share capital.

(c)   **Called-up capital**. When shares are issued or allotted, a company does not always expect to be paid the full amount for the shares at once. It might instead call up only a part of the issue price, and wait until a later time before it calls up the remainder.

For example, if a company allots 400,000 ordinary shares of £1, it might call up only, say, 75 pence per share. The issued share capital would be £400,000, but the called up share capital would only be £300,000.

(d)   **Paid-up capital**. Like everyone else, investors are not always prompt or reliable payers. When capital is called up, some shareholders might delay their payment (or even default on payment). Paid-up capital is the amount of called-up capital that has been paid.

For example, if a company issues 400,000 ordinary shares of £1 each, calls up 75 pence per share, and receives payments of £290,000, we would have:

	£
Issued capital	400,000
Called-up capital	300,000
Paid-up capital	290,000
Called-up capital not paid	10,000

The balance sheet of the company would then include called up capital not paid on the assets side, as a debtor:

	£
Called-up capital not paid	10,000
Cash at bank	290,000
	300,000
Called-up share capital	
400,000 ordinary shares of £1, with 75p per share called up.	300,000

Question

Distinguish between authorised and issued share capital.

Answer

Look back to paragraph 2.2 (a) and (b)

2.3 Ordinary and preference shares

FAST FORWARD

At this stage it is relevant to distinguish between the various types of shares most often encountered: **preference shares** and **ordinary shares**.

2.3.1 Preference shares

Key term

> **Preference shares** are shares which confer certain preferential rights on their holder.

Preference shares are now rather old-fashioned and are rarely issued, although they do have occasional resurgences of popularity.

They carry the right to a final dividend which is expressed as a percentage of their nominal value: eg a 6% £1 preference share carries a right to an annual dividend of 6p. Preference dividends have priority over ordinary dividends; in other words, if the directors of a company wish to pay a dividend (which they are not obliged to do) they must pay any preference dividend first. Otherwise, no ordinary dividend may be paid.

The rights attaching to preference shares are set out in the company's constitution. They may vary from company to company, but typically:

(a) Preference shareholders have a **priority right** over ordinary shareholders to a **return of their capital** if the company goes into liquidation.

(b) Preference shares do **not carry a right to vote**.

(c) If the preference shares are cumulative, it means that before a company can pay an ordinary dividend it must not only pay the current year's preference dividend, but must also make good any arrears of preference dividends unpaid in previous years.

2.3.2 Classification of preference shares

Preference shares may be classified in one of two ways.

- **Redeemable**
- **Irredeemable**

Redeemable preference shares mean that the company will redeem (repay) the nominal value of those shares at a late date. For example, 'redeemable 5% £1 preference shares 20X9' means that the company will pay these shareholders £1 for every share they hold on a certain date in 20X9. The shares will then be cancelled and no further dividends paid. Redeemable preference shares are treated like loans and are included as long-term liabilities in the balance sheet. Remember to reclassify as current liabilities if the redemption is due within 12 months. Dividends paid on redeemable preference shares are treated like interest paid on loans and are included in finance costs in the profit and loss account.

Irredeemable preference shares are treated just like other shares. They form part of equity and their dividends are treated as appropriations of profit.

> In the exam, the question will specifically state whether the preference shares are redeemable or irredeemable.

2.3.3 Ordinary shares

Ordinary shares are by far the most common. They carry no right to a fixed dividend but are entitled to all profits left after payment of any preference dividend. Generally however, only a part of such remaining profits is distributed, the rest being kept in reserve (see below).

> **Ordinary shares** are shares which are not preferential with regard to dividend payments. Thus a holder only receives a dividend after fixed dividends have been paid to preference shareholders.

The amount of ordinary dividends fluctuates, although there is a general expectation that it will increase from year to year. Should the company be wound up, any surplus not distributed is shared between the ordinary shareholders. Ordinary shares normally carry voting rights.

Ordinary shareholders are thus the effective owners of a company. They own the 'equity' of the business, and any reserves of the business (described later) belong to them. Ordinary shareholders are sometimes referred to as equity shareholders. Preference shareholders are in many ways more like creditors (although legally they are members, not creditors).

It should be emphasised that the precise rights attached to preference, deferred and ordinary shares vary from company to company; the distinctions noted above are generalisations.

2.4 Example: Dividends, ordinary shares and preference shares

Garden Gloves Ltd has issued 50,000 ordinary shares of 50 pence each and 20,000 7% preference shares of £1 each. Its profits after taxation for the year to 30 September 20X5 were £8,400. The board of directors has decided to pay an ordinary dividend (ie a dividend on ordinary shares) which is 50% of profits after tax and preference dividend.

Required

Show the amount in total of dividends and of retained profits, and calculate the dividend per share on ordinary shares.

Solution

	£
Profit after tax	8,400
Preference dividend (7% of £1 × 20,000)	1,400
Profit after tax and preference dividend	7,000
Ordinary dividend (50% of earnings)	3,500
Retained profit (also 50% of earnings)	3,500

The ordinary dividend is 7 pence per share (£3,500 ÷ 50,000 ordinary shares).

The appropriation of profit would be shown as follows:

		£	£
Profit after tax			8,400
Dividends:	preference	1,400	
	ordinary	3,500	
			4,900
Retained profit			3,500

As we will see later, appropriations of profit do not appear in the profit and loss account, but are shown as movements on reserves.

2.5 The market value of shares

The nominal value of shares will be different from their market value, which is the price at which someone is prepared to purchase shares in the company from an existing shareholder. If Mr A owns 1,000 £1 shares in Z Ltd he may sell them to B for £1.60 each.

This transfer of existing shares does not affect Z Ltd's own financial position in any way and, apart from changing the register of members, Z Ltd does not have to bother with the sale by Mr A to Mr B at all. There are certainly no accounting entries to be made for the share sale.

Shares in private companies do not change hands very often, hence their market value is often hard to estimate. Public companies are usually (not always) quoted; a quoted company is one whose shares are traded on The Stock Exchange and it is the market value of the shares which is quoted.

2.6 Debenture loans

FAST FORWARD

Limited companies may issue **debenture stock** (debentures) or loan stock. These are **long-term liabilities** described on the balance sheet as loan capital.

They are different from share capital in the following ways.

(a)   **Shareholders** are **members** of a company, while **providers of loan capital** are **creditors**.

(b)   **Shareholders** receive **dividends** (appropriations of profit) whereas the holders of loan capital are entitled to a **fixed rate of interest** (an expense charged against revenue).

(c)   Loan capital holders can take legal action against a company if their interest is not paid when due, whereas **shareholders cannot enforce the payment of dividends**.

(d)   **Debentures** or loan stock are often **secured on company assets**, whereas shares are not.

The holder of loan capital is generally in a less risky position than the shareholder. He has greater security, although his income is fixed and cannot grow, unlike ordinary dividends. As remarked earlier, preference shares are in practice very similar to loan capital, not least because the preference dividend is normally fixed.

Interest is calculated on the nominal value of loan capital, regardless of its market value. If a company has £700,000 (nominal value) 12% debentures in issue, interest of £84,000 will be charged in the profit and loss account per year. Interest is usually paid half-yearly; examination questions often require an accrual to be made for interest due at the year-end.

For example, a company has £700,000 of 12% debentures in issue and pays interest on 30 June and 31 December each year. It ends its accounting year on 30 September. There would be an accrual of three months' unpaid interest (3/12 × £84,000) = £21,000 at the end of each accounting year that the debentures are still in issue.

Advantages of raising finance by borrowing by debentures

(a)   Debenture holders are creditors, not shareholders, and so do not affect the **control** of the company.

(b)   The interest rate is fixed and a known cost.

(c)   The interest is usually allowable for offset against the company's corporation tax.

(d)   If a debenture is secured as assets the interest rate will normally be lower than, say, an overdraft.

Disadvantages of raising finance by borrowing debenture

(a)   Debenture interest **must** be paid, whereas directors do not need to pay shareholders a dividend.

(b)   Debenture holders can force the sale of any assets used as security, if their loan is not repaid on the due date.

3 Reserves

The net fixed assets of a company, plus the working capital (ie current assets minus current liabilities) minus the long-term liabilities, are 'financed' by the shareholders' funds.

Shareholders' funds consists of both:

(a)   The nominal value of issued capital (minus any amounts not yet called up on issued shares).

(b)   Reserves.

The share capital itself might consist of both ordinary shares and preference shares. All reserves, however, are owned by the ordinary shareholders, who own the 'equity' in the company. We looked at share capital in detail above.

3.1 Reserves

In the case of a sole trader, the proprietor's interest = net assets of the business, and in the case of a partnership, partners' funds = net assets. For a company the equation is:

> Shareholders' funds = net assets
>
> Furthermore:
>
> Shareholders' funds = share capital and reserves

A company's share capital will remain fixed from year to year, unless new shares are issued. Reserves are difficult to define neatly since different reserves arise for different reasons, but it follows from the above that:

Reserves = net assets minus share capital

So the total amount of reserves in a company varies, according to changes in the net assets of the business.

A typical balance sheet may show a number of reserves.

A distinction should be made between:

(a)   **Statutory reserves**, which are reserves which a company is required to set up by law, eg the revaluation reserve, and which are not available for the distribution of dividends.

(b)   **Non-statutory reserves**, which are reserves consisting of profits which are distributable as dividends, if the company so wishes.

3.2 The share premium account

There are a number of statutory (or **capital**) reserves. One is the revaluation reserve, which we met in Chapter 9. However, the most important one at this stage is the **share premium account**. Section 130 of the Companies Act 1985 states that 'where a company issues shares at a premium, whether for cash or otherwise, a sum equal to.... the premiums on those shares shall be transferred to the share premium account'.

By **'premium'** is meant the difference between the issue price of the share and its nominal value. When a company is first incorporated (set up) the issue price of its shares will probably be the same as their nominal value and so there would be no share premium. If the company does well the market value of its shares will increase, but not the nominal value. The price of any new shares issued will be approximately their market value.

The difference between cash received by the company and the nominal value of the new shares issued is transferred to the share premium account. For example, if X Ltd issues 1,000 £1 ordinary shares at £2.60 each the book entry will be:

		£	£
DEBIT	Cash	2,600	
CREDIT	Ordinary share capital		1,000
	Share premium account		1,600

A **share premium account** only comes into being when a company issues shares at a price in excess of their nominal value. The market price of the shares, once they have been issued, has no bearing at all on the company's accounts, and so if their market price goes up or down, the share premium account would remain unaltered.

A **share premium account** is an account into which sums received as payment for shares in excess of their nominal value must be placed.

Once established, the share premium account constitutes capital of the company which cannot be paid out in dividends. The share premium account will increase in value if and when new shares are issued at a price above their nominal value.

The share premium account can be 'used' – and so decrease in value – only in certain very limited ways. One use of the share premium account, however, is to 'finance' the issue of bonus shares, which are described later in this section.

The share premium account cannot be distributed as dividend under any circumstances.

The reason for creating statutory reserves is to **maintain the capital** of the company. This capital 'base' provides some **security for the company's creditors**, bearing in mind that the liability of shareholders is limited in the event that the company cannot repay its debts. It would be most unjust – and illegal – for a company to pay its shareholders a dividend out of its base capital when it is not even able to pay back its debts.

Another reason why statutory reserves cannot be distributed is the fact that they often represent unrealised profits. A profit does arise when assets are revalued but it is not realised into cash. It is a generally accepted accounting principle that profit can only be distributed when it is realised because an unrealised profit can disappear if the value of the revalued asset subsequently drops.

You may be asked to explain why statutory reserves cannot be distributed.

Question

Share premium

What are the ledger entries needed to record the issue of 200,000 £1 ordinary shares at a premium of 30p and paid for in full by cheque?

Answer

		£	£
DEBIT	Bank	260,000	
CREDIT	Share capital		200,000
CREDIT	Share premium		60,000

Question

Share issue

AB Ltd issues 5,000 50p shares for £6,000. What are the entries for share capital and share premium in the balance sheet?

	Share capital	Share premium
A	£5,000	£1,000
B	£1,000	£5,000
C	£3,500	£3,500
D	£2,500	£3,500

Did you notice that the shares are 50p each, not £1? The shares were issued for £1.20 each (£6,000/5,000 shares). Of this 50p is share capital and 70p is share premium. Therefore option D is the correct answer.

3.3 Revaluation surplus

We looked at the revaluation of fixed assets in Chapter 9. The result of an upward revaluation is a '**revaluation surplus**'. This is **non-distributable** as it represents unrealised profits on the revalued assets. It is another capital reserve. The relevant part of a revaluation surplus can only become realised if the asset in question is sold, thus realising the gain. The revaluation surplus may fall, however, if an asset which had previously been revalued upwards suffered a fall in value in the next revaluation.

3.4 Other reserves

We are concerned here with non-statutory reserves, which the company managers may choose to set up. These may have a specific purpose (eg plant and machinery replacement reserve) or not (eg general reserve). The creation of these reserves usually indicates a general intention not to distribute the profits involved at any future date, although legally any such reserves, being non-statutory, remain available for the payment of dividends.

Profits are transferred to these reserves by making an appropriation out of profits, usually profits for the year. Typically, you might come across the following.

	£	£
Profit after taxation		100,000
Appropriations of profit		
Dividend	60,000	
Transfer to general reserve	10,000	
		70,000
Retained earnings for the year		30,000
Retained earnings b/f		250,000
Retained earnings c/f		280,000

3.4.1 Dividends

Dividends are appropriations of profit after tax.

Shareholders who are also managers of their company will receive a salary as a manager. They are also entitled to a share of the profits made by the company.

Many companies pay dividends in two stages during the course of their accounting year.

(a) In mid year, after the half-year financial results are known, the company might pay an **interim dividend**.

(b) At the end of the year, the company might propose a further **final dividend**.

The total dividend for the year is the sum of the interim and the final dividend. (Not all companies by any means pay an interim dividend. Interim dividends are, however, commonly paid out by larger limited companies.)

At the end of an accounting year, a company's managers may have proposed a final dividend payment, but this will not yet have been paid. The final dividend **does not appear in the accounts** but will be disclosed in the notes.

Exam focus point

Dividends which have been **paid** are shown in the statement of movement in reserves (see Section 3.7). They are not shown in the profit and loss account, although they are deducted from retained earnings in the balance sheet. **Proposed** dividends are not adjusted for, they are simply disclosed by note.

The terminology of dividend payments can be confusing, since they may be expressed either in the form, as 'x cents per share' or as 'y%. In the latter case, the meaning is always 'y% of the *par value* of the shares in issue'. For example, suppose a company's issued share capital consists of 100,000 50p ordinary shares which were issued at a premium of 10p per share. The company's balance sheet would include the following.

		£
Ordinary shares:	100,000 50p ordinary shares	50,000
Share premium account	(100,000 × 10p)	10,000

If the managers wish to pay a dividend of £5,000, they may propose either:

(a)   a dividend of 5p per share (100,000 × 5p = £5,000); or
(b)   a dividend of 10% (10% × £50,000 = £5,000).

Not all profits are distributed as dividends; some will be retained in the business to finance future projects.

Question   Dividend

A company has authorised share capital of 1,000,000 50p ordinary shares and an issued share capital of 800,000 50p ordinary shares. If an ordinary dividend of 5% is declared, what is the amount payable to shareholders?

A   £50,000
B   £20,000
C   £40,000
D   £25,000

Answer

B   800,000 × 50p × 5% = £20,000.

3.5 Profit and loss reserve (retained profits)

The most significant **non-statutory reserve** (revenue reserve) is variously described as:

(a)   Revenue reserve
(b)   Retained profits
(c)   Retained earnings
(d)   Undistributed profits
(e)   Profit and loss account
(f)   Unappropriated profits

These are **profits** earned by the company and **not appropriated** by dividends, taxation or transfer to another reserve account.

Provided that a company is earning profits, this reserve generally increases from year to year, as most companies do not distribute all their profits as dividends. Dividends can be paid from it: even if a loss is made in one particular year, a dividend can be paid from previous years' retained profits.

For example, if a company makes a loss of £100,000 in one year, yet has unappropriated profits from previous years totalling £250,000, it can pay a dividend not exceeding £150,000. One reason for retaining some profit each year is to enable the company to pay dividends even when profits are low (or non-existent). Another reason is usually shortage of cash.

Very occasionally, you might come across a debit balance on the profit and loss account. This would indicate that the company has **accumulated losses**.

3.6 Distinction between reserves and provisions

A **reserve** is an appropriation of distributable profits for a specific purpose (eg plant replacement) while a provision is an amount charged against revenue as an expense. A provision relates either to a diminution in the value of an asset or a known liability (eg audit fees), the amount of which cannot be established with any accuracy.

Provisions or allowances (for depreciation etc) are dealt with in company accounts in the same way as in the accounts of other types of business.

3.7 Statement of movements in reserves

In the published accounts, a company has to provide a statement of movements on reserves, which details the movements for all its reserves.

STATEMENT OF MOVEMENTS IN RESERVES

	Share premium £	Revaluation £	General £	Profit & loss £
At 1 January 20X8	5,000	20,000	750	250
Profit for the period	-	-	-	100
Dividends	-	-	-	(60)
Transfer to general reserve	-	-	10	(10)
Share issue	500	-	-	-
Revaluation	-	5,000	-	-
At 31 December 20X8	5,500	25,000	760	280

4 Bonus and rights issues

A company can increase its share capital by means of a **bonus issues** or a **rights issue**.

4.1 Bonus issues

A company may wish to increase its share capital without needing to raise additional finance by issuing new shares. For example, a profitable company might expand from modest beginnings over a number of years. Its profitability would be reflected in large balances on its reserves, while its original share capital might look like that of a much smaller business.

It is open to such a company to **re-classify some of its reserves as share capital**. This is purely a paper exercise which **raises no funds**. Any reserve may be re-classified in this way, including a share premium account or other statutory reserve. Such a re-classification **increases the capital base** of the company and gives **creditors greater protection**.

4.1.1 Advantages

* Increases capital without diluting current shareholders' holdings
* Capitalises reserves so they cannot be paid as dividends

4.1.2 Disadvantages

* Does not raise any cash
* May jeopardise payment of future dividends if profits fall

4.2 Example: Bonus issue

BUBBLES LIMITED
BALANCE SHEET (EXTRACT)

Funds employed	£'000	£'000
Share capital		
£1 ordinary shares (fully paid)		1,000
Reserves		
Share premium	500	
Undistributed profit	2,000	
		2,500
Shareholders' funds		3,500

Bubbles decided to make a '3 for 2' bonus issue (ie 3 new shares for every 2 already held). So shares with a nominal value of £1,500,000 need to be issued.

The double entry is

		£'000	£'000
DEBIT	Share premium	500	
	Undistributed profit	1,000	
CREDIT	Ordinary share capital		1,500

After the issue the balance sheet is as follows

	£'000
Share capital	
£1 ordinary shares (fully paid)	2,500
Reserves	
Undistributed profit	1,000
Shareholders' funds	3,500

1,500,000 new ('bonus') shares are issued to existing shareholders, so that if Mr X previously held 20,000 shares he will now hold 50,000. The total value of his holding should theoretically remain the same however, since the net assets of the company remain unchanged and his share of those net assets remains at 2% (ie 50,000/2,500,000; previously 20,000/1,000,000).

4.3 Rights issues

A rights issue (unlike a bonus issue) is an issue of shares for cash. The 'rights' are offered to existing shareholders, who can sell them if they wish.

4.3.1 Advantages

- Raises cash for the company
- Keeps reserves available for future dividends

4.3.2 Disadvantages

- Dilutes shareholders' holdings if they do not take up their rights

4.4 Example: Rights issue

Bubbles Ltd (above) decides to make a rights issue, shortly after the bonus issue. The terms are '1 for 5 @ £1.20' (ie one new share for every five already held, at a price of £1.20). Assuming that all shareholders take up their rights (which they are not obliged to) the double entry is:

		£'000	£'000
DEBIT	Cash	600	
CREDIT	Ordinary share capital		500
	Share premium		100

Mr X who previously held 50,000 shares will now hold 60,000, and the value of his holding should increase (all other things being equal) because the net assets of the company will increase. The new balance sheet will show:

	£'000	£'000
Share capital		
£1 ordinary shares		3,000
Reserves		
Share premium	100	
Undistributed profit	1,000	
		1,100
Shareholders' funds		4,100

The increase in funds of £600,000 represents the cash raised from the issue of 500,000 new shares at a price of £1.20 each.

Rights issues are a popular way of **raising cash** by issuing shares and they are **cheap to administer**. In addition, **shareholders retain control** of the business as their holding is not diluted.

The disadvantages of a rights issue is that shareholders are **not obliged** to take up their rights and so the issue could fail to raise the money required. For this reason companies usually try to find a broker to 'underwrite' the issue, ie who will buy any rights not taken up by the shareholders.

Question   Bonus and rights issue

X Ltd has the following capital structure:

	£
400,000 ordinary shares of 50p	200,000
Share premium account	70,000
Retained profits	230,000
Shareholders' funds	500,000

Show its capital structure following:

(a)   A '1 for 2' bonus issue
(b)   A rights issue of '1 for 3' at 75p following the bonus issue, assuming all rights taken up

Answer

(a)

	£
600,000 ordinary shares of 50p	300,000
Retained profits	200,000
Shareholders funds	500,000

(b)

	£
800,000 ordinary shares of 50p	400,000
Share premium account	50,000
Retained profits	200,000
Shareholders funds	650,000

The bonus issue was financed by the whole of the share premium account and £30,000 retained profits. The share premium account has funds again following the rights issue. Note that the bonus issue leaves shareholders funds unchanged. The rights issue will have brought in cash of £150,000 (200,000 × 75p) and shareholders funds are increased by this amount.

5 Ledger accounts and limited companies

Limited companies keep ledger accounts, and the only difference between the ledger accounts of companies and sole traders is the nature of some of the transactions, assets and liabilities for which accounts need to be kept.

For example, there will be an account for each of the following items:

(a)   *Taxation*

   (i)   Tax charged against profits will be accounted for by:

   DEBIT   P&L account
   CREDIT   Taxation account

   (ii)   The outstanding balance on the taxation account will be a liability in the balance sheet, until eventually paid, when the accounting entry would be:

   DEBIT   Taxation account
   CREDIT   Cash

(b)   *Dividends*

   A separate account will be kept for the dividends for each different class of shares (eg preference, ordinary).

   (i)   Dividends declared out of profits will be disclosed in the notes if they are unpaid at the year end.

   (ii)   When dividends are paid, we have:

   DEBIT   Dividends paid account
   CREDIT   Cash

Exam focus point

No dividends payable will be shown at the year end.

(c)   *Loan stock and debentures*

   Loan stock being a long-term liability will be shown as a credit balance in a loan stock account.

   Interest payable on such loans is not credited to the loan account, but is credited to a separate creditors account for interest until it is eventually paid: ie

   DEBIT   Interest account (an expense, chargeable against profits)
   CREDIT   Interest payable (a current liability until eventually paid)

(d)   *Share capital and reserves*

   There will be a separate account for:

   (i)   each different class of share capital (always a credit balance b/f).
   (ii)   each different type of reserve (nearly always a credit balance b/f).

Chapter Roundup

- As we should expect, the accounting rules and conventions for recording the business transactions of limited companies and then preparing their final accounts are much the same as for sole traders. However there are some important differences as well.

- There is a legal requirement for companies in the UK to keep **accounting records** which are sufficient to show and explain the company's transactions.

- In preparing a balance sheet you must be able to deal with:
    - ordinary and preference share capital
    - reserves
    - loan stock

    The proprietors' capital in a limited company consists of share capital.

- At this stage it is relevant to distinguish between the various types of shares most often encountered: **preference shares** and **ordinary shares**.

- Limited companies may issue **debenture stock** (debentures) or loan stock. These are **long-term liabilities** described on the balance sheet as loan capital.

- The net fixed assets of a company, plus the working capital (ie current assets minus current liabilities) minus the long-term liabilities, are 'financed' by the shareholders' funds.

- A company can increase its share capital by means of a **bonus issues** or a **rights issue**.

Quick Quiz

1   What is the meaning of limited liability?

    A   Shareholders are responsible for the company's debts.
    B   Shareholders are responsible only for the amount paid on the shares.

2   What is the difference between issued capital and called-up capital?

3   What are the differences between ordinary shares and preference shares?

4   What are the differences between debentures and share capital?

5   A company issues 50,000 £1 shares at a price of £1.25 per share. How much should be posted to the share premium account?

    A   £50,000
    B   £12,500
    C   £62,500
    D   £60,000

6   Distinguish between a bonus (capitalisation) issue and a rights issue.

7   A company has a balance on share premium account of £50,000 and on retained profits of £75,000. Issued share capital is 400,000 25p shares. The company decides to make a bonus issue of one for one. What are the closing balances on share premium and retained profits?

	Share premium	Retained profits
A	£25,000	Nil
B	£10,000	£15,000
C	Nil	£25,000
D	Nil	£(275,000)

1   B   The maximum amount that a shareholder has to pay is the amount paid on his shares.

2   Issued share capital is the par value of shares issued to shareholders. Called-up share capital is the amount payable to date by the shareholders.

3   Ordinary shares can be paid any or no dividend. The dividend attaching to preference shares is set from the start.

4   Debentures are long-term loans, and so debentureholders are long-term creditors. Equity shareholders own the company.

5   B   (50,000 × 25p)

6   A bonus issue is financed by capitalising revenue reserves. A rights issue is paid for by the shareholders taking up the shares.

7   C   Capitalisation of 1:1 means a further 400,000 25p share are issued. This represents £100,000. This £100,000 is taken from share premium account first (£50,000) and the balance of £50,000 is taken from retained earnings.

Now try the questions below from the Exam Question Bank

Number	Level	Marks	Time
Q41	Examination	1	1 min
Q42	Examination	2	2 mins
Q43	Examination	2	2 mins
Q44	Examination	2	2 mins

21

Preparation of financial statements for companies

Topic list	Syllabus reference
1 The final accounts of limited companies	F1(d), F2(a), F2(g)
2 Items in the profit and loss account	F1(e)-(f), F2(a)-(g)
3 Items in the balance sheet	F1(a), F1(d)
4 The current/long-term distinction	D8(l)
5 Company accounts for internal purposes	F1(d), F2(a), F2(c)
6 FRS 3 *Reporting financial performance*	D10(j)-(k)
7 Published accounts	F1(c), F1(d), F2(a)-(d)

Introduction

You now come to the point in your studies for Paper F3 when you can look at the form and content of the financial statements of **limited companies**. Your later financial accounting studies will be concerned almost entirely with company accounts so it is vital that you acquire a sound understanding of the basic concepts now.

The financial statements of limited companies are usually governed by national legislation and accounting standards. We will look at the Companies Act formats and explain those items in the financial statements which have not yet appeared in the text.

We will look at another FRS which has a significant impact on the content and form of company accounts, FRS 3 *Reporting financial performance*.

All these standards are concerned with financial statements produced for external reporting purposes (ie to external users), but companies also produce financial accounts for internal purposes, and we will look at the different approach in preparing accounts for internal as well as external use.

Study guide

		Intellectual level
D8	**Debtors and creditors**	
(l)	Classify items as current or long-term liabilities in the balance sheet	1
D10	**Capital structure and finance costs**	
(j)	Identify the components of the statement of movement in reserves	1
(k)	Identify the components of the statement of total recognised gains and losses	1
F1	**Balance sheets**	
(a)	Recognise how the balance sheet equation and business entity convention underlie the balance sheet	1
(c)	Identify and report reserves in a company balance sheet	1
(d)	Prepare extracts of a balance sheet from given information	1
(e)	Understand why 'profit and loss' appears in a company balance sheet	1
F2	**Profit and loss accounts**	
(a)	Prepare extracts of a profit and loss account from given information	1
(b)	Understand how accounting concepts apply to revenue and expenses	1
(c)	Calculate revenue, cost of sales, gross profit and net profit from given information	1
(d)	Disclose items of income and expenditure in the profit and loss account	1
(e)	Record corporation tax in the profit and loss account of a company, including the under and over provision of tax in the prior year	1
(f)	Understand the interrelationship between the balance sheet and profit and loss account	1
(g)	Identify items requiring separate disclosure on the face of the profit and loss account	1

Exam guide

Your later financial accounting studies will be concerned almost entirely with company accounts so it is vital that you acquire a sound understanding of the basic published formats. This is a key exam area.

1 The final accounts of limited companies

FAST FORWARD

> The preparation and publication of the final accounts of limited companies in the UK are governed by the Companies Act 2006.

At this stage we are concerned with the preparation of limited company accounts for **internal use**. If you are asked to produce such a set of final accounts, you need not follow the detailed regulations laid down by the Act. However, the general format of the balance sheet and profit and loss account of a limited company is shown below, with some simplifications.

TYPICAL COMPANY LIMITED BALANCE SHEET AS AT...

		£	£	£
Fixed assets				
Intangible assets	Development costs		X	
	Concessions, patents, licences, trademarks		X	
	Goodwill		X	
				X
Tangible assets	Land and buildings		X	
	Plant and machinery		X	
	Fixtures, fittings, tools and equipment		X	
	Motor vehicles		X	
				X
Investments				X
				X
Current assets	Stocks		X	
	Debtors and prepayments		X	
	Investments		X	
	Cash at bank and in hand		X	
			X	
Creditors: amounts falling due within one year (ie current liabilities)				
	Debenture loans (nearing their redemption date)	X		
	Bank overdraft and loans	X		
	Trade creditors	X		
	Bills of exchange payable	X		
	Taxation	X		
	Accruals	X		
			(X)	
Net current assets				X
Total assets less current liabilities				X
Creditors: amounts falling due after more than one year (ie long term liabilities)				
	Debenture loans		X	
	Taxation		X	
				(X)
				X
Capital and reserves	Called up share capital			
	Ordinary shares		X	
	Preference shares		X	
				X
Reserves	Share premium account		X	
	Revaluation reserve		X	
	Other reserves		X	
	Profit and loss account (retained profits)		X	
				X
				X

The profit and loss account of a company might have a format roughly similar to the one on the following page.

TYPICAL COMPANY LIMITED
PROFIT AND LOSS ACCOUNT FOR THE YEAR ENDED...

	£	£
Turnover		X
Cost of sales		(X)
Gross profit		X
Distribution costs	X	
Administrative expenses	X	
		(X)
		X
Other operating income	X	
Income from fixed asset investments	X	
Other interest receivable and similar income	X	
		X
		X
Interest payable		(X)
Profit before taxation		X
Tax		(X)
Profit after tax		X

You may be asked to produce a set of accounts for **external use**, in which case you will have to follow the statutory format in all respects. This is covered in Section 7 of this chapter.

We will now consider some of the components in more detail in the following sections.

2 Items in the profit and loss account

2.1 Cost of sales

This represents the summary of the detailed workings we have used in a sole trader's financial statements.

2.2 Expenses

Notice that expenses are gathered under a number of headings. Any detail needed will be given in the notes to the financial statements.

2.2.1 Managers' salaries

The salary of a sole trader or a partner in a partnership is not a charge to the profit and loss account but is an appropriation of profit. The **salary of a manager or member of management board of a limited liability company**, however, is an **expense in the profit and loss account**, even when the manager is a shareholder in the company. Management salaries are included in **administrative expenses.**

2.3 Finance cost

This is interest **payable** during the period. Remember (from the previous chapter) that this may include accruals for interest payable on debentures.

2.4 Taxation

Taxation affects both the balance sheet and the profit and loss account.

All companies pay some kind of corporate taxation on the profits they earn. The rate of corporation tax will vary for different types or size of company.

Note that because a company has a **separate legal personality, its tax is included in its accounts**. An unincorporated business would not show personal income tax in its accounts, as it would not be a business expense but the personal affair of the proprietors.

(a) The **charge for tax on profits for the year** is shown as a **deduction from net profit**.

(b) In the balance sheet, **tax payable** to the government is generally shown as a **current liability** as it is usually due within 12 months of the year end.

(c) For various reasons, the tax on profits in the profit and loss account and the tax payable in the balance sheet are not normally the same amount.

2.4.1 Example: taxation

A company has a tax liability brought forward of £15,000. The liability is finally agreed at £17,500 and this is paid during the year. The company estimates that the tax liability based on the current year's profit, will be £20,000. Prepare the tax liability account for the year.

Solution

TAX LIABILITY ACCOUNT

	£		£
Cash paid	17,500	Balance b/f	15,000
		Profit and loss a/c	22,500
Balance c/f	20,000		
	37,500		37,500

Notice that the profit and loss account charge consists of the following:

	£
Underprovision for prior year (17,500 – 15,000)	2,500
Provision for current year	20,000
	22,500

Notice also that the balance carried forward consists solely of the provision for the current year.

2.5 Accounting concepts

You will notice from the above that the accounting concepts apply to revenue and expenses. In particular, the matching concept applies and so expect to have to adjust for accruals and prepayments.

2.6 Interrelationship of profit and loss account and balance sheet

When we were dealing with the financial statements of sole traders, we transferred the net profit to the capital account. In the case of limited companies, the net profit is transferred to retained profits in the statement of movements in reserves. The closing balance of the accounts are then transferred to the balance sheet.

3 Items in the balance sheet

3.1 Intangible fixed assets

Intangible fixed assets represent amounts of money paid by a business to acquire benefits of a long-term nature. **Deferred development expenditure** is an intangible asset discussed in detail in an earlier chapter.

If a company purchases some **patent rights**, or a concession from another business, or the right to use a trademark, the cost of the purchase can be accounted for as the purchase of an intangible fixed asset. These assets must then be **amortised** (depreciated) over their economic life.

3.2 Tangible fixed assets

As with any other type of business, tangible fixed assets are shown in the balance sheet at their net book value (ie at cost less provision for depreciation). Sometimes, a fixed asset, such as a building, might be revalued to a current market value. Depreciation would then be based on the revalued amount, and the balance sheet value of the asset would be the revalued amount less provision for depreciation on the revalued amount.

3.3 Investments

Investments are fixed assets if the company intends to hold on to them for a long time, and current assets if they are only likely to be held for a short time before being sold (eg to invest funds not needed for say six months).

3.4 Other assets

Other assets are exactly the same as those found in a sole trader's accounts.

3.5 Liabilities

These are split between current and long-term liabilities (see Section 4).

3.6 Concepts

The balance sheet relies on the accounting concept that:

Assets – liabilities = capital

As this is a version of the accounting equation, you will not be surprised to learn, therefore, that the accounting equation is also called the **balance sheet equation**. The balance sheet is also prepared according to the **business entity** convention.

4 The current/long-term distinction

The term **'creditors: amounts falling due within one year'** is used in the Companies Act 2006 as an alternative phrase meaning 'current liabilities'. You will therefore come across this term increasingly often as you progress through your accountancy studies.

The sub-headings in Section 1 show the main types of liabilities. Refer back to Chapter 13 for a definition of a liability, as opposed to a provision.

Similarly, the term '**creditors : amounts falling due after more than one year**' is the Companies Act 2006 term for long-term liabilities.

5 Company accounts for internal purposes

We can now try to draw together several of the items described in this chapter into an illustrative example. Study it carefully.

5.1 Example: Wislon Ltd

The accountant of Wislon Ltd has prepared the following trial balance as at 31 December 20X7.

	£'000
50p ordinary shares (fully paid)	350
7% £1 preference shares (fully paid)	100
10% debentures (secured)	200
Retained profit 1.1.X7	242
General reserve 1.1.X7	171
Freehold land and buildings 1.1.X7 (cost)	430
Plant and machinery 1.1.X7 (cost)	830
Provision for depreciation:	
Freehold buildings 1.1.X7	20
Plant and machinery 1.1.X7	222
Stock 1.1.X7	190
Sales	2,695
Purchases	2,152
Preference dividend	7
Ordinary dividend (interim)	8
Debenture interest	10
Wages and salaries	254
Light and heat	31
Sundry expenses	113
Suspense account	135
Debtors	179
Creditors	195
Cash	126

Notes

(a) Sundry expenses include £9,000 paid in respect of insurance for the year ending 1 September 20X8. Light and heat does not include an invoice of £3,000 for electricity for the three months ending 2 January 20X8, which was paid in February 20X8. Light and heat also includes £20,000 relating to salesmen's commission.

(b) The suspense account is in respect of the following items:

	£'000
Proceeds from the issue of 100,000 ordinary shares	120
Proceeds from the sale of plant	300
	420
Less consideration for the acquisition of Mary & Co	285
	135

(c) The net assets of Mary & Co were purchased on 3 March 20X7. Assets were valued as follows:

	£'000
Investments	230
Stock	34
	264

All the stock acquired was sold during 20X7. The investments were still held by Wislon at 31.12.X7.

(d) The freehold property was acquired some years ago. The buildings element of the cost was estimated at £100,000 and the estimated useful life of the assets was fifty years at the time of purchase. As at 31 December 20X7 the property is to be revalued at £800,000.

(e) The plant which was sold had cost £350,000 and had a net book value of £274,000 as on 1.1.X7. £36,000 depreciation is to be charged on plant and machinery for 20X7.

(f)   The debentures have been in issue for some years. The 50p ordinary shares all rank for dividends at the end of the year.

(g)   The directors wish to provide for:

     (i)   Debenture interest due

     (ii)   A transfer to general reserve of £16,000

     (iii)   Audit fees of £4,000

(h)   Stock as at 31 December 20X7 was valued at £220,000 (cost).

(i)   Taxation is to be ignored.

Required

Prepare the final accounts of Wislon Ltd in a form suitable for internal purposes.

5.2 Approach and suggested solution

(a)   Normal adjustments are needed for accruals and prepayments (insurance, light and heat, debenture interest and audit fees). The debenture interest accrued is calculated as follows:

	£'000
Charge needed in P & L account (10% × £200,000)	20
Amount paid so far, as shown in trial balance	10
Accrual – presumably six months' interest now payable	10

	£'000
The accrued expenses shown in the balance sheet comprise:	
Debenture interest	10
Light and heat	3
Audit fee	4
	17

(b)   The misposting of £20,000 to light and heat is also adjusted, by reducing the light and heat expense, but charging £20,000 to salesmen's commission.

(c)   Depreciation on the freehold building is calculated as $\dfrac{£100,000}{50} = £2,000$.

The NBV of the freehold property is then £430,000 – £20,000 – £2,000 = £408,000 at the end of the year. When the property is revalued a reserve of £800,000 – £408,000 = £392,000 is then created.

(d)   The profit on disposal of plant is calculated as proceeds £300,000 (per suspense account) less NBV £274,000, ie £26,000. The cost of the remaining plant is calculated at £830,000 – £350,000 = £480,000. The depreciation provision at the year end is:

	£'000
Balance 1.1.X7	222
Charge for 20X7	36
Less depreciation on disposals (350 – 274)	(76)
	182

(e)   Goodwill arising on the purchase of Mary & Co is:

	£'000
Consideration (per suspense account)	285
Assets at valuation	264
Goodwill	21

In the absence of other instructions, this is shown as an asset on the balance sheet. The investments, being owned by Wislon at the year end, are also shown on the balance sheet, whereas Mary's stock, acquired and then sold, is added to the purchases figure for the year.

(f) The other item in the suspense account is dealt with as follows:

	£'000
Proceeds of issue of 100,000 ordinary shares	120
Less nominal value 100,000 × 50p	50
Excess of consideration over nominal value (= share premium)	70

(g) The transfer to general reserve increases that reserve to £171,000 + £16,000 = £187,000.

WISLON LIMITED
TRADING AND PROFIT AND LOSS ACCOUNT
FOR THE YEAR ENDED 31 DECEMBER 20X7

	£'000	£'000	£'000
Sales			2,695
Less cost of sales			
Opening stock		190	
Purchases		2,186	
		2,376	
Less closing stock		220	
			2,156
Gross profit			539
Profit on disposal of plant			26
			565
Less expenses			
Wages, salaries and commission		274	
Sundry expenses		107	
Light and heat		14	
Depreciation: freehold buildings		2	
plant		36	
Audit fees		4	
Debenture interest		20	
			457
Net profit			108
Movement on retained profits			
Profit for the period			108
Transfer to general reserve			(16)
Dividends: preference (paid)	7		
ordinary: interim (paid)	8		(15)
Retained profit for the year			77
Retained profit brought forward			242
Retained profit carried forward			319

WISLON LIMITED
BALANCE SHEET AS AT 31 DECEMBER 20X7

	Cost/val'n £'000	Dep'n £'000	£'000
Fixed assets			
Intangible assets			
Goodwill			21
Tangible assets			
Freehold property	800	–	800
Plant and machinery	480	182	298
	1,280	182	
Investments			230
			1,349
Current assets			
Stock		220	
Debtors		179	
Prepayment		6	
Cash		126	
		531	
Creditors: amounts falling due within one year			
Creditors	195		
Accrued expenses	17		
		212	
Net current assets			319
Total assets less current liabilities			1,668
Creditors: amounts falling due after more than one year			
10% debentures (secured)			(200)
			1,468
Capital and reserves			
Called up share capital			
50p ordinary shares		400	
7% £1 preference shares		100	
			500
Reserves			
Share premium		70	
Revaluation reserve		392	
General reserve		187	
Profit and loss account		319	
			968
			1,468

6 FRS 3 *Reporting financial performance*

Before we launch into the details of FRS 3, it is worth considering briefly why the changes were necessary. So what was wrong with the profit and loss account before FRS 3?

6.1 Comparisons

Before FRS 3, it was difficult to make comparisons between one year and another because there was no information about the turnover and profit drawn from activities that ceased during the year (and so will not continue next year) and new activities that did not exist last year.

To try to deal with this problem, FRS 3 requires an analysis of the profit and loss account as far as the figure of profit on ordinary activities before interest into three elements.

(a) **Continuing operations**
(b) **New acquisitions**
(c) **Discontinued operations**

This is discussed in more detail in Section 6.5 below.

Someone needing to make comparisons between this year's and last year's turnover and profit, will thus be **comparing like with like**. Similarly, someone needing to forecast next year's turnover and profit can now see how much of this year's operations will continue into the future.

To facilitate the comparison with previous years, FRS 3 requires the comparative figures for the previous year (which have to be disclosed alongside those for the current year in published accounts) to be **restated** so as to show as continuing activities only those which are still continuing in the current year.

6.2 Manipulation

Another reason for introducing FRS 3 was to put an end to the **manipulation** of the profit and loss account by means of **exceptional and extraordinary items**. These, and the changes introduced in FRS 3 are discussed in more detail later in this section, but here we just look briefly at the problem which FRS 3 needed to remedy.

6.2.1 Effect on profit after tax

The forerunner to FRS 3, SSAP 6 *Extraordinary items and prior year adjustments* recognised that large and unusual 'one-off' items in a profit and loss account could distort results and make year-on-year comparisons difficult. It identified two such items, defined informally here, and prescribed two kinds of accounting treatment for the items in question.

(a) **Exceptional items**. These are part of the normal course of a company's business, but hardly ever happen. They were to be disclosed separately but *included* in the calculation of profit on *ordinary* activities before tax.

(b) **Extraordinary items**. These hardly ever happen and are *not* part of a company's ordinary activities. They are to be disclosed separately and *excluded* from the calculation of profit on ordinary activities before, and hence after, tax.

6.3 Main elements of FRS 3

The main elements of FRS 3 are as follows.

(a) New structure of the profit and loss account
(b) Extraordinary items
(c) Statement of total recognised gains and losses
(d) Other new disclosures
(e) Earnings per share

You only need to know about (a) to (d) for your syllabus.

6.4 Exceptional and extraordinary items

AST FORWARD

FRS 3 lays down the rules for dealing with 'out of the ordinary' items and how they are shown in the P & L account. FRS 3 restricts the way companies could manipulate the figures.

6.4.1 Exceptional items

ey term

FRS 3 defines **exceptional items** as:
'Material items which derive from events or transactions that fall within the ordinary activities of the reporting entity and which individually or, if of a similar type, in aggregate, need to be disclosed by virtue of their *size or incidence* if the financial statements are to give a true and fair view.'

6.4.2 Definition of ordinary activities

'Any activities which are undertaken by a reporting entity as part of its business and such related activities in which the reporting entity engages in furtherance of, incidental to, or arising from these activities. Ordinary activities include the effects on the reporting entity of any event in the various environments in which it operates including the political, regulatory, economic and geographical environments irrespective of the frequency or unusual nature of the event.'

There are two types of exceptional item and their accounting treatment is as follows.

(a)   Firstly, there are **three categories** of exceptional items which must be **shown separately** on the face of the profit and loss account after operating profit and before interest and allocated appropriately to discontinued and continued activities.

      (i)   Profit or loss on the sale or termination of an operation.

      (ii)   Costs of a fundamental reorganisation or restructuring that has a material effect on the nature and focus of the reporting entity's operations.

      (iii)   Profit or loss on disposal of fixed assets.

      For both items (i) and (iii) profit and losses may not be offset within categories.

(b)   **Other items** should be allocated to the **appropriate statutory format heading** and attributed to continuing or discontinued operations as appropriate. If the item is sufficiently material that it is needed to show a true and fair view it must be disclosed on the face of the profit and loss account.

In both (a) and (b) an adequate description must be given in the notes to the accounts.

FRS 3 does not give examples of the type of transaction which is likely to be treated as exceptional. However, its predecessor on the subject, SSAP 6, gave a useful list of examples of items which if of a sufficient size might normally be treated as exceptional.

(a)   Abnormal charges for bad debts and write-offs of stock and work in progress.

(b)   Abnormal provisions for losses on long-term contracts.

(c)   Settlement of insurance claims.

6.4.3 Extraordinary items

Under SSAP 6 and SSAP 3 (the replaced standard on earnings per share) the term extraordinary item was one of great significance. However, the ASB publicly stated that it does not envisage such items to appear on a company's profit and loss account and did not provide any examples of things that would be classified as 'extraordinary' rather than 'exceptional'. Its decline in importance has been achieved by tightening of the definition of an extraordinary item.

Key term

> **Extraordinary items** are defined as material items possessing a high degree of abnormality which arise from events or transactions that fall outside the ordinary activities of the reporting entity and which are not expected to recur.

Extraordinary items should be shown on the face of profit and loss account before dividends. Tax on the extraordinary item should be shown separately. A description of the extraordinary items should be given in the notes to the accounts.

6.5 FRS 3 Statements and notes

FAST FORWARD

> FRS 3 introduced a new statement and a variety of new notes to expand the information required in published accounts.

6.5.1 Statement of total recognised gains and losses

Key term

> The **statement of total recognised gains and losses** brings together the profit as shown in the profit and loss account and other gains or losses including unrealised gains and losses.

The profit and loss account can only deal with *realised* profits. An example of realised profits might be profits resulting from the sale proceeds already received or about to be received.

A company can also make substantial **unrealised profits** and losses, for example through changes in the *value* of its fixed assets. These are **recognised**, in the case of asset revaluation, by increasing the value of the assets in the balance sheet, the double entry being to a revaluation reserve included in shareholders' funds.

Question

Recognised not realised

Can you think of two other types of gains and losses which might be recognised during a period but which are not realised and do not pass through the profit and loss account?

Answer

(a)   Gains or losses arising on the translation of foreign currency, for example with overseas investments

(b)   Gains or losses on long-term trade investments

Attention!

> Generally speaking, realised profits and losses have been recognised in the profit and loss account; unrealised profits and loses may be recognised in the balance sheet. FRS 3 argues that users of accounts need to know about the unrealised movements. The statement brings all the information together.

The ASB regards the statement of total recognised gains and losses as very important, and accords it the status of a **primary statement**. This means that it must be presented with the same prominence as the balance sheet, the profit and loss account and the cash flow statement. Below is a specimen statement.

STATEMENT OF TOTAL RECOGNISED GAINS AND LOSSES

	£m
Profit for the financial year	
(ie profit after tax and extraordinary items if any)	29
Unrealised surplus on revaluation of properties	4
Unrealised loss on trade investment	(3)
	30
Foreign currency translation differences	(2)
Total gains and losses recognised since last annual report	28

The statement is, is useful in that it brings together information from different sources: the profit and loss account, the balance sheet and the supporting notes for the asset revaluations. It shows, in this instance, that the total recognised gain for the entity is less than the profit for the period.

7 Published accounts

Now we will see how the financial statements of Wislon would appear if presented for **external** purposes using the standard CA 2006 formats.

WISLON LIMITED
PROFIT AND LOSS ACCOUNT FOR THE YEAR ENDED 31 DECEMBER 20X7

	£'000
Turnover	2,695
Cost of sales	2,156
Gross profit	539
Administrative expenses	437
Operating profit	102
Other income	26
Interest payable and similar charges	20
Profit on ordinary activities before taxation	108
Tax on profit on ordinary activities	0
Profit on ordinary activities after taxation	108

WISLON LIMITED
BALANCE SHEET AS AT 31 DECEMBER 20X7

	£'000	£'000
Fixed assets		
Intangible assets		21
Tangible assets		1,098
Fixed asset investments		230
		1,349
Current assets		
Stocks	220	
Debtors	185	
Cash at bank and in hand	126	
	531	
Creditors: amounts falling due within one year	212	
Net current assets		319
Total asset less current liabilities		1,668
Creditors: amounts falling due after more than one year		200
		1,468
Capital and reserves		
Called up share capital		500
Share premium account		70
Revaluation reserve		392
General reserve		187
Profit and loss account		319
		1,468

WISLON LIMITED
STATEMENT OF MOVEMENTS IN RESERVES

	Share capital £'000	Share premium £'000	Reval'n reserve £'000	General reserve £'000	Profit & loss a/c £'000
At 1 January 20X7	450	-	-	171	242
Share issue	50	70	-	-	-
Revaluation	-	-	392	-	-
Profit for the year	-	-	-	-	108
Dividends paid	-	-	-	-	(15)
Transfers	-	-	-	16	(16)
At 31 December 20X7	500	70	392	187	319

Note that in accounts for publication there is less detail on the face of the profit and loss account. All expenses except interest are grouped under Distribution costs or Administrative expenses, with a breakdown contained in the notes. Similarly, Cost of sales is a one-line item – the details of purchases and opening and closing stock can be shown in a working.

In the balance sheet, details of fixed assets go to the notes as does breakdown of share capital. If an exam question asks for accounts suitable for publication, remember to put all the breakdowns into notes. This is good practice for any accounts preparation question.

In the case of Wilson we would have the following notes:

	£'000
Administrative expenses	
Wages and salaries	274
Sundry expenses	107
Light and heat	14
Depreciation	38
Audit fee	4
	437
Other income	
Profit on disposal of plant	26

Fixed assets
Breakdown as shown on original balance sheet.

One of the competences you require to fulfil performance criteria 10 of the PER is the ability to compile financial statements and accounts in line with appropriate standards and guidelines. You can apply the knowledge you obtain from this section of the text to help demonstrate this competence.

Chapter Roundup

- The preparation and publication of the final accounts of limited companies in the UK are governed by the Companies Act 2006.

- The introduction of FRS 3 *Reporting financial performance* has meant significant changes to company published accounts. All the changes were intended to improve the quality of information provided to shareholders.

- FRS 3 lays down the rules for dealing with 'out of the ordinary' items and how they are shown in the P & L account. FRS 3 restricts the way companies could manipulate the figures.

- FRS 3 introduced a new statement and a variety of new notes to expand the information required in published accounts.

1   According to the Companies Act 2006, companies have to produce their accounts within what period?

   A   Within 6 months of the balance sheet date
   B   Within 9 months of the balance sheet date

2   Managers' salaries are appropriations of profit.

   A   True
   B   False

3   Which of the following items are fixed assets?

   (i)   Land
   (ii)   Machinery
   (iii) Bank loan
   (iv)   Stock

   A   (i) only
   B   (i) and (ii)
   C   (i), (ii) and (iii)
   D   (ii), (iii) and (iv)

4   How is a bank overdraft classified in the balance sheet?

   A   Fixed asset
   B   Current asset
   C   Current liability
   D   Long-term liability

5   In the published accounts of XYZ Co, the profit for the period is £3,500,000. The balance of retained profits at the beginning of the year is £500,000. If dividends of £2,500,000 were paid, what is the closing balance of retained profit?

   A   £4,000,000
   B   £1,500,000
   C   £500,000
   D   £1,000,000

6   Which of the following occurrences would be treated as extraordinary under FRS 3?

   A   Restructuring
   B   Natural disasters
   C   Revaluation
   D   Discontinued operations

Answers to Quick Quiz

1   B

2   B   False. Managers' salaries are an expense charged to the profit and loss account.

3   B   Item (iii) is a liability and item (iv) is a current asset.

4   C   A bank overdraft is strictly payable on demand and so it is a current liability.

5   B

	£'000
Retained profits	
Opening balance	500
Profit for the period	3,500
	4,000
Dividends paid	(2,500)
Closing balance	1,500

6   B   The others are normal trading activities.

Now try the question below from the Exam Question Bank

Number	Level	Marks	Time
Q45	Examination	2	2 mins

22

Events after the balance sheet date

Topic list	Syllabus reference
1 FRS 21 Events after the balance sheet date	F3(a)-(c)

Introduction

You will see in FRS 21 (previously SSAP 17) the application of the accounting concept of prudence, which you learnt about in Chapter 3. This FRS is important for your auditing studies later and must be thoroughly learnt. It is more straightforward in theory than in practice.

Study guide

		Intellectual level
F3	**Events after the balance sheet date**	
(a)	Define an event after the balance sheet date in accordance with FRSs	1
(b)	Classify events as adjusting or non-adjusting	1
(c)	Distinguish between how adjusting and non-adjusting events are reported in the financial statements	1

Exam guide

This is an important area which is likely to come up regularly. Learn the rules and be confident you can decide upon the correct accounting treatment for a given situation.

1 FRS 21 Events after the balance sheet date

FAST FORWARD

Events after the balance sheet date which provide **additional evidence** of conditions existing at the balance sheet date, will cause **adjustments** to be made to the assets and liabilities in the financial statements.

1.1 Definitions

FRS 21 defines events after balance sheet date as follows.

Key term

Events after the balance sheet date are those events, favourable and unfavourable, that occur between the balance sheet date and the date when the financial statements are authorised for issue.'

FRS 21 makes a distinction between 'adjusting events' and 'non-adjusting events'.

1.2 Adjusting events

FRS 21 defines adjusting events as follows.

Key term

Adjusting events are events after the balance sheet date 'that provide evidence of conditions that existed at the balance sheet date.

Adjusting events mean that the accounts must be revised to reflect the new information.

1.3 Examples of adjusting events

FRS 21 cites a number of events after the balance sheet date which normally should be classified as adjusting events. They include:

(a) The settlement after the balance sheet date of a court case that confirms that the entity had a present obligation at the balance sheet date. The adjustment may be to a provision under FRS 12 or to set up a new provision because it is no longer a contingent liability.

(b) The receipt of information indicating that an asset was impaired at the balance sheet date, or that the amount of impairment needs to be adjusted. For example,

   (i)   Bankruptcy of a customer after the balance sheet date.

   (ii)   Sale of inventories (stock) after the balance sheet date may give evidence of their NRV at the balance sheet date.

(c) The determination after the balance sheet date of the cost of assets purchased or the proceeds from assets sold before the balance sheet date.

(d)   The determination of the amount of any profit-sharing or bonus payments if there was a present legal or constructive obligation at the balance sheet to make such payments due to events before that date.

(e)   The discovery of fraud or errors that show the financial statements are incorrect.

Some events occurring after the balance sheet date, such as a deterioration in the company's operating results and in its financial position, may indicate a need to consider whether it is appropriate to use the going concern concept in the preparation of financial statements. Consequently such events may fall to be treated as adjusting events.

Note that the declaration of dividends after the balance sheet date is no longer an adjusting event (it was under SSAP 17).

1.4 Non-adjusting events

FRS 21 states:

> **Non-adjusting events** those that are indicative of conditions that arose after the balance sheet date.'

Consequently they do not result in changes in amounts in financial statements. They may, however, be of such materiality that their disclosure is required by way of notes to ensure that financial statements are not misleading.

1.5 Examples of non-adjusting events

Again, a number of examples are given in FRS 21.

(a)   Decline in market value of investments.

(b)   Declaration of dividends after the balance sheet date (to be disclosed instead in the notes to the financial statements).

If non-adjusting events are material, then disclosure is made in the notes to the accounts of:

(a)   The nature of the event; and

(b)   An estimate of its financial effect or a statement that such an estimate cannot be made.

1.6 Examples of non-adjusting events requiring disclosure

The FRS gives a number of examples of events after the balance sheet date needing disclosure.

(a)   A major business combination after the balance sheet date or disposing of a major subsidiary.

(b)   Announcing a plan to discontinue an operation.

(c)   Major purchases and disposals of assets, or expropriation of major assets by government.

(d)   The destruction of a major production plant by a fire.

(e)   Announcing, or commencing the implementation of, a major restructuring.

(f)   Major ordinary share transactions and potential ordinary share transactions.

(g)   Abnormally large changes in asset prices or foreign exchange rates.

(h)   Changes in tax rates, or tax laws enacted or announced, that have a significant effect on current and deferred tax assets and liabilities.

(i)   Entering into significant commitments or contingent liabilities eg by issuing significant guarantees.

(j)   Commencing major litigation arising solely out of events that occurred after the balance sheet date.

1.7 Disclosure requirements

Financial statements should be prepared on the basis of **conditions existing** at the **balance sheet** date and should also disclose the date on which they were approved by the board of directors (so that users can establish the duration of the 'events after the balance sheet period'). The standard is not intended to apply to events occurring after the date of board approval, but recommends that if such events are material the directors should consider publishing the relevant information so that users of financial statements are not misled.

FRS 21 states that a material event after the balance sheet date requires **changes** in the amounts to be included in financial statements where:

(a)   It is an **adjusting event**.

(b)   It indicates that application of the **going concern** concept to the whole or a material part of the company is **not appropriate**.

Separate disclosure of adjusting events is not normally required as they do no more than provide additional evidence in support of items in financial statements. However in exceptional circumstances, where a non-adjusting event is reclassified as an adjusting event, full disclosure of the adjustment is required.

The CA 2006 requires that all liabilities and losses which have arisen or are likely to arise in respect of the financial year to which the accounts relate (or a previous financial year) shall be taken into account, including those that only become apparent between the balance sheet date and the date on which it is signed on behalf of the board of directors.

The Act therefore gives some statutory enforcement to the provisions in FRS 21 in respect of adjusting events after the balance sheet date, but refers to 'liabilities and losses' only, and not to 'gains'.

FRS 21 also requires that a material event after the balance sheet date should be **disclosed** where:

(a)   It is a **non-adjusting event** of such materiality that its non-disclosure would affect the ability of the users of financial statements to reach a proper understanding of the financial position.

(b)   It is the reversal or maturity after the year end of a transaction entered into before the year end, the substance of which was primarily to alter the appearance of the company's balance sheet.

In delaying whether a non-adjusting event is material enough to need disclosure, consider whether the users of financial statements would be misled if the disclosure was omitted.

The CA 2006 requires that the directors' report should contain particulars of any important events affecting the company (or its subsidiaries) which have occurred since the end of the year.

Although this gives some statutory backing to the provisions of FRS 21 in respect of non-adjusting events after the balance sheet date, it suggests the information be given in the directors' report rather than the notes to the accounts (as required by FRS 21).

Exam focus point

There was an article on events after the balance sheet date in *Student Accountant* dated 15 March 2007. We recommend that you read this article.

Question

Adjusting or non-adjusting

State whether the following events after the balance sheet date are adjusting or non-adjusting:

(a)   Purchase of an investment
(b)   A change in the rate of corporation tax, applicable to the previous year
(c)   An increase in pension benefits
(d)   Losses due to fire
(e)   An irrecoverable debt suddenly being paid
(f)   The receipt of proceeds of sales or other evidence concerning the net realisable value of stock
(g)   A sudden decline in the value of property held as a fixed asset
(h)   A merger

Answer

(e) and (f) are adjusting; the others are non-adjusting.

Question

In the case of item (g) in the question above, the following additional information is available. A factory held as a fixed asset with a NBV of £500,000 in the balance sheet. Due to the sudden abandonment of the local council's redevelopment plans in the Northwich area, the market value of the property has fallen to £250,000. Draft a note to the company financial statements.

Answer

Note: Event after the balance sheet date

After the balance sheet date, the local council abandoned its redevelopment plans for the Northwich area. The company has a factory in that area and the market value of that property has now fallen to £250,000. The factory is shown in the accounts with a net book value of £500,000 at the balance sheet date.

Tutorial note: When drafting these type of notes give all the information that is available in the question.

Exam focus point

Expect to be asked whether an item is adjusting or non-adjusting. You may well be asked to adjust for an adjusting item.

Chapter Roundup

- **Events after the balance sheet date** which provide **additional evidence** of conditions existing at the balance sheet date, will cause **adjustments** to be made to the assets and liabilities in the financial statements.

Quick Quiz

1   When does an event after the balance sheet date require changes to the financial statements?

   A   Never
   B   If it provides further evidence of conditions existing at the balance sheet date

2   What disclosure is required when it is not possible to estimate the financial effect of an event not requiring adjustment?

   A   No disclosure
   B   A note to the accounts giving what information is available

3   Which of the following items are adjusting events?

   (i)   Stock found to have deteriorated
   (ii)   Dividends proposed at the year end
   (iii)   A building destroyed by fire after the balance sheet date

   A   (i) only
   B   (ii) only
   C   (iii) only
   D   None of the above

4	Which of the following items are non-adjusting events?

(i)	Stock destroyed by flood two days before the balance sheet date

(ii)	A customer goes bankrupt

(iii)	Fall in value of an investment between the balance sheet date and the date the financial statements are finalised

A	(i) only
B	(ii) only
C	(iii) only
D	None of the above

5	A debtor has been written off as irrecoverable. However the customer suddenly pays the written off amount after the balance sheet date. Is this event

A	Adjusting
B	Non-adjusting

Answers to Quick Quiz

1	B	Assets and liabilities should be adjusted for events after the balance sheet date when these provide additional evidence for estimates existing at the balance sheet date.

2	B	A statement of the nature of the event and the fact that a financial estimate of the event can not be made.

3	A

4	C

5	A

Now try the questions below from the Exam Question Bank			
Number	**Level**	**Marks**	**Time**
Q46	Examination	1	1 min
Q47	Examination	2	2 mins

Cash flow statements

23

Topic list	Syllabus reference
1 FRS 1 Cash flow statements	F5(a)-(h)
2 Preparing a cash flow statement	F5(g)

Introduction

In the long run, a profit will result in an increase in the company's cash balance but, as Keynes observed, 'in the long run we are all dead'. In the short run, the making of a profit will not necessarily result in an increased cash balance. The observation leads us to two questions:

- What is the difference between cash and profit?
- How useful are the profit and loss account and balance sheet in demonstrating whether a company has sufficient cash to finance its operations?

The importance of the distinction between cash and profit and the scant attention paid to this by the profit and loss account has resulted in the development of cash flow statements.

Study guide

		Intellectual level
F5	**Cash flow statements (excluding partnerships)**	
(a)	Differentiate between profit and cash flow	1
(b)	Understand the need for management to control cash flow	1
(c)	Recognise the benefits and drawbacks to users of the financial statements of a cash flow statement	1
(d)	Classify the effect of transactions on cash flows	1
(e)	Calculate the figures needed for the cash flow statement including:	1
(i)	Net cash inflow from operating activities	
(ii)	Return on investments or servicing of finance	
(iii)	Taxation	
(iv)	Capital expenditure	
(v)	Equity dividends paid	
(vi)	Management of liquid resources	
(vii)	Financing	
(f)	Calculate the cash flow from operating activities using the indirect and direct methods	1
(g)	Prepare extracts from cash flow statements from given information	1
(h)	Identify the treatment of given transactions in a company's cash flow statement	1

Exam guide

This chapter adopts a systematic approach to the preparation of cash flow statements in examinations; you should learn this method and you will then be equipped for any questions in the exam itself. A **question is certain** to appear in the exam. However you will be asked only for a part of the cash flow statement (eg cash flows from operating activities) and not for a full statement.

Exam focus point

> At the 2009 ACCA Teachers' Conference, the examiner highlighted cash flow statements as another area consistently answered badly in the exam. She also recommended practising full questions in this key area. It will not only help you through F3 but is an essential skill for F7.

1 FRS 1 Cash flow statements

FAST FORWARD

> Cash flow is a useful measure of a company's performance.

It has been argued that 'profit' does not always give a useful or meaningful picture of a company's operations. Readers of a company's financial statements might even be **misled by a reported profit figure**.

(a)   Shareholders might believe that if a company makes a profit after tax, of say, £100,000 then this is the amount which it could afford to pay as a dividend. Unless the company has sufficient cash available to stay in business and also to pay a dividend, the shareholders' expectations would be wrong.

(b)   Employees might believe that if a company makes profits, it can afford to pay higher wages next year. This opinion may not be correct: the ability to pay wages depends on the availability of cash.

(c)   Cash is the lifeblood of the business. Survival of a business entity depends not so much on profits as on its ability to pay its debts when they fall due. Such payments might include 'profit and loss' items such as material purchases, wages, interest and taxation etc, but also capital payments for new fixed assets and the repayment of loan capital when this falls due (for example on the redemption of debentures).

From these examples, it may be apparent that a company's performance and prospects depend not so much on the 'profits' earned in a period, but more realistically on liquidity or **cash flows**.

The great advantage of a cash flow statement is that it is unambiguous and provides information which is additional to that provided in the rest of the accounts. It also describes the cash flows of an organisation by activity and not by balance sheet classification.

1.1 Basic cash flow statement

A very basic cash flow statement follows.

	£
Net cash flow from operating activities	X
Returns on investment and servicing of finance	X
Taxation	X
Capital expenditure	X
Equity dividends paid	X
Management of liquid resources	X
Financing	X
Increase/(decrease) in cash	X/(X)

1.2 Net cash flow from operating activities

One way of arriving at net cash flow from operating activities is to start from operating profit and adjust for non-cash items, such as depreciation, debtors etc. This is known as the **indirect method**. A proforma calculation is given below.

Formula to learn

	£
Operating profit (P&L)	X
Add depreciation	X
Loss (profit) on sale of fixed assets	X
(Increase)/decrease in stocks	(X)/X
(Increase)/decrease in debtors	(X)/X
Increase/(decrease) in creditors	X/(X)
Net cash flow from operating activities	X

It is important to understand why certain items are added and others subtracted. Note the following points.

(a)   Depreciation is not a cash expense, but is deducted in arriving at the profit figure in the profit and loss account. It makes sense, therefore, to eliminate it by adding it back.

(b)   By the same logic, a loss on a disposal of a fixed asset (arising through underprovision of depreciation) needs to be added back and a profit deducted.

(c)   An increase in stocks means less cash – you have spent cash on buying stock.

(d)   An increase in debtors means debtors have not paid as much, therefore less cash.

(e)   If we pay off creditors, causing the figure to decrease, again we have less cash.

Exam focus point

> You will probably need to use the **indirect method** in examination questions based around FRS 1 (see below).

The **direct method** is illustrated in the question Rene plc, later in this chapter. The pro-forma is shown below.

	£
Cash received from customers	X
Cash payments to suppliers	X
Cash payments to and on behalf of employees	X
Net cash flow from operating activities	X

Question

Indirect method

Quest Ltd has operating profit for the year to 31 December 20X6 of £850, after charging £650 for depreciation and making a profit on sale of a car of £120.

The balance sheet for the year shows the following entries:

	20X6	20X5
Stock	586	763
Trade debtors	1021	589
Trade creditors	443	1431

Required

Calculate the net cash from operating activities

Answer

	£
Operating profit	850
Add depreciation	650
Deduct profit on disposal	(120)
Add decrease in stocks	177
Deduct increase in debtors	(432)
Deduct decrease in creditors	(988)
Net cash from operating activities	137

1.3 Return on investments or servicing of finance

Cash flows from investing activities and servicing of finance are calculated separately in the cash flow statement.

The pro-forma for return on investments

Interest paid	(X)
Interest received	X
Dividends received	X
Cash flow from investing activities and servicing of finance	X

Example

Pearl Ltd acquired a new factory in the year to 30 June 20X6 for a cost of £805,000. They sold their old factory for £425,000. They also received interest on surplus funds of £350,000. Calculate cash flows arising from investing activities.

Solution

	£
Interest received	350,000
Return on investments	350,000

Note. The movements on fixed assets will be part of the capital expenditure calculation.

1.4 Cash flows from financing activities

The pro-forma to learn for this part of the cash flow statement is:

Proceeds from issue of share capital	X
Proceeds from long-term borrowing	X
Cash flow from financing activities	X

Example

Spear Ltd issued 87,500 £1 shares at par during the year to 31 December 20X6. Loans taken out increased from £18,000 at the beginning of the year to £30,000 at the end of the year. The company declared a dividend of 10p per share. Calculate the cash flows from financing activities.

	£
Proceeds from issue of shares	87,500
Increase in loans	12,000
Cash flows from financing activities	99,500

Please note that only dividends *paid* in the period represent cash flows.

1.5 FRS 1 Cash flow statements (revised)

FRS 1 sets out the structure of a cash flow statement and it also sets the minimum level of disclosure. Examination questions are likely to be computational, but some discussion and interpretation may be required.

In October 1996 the ASB issued a revised version of FRS 1 *Cash flow statements*. The revision of FRS 1 was part of a normal process of revision, but it also responded to various criticisms of the original FRS 1.

1.6 Objective

The FRS begins with the following statement.

'The objective of this FRS is to ensure that reporting entities falling within its scope:

(a)   Report their cash generation and cash absorption for a period by highlighting the significant components of cash flow in a way that facilitates comparison of the cash flow performance of different businesses.

(b)   Provide information that assists in the assessment of their liquidity, solvency and financial adaptability.'

1.7 Scope

The FRS applies to all financial statements intended to give a true and fair view of the financial position and profit or loss (or income and expenditure), except those of various exempt bodies in group accounts situations or where the content of the financial statement is governed by other statutes or regulatory regimes. In addition, small entities are excluded as defined by companies legislation.

1.8 Format of the cash flow statement

An example is given of the format of a cash flow statement for a single company and this is reproduced in Section 1.12.

A cash flow statement should list its cash flows for the period classified under the following **standard headings**:

(a)   **Operating activities** (using either the direct or indirect method)
(b)   **Returns on investments and servicing of finance**
(c)   **Taxation**
(d)   **Capital expenditure** and financial investment

(e)   **Acquisitions and disposals**
(f)   **Equity dividends paid**
(g)   **Management of liquid resources**
(h)   **Financing**

The last two headings can be shown in a single section provided a subtotal is given for each heading. Acquisitions and disposals **are not on your syllabus**; the heading is included here for completeness.

Individual categories of inflows and outflows under the standard headings should be disclosed separately either in the cash flow statements or in a note to it unless they are allowed to be shown net. Cash inflows and outflows may be shown net if they relate to the management of liquid resources or financing and the inflows and outflows:

(a)   Relate in substance to a single financing transaction (unlikely to be a concern in Paper F3).
(b)   Or are due to short maturities and high turnover occurring from rollover or reissue (for example, short-term deposits).

The requirement to show cash inflows and outflows separately does not apply to cash flows relating to operating activities.

Each cash flow should be classified according to the substance of the transaction giving rise to it.

1.9 Links to other primary statements

Because the information given by a cash flow statement is best appreciated in the context of the information given by the other primary statements, the FRS requires **two reconciliations**, between:

(a)   **Operating profit and the net cash flow from operating activities**
(b)   **The movement in cash in the period and the movement in net debt**.

Neither reconciliation forms part of the cash flow statement but each may be given either adjoining the statement or in a separate note.

The reconciliation in point (a) above has already been given in the formula to learn in Section 1.2.

The **movement in net debt** should identify the following components and reconcile these to the opening and closing balance sheet amount:

(a)   The cash flows of the entity
(b)   Other non-cash changes
(c)   The recognition of changes in market value and exchange rate movements

1.10 Definitions

The FRS includes the following important definitions (only those of direct concern to your syllabus are included here). Note particularly the definitions of cash and liquid resources.

(a)   An **active market** is a market of sufficient depth to absorb the investment held without a significant effect on the price. (This definition affects the definition of liquid resources below.)
(b)   **Cash** is cash in hand and deposits repayable on demand with any qualifying financial institution, less overdrafts from any qualifying financial institution repayable on demand. Deposits are repayable on demand if they can be withdrawn at any time without notice and without penalty or if a maturity or period of notice of not more than 24 hours or one working day has been agreed. Cash includes cash in hand and deposit denominated in foreign currencies.
(c)   **Cash flow** is an increase or decrease in an amount of cash.
(d)   **Liquid resources** are current asset investments held as readily disposable stores of value. A readily disposable investment is one that:
(i)   Is disposable by the reporting entity without curtailing or disrupting its business
(ii)   Is either:

          (1)   Readily convertible into known amounts of cash at or close to its carrying amount, or

          (2)   Traded in an active market.

(e)   **Net debt** is the borrowings of the reporting entity less cash and liquid resources. Where cash and liquid resources exceed the borrowings of the entity reference should be to 'net funds' rather than to 'net debt'.

(f)   **Overdraft** is a borrowing facility repayable on demand that is used by drawing on a current account with a qualifying financial institution.

1.11 Classification of cash flows by standard heading

The FRS looks at each of the cash flow categories in turn.

1.11.1 Operating activities

Cash flows from operating activities are in general the cash effects of transactions and other events relating to operating or trading activities, normally shown in the profit and loss account in arriving at operating profit. They include cash flows in respect of operating items relating to provisions, whether or not the provision was included in operating profit.

A reconciliation between the **operating profit** reported in the profit and loss account and the **net cash flow from operating activities** should be given either adjoining the cash flow statement or as a note. The reconciliation is not part of the cash flow statement: if adjoining the cash flow statement, it should be clearly labelled and kept separate. The reconciliation should disclose separately the movements in stocks, debtors and creditors related to operating activities and other differences between cash flows and profits.

1.11.2 Returns on investments and servicing of finance

These are receipts resulting from the ownership of an investment and payments to providers of finance and non-equity shareholders (eg the holders of preference shares).

Cash inflows from returns on investments and servicing of finance include:

(a)   Interest received, including any related tax recovered

(b)   Dividends received, net of any tax credits

Cash outflows from returns on investments and servicing of finance include:

(a)   Interest paid (even if capitalised), including any tax deducted and paid to the relevant tax authority.

(b)   Cash flows that are treated as finance costs (this will include issue costs on debt and non-equity share capital).

(c)   The interest element of finance lease rental payments.

(d)   Dividends paid on non-equity shares of the entity.

1.11.3 Taxation

These are cash flows to or from taxation authorities in respect of the reporting entity's revenue and capital profits. VAT and other sales taxes are discussed below.

(a)   Taxation cash inflows include cash receipts from the relevant tax authority of tax rebates, claims or returns of overpayments.

(b)   Taxation cash outflows include cash payments to the relevant tax authority of tax, including payments of advance corporation tax.

1.11.4 Capital expenditure and financial investment

These cash flows are those related to the acquisition or disposal of any fixed asset other than one required to be classified under 'acquisitions and disposals' (discussed below), and any current asset investment not included in liquid resources (also dealt with below). If no cash flows relating to financial investment fall to be included under this heading the caption may be reduced to 'capital expenditure'.

The cash inflows here include:

(a)   Receipts from sales or disposals of property, plant or equipment.
(b)   Receipts from the repayment of the reporting entity's loans to other entities.

Cash outflows in this category include:

(a)   Payments to acquire property, plant or equipment
(b)   Loans made by the reporting entity

1.11.5 Acquisitions and disposals

These cash flows are related to the acquisition or disposal of any trade or business, or of an investment in an entity that is either an associate, a joint venture, or a subsidiary undertaking (**these group matters are beyond the scope of your syllabus**).

(a)   Cash inflows here include receipts from sales of trades or businesses.
(b)   Cash outflows here include payments to acquire trades or businesses.

1.11.6 Equity dividends paid

The cash outflows are dividends paid on the reporting entity's equity shares.

1.11.7 Management of liquid resources

This section should include cash flows in respect of liquid resources as defined above. Each entity should explain what it includes as liquid resources and any changes in its policy. The cash flows in this section can be shown in a single section with those under 'financing' provided that separate subtotals for each are given.

Cash inflows include:

(a)   Withdrawals from short-term deposits not qualifying as cash
(b)   Inflows from disposal or redemption of any other investments held as liquid resources

Cash outflows include:

(a)   Payments into short-term deposits not qualifying as cash
(b)   Outflows to acquire any other investments held as liquid resources

1.11.8 Financing

Financing cash flows comprise receipts or repayments of principal from or to external providers of finance. The cash flows in this section can be shown in a single section with those under 'management of liquid resources' provided that separate subtotals for each are given.

Financing cash inflows include:

(a)   Receipts from issuing shares or other equity instruments
(b)   Receipts from issuing debentures, loans and from other long-term and short-term borrowings (other than overdrafts)

Financing cash outflows include:

(a)   Repayments of amounts borrowed (other than overdrafts)
(b)   The capital element of finance lease rental payments
(c)   Payments to reacquire or redeem the entity's shares
(d)   Payments of expenses or commission on any issue of equity shares

1.12 Example: Single company

The following example is provided by the standard for a single company.

XYZ LIMITED

CASH FLOW STATEMENT FOR THE YEAR ENDED 31 DECEMBER 1996

Reconciliation of operating profit to net cash inflow from operating activities

	£'000
Operating profit	6,022
Depreciation charges	899
Increase in stocks	(194)
Increase in debtors	(72)
Increase in creditors	234
Net cash inflow from operating activities	6,899

CASH FLOW STATEMENT

	£'000
Net cash inflow from operating activities	6,889
Returns on investments and servicing of finance (note 1)	2,999
Taxation	(2,922)
Capital expenditure (note 1)	(1,525)
	5,441
Equity dividends paid	(2,417)
	3,024
Management of liquid resources (note 1)	(450)
Financing (note 1)	57
Increase in cash	2,631

Reconciliation of net cash flow to movement in net debt (note 2)

	£'000	£'000
Increase in cash in the period	2,631	
Cash to repurchase debenture	149	
Cash used to increase liquid resources	450	
Change in net debt*		3,230
Net debt at 1.1.96		(2,903)
Net funds at 31.12.96		327

*In this example all changes in net debt are cash flows.

The reconciliation of operating profit to net cash flows from operating activities can be shown in a note.

NOTES TO THE CASH FLOW STATEMENT

1 *Gross cash flows*

	£'000	£'000
Returns on investments and servicing of finance		
Interest received	3,011	
Interest paid	(12)	
		2,999
Capital expenditure		
Payments to acquire intangible fixed assets	(71)	
Payments to acquire tangible fixed assets	(1,496)	
Receipts from sales of tangible fixed assets	42	
		(1,525)
Management of liquid resources		
Purchase of treasury bills	(650)	
Sale of treasury bills	200	
		(450)
Financing		
Issue of ordinary share capital	211	
Repurchase of debenture loan	(149)	
Expenses paid in connection with share issues	(5)	
		57

Note. These gross cash flows can be shown on the face of the cash flow statement, but it may sometimes be neater to show them as a note like this.

2   *Analysis of changes in net debt*

	As at 1 Jan 1996 £'000	Cash flows £'000	Other changes £'000	At 31 Dec 1996 £'000
Cash in hand, at bank	42	847		889
Overdrafts	(1,784)	1,784		
		2,631		
Debt due within 1 year	(149)	149	(230)	(230)
Debt due after 1 year	(1,262)		230	(1,032)
Current asset investments	250	450		700
Total	(2,903)	3,230	–	327

Question   Format

Close the book for a moment and jot down the format of the cash flow statement.

2 Preparing a cash flow statement

FAST FORWARD

You need to be aware of the format laid out in FRS 1.

Exam focus point

In essence, preparing a cash flow statement is very straightforward. You should therefore simply learn the format and apply the steps noted in the example below.

Note that the following items are treated in a way that might seem confusing, but the treatment is logical if you think in terms of **cash**.

(a)   Increase in stock is treated as **negative** (in brackets). This is because it represents a cash **outflow**; cash is being spent on stock.

(b)   An increase in debtors would be treated as **negative** for the same reasons; more debtors means less cash.

(c)   By contrast an increase in creditors is **positive** because cash is being retained and not used to pay off creditors. There is therefore more of it.

2.1 Example: Preparation of a cash flow statement

Kane Ltd's profit and loss account for the year ended 31 December 20X2 and balance sheets at 31 December 20X1 and 31 December 20X2 were as follows.

KANE LIMITED
PROFIT AND LOSS ACCOUNT FOR THE YEAR ENDED 31 DECEMBER 20X2

	£'000	£'000
Sales		720
Raw materials consumed	70	
Staff costs	94	
Depreciation	118	
Loss on disposal	18	
		300
Operating profit		420
Interest payable		28
Profit before tax		392
Taxation		124
Profit after tax		268

KANE LIMITED
BALANCE SHEETS AS AT 31 DECEMBER

	20X2		20X1	
	£'000	£'000	£'000	£'000
Fixed assets				
Cost		1,596		1,560
Depreciation		318		224
		1,278		1,336
Current assets				
Stock	24		20	
Trade debtors	66		50	
Recoverable corporation tax	10		8	
Bank	48		56	
	148		134	
Current liabilities				
Trade creditors	12		6	
Taxation	102		86	
	114		92	
Net current assets		34		42
		1,312		1,378
Long-term liabilities				
Long-term loans		200		500
		1,112		878
Share capital		360		340
Share premium		36		24
Profit and loss		716		514
		1,112		878

Dividends totalling £66,000 were paid during the year.

During the year, the company paid £90,000 for a new piece of machinery.

Required

Prepare a cash flow statement for Kane Ltd for the year ended 31 December 20X2 in accordance with the requirements of FRS 1 (revised).

Solution

Step 1. Set out the proforma cash flow statement with all the headings required by FRS 1 (revised). You should leave plenty of space. Ideally, use three or more sheets of paper, one for the main statement, one for the notes (particularly if you have a separate note for the gross cash flows) and one for your workings. It is obviously essential to know the formats very well.

Step 2. Complete the reconciliation of operating profit to net cash inflow as far as possible. When preparing the statement from balance sheets, you will usually have to calculate such items as depreciation, loss on sale of fixed assets and profit for the year (see Step 4).

Step 3. Calculate the figures for tax paid, purchase or sale of fixed assets, issue of shares and repayment of loans if these are not already given to you (as they may be). Note that you may not be given the tax charge in the profit and loss account. You will then have to assume that the tax paid in the year is last year's year-end provision and calculate the charge as the balancing figure.

Step 4. If you are not given the profit figure, open up a working for the profit and loss account. Using the opening and closing balances, the taxation charge and dividends paid you will be able to calculate profit for the year as the balancing figure to put in the statement.

Step 5. Complete Note 1, the gross cash flows, if asked for it. Alternatively, the information may go straight into the statement.

Step 6. You will now be able to complete the statement by slotting in the figures given or calculated.

Step 7. Complete Note 2, the analysis of changes in net debt, if asked.

KANE LIMITED
CASH FLOW STATEMENT FOR THE YEAR ENDED 31 DECEMBER 20X2
Reconciliation of operating profit to net cash inflow

	£'000
Operating profit	420
Depreciation charges	118
Loss on sale of tangible fixed assets	18
Increase in stocks	(4)
Increase in debtors	(16)
Increase in creditors	6
Net cash inflow from operating activities	542

CASH FLOW STATEMENT

	£'000	£'000
Net cash flows from operating activities		542
Returns on investment and servicing of finance		
Interest paid		(28)
Taxation		
Corporation tax paid (W1)		(110)
Capital expenditure		
Payments to acquire tangible fixed assets	(90)	
Receipts from sales of tangible fixed assets	12	
Net cash outflow from capital expenditure		(78)
		326
Equity dividends paid		(66)
		260
Financing		
Issues of share capital (360 + 36 – 340 – 24)	32	
Long-term loans repaid (500 – 200)	(300)	
Net cash outflow from financing		(268)
Decrease in cash		(8)

NOTES TO THE CASH FLOW STATEMENT

Analysis of changes in net debt

	At 1 Jan 20X2 £'000	Cash flows £'000	At 31 Dec 20X2 £'000
Cash in hand, at bank	56	(8)	48
Debt due after 1 year	(500)	300	(200)
Total	(444)	292	(152)

Workings

1   Corporation tax paid

	£'000
Opening CT payable (86 – 8)	78
Charge for year	124
Net CT payable at 31.12.X2 (102 – 10)	(92)
Paid	110

2   Fixed asset disposals

COST

	£'000		£'000
At 1.1.X2	1,560	At 31.12.X2	1,596
Purchases	90	Disposals	54
	1,650		1,650

ACCUMULATED DEPRECIATION

	£'000		£'000
At 31.1.X2	318	At 1.1.X2	224
Depreciation on disposals	24	Charge for year	118
	342		342

	£'000
NBV of disposals	30
Net loss reported	(18)
Proceeds of disposals	12

One of the competences you require to fulfil performance objective 11 of the PER is the ability to analyse and interpret financial data. You can apply the knowledge you obtain from this chapter to help to demonstrate this competence.

Question

The summarised accounts of Rene plc for the year ended 31 December 20X8 are as follows.

RENE PLC
BALANCE SHEET AS AT 31 DECEMBER 20X8

	20X8		20X7	
	£'000	£'000	£'000	£'000
Fixed assets				
Tangible assets		628		514
Current assets				
Stocks	214		210	
Debtors	168		147	
Cash	7		–	
	389		357	
Creditors: amounts falling due within one year				
Trade creditors	136		121	
Tax payable	39		28	
Overdraft	–		14	
	175		163	
Net current assets		214		194
Total assets less current liabilities		842		708
Creditors: amounts falling due after more than one year				
10% debentures		(80)		(50)
		762		658
Capital and reserves				
Share capital (£1 ords)		250		200
Share premium account		70		60
Revaluation reserve		110		100
Profit and loss account		332		298
		762		658

RENE PLC
PROFIT AND LOSS ACCOUNT
FOR THE YEAR ENDED 31 DECEMBER 20X8

	£'000
Sales	600
Cost of sales	(319)
Gross profit	281
Other expenses (including depreciation of £42,000)	(194)
Profit before tax	87
Tax	(31)
Profit after tax	56

You are additionally informed that there have been no disposals of fixed assets during the year. New debentures were issued on 1 January 20X8. Wages for the year amounted to £86,000. Dividends paid were £22,000.

Required

Produce a cash flow statement using the direct method suitable for inclusion in the financial statements, as per FRS 1 (revised).

RENE PLC
CASH FLOW STATEMENT
FOR THE YEAR ENDED 31 DECEMBER 20X8

	£'000	£'000
Operating activities		
Cash received from customers (W1)	579	
Cash payments to suppliers (W2)	(366)	
Cash payments to and on behalf of employees	(86)	
		127
Returns on investments and servicing of finance		
Interest paid		(8)
Taxation		
UK corporation tax paid (W4)		(20)
Capital expenditure		
Purchase of tangible fixed assets (W5)	(146)	
Net cash outflow from capital expenditure		(146)
		(47)
Equity dividends paid		(22)
Financing		
Issue of share capital	60	
Issue of debentures	30	
Net cash inflow from financing		90
Increase in cash		21

NOTES TO THE CASHFLOW STATEMENT

1   Reconciliation of operating profit to net cash inflow from operating activities

	£'000
Operating profit (87 + 8)	95
Depreciation	42
Increase in stock	(4)
Increase in debtors	(21)
Increase in creditors	15
	127

2   Reconciliation of net cash flow to movement in net debt

	£'000
Net cash inflow for the period	21
Cash received from debenture issue	(30)
Change in net debt	(9)
Net debt at 1 January 20X8	(64)
Net debt at 31 December 20X8	(73)

3   Analysis of changes in net debt

	At 1 January 20X8 £'000	Cash flows £'000	At 31 December 20X8 £'000
Cash at bank	–	7	7
Overdrafts	(14)	14	–
		21	
Debt due after 1 year	(50)	(30)	(80)
Total	(64)	(9)	(73)

Workings

1   Cash received from customers

DEBTORS CONTROL ACCOUNT

	£'000		£'000
B/f	147	Cash received (bal)	579
Sales	600	C/f	168
	747		747

2   Cash paid to suppliers

CREDITORS CONTROL ACCOUNT

	£'000		£'000
Cash paid (bal)	366	B/f	121
C/f	136	Purchases (W3)	381
	502		502

3   Purchases

	£'000
Cost of sales	319
Opening stock	(210)
Closing stock	214
Expenses (194 – 42 – 86 – 8 debenture interest)	58
	381

4   Taxation

TAXATION

	£'000		£'000
∴ Tax paid	20	Balance b/f	28
Balance c/f	39	Charge for year	31
	59		59

5   Purchase of fixed assets

	£'000
Opening fixed assets	514
Less depreciation	(42)
Add revaluation (110 – 100)	10
	482
Closing fixed assets	628
Difference = additions	146

Exam focus point

In the December 2008 exam, there was a question requiring the calculation of the purchase of fixed assets for the cash flow statement. Only 38% answered the question correctly. Make sure you use a T account to calculate the figure or a working as shown above.

2.2 The advantages of cash flow accounting

The advantages of cash flow accounting are as follows.

(a)   Survival in business depends on the ability to generate cash. Cash flow accounting directs attention towards this critical issue.

(b)   Cash flow is more comprehensive than 'profit' which is dependent on accounting conventions and concepts.

(c)   Creditors (long and short-term) are more interested in an entity's ability to repay them than in its profitability. Whereas 'profits' might indicate that cash is likely to be available, cash flow accounting is more direct with its message.

(d)   Cash flow reporting provides a better means of comparing the results of different companies than traditional profit reporting.

(e)   Cash flow reporting satisfies the needs of all users better.

(i) For management, it provides the sort of information on which decisions should be taken: (in management accounting, 'relevant costs' to a decision are future cash flows); traditional profit accounting does not help with decision-making.

(ii) For shareholders and auditors, cash flow accounting can provide a satisfactory basis for stewardship accounting.

(iii) As described previously, the information needs of creditors and employees will be better served by cash flow accounting.

(f) Cash flow forecasts are easier to prepare, as well as more useful, than profit forecasts.

(g) They can in some respects be audited more easily than accounts based on the accruals concept.

(h) The accruals concept is confusing, and cash flows are more easily understood.

(i) Cash flow accounting should be both retrospective, and also include a forecast for the future. This is of great information value to all users of accounting information.

(j) Forecasts can subsequently be monitored by the publication of variance statements which compare actual cash flows against the forecast.

(k) Management need to control cash flows and the cash flow statement shows exactly which activities are generating and which using cash.

Question

Disadvantages

Can you think of some possible disadvantages of cash flow accounting?

Answer

The main disadvantages of cash accounting are essentially the advantages of accruals accounting (proper matching of related items). There is also the practical problem that few businesses keep historical cash flow information in the form needed to prepare a historical cash flow statement and so extra record keeping is likely to be necessary.

xam focus
oint

You could be asked to consider the usefulness of a cash flow statement as well as having to prepare items from it.

Chapter Roundup

- Cash flow is a useful measure of a company's performance.
- You need to be aware of the format laid out in FRS 1.

Quick Quiz

1   What is the objective of FRS 1?

    A   To provide additional information about profits and losses
    B   To provide additional information about generation of cash

2   Which of the following headings is not a classification of cash flows in FRS 1?

    A   Operating activities
    B   Financial investment
    C   Administration
    D   Financing

3   What is the 'indirect method' of preparing a cash flow statement?

4   A company has the following information about its fixed assets.

	20X7	20X6
	£'000	£'000
Cost	750	600
Accumulated depreciation	250	150
Net book value	500	450

Plant with a net book value of £75,000 (original cost £90,000) was sold for £30,000 during the year.

What is the cash flow from capital expenditure for the year?

    A   £95,000 inflow
    B   £210,000 inflow
    C   £210,000 outflow
    D   £95,000 outflow

5   A company has the following extract from a balance sheet.

	20X7	20X6
	£'000	£'000
Share capital	2,000	1,000
Share premium	500	–
Debenture	750	1,000

What is the cash flow from financing for the year?

    A   £1,250 inflow
    B   £1,750 inflow
    C   £1,750 outflow
    D   £1,250 outflow

6   When adjusting profit before tax to arrive at cash generated from operating activities, a decrease in debtors is added to operating profit. Is this statement

    A   True
    B   False

1   B   To provide information to users about the company's ability to generate cash and cash absorption.

2   C.   Administration costs are a classification in the profit and loss account, not the cash flow statement.

3   The operating cash flow is arrived at by adjusting net profits (or loss) for non-cash items and changes in stock, trade debtors and trade creditors.

4   C

FIXED ASSETS

	£'000		£'000
Opening balance	600	Disposals	90
Purchases (bal fig)	240	Closing balance	750
	840		840

Purchase of fixed assts	240,000
Proceeds of sale of fixed assets	(30,000)
Net cash outflow	210,000

5   A

	£'000
Issue of share capital (2,000 + 500 – 1,000)	1,500
Repayment of debentures (1,000 – 750)	(250)
Net cash inflow	1,250

6   A   True

Now try the questions below from the Exam Question Bank

Number	Level	Marks	Time
Q48	Examination	2	2 mins
Q49	Examination	2	2 mins
Q50	Examination	2	2 mins

Miscellaneous topics

Information technology

Topic list	Syllabus reference
1 Accounting packages	C3(d)-(e)
2 Accounting modules	C3(b)-(e)
3 Databases	C3(b)
4 Practical experience	C3(b)

Introduction

We referred briefly to computerised accounting systems earlier in this text. These days, most accounting systems are computerised and anyone training to be an accountant should be able to work with them.

The most important point to remember is that the **principles of computerised accounting are the same as those of manual accounting**. You should by now have a good grasp of these principles.

The first section of this chapter talks about accounting **packages**. This is a rather general term, but most of us can probably name the accounting package that we use at work.

An accounting package consists of several accounting **modules**, eg sales ledger, cash book. An exam question may take one of these modules and ask you to describe inputs, processing and outputs. Alternatively, you may be asked to outline the advantages of computer processing over manual processing, for example, for debtors or payroll.

Questions may ask you to discuss the advantages and disadvantages of **databases**. These are discussed in Section 3.

Study guide

		Intellectual level
C3	**Accounting systems and the impact of information technology on financial reporting**	
(b)	Understand the basic function and form of accounting records in a typical computerised system	1
(c)	Compare manual and computerised accounting systems	1
(d)	Identify advantages and disadvantages of computerised accounting systems	1
(e)	Understand the uses of integrated accounting software packages	1

Exam guide

You should be prepared for questions comparing manual and computerised systems. Do not neglect this chapter. You need to study the **full range** of the syllabus.

1 Accounting packages

> **FAST FORWARD**
>
> The syllabus for this paper requires you to know about the use of computers in financial accounting practice.

Exam focus point

> Questions will *not* be set on the technical aspects of how computers work.

We shall assume, therefore, that you know that a modern computer generally consists of a keyboard, a television-like screen, a box-like disk drive which contains all the necessary electronic components for data processing, and a printer. This is the computer hardware.

The computer hardware described above is also known as a personal computer (PC), but the technical name is a **micro-computer**.

Key term

> **Computer programs** are the instructions that tell the electronics how to process data. The general term used for these is **software**.

Software is what we are concerned with in this text, and in particular 'applications software', that is packages of computer programs that carry out specific tasks.

(a)   Some applications are devoted specifically to an accounting task, for example a payroll package, a fixed asset register or a stock control package.

(b)   Other applications have many uses in business, including their use for accounting purposes. Packages of this sort that we shall describe are databases and spreadsheets.

1.1 Accounting packages

> **FAST FORWARD**
>
> One of the most important facts to remember about computerised accounting is that **in principle, it is exactly the same as manual accounting**.

Accounting functions retain the same names in computerised systems as in more traditional written records. Computerised accounting still uses the familiar ideas of day books, ledger accounts, double entry, trial balance and financial statements. The principles of working with computerised sales, purchase and nominal ledgers are exactly what would be expected in the manual methods they replace.

The only difference is that these various books of account have become invisible. Ledgers are now computer files which are held in a computer-sensible form, ready to be called upon.

1.1.1 Advantages

However, the advantages of accounting packages compared with a manual system are as follows.

(a)   The packages can be used by **non-specialists**.

(b)   A large amount of **data can be processed very quickly**.

(c)   Computerised systems are **more accurate** than manual systems.

(d)   A computer is capable of handling and processing **large volumes** of data.

(e)   Once the data has been input, computerised systems can **analyse data** rapidly to present useful control information for managers such as a trial balance or a debtors schedule.

1.1.2 Disadvantages

The advantages of computerised accounting system far outweigh the disadvantages, particularly for large businesses. However, the following may be identified as possible disadvantages.

(a)   The initial **time and costs** involved in installing the system, training personnel and so on.

(b)   The need for **security checks** to make sure that unauthorised personnel do not gain access to data files.

(c)   The necessity to develop a **system of coding** (see below) and checking.

(d)   **Lack of 'audit trail'**. It is not always easy to see where a mistake has been made.

(e)   Possible **resistance** on the part of staff to the introduction of the system.

1.2 Coding

Computers are used more efficiently if vital information is expressed in the form of codes. For example, nominal ledger accounts will be coded individually, perhaps by means of a two-digit code: eg

00	Ordinary share capital
01	Share premium
05	Profit and loss account
15	Purchases
22	Debtors ledger control account
41	Creditors ledger control account
42	Interest
43	Dividends etc

In the same way, individual accounts must be given a unique code number in the sales ledger and purchase ledger.

1.3 Example: Coding

When an invoice is received from a supplier (code 1234) for £3,000 for the purchase of raw materials, the transaction might be coded for input to the computer as:

Supplier Code	Nominal ledger Debit	Credit	Value	Stock Code	Quantity
1234	15	41	£3,000	56742	150

Code 15 might represent purchases and code 41 the creditors control account. This single input could be used to update the purchase ledger, the nominal ledger, and the stock ledger. The stock code may enable further analysis to be carried out, perhaps allocating the cost to a particular department or product. Thus the needs of both financial accounting and cost accounting can be fulfilled at once.

1.4 Using an accounting package

When a user begins to work with an accounting package he will usually be asked to key in a **password**. Separate passwords can be used for different parts of the system, for example for different ledgers if required. The user will then be presented with a 'menu' of options such as 'enter new data' or 'print report' or a Windows-type screen with buttons and icons. By selecting the appropriate option the user will then be guided through the actions needed to enter the data or generate the report.

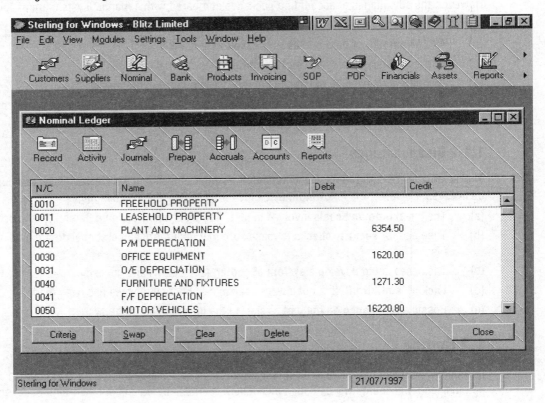

Attention!

If you are not already using one, get some experience between now and the exam, of using an accounting package.

One of the competences you require to fulfil performance objective 6 of the PER is the ability to use standard software packages including word processing and spreadsheet applications. You can apply the knowledge you obtain from this section of the text to help to demonstrate this competence.

1.5 Modules

Key term

A **module** is a program which deals with one particular part of a business accounting system.

An accounting package will consist of several modules. A simple accounting package might consist of only one module (in which case it is called a stand-alone module), but more often it will consist of several modules. The name given to a set of several modules is a **suite**. An accounting package, therefore, might have separate modules for:

(a)   Invoicing
(b)   Stock
(c)   Sales ledger
(d)   Purchase ledger
(e)   Nominal ledger
(f)   Payroll
(g)   Cash book
(h)   Job costing
(i)   Fixed asset register
(j)   Report generator

1.6 Integrated software

Each module may be integrated with the others, so that data entered in one module will be passed automatically or by simple operator request through into any other module where the data is of some relevance. For example, if there is an input into the invoicing module authorising the despatch of an invoice to a customer, there might be **automatic links**:

(a)   To the sales ledger, to update the file by posting the invoice to the customer's account.
(b)   To the stock module, to update the stock file by:

   (i)   Reducing the quantity and value of stock in hand
   (ii)   Recording the stock movement

(c)   To the nominal ledger, to update the file by posting the sale to the sales account.
(d)   To the job costing module, to record the sales value of the job on the job cost file.
(e)   To the report generator, to update the sales analysis and sales totals which are on file and awaiting inclusion in management reports.

A diagram of an **integrated accounting system** is given below.

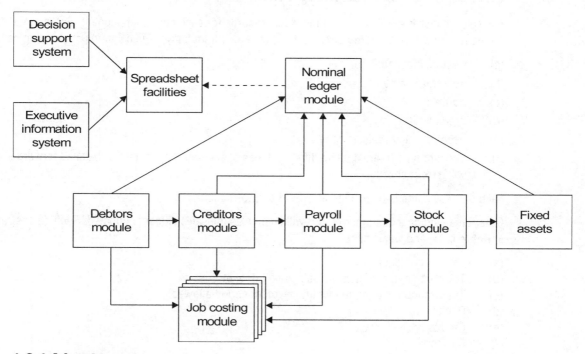

1.6.1 Advantages

(a)   It becomes possible to make just one entry in one of the ledgers which automatically updates the others.
(b)   Users can specify reports, and the software will automatically extract the required data from *all* the relevant files.
(c)   Both of the above simplify the workload of the user, and the irritating need to constantly load and unload disks is eliminated.

1.6.2 Disadvantages

(a)   Usually, it requires more computer memory than separate (stand-alone) systems - which means there is less space in which to store actual data.
(b)   Because one program is expected to do everything, the user may find that an integrated package has fewer facilities than a set of specialised modules. In effect, an integrated package could be 'Jack of all trades but master of none'.

2 Accounting modules

An accounting package consists of a number of 'modules' which perform all the tasks needed to maintain a normal accounting function like purchase ledger or payroll.

2.1 Accounting for debtors

A computerised sales ledger will be expected to keep the sales ledger up-to-date, and also it should be able to produce certain output (eg statements, sales analysis reports, responses to file interrogations etc). The output might be produced daily (eg day book listings), monthly (eg statements), quarterly (eg sales analysis reports) or periodically (eg responses to file interrogations, or customer name and address lists printed on adhesive labels for despatching circulars or price lists).

What we need to do is to have a closer look at the forms that input, output and processing take within a sales ledger. We will begin by thinking about what data we would expect to see in a sales ledger.

2.1.1 Data held on a sales ledger file

The sales ledger **file** will consist of individual **records** for each customer account. Some of the data held on the record will be **standing data** (ie it will change infrequently). Typical items of standing data are:

(a)   Customer account number
(b)   Customer name
(c)   Address
(d)   Credit limit
(e)   Account sales analysis code
(f)   Account type (there are two different types of account – open item or balance forward – which we will look at shortly)

Each of these items is referred to as a **field** of information.

Other data held on a customer record will change as the sales ledger is updated. Such data is called **variable data**, and will include:

(a)   Transaction data
(b)   Transaction description (eg sale, credit note etc)
(c)   Transaction code (eg to identify payment period allowed)
(d)   Debits
(e)   Credits
(f)   Balance

The file which contains these customer records - the sales ledger - is sometimes called a **master file**. If it is updated from another file containing various transactions, then that file is called a **transactions file**. Developments in the way computers store information mean that you are not likely to see these terms much any more – people more often talk about 'databases' of information.

Question

What is the relationship between a file, a field and a record?

Answer

A file is made up of records which are made up of fields. Make sure you learn any new terminology like this, because it will make your answers to examination questions far more convincing.

2.1.2 Input to a sales ledger system

Bearing in mind what we expect to find in a sales ledger, we can say that typical data input into sales ledger system is as follows.

(a) **Amendments**

(i) Amendments to customer details, eg change of address, change of credit limit, etc
(ii) Insertion of new customers
(iii) Deletion of old 'non-active' customers

(b) **Transaction data relating to:**

(i) Sales transactions, for invoicing
(ii) Customer payments
(iii) Credit notes
(iv) Adjustments (debit or credit items)

Some computerised sales ledgers produce invoices, so that basic sales data is input into the system. But other businesses might have a specialised invoicing module, so that the sales ledger package is not expected to produce invoices. The invoice details are already available (as output from the specialised module) and are input into the sales ledger system rather than basic sales data. So item (b)(i) of the list of typical data should read as follows.

(b) (i) Sales transactions, for invoicing (if the sales ledger is expected to produce invoices) or invoice details (if already available from a specialised invoicing module).'

2.1.3 Processing in a sales ledger system

The primary action involved in updating the sales ledger is modifying the amount outstanding on the customer's account. How the amount is modified depends on what data is being input (ie whether it is an invoice, credit note, remittance etc).

When processing starts, the balance on an account is called the *brought-forward* balance. When processing has finished, the balance on the account is called the *carried-forward* balance. These terms are often abbreviated to b/f and c/f.

What a computer does is to add or subtract whatever you tell it to from the b/f balance, and end up with a c/f balance.

	£	£
Brought forward account balance		X
Add:		
Invoice value	X	
Adjustments (+)	X	
		X
		X
Deduct:		
Credit note value	X	
Adjustments (-)	X	
Remittances	X	
		X
Carried forward account balance		X

This method of updating customer accounts is called the balance forward method.

Most systems also offer users the **open item** method of processing the data, which is much neater. Under this method, the user identifies specific invoices, and credits individual payments against specific invoices. Late payments of individual invoices can be identified and chased up. The customer's outstanding balance is the sum of the unpaid open items. The open item method follows best accounting practice, but it is more time consuming than the balance forward method.

2.1.4 Outputs from a sales ledger system

Typical outputs in a computerised sales ledger are as follows.

(a) **Day book listing**. A list of all transactions posted each day. This provides an audit trail - ie it is information which the auditors of the business can use when carrying out their work. Batch and control totals will be included in the listing.

(b) **Invoices** (if the package is one which is expected to produce invoices.)

(c) **Statements**. End of month statements for customers.

(d) **Aged debtors list**. Probably produced monthly.

(e) **Sales analysis reports**. These will analyse sales according to the sales analysis codes on the sales ledger file.

(f) **Debtors reminder letters**. Letters can be produced automatically to chase late payers when the due date for payment goes by without payment having been received.

(g) **Customer lists** (or perhaps a selective list). The list might be printed on to adhesive labels, for sending out customer letters or marketing material.

(h) **Responses to enquiries**, perhaps output on to a VDU screen rather than as printed copy, for fast response to customer enquiries.

(i) **Output onto disk file for other modules** - eg to the stock control module and the nominal ledger module, if these are also used by the organisation, and the package is not an integrated one.

2.1.5 The advantages of a computerised debtor system

The advantage of such a system, in addition to the advantages of computerised accounting generally, is its ability to assist in sales administration and marketing by means of outputs such as those listed above.

2.2 Purchase ledger

A computerised purchase ledger will certainly be expected to keep the purchase ledger up-to-date, and also it should be able to output various reports requested by the user. In fact, a computerised purchase ledger is much the same as a computerised sales ledger, except that it is a sort of mirror image as it deals with purchases rather than sales.

Question   Purchase ledger file

What sort of data would you expect to be held on a purchase ledger file?

Answer

The purchase ledger will consist of individual records for each supplier account. Just as for customer accounts, some of the data held on record will be *standing* data, and some will be *variable* data. Standing data will include:

(a) Account number
(b) Name
(c) Address
(d) Credit details
(e) Bank details (eg method of payment)
(f) Cash discount details, if appropriate

Variable data will include:

(a) Transaction date
(b) Transaction description

(c)   Transaction code
(d)   Debits
(e)   Credits
(f)   Balance

2.2.1 Inputs to a purchase ledger system

Bearing in mind what we expect to see held on a purchase ledger, typical data input into a purchase ledger system is:

(a)   Details of purchases recorded on invoices
(b)   Details of returns to suppliers for which credit notes are received
(c)   Details of payments to suppliers
(d)   Adjustments

2.2.2 Processing in a purchase ledger system

The primary action involved in updating the purchase ledger is adjusting the amounts outstanding on the supplier accounts. These amounts will represent money owed to the suppliers. This processing is identical to updating the accounts in the sales ledger, except that the sales ledger balances are debits (debtors) and the purchase ledger balances are credits (creditors). Again, the open item approach is the best.

2.2.3 Outputs from a purchase ledger system

Typical outputs in a computerised purchase ledger are as follows.

(a)   Lists of transactions posted - produced every time the system is run.

(b)   An analysis of expenditure for nominal ledger purposes. This may be produced every time the system is run or at the end of each month.

(c)   List of creditors balances together with a reconciliation between the total balance brought forward, the transactions for the month and the total balance carried forward.

(d)   Copies of creditors' accounts. This may show merely the balance b/f, current transactions and the balance c/f. If complete details of all unsettled items are given, the ledger is known as an **open-ended ledger**. (This is similar to the open item or balance forward methods with a sales ledger system.)

(e)   Any purchase ledger system can be used to produce details of payments to be made. For example:
    (i)   Remittance advices (usually a copy of the ledger account)
    (ii)   Cheques
    (iii)   Credit transfer listings

(f)   Other special reports may be produced for:
    (i)   Costing purposes
    (ii)   Updating records about fixed assets
    (iii)   Comparisons with budget
    (iv)   Aged creditors list

2.3 Nominal ledger

The nominal ledger (or general ledger) is an accounting record which summarises the financial affairs of a business. It is the nucleus of an accounting system. It contains details of assets, liabilities and capital, income and expenditure and so profit or loss. It consists of a large number of different accounts, each account having its own purpose or 'name' and an identity or code.

A nominal ledger will consist of a large number of coded accounts. For example, part of a nominal ledger might be as follows.

Account code	Account name
100200	Plant and machinery (cost)
100300	Motor vehicles (cost)
100201	Plant and machinery depreciation
100301	Vehicles depreciation
300000	Total debtors
400000	Total creditors
500130	Wages and salaries
500140	Rent and rates
500150	Advertising expenses
500160	Bank charges
500170	Motor expenses
500180	Telephone expenses
600000	Sales
700000	Cash

A business will, of course, choose its own codes for its nominal ledger accounts. The codes given in this table are just for illustration.

It is important to remember that a computerised nominal ledger works in exactly the same way as a manual nominal ledger, although there are some differences in terminology. For instance, in a manual system, the sales and debtors accounts were posted from the sales day book (not the sales ledger). But in a computerised system, the sales day book is automatically produced as part of the 'sales ledger module'. So it may *sound* as if you are posting directly from the sales ledger, but in fact the day book is part of a computerised sales ledger.

2.3.1 Inputs to the nominal ledger

Inputs depend on whether the accounting system is integrated or not.

(a)   If the system is integrated, then as soon as data is put into the sales ledger module (or anywhere else for that matter), the relevant nominal ledger accounts are updated. There is nothing more for the system user to do.

(b)   If the system is not integrated then the output from the sales ledger module (and anywhere else) has to be input into the nominal ledger. This is done by using journal entries. For instance.

DEBIT	A/c 300000	£3,000	
CREDIT	A/c 600000		£3,000

Where 600000 is the nominal ledger code for sales, and 300000 is the code for debtors.

Regardless of whether the system is integrated or not, the actual data needed by the nominal ledger package to be able to update the ledger accounts includes:

(a)   Date
(b)   Description
(c)   Amount
(d)   Account codes (sometimes called distinction codes)

2.3.2 Outputs from the nominal ledger

The main outputs apart from listings of individual nominal ledger accounts are:

(a)   The trial balance
(b)   Financial statements

3 Databases

FAST FORWARD

A database may be described as a 'pool' of data, which can be used by any number of applications. Its use is not restricted to the accounts department.

A stricter definition is provided in the *Computing Terminology* of the Chartered Institute of Management Accountants (CIMA).

Key term

'Frequently a much abused term, in its strict sense a **database** is a file of data structured in such a way that it may serve a number of applications without its structure being dictated by any one of those applications. The idea is that programs are written around the database rather than files being structured to meet the needs of specific programs. The term is also rather loosely applied to simple file management software.'

The software that runs the database is called the database management system (DBMS). The CIMA's definition is as follows.

Key term

'Technically, a **database management system** is a system which uses a database philosophy for the storage of information. In practice this term is often used to describe any system which enables the definition, storage and retrieval of information from discrete files within a system. Thus many simple file-handling systems are frequently referred to as "database systems".'

The database approach can also be summarised diagrammatically.

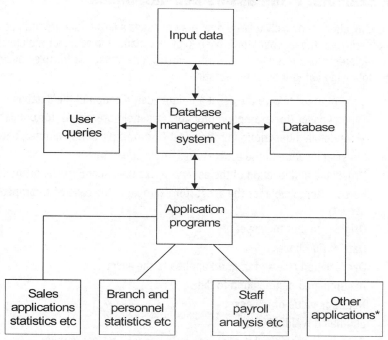

* The range of applications which make use of a database will vary widely, depending on what data is held in the database files.

Note the following from the diagram.

(a) Data is input, and the DBMS software organises it into the database. If you like, you can think of the database as a vast library of fields and records, waiting to be used.

(b) Various application programs (sales, payroll etc) are 'plugged into' the DBMS software so that they can use the database, or the same application used by different departments can all use the database.

(c) As there is only one pool of data, there is no need for different departments to keep many different files with duplicated information.

3.1 Objectives of a database

The main virtues of a database are as follow.

(a) There is **common data** for all users to share.

(b) The extra effort of keeping **duplicate files** in different departments is avoided.

(c) Conflicts between departments who use **inconsistent data are avoided**.

A database should have four major objectives.

(a) It should be **shared**. Different users should be able to access the *same data* in the database for their own processing applications (and at the *same time* in some systems) thus removing the need for duplicating data on different files.

(b) The **integrity** of the database must be preserved. This means that one user should not be allowed to alter the data on file so as to spoil the database records for other users. However, users must be able to update the data on file, and so make valid alterations to the data.

(c) The database system should provide for the needs of different users, who each have their own processing requirements and data access methods. In other words, the database should provide for the **operational requirements of all its users**.

(d) The database should be capable of **evolving**, both in the short term (it must be kept updated) and in the longer term (it must be able to meet the future data processing needs of users, not just their current needs).

3.2 Example: Fixed assets and databases

An organisation, especially a large one, may possess a large quantity of fixed assets. Before computerisation these would have been kept in a manual fixed asset register. A database enables this fixed asset register to be stored in an electronic form. A database file for fixed assets might contain most or all of the following categories of information.

(a) Code number to give the asset a unique identification in the database

(b) Type of asset (for example motor car, leasehold premises), for published accounts purposes

(c) More detailed description of the asset (for example serial number, car registration number, make)

(d) Physical location of the asset (for example address)

(e) Organisational location of the asset (for example accounts department)

(f) Person responsible for the asset (for example in the case of a company-owned car, the person who uses it)

(g) Original cost of the asset

(h) Date of purchase

(i) Depreciation rate and method applied to the asset

(j) Accumulated depreciation to date

(k) Net book value of the asset

(l) Estimated residual value

(m) Date when the physical existence of the asset was last verified

(n) Supplier

Obviously, the details kept about the asset would depend on the type of asset it is.

Any kind of computerised fixed asset record will improve efficiency in accounting for fixed assets because of the ease and speed with which any necessary calculations can be made. Most obvious is the calculation of the depreciation provision which can be an extremely onerous task if it is done monthly and there are frequent acquisitions and disposals and many different depreciation rates in use.

The particular advantage of using a database for the fixed asset function is its flexibility in generating reports for different purposes. Aside from basic cost and net book value information a database with fields such as those listed above in the record of each asset could compile reports analysing assets according to location say, or by manufacturer. This information could be used to help compare the performance of different divisions, perhaps, or to assess the useful life of assets supplied by different manufacturers. There may be as many more possibilities as there are permutations of the individual pieces of data.

4 Practical experience

FAST FORWARD

> Reading about computer systems and packages is no substitute for using one.

You should make every effort to gain experience in using an accounting package.

Chapter Roundup

- The syllabus for this paper requires you to know about the use of computers in financial accounting practice.

- One of the most important facts to remember about computerised accounting is that **in principle, it is exactly the same as manual accounting**.

- An accounting package consists of a number of 'modules' which perform all the tasks needed to maintain a normal accounting function like purchase ledger or payroll.

- A database may be described as a 'pool' of data, which can be used by any number of applications. Its use is not restricted to the accounts department.

- Reading about computer systems and packages is no substitute for using one.

Quick Quiz

1   What is one of the advantages of computerised accounting?

   A   Use by non-specialists
   B   Need for security checks

2   What are the disadvantages?

3   What is an accounting suite?

   A   Where accounting information is produced
   B   A set of several different modules

4   What sort of data is input into a sales ledger system?

   A   Amendments
   B   Transaction data
   C   Adjustments to terms
   D   All of the above

5   What is the open item method of processing?

6   What should be the four major objectives of a database?

7   What are the advantages of using a database to maintain fixed asset records?

   A   Amount of detail
   B   Ease of calculation
   C   Both of the above

Answers to Quick Quiz

1   A

2   See Paragraph 1.1.2.

3   B   A set of several different modules.

4   D

5   Payments are credited to specific invoices, so that late payment of invoices can be identified.

6   See Paragraph 3.1.

7   C   The amount of detail that can be kept about each individual asset and the ease in analysing this
             information into different reports and calculations (eg depreciation, profit on sale).

Now try the question below from the Exam Question Bank

Number	Level	Marks	Time
Q51	Examination	1	1 min

Exam question and answer bank

1   Which of the following are differences between sole traders and limited liability companies?

    (1)   A sole traders' financial statements are private; a company's financial statements are sent to shareholders and may be publicly filed

    (2)   Only companies have capital invested into the business

    (3)   A sole trader is fully and personally liable for any losses that the business might make; a company's shareholders are not personally liable for any losses that the company might make.

    A   1 and 2 only
    B   2 and 3 only
    C   1 and 3 only
    D   1, 2 and 3   **(2 marks)**

2   What is the role of the Financial Reporting Review Panel?

    A   To create a set of accounting standards
    B   To ensure public and large private companies comply with relevant reporting requirements   **(1 mark)**

3   In times of rising prices, what effect does the use of the historical cost concept have on a company's asset values and profit?

    A   Asset values and profit both understated
    B   Asset values and profit both overstated
    C   Asset values understated and profit overstated
    D   Asset values overstated and profit understated.   **(2 marks)**

4   The ASB's *Statement of principles for financial reporting* gives qualitative characteristics that make financial information reliable.

    Which of the following are examples of those qualitative characteristics?

    A   Faithful representation, neutrality and prudence
    B   Neutrality, comparability and true and fair view
    C   Prudence, comparability and accruals
    D   Neutrality, accruals and going concern   **(2 marks)**

5   A company has made a material change to an accounting policy in preparing its current financial statements.

    Which of the following disclosures are required by FRS 18 *Accounting policies* in the financial statements?

    1   The reasons for the change.

    2   The amount of the adjustment in the current period and in comparative information for prior periods.

    3   An estimate of the effect of the change on the next five accounting periods.

    A   1 and 2 only
    B   1 and 3 only
    C   2 and 3 only
    D   1, 2 and 3   **(2 marks)**

6   Which of the following statements are correct?

(1)   Materiality means that only items having a physical existence may be recognised as assets.

(2)   The substance over form convention means that the legal form of a transaction must always be shown in financial statements even if this differs from the commercial effect.

(3)   The money measurement concept is that only items capable of being measured in monetary terms can be recognised in financial statements.

A   2 only
B   1, 2 and 3
C   1 only
D   3 only   (2 marks)

7   Which of the following explains the imprest system of operating petty cash?

A   Weekly expenditure cannot exceed a set amount.
B   The exact amount of expenditure is reimbursed at intervals to maintain a fixed float.
C   All expenditure out of the petty cash must be properly authorised.
D   Regular equal amounts of cash are transferred into petty cash at intervals.   (2 marks)

8   Which of the following documents should accompany a payment made to a supplier?

A   Supplier statement
B   Remittance advice
C   Purchase invoice   (1 mark)

9   Is the following statement true or false?

The business entity concept requires that a business is treated as being separate from its owners

A   True
B   False   (1 mark)

10   A company's motor vehicles at cost account at 30 June 20X6 is as follows:

Motor vehicles – cost

	£		£
Balance b/f	35,800	Disposal	12,000
Additions	12,950	Balance c/f	36,750
	48,750		48,750

What opening balance should be included in the following period's trial balance for motor vehicles – cost at 1 July 20X6?

A   £36,750 DR
B   £48,750 DR
C   £36,750 CR
D   £48,750 CR   (2 marks)

11   VAT should be included in the profit and loss account of a registered trader.

Is this statement true or false?

A   True
B   False   (1 mark)

12 According to SSAP 9 *Stocks and long-term contracts*, which of the following costs should be included in valuing the stock of a manufacturing company?

(1) Carriage inwards
(2) Carriage outwards
(3) Depreciation of factory plant
(4) General administrative overheads

A All four items
B 1, 2 and 4 only
C 2 and 3 only
D 1 and 3 only

(2 marks)

13 A company values its stock using the first in, first out (FIFO) method. At 1 May 20X5 the company had 700 engines in stock, valued at £190 each.

During the year ended 30 April 20X6 the following transactions took place:

20X5

| 1 July | Purchased | 500 engines | at £220 each |
| 1 November | Sold | 400 engines | for £160,000 |

20X6

| 1 February | Purchased | 300 engines | at £230 each |
| 15 April | Sold | 250 engines | for £125,000 |

What is the value of the company's closing stock of engines at 30 April 20X6?

A £188,500
B £195,500
C £166,000
D £106,000

(2 marks)

14 At 31 December 20X4 Q, a limited liability company, owned a building that cost £800,000 on 1 January 20W5. It was being depreciated at two per cent per year.

On 1 January 20X5 a revaluation to £1,000,000 was recognised. At this date the building had a remaining useful life of 40 years.

What is the depreciation charge for the year ended 31 December 20X5 and the revaluation reserve balance as at 1 January 20X5?

	Depreciation charge for year ended 31 December 20X5 £	Revaluation reserve as at 1 January 20X5 £
A	25,000	200,000
B	25,000	360,000
C	20,000	200,000
D	20,000	360,000

(2 marks)

15 The plant and machinery account (at cost) of a business for the year ended 31 December 20X5 was as follows:

Plant and machinery – cost

20X5	£	20X5	£
1 Jan Balance	240,000	31 March Transfer disposal account	60,000
30 June Cash – purchase of plant	160,000	31 Dec Balance	340,000
	400,000		400,000

The company's policy is to charge depreciation at 20% per year on the straight line basis, with proportionate depreciation in the years of purchase and disposal.

What should be the depreciation charge for the year ended 31 December 20X5?

A   £68,000
B   £64,000
C   £61,000
D   £55,000

(2 marks)

16 Gareth, a VAT registered trader purchased a computer for use in his business. The invoice for the computer showed the following costs related to the purchase:

	£
Computer	890
Additional memory	95
Delivery	10
Installation	20
Maintenance (1 year)	25
	1,040
VAT (17.5%)	182
Total	1,222

How much should Gareth capitalise as a fixed asset in relation to the purchase?

A   £1,222
B   £1,040
C   £890
D   £1,015

(2 marks)

17 What is the correct double entry to record the depreciation charge for a period?

A   DR   Depreciation expense
     CR Accumulated depreciation

B   DR   Accumulated depreciation
     CR Depreciation expense

(1 mark)

18 Which of the following statements are correct?

(1)   Capitalised development expenditure must be amortised over a period not exceeding five years.

(2)   Capitalised development costs are shown in the balance sheet under the heading of Fixed Assets

(3)   If certain criteria are met, research expenditure must be recognised as an intangible asset.

A   2 only
B   2 and 3
C   1 only
D   1 and 3

(2 marks)

19 Theta prepares its financial statements for the year to 30 April each year. The company pays rent for its premises quarterly in advance on 1 January, 1 April, 1 July and 1 October each year. The annual rent was £84,000 per year until 30 June 20X5. It was increased from that date to £96,000 per year.

What rent expense and end of year prepayment should be included in the financial statements for the year ended 30 April 20X6?

	Expense	Prepayment
A	£93,000	£8,000
B	£93,000	£16,000
C	£94,000	£8,000
D	£94,000	£16,000

(2 marks)

20 A company receives rent from a large number of properties. The total received in the year ended 30 April 20X6 was £481,200.

The following were the amounts of rent in advance and in arrears at 30 April 20X5 and 20X6:

	30 April 20X5 £	30 April 20X6 £
Rent received in advance	28,700	31,200
Rent in arrears (all subsequently received)	21,200	18,400

What amount of rental income should appear in the company's profit and loss account for the year ended 30 April 20X6?

A   £486,500
B   £460,900
C   £501,500
D   £475,900

(2 marks)

21 At 30 June 20X5 a company's allowance for debtors was £39,000. At 30 June 20X6 trade debtors totalled £517,000. It was decided to write off debts totalling £37,000 and to adjust the allowance for debtors to the equivalent of 5 per cent of the trade debtors based on past events.

What figure should appear in the profit and loss account for the year ended 30 June 20X6 for these items?

A   £61,000
B   £22,000
C   £24,000
D   £23,850

(2 marks)

22 How should a contingent liability be included in a company's financial statements if the likelihood of a transfer of economic benefits to settle it is remote?

A   Disclosed by note with no provision being made
B   No disclosure or provision is required

(1 mark)

23   The following control account has been prepared by a trainee accountant:

Debtors ledger control account

	£		£
Opening balance	308,600	Cash received from credit customers	147,200
Credit sales	154,200	Discounts allowed to credit customers	1,400
Cash sales	88,100	Interest charged on overdue accounts	2,400
Contras against credit balances in creditors ledger	4,600	Bad debts written off	4,900
		Allowance for debtors	2,800
		Closing balance	396,800
	555,500		555,500

What should the closing balance be when all the errors made in preparing the debtors ledger control account have been corrected?

A   £395,200
B   £304,300
C   £309,500
D   £307,100   (2 marks)

24   Alpha received a statement of account from a supplier Beta, showing a balance to be paid of £8,950. Alpha's purchase ledger account for Beta shows a balance due to Beta of £4,140.

Investigation reveals the following:

(1)   Cash paid to Beta £4,080 has not been allowed for by Beta
(2)   Alpha's ledger account has not been adjusted for £40 of cash discount disallowed by Beta.

What discrepancy remains between Alpha's and Beta's records after allowing for these items?

A   £690
B   £770
C   £9,850
D   £9,930   (2 marks)

25   Mountain sells goods on credit to Hill. Hill receives a 10% trade discount from Mountain and a further 5% settlement discount if goods are paid for within 14 days. Hill bought goods with a list price of £200,000 from Mountain. VAT is at 17.5%.

What amount should be included in Mountain's sales ledger for this transaction?

A   £235,000
B   £211,500
C   £200,925
D   £209,925   (2 marks)

26   The total of the list of balances in Valley's purchase ledger was £438,900 at 30 June 20X6. This
      balance did not agree with Valley's purchase ledger control account balance. The following errors
      were discovered:

      1   A contra entry of £980 was recorded in the purchase ledger control account, but not in the
             purchase ledger.
      2   The total of the purchase returns daybook was undercast by £1,000.
      3   An invoice for £4,344 was posted to the supplier's account as £4,434.

      What amount should Valley report in its balance sheet as trade creditors at 30 June 20X6?

      A   £436,830
      B   £438,010
      C   £439,790
      D   £437,830   (2 marks)

27   The following bank reconciliation statement has been prepared by a trainee accountant:

                                                      £
      Overdraft per bank statement   3,860
      less: Outstanding cheques   9,160
                                                   5,300
      add: Deposits credited after date   16,690
      Cash at bank as calculated above   21,990

      What should be the correct balance per the cash book?

      A   £21,990 balance at bank as stated
      B   £3,670 balance at bank
      C   £11,390 balance at bank
      D   £3,670 overdrawn.   (2 marks)

28   In preparing a company's bank reconciliation statement at March 20X6, the following items are
      causing the difference between the cash book balance and the bank statement balance:

      (1)   Bank charges £380
      (2)   Error by bank £1,000 (cheque incorrectly debited to the account)
      (3)   Lodgements not credited £4,580
      (4)   Outstanding cheques £1,475
      (5)   Direct debit £350
      (6)   Cheque paid in by the company and dishonored £400.

      Which of these items will require an entry in the cash book?

      A   2, 4 and 6
      B   1, 5 and 6
      C   3, 4 and 5
      D   1, 2 and 3   (2 marks)

29   The debit side of a company's trial balance totals £800 more than the credit side.

      Which one of the following errors would fully account for the difference?

      A   £400 paid for plant maintenance has been correctly entered in the cash book and credited to
             the plant asset account.
      B   Discount received £400 has been debited to discount allowed account
      C   A receipt of £800 for commission receivable has been omitted from the records
      D   The petty cash balance of £800 has been omitted from the trial balance.   (2 marks)

30   A company's profit and loss account for the year ended 31 December 20X5 showed a net profit of £83,600. It was later found that £18,000 paid for the purchase of a motor van had been debited to the motor expenses account. It is the company's policy to depreciate motor vans at 25 per cent per year on the straight line basis, with a full year's charge in the year of acquisition.

What would the net profit be after adjusting for this error?

     A   £106,100
     B   £70,100
     C   £97,100
     D   £101,600   **(2 marks)**

31   Q's trial balance failed to agree and a suspense account was opened for the difference.

Q does not keep debtors and creditors control accounts. The following errors were found in Q's accounting records:

     (1)   In recording an issue of shares at par, cash received of £333,000 was credited to the ordinary share capital account as £330,000

     (2)   Cash £2,800 paid for plant repairs was correctly accounted for in the cash book but was credited to the plant asset register

     (3)   The petty cash book balance £500 had been omitted from the trial balance

     (4)   A cheque for £78,400 paid for the purchase of a motor car was debited to the motor vehicles account as £87,400.

Which of the errors will require an entry to the suspense account to correct them?

     A   1, 2 and 4 only
     B   1, 2, 3 and 4
     C   1 and 4 only
     D   2 and 3 only   **(2 marks)**

32   The bookkeeper of Field made the following mistakes:

Discounts allowed £3,840 was credited to the discounts received account

Discounts received £2,960 was debited to the discounts allowed account

Which journal entry will correct the errors?

		DR	CR
A	Discounts allowed	£7,680	
	Discounts received		£5,920
	Suspense account		£1,760
B	Discounts allowed	£880	
	Discounts received	£880	
	Suspense account		£1,760
C	Discounts allowed	£6,800	
	Discounts received		£6,800
D	Discounts allowed	£3,840	
	Discounts received		£2,960
	Suspense account		£880

                                                                        (2 marks)

33 A sole trader took some goods costing £800 from stock for his own use. The normal selling price of the goods is £1,600.

Which of the following journal entries would correctly record this?

		Dr £	Cr £
A	Drawings account	800	
	Stock account		800
B	Drawings account	800	
	Purchases account		800
C	Sales account	1,600	
	Drawings account		1,600

(1 mark)

34 Which of the following calculates a trader's net profit for a period?

A   Closing net assets + drawings – capital introduced – opening net assets
B   Closing net assets – drawings + capital introduced – opening net assets
C   Closing net assets – drawings – capital introduced – opening net assets
D   Closing net assets + drawings + capital introduced – opening net assets.

(2 marks)

35 A fire on 30 September destroyed some of a company's stock and its stock records.

The following information is available:

	£
Stock 1 September	318,000
Sales for September	612,000
Purchases for September	412,000
Stock in good condition at 30 September	214,000

Standard gross profit percentage on sales is 25%

Based on this information, what is the value of the stock lost?

A   £96,000
B   £271,000
C   £26,400
D   £57,000

(2 marks)

36 The stock value for the financial statements of Q for the year ended 31 May 20X6 was based on a stock count on 4 June 20X6, which gave a total stock value of £836,200.

Between 31 May and 4 June 20X6, the following transactions took place:

	£
Purchases of goods	8,600
Sales of goods (profit margin 30% on sales)	14,000
Goods returned by Q to supplier	700

What adjusted figure should be included in the financial statements for stock at 31 May 20X6?

A   £838,100
B   £853,900
C   £818,500
D   £834,300

(2 marks)

37   Annie is a sole trader who does not keep full accounting records. The following details relate to her transactions with credit customers and suppliers for the year ended 30 June 20X6:

	£
Trade debtors, 1 July 20X5	130,000
Trade creditors, 1 July 20X5	60,000
Cash received from customers	686,400
Cash paid to suppliers	302,800
Discounts allowed	1,400
Discounts received	2,960
Contra between purchase and sales ledgers	2,000
Trade debtors, 30 June 20X6	181,000
Trade creditors, 30 June 20X6	84,000

What figure should appear in Annie's profit and loss account for the year ended 30 June 20X6 for purchases?

A   £331,760
B   £740,800
C   £283,760
D   £330,200   (2 marks)

38   P and Q are in partnership, sharing profits equally.

On 30 June 20X5, R joined the partnership and it was agreed that from that date all three partners should share equally in the profit.

In the year ended 31 December 20X5 the profit amounted to £300,000, accruing evenly over the year, after charging a bad debt of £30,000 which it was agreed should be borne equally by P and Q only.

What should P's total profit share be for the year ended 31 December 20X5?

A   £ 95,000
B   £122,500
C   £125,000
D   £110,000   (2 marks)

39   Goodwill should never be shown on the balance sheet of a partnership.

Is the following statement true or false?

A   True
B   False   (1 mark)

40   A and B are in partnership sharing profits and losses in the ratio 3:2 respectively. Profit for the year was £86,500. The partners' capital and current account balances at the beginning of the year were as follows:

	A £	B £
Current accounts	5,750CR	1,200CR
Capital accounts	10,000CR	8,000CR

A's drawings during the year were £4,300, and B's were £2,430.

What should A's current account balance be at the end of the year?

A   £57,650
B   £51,900
C   £61,950
D   £53,350   (2 marks)

41   Should dividends paid appear on the face of a company's profit and loss account?

      A   Yes

      B   No   **(1 mark)**

42   Which of the following journal entries are correct, according to their narratives?

		Dr £	CR £
1	Suspense account	18,000	
	Rent received account		18,000
	Correction of error in posting £24,000 cash received for rent to the rent received account as £42,000		
2	Share premium account	400,000	
	Share capital account		400,000
	1 for 3 bonus issue on share capital of 1,200,000 50p shares		
3	Trade investment in X	750,000	
	Share capital account		250,000
	Share premium account		500,000
	500,000 50p shares issued at £1.50 per share in exchange for shares in X		

      A   1 and 2

      B   2 and 3

      C   1 only

      D   3 only   **(2 marks)**

43   Which of the following should appear in a company's statement of total recognised gains and losses?

      1   Profit for the financial year

      2   Amortisation of capitalised development costs

      3   Surplus on revaluation of fixed assets

      A   All three items

      B   2 and 3 only

      C   1 and 3 only

      D   1 and 2 only   **(2 marks)**

44   At 31 December 20X4 a company's capital structure was as follows:

£

Ordinary share capital
(500,000 shares of 25p each)   125,000
Share premium account   100,000

In the year ended 31 December 20X5 the company made a rights issue of 1 share for every 2 held at £1 per share and this was taken up in full. Later in the year the company made a bonus issue of 1 share for every 5 held, using the share premium account for the purpose.

What was the company's capital structure at 31 December 20X5?

Ordinary share capital   Share premium account

	£	£
A	450,000	25,000
B	225,000	250,000
C	225,000	325,000
D	212,500	262,500

(2 marks)

45   At 31 December 20X5 the following require inclusion in a company's financial statements:

(1)   On 1 January 20X5 the company made a loan of £12,000 to an employee, repayable on 1 January 20X6, charging interest at 2 per cent per year. On the due date she repaid the loan and paid the whole of the interest due on the loan to that date.

(2)   The company has paid insurance £9,000 in 2005, covering the year ending 31 August 20X6.

(3)   In January 20X6 the company received rent from a tenant £4,000 covering the six months to 31 December 20X5.

For these items, what total figures should be included in the company's balance sheet at 31 December 20X5?

	Current assets	Current liabilities
	£	£
A	10,000	12,240
B	22,240	nil
C	10,240	nil
D	16,240	6,000

(2 marks)

46   Should details of material adjusting or material non-adjusting events after the balance sheet date be disclosed in the notes to financial statements according to FRS 21 *Events After the Balance Sheet Date?*

A   Adjusting events
B   Non-Adjusting events
(1 mark)

47   Which of the following material events after the balance sheet date and before the financial statements are approved are adjusting events?

(1)   A valuation of property providing evidence of impairment in value at the balance sheet date.
(2)   Sale of stock held at the balance sheet date for less than cost.
(3)   Discovery of fraud or error affecting the financial statements.
(4)   The insolvency of a customer with a debt owing at the balance sheet date which is still outstanding.

A   1, 2, 3 and 4
B   1, 2 and 4 only
C   3 and 4 only
D   1, 2 and 3 only.
(2 marks)

48   Part of a company's cash flow statement is shown below:

	£'000
Operating profit	8,640
Depreciation charges	(2,160)
Increase in stock	(330)
Increase in trade creditors	440

The following criticisms of the extract have been made:

(1)   Depreciation charges should have been added, not deducted.
(2)   Increase in stock should have been added, not deducted.
(3)   Increase in trade creditors should have been deducted, not added.

Which of the criticisms are valid?

A   2 and 3 only
B   1 only
C   1 and 3 only
D   2 only   **(2 marks)**

49   Which of the following items could appear in a company's cash flow statement?

(1)   Surplus on revaluation of fixed assets
(2)   Proceeds of issue of shares
(3)   Proposed dividend
(4)   Dividends received

A   1 and 2
B   3 and 4
C   1 and 3
D   2 and 4   **(2 marks)**

50   Which of the following statements are correct?

(1)   A cash flow statement prepared using the direct method produces a different figure for
       operating cash flow from that produced if the indirect method is used.
(2)   Rights issues of shares do not feature in cash flow statements.
(3)   A surplus on revaluation of a fixed asset will not appear as an item in a cash flow statement
(4)   A profit on the sale of a fixed asset will appear as an item under Capital Expenditure in a
       cash flow statement.

A   1 and 4
B   2 and 3
C   3 only
D   2 and 4   **(2 marks)**

51   Is the following statement true or false?

A computerised accounting system operates using the principle of double entry accounting.

A   True
B   False   **(1 mark)**

1	C	
2	B	
3	C	
4	A	
5	A	FRS 18 does not require future predictions, so 3 is wrong.
6	D	
7	B	
8	B	
9	A	
10	A	
11	B	False. VAT for a registered trader is removed from income and expenses.
12	D	
13	A	(300@230) + (500@220) + (50@190) = 188,500
14	B	1,000,000/40years = 25,000; 1,000,000 − (800,000 − (800,000*2%*10years)) = 360,000
15	D	(240,000*20%) + (6/12*160,000*20%) − (9/12*60,000*20%) = 55,000
16	D	890 + 95 + 10 + 20 = 1,015
17	A	
18	A	
19	D	(84,000*2/12) + (96,000*10/12) = 94,000; 96,000*2/12 = 16,000

20   D

Rent receivable

	£		£
O/Balance	21,200	O/Balance	28,700
Profit and Loss	475,900	Cash received	481,200
C/Balance	31,200	C/Balance	18,400
	528,300		528,300

21   B   37,000 + ((517,000 − 37,000)*5%) −39,000) = 22,000. The allowance needed is £24,000, resulting in a reduction of £15,000.

22   B

23   D

Debtors ledger control account

	£		£
Opening balance	308,600	Contras	4,600
Credit sales	154,200	Cash received	147,200
Interest charged	2,400	Discounts allowed	1,400
		Bad debts	4,900
		Closing balance	307,100
	465,200		465,200

24   A   (8,950 − 4,080) − (4,140 + 40) = 690

25   D

List Price	200,000
Trade discount	(20,000)
	180,000
VAT (17.5%*95%*180,000)	29,925
	209,925

26   D   438,900 − 980-90 = 437,830

27	B	$-3,860 - 9,160 + 16,690 = 3,670$. Remember that the opening balance is overdrawn.
28	B	
29	B	
30	C	$83,600 + 18,000 - (18,000*25\%) = 97,100$
31	B	
32	B	
33	B	
34	A	
35	D	$(318,000 + 412,000 - 214,000) - (612,000*75\%) = 57,000$
36	A	$836,200 - 8,600 + (14,000*70\%) + 700 = 838,100$

37   A

Purchase ledger

	£		£
Cash paid	302,800	O/balance	60,000
Discounts received	2,960	Purchases (bal. fig)	331,760
Contra	2,000		
C/balance	84,000		
	391,760		391,760

38	B	$((300,000 + 30,000) / 2 * ½) + (300,000 + 30,000) / 2 * 1/3) - (30,000 * ½) = 122,500$
39	A	
40	D	$5,750 + (86,500*3/5) - 4,300 = 53,350$
41	B	Dividends appear in the statement of movements on reserves.
42	D	
43	C	
44	B	$125,000 + (500,000*1/2*25p) + (750,000*1/5*25p) = 225,000; 100,000 + (500,000*1/2*75p) - (750,000*1/5*25p) = 250,000$
45	B	$12,000 + (12,000*2\%) + (9,000*8/12) + 4,000 = 22,240$
46	B	
47	A	
48	B	
49	D	
50	C	
51	A	

Index

Review Form & Free Prize Draw – Paper F3 Financial Accounting (UK) (6/09)

All original review forms from the entire BPP range, completed with genuine comments, will be entered into one of two draws on 31 January 2010 and 31 July 2010. The names on the first four forms picked out on each occasion will be sent a cheque for £50.

Name: _____   Address: _____

_____

_____

How have you used this Text?
(Tick one box only)

☐ Home study (book only)

☐ On a course: college _____

☐ With 'correspondence' package

☐ Other _____

Why did you decide to purchase this Text? *(Tick one box only)*

☐ Have used BPP Texts in the past

☐ Recommendation by friend/colleague

☐ Recommendation by a lecturer at college

☐ Saw advertising

☐ Saw information on BPP website

☐ Other _____

During the past six months do you recall seeing/receiving any of the following?
(Tick as many boxes as are relevant)

☐ Our advertisement in *ACCA Student Accountant*

☐ Our advertisement in *Pass*

☐ Our advertisement in *PQ*

☐ Our brochure with a letter through the post

☐ Our website www.bpp.com

Which (if any) aspects of our advertising do you find useful?
(Tick as many boxes as are relevant)

☐ Prices and publication dates of new editions

☐ Information on Text content

☐ Facility to order books off-the-page

☐ None of the above

Which BPP products have you used?

Text	☑	Success CD	☐	Learn Online	☐
Kit	☐	i-Learn	☐	Home Study Package	☐
Passcard	☐	i-Pass	☐	Home Study PLUS	☐

Your ratings, comments and suggestions would be appreciated on the following areas.

	Very useful	Useful	Not useful
Introductory section (Key study steps, personal study)	☐	☐	☐
Chapter introductions	☐	☐	☐
Key terms	☐	☐	☐
Quality of explanations	☐	☐	☐
Case studies and other examples	☐	☐	☐
Exam focus points	☐	☐	☐
Questions and answers in each chapter	☐	☐	☐
Fast forwards and chapter roundups	☐	☐	☐
Quick quizzes	☐	☐	☐
Question Bank	☐	☐	☐
Answer Bank	☐	☐	☐
Index	☐	☐	☐

Overall opinion of this Study Text	Excellent ☐	Good ☐	Adequate ☐	Poor ☐

Do you intend to continue using BPP products?   Yes ☐   No ☐

On the reverse of this page are noted particular areas of the text about which we would welcome your feedback. The BPP author of this edition can be e-mailed at: janiceross@bpp.com

Please return this form to: Lesley Buick, ACCA Publishing Manager, BPP Learning Media, FREEPOST, London, W12 8BR

Review Form & Free Prize Draw (continued)

TELL US WHAT YOU THINK

Please note any further comments and suggestions/errors below

Free Prize Draw Rules

1   Closing date for 31 January 2010 draw is 31 December 2009. Closing date for 31 July 2010 draw is 30 June 2010.

2   Restricted to entries with UK and Eire addresses only. BPP employees, their families and business associates are excluded.

3   No purchase necessary. Entry forms are available upon request from BPP Learning Media. No more than one entry per title, per person. Draw restricted to persons aged 16 and over.

4   Winners will be notified by post and receive their cheques not later than 6 weeks after the relevant draw date.

5   The decision of the promoter in all matters is final and binding. No correspondence will be entered into.